Sport Consumer Behaviour

All successful marketing strategies in sport must take into account the complex behaviour of consumers. This book offers a complete introduction to consumer behaviour in sport, combining theory and cutting-edge research with practical guidance and advice to enable students and industry professionals to become more effective practitioners. Written by three of the world's leading sports marketing academics, it covers a wide range of areas including:

- sport consumer motivation
- the segmentation of the sport consumer market
- the external and environmental factors that influence sport consumer behaviour
- sport consumer personalities and attitudes
- service quality and customer satisfaction.

These chapters are followed by a selection of international case studies on topics such as female sport fans, college sports, marathons and community engagement. The book's companion website also provides additional resources exclusively for instructors and students, including test banks, slides and useful web links.

As the only up-to-date book to focus on consumer behaviour in sport and events, *Sport Consumer Behaviour: Marketing Strategies* offers a truly global perspective on this rapidly growing subject. This book is an invaluable resource for anyone involved in the sport and events industries, from students and academics to professional marketers.

Daniel C. Funk is a Professor and Washburn Senior Research Fellow in the Department of Sport and Recreation Management within the School of Sport, Tourism and Hospitality Management at Temple University, USA. His research examines sport consumer experience through the investigation of internal and external factors that shape attitudes and behaviour in related industry sectors. He has been recognized as a Research Fellow for the Sport Marketing Association and the North American Society for Sport Management. Dr Funk has published articles and chapters in a variety of academic journals and textbooks and served as Editor for *Sport Marketing Quarterly*.

Kostas Alexandris is an Associate Professor at Aristotle University of Thessaloniki, Greece. He earned his PhD from the University of Manchester, UK. He was previously a faculty member of the University of Illinois at Urbana-Champaign. Dr Alexandris has published more than 60 research articles in international academic journals and several book chapters on topics related to sport, leisure, tourism consumer behaviour and marketing. He is an Associate Editor of the *Journal of Leisure Research* and serves on the Editorial Boards of *Sport Management Review*, the *Journal of Service Theory and Practice*, *Sport Marketing Quarterly*, *Managing Sport and Leisure and International Journal of Sport Management*. He is also the editor of the book *Performance Measurement and Leisure Management*, published by Routledge.

Heath McDonald is Professor of Marketing and the Associate Dean in the Faculty of Business and Law at Swinburne University, Australia. He is an expert in the field of customer acquisition and retention, particularly in subscription markets. His academic research work has been published in journals in the fields of Marketing, Sport Management and Hospitality. Dr McDonald also sits on the Editorial Boards of the *Journal of Sport Management*, *Sport Management Review*, *Sport Marketing Quarterly* and *Sport, Business and Management*.

Sport Consumer Behaviour

Marketing Strategies

**Daniel C. Funk, Kostas Alexandris
and Heath McDonald**

 Routledge
Taylor & Francis Group

LONDON AND NEW YORK

First published 2016
by Routledge
2 Park Square, Milton Park, Abingdon, Oxon OX14 4RN

and by Routledge
711 Third Avenue, New York, NY 10017

Routledge is an imprint of the Taylor & Francis Group, an informa business

British Library Cataloguing-in-Publication Data
A catalogue record for this book is available from the British Library

Library of Congress Cataloging in Publication Data
A catalog record for this book has been requested

ISBN: 978-1-138-91248-9 (hbk)
ISBN: 978-1-138-91249-6 (pbk)
ISBN: 978-1-315-69190-9 (ebk)

Typeset in Berling and Futura
by Florence Production Ltd, Stoodleigh, Devon, UK

Visit the companion website: www.routledge.com/cw/funk

Contents

Part 4: Outputs: sport consumer connections and satisfaction 167

Illustrations

FIGURES

TABLES

Acknowledgements

We would like to thank the following companies, businesses, journals, and research units for offering us their reports to use them as case studies and examples in the book:

- IEG (www.sponsorship.com)
- IHRSA (www.ihrsa.org)
- REPUCOM (http://repucom.net)
- RESEARCH UNIT OF SOCIAL KINESIOLOGY AND SPORT MANAGEMENT, Department of Kinesiology, Faculty of Kinesiology and Rehabilitation Sciences, KU Leuven, (https://faber.kuleuven.be)
- SPORTCAL – SPORTS MARKET INTELLIGENCE (www.sportcal.com)
- SPORTS BUSINESS DAILY, (www.sportsbusinessdaily.com) www.sportsbusiness daily.com/Journal/Issues/2013/10/14/Leagues-and-Governing-Bodies/NFL-women. aspx
- SPORTS DESTINATION MANAGEMENT (http://www.sportsdestinations.com)

Thank you to the following graduate students at Temple University for their help in developing material for this book: James Du, Bradley Baker, Miae Lee, Xiaochen Zhou, and Anthony Pizzo.

Preface

The book is divided into seven parts with 14 chapters, case studies and topics of interest. Teaching materials are also provided for each chapter including Powerpoint slides and chapter quizzes on the companion website.

PART 1: INTRODUCTION AND CONSUMER SEGMENTATION

Part 1 provides an overview of consumer behaviour with a discussion of how sport consumers make decisions and sport managers can apply this knowledge. Chapter 1 provides an introductory chapter framing the context of sport consumer experiences and behaviour in sport. Discussion related to the specific characteristics of the sport context is provided. The chapter introduces and describes a sport consumer decision-making model that sets the basis for introducing the inputs, processes and outputs in subsequent parts of the book. Chapter 2 presents information on a key application of sport consumer behaviour understanding in the form of segmentation strategies. A series of segmentation studies (socio-demographic, psychographic, behavioural segmentation) are presented with emphasis on sport marketing applications.

PART 2: INPUTS: EXTERNAL FORCES AND BRANDING

Part 2 examines external inputs that shape sport consumer experiences, which include branding activities used by sport organizations and environmental factors. Chapter 3 discusses the sport product and the sport consumer. A discussion of the sport industry, types of sport consumers and unique characteristics of sport consumers is provided. The issue of branding the sport product is also analysed in this chapter. Chapter 4 examines the role of external factors related to the socio-culture environment, which shapes the sport consumer's perspective and experiences. The environmental factors include families and references groups, various cohorts and cultures and subcultures.

PART 3: PROCESSES: INTERNAL PSYCHOLOGICAL COMPONENTS

Part 3 includes key internal processes that influence the evaluation of external inputs by the sport consumer. Chapter 5 describes types of motivations and defines the motivation process. The chapter offers examples of motivational theories, outcomes and methods to measure this important process. Chapter 6 defines perceived constraints and introduces a constraint decision-making model and the process of negotiation constraints. The chapter discusses key socio-culture constraints on the influence of sport consumer engagement. Chapter 7 introduces the attitude concept and presents various models that describe its composition and formation. The chapter describes attitude change and how sponsorship is evaluated. Chapter 8 describes personality theory and traits and offers a review of sport consumer research using personality. The chapter concludes with a discussion of brand personality research and its application to sport context.

PART 4: OUTPUTS: SPORT CONSUMER CONNECTIONS AND SATISFACTION

Part 4 presents a discussion of key psychological outputs that result from the evaluation process of various sport experiences. Chapter 9 introduces a stage-based theoretical framework to illustrate how emotional connections can develop within four stages. The chapter proposes marketing strategies that can facilitate movement within the stages and describe how attitudes and behaviour correspond. Chapter 10 provides a detailed discussion for each stage of the framework and identifies key internal and external forces that shape the developmental progression. Chapter 11 introduces the sport involvement concept and provides conceptual and methodological approaches used in sport research. The chapter concludes with a description for how sport involvement is used to operationalize a theoretical framework to stage place consumers into one of four stages. Chapter 12 defines the construct of team identification and describes its origins and application in sport research with key consequences. The chapter concludes with a discussion of optimal distinctiveness and multiple in-groups that exist. Chapter 13 introduces the concepts of service quality and customer satisfaction. The chapter describes how sport consumer's perception of quality are formed and managed and concludes with a discussion of key determinants of sport customer satisfaction and its impact on loyalty and word of mouth.

PART 5: AN ALTERNATIVE PERSPECTIVE ON SPORT CONSUMER BEHAVIOUR

Part 5 introduces a different view of consumer behaviour that challenges the fundamental assumption in previous chapters that sport is a unique context. Chapter 14 examines whether established empirical generalizations, or laws, observed across a number of contexts are applicable to sport. This chapter addresses Double Jeopardy, which proposes that small market share brands not only have fewer buyers than their larger competitors, but also attract less loyal consumers. In addition, the Duplication of Purchase concept, which suggests that brands have been found to share customers in line with other brands' market share.

PART 6: CASE STUDIES

Part 6 offers 6 case studies to provide students with an opportunity to apply theory to practice. Each case presents a detailed examination of a specific sport or event context to help the student gain an in-depth understanding of concepts and theory presented in the book. The cases offer a range of activities and tasks designed to further their knowledge about sport consumer behaviour.

PART 7: TOPICS OF INTEREST FOR SPORT MARKETING

The final section of the book provides students with various topics related to sport consumer behaviour. Various topics are listed with respect to sport marketing that can be examined.

PART 1

Introduction and consumer segmentation

CHAPTER 1

Introduction to sport consumer behaviour and decision-making

This chapter's objectives are to:

- introduce the concept of sport experience design
- describe sport consumer behaviour and provide a definition
- discuss resources of *time, money* and *effort* related to sport experiences
- introduce a sport consumer behaviour decision-making model
- describe sport marketing actions.

1.0 INTRODUCTION

A fundamental purpose of any business is to maximize profits, mostly by designing and delivering products and services to meet the needs and wants of consumers. Sport organizations are not immune to such profit motives. Sport typically involves experiences that are largely considered subjective in nature and based on the interactions between individual consumers and physical environments. From a management perspective, the sport organization's key function is to enhance such interactions in order to maximize the experience. From a consumer perspective, the sport interaction involves an individual's psychological and physical responses, and includes beliefs, emotions and perceptions that occur before, during and after the use or anticipated use of a sport product or service. The focus of this book is on the consumer perspective, with an emphasis on understanding behaviour within the sport and recreation context.

A key benchmark for any sport organization is to provide a positive and pleasurable consumer experience. The fundamental assumption is that satisfaction with the sport experience will enhance consumer engagement. However, the psychological and physical features that contribute to this experience are less obvious. There is a general consensus among academic scholars and practitioners that sport consumers can be complicated to understand; they are often diverse, inconsistent, stubborn, emotional, selective, logical and prone to making irrational decisions. All of which makes predicting their behaviour somewhat challenging.

So, how does sport management construct the optimal experience to maximize profits? A difficult question to answer, but a good start is to focus on the design elements of the sport experience.

1.1 SPORT EXPERIENCE DESIGN

The concept of sport experience design (SX design) represents the process of enhancing customer engagement by improving the use and pleasure provided in interactions between the customer and the delivery of the sport product or service. There are three main factors that influence SX design: the sport user; the sport context; and the sport management system. The sport consumer has psychological tendencies related to perceptions, personalities, desires and emotions, as well as personal characteristics related to demographics. For example, what motivates a 36-year-old female to wear a team logoed T-shirt while watching a basketball game. The sport context is the physical and virtual environments in which the specific sport behaviour takes place. For example, attending a live sporting event in a stadium or using a website to purchase a ticket or a sweatshirt. The sport management system is the process through which a sport organization creates and delivers the sport product or service to the customer. For example, the way a professional football organization stages a home game and manages the customer interactions via various touchpoints (e.g. website, media, parking, stadium atmosphere, employees and concessions). In combination, all three factors are important for understanding how to create the optimal SX design.

An example of this SX design approach is provided by Kaan Turnali (2014) in his five-part series entitled *Fan experience matters: Design elements* (http://forbes.com/sites/sap/2014/05/04/the-fan-experience-matters-design-elements/). Turnali used an SX design perspective to illustrate how the three SX design factors previously discussed relate to sport spectators and fans. He identified five key sport experience design elements that sport management should consider: 1) The fan experience should not be considered a one-size-fits-all proposition; 2) The fan experience can be both art and science; 3) The fan experience should be based on continuous engagement; 4) The fan experience is about making a special connection; and 5) The fan experience can be improved through continued research and evaluation.

Turnali stressed the importance of the consumer perspective in evaluating the design and delivery of the sport product or service. That is, a manager should examine the sport experience as a spectator or fan, and not as a professional working in an office. He proposed the use of the 'empathy principle' by sport managers to capture the essence of the customer's journey as he/she interacts with various touchpoints, whether physical or virtual. This will allow a sport manager to get inside the head of the consumer and feel what it's like to be that consumer as he/she engages in the sport experience.

The SX design perspective incorporates both sport consumer and sport management perspectives by focusing on the quality of interactions that occur. As a management responsibility, the process of engaging sport customers by improving the interactions between the sport consumer and the delivery of the sport product or service is critical. As a result, most sport organizations devote considerable resources to creating sport management systems and contexts to optimize the sport consumer experience and maximize profits. However, providing the optimal sport consumer experience can be challenging without understanding the perceptions, desires and emotions of sport consumers. There are a wide variety of personal, psychological and environmental forces that can influence sport consumer decision-making and behaviour. In order to assists sport managers, this book examines these forces and how they shape interactions with the delivery of sport products and services from a sport consumer behaviour perspective.

1.2 SPORT CONSUMER BEHAVIOUR BACKGROUND

Consumer behaviour as an academic field of study is generally considered a separate discipline from marketing. It emerged in the early 1980s from a variety of disciplines including psychology, sociology, anthropology, economics and general education to examine consumption in many forms and contexts. Consumer behaviour is primarily concerned with investigating psychological and physical factors that influence an individual's decision making, in order to explain or predict behaviour patterns (Schiffman & Kanuk, 2010). From this perspective, researchers seek to answer questions related to consumer behaviour to inform management practices. The answers to these questions are of value for the development of marketing initiatives by organization, to optimize the delivery of its products and services.

The study of sport consumer behaviour emerged as a subset of the general field of consumer behaviour within the sport management academic discipline. This divergence was largely based on the assumptions that sport has unique characteristics as well as a wider variety of products and services. These characteristic differences can include the intangibility and inconsistent nature of the sport product or service, the level of know-ledge that sport consumers possess, the emotions created from watching or participating in sport, fluctuations in supply and demand, the manner in which sport is consumed in the presence of others and reliance on product extensions. A more detailed discussion of these characteristics appears in Chapter 2. In order to study sport consumer behaviour, researchers initially used knowledge derived from social psychology to explain why sport consumers attend or participate in sport events, use sport media and technology and purchase and wear sport merchandise. As the study of sport consumers continued to grow, knowledge from marketing and economics has been used to help explain sport consumer behaviour and decision making.

The various approaches utilized to study sport consumers highlight the complexity of explaining and predicting behaviour in the sports context. The sport consumer can purchase and use tangible and intangible products and services that have physical and experiential features. For example, purchasing and wearing a professional football team logoed hat; then attending a home match at a stadium and being part of an exciting crowd atmosphere when the team wins. In order to provide a foundation to guide our under-standing, a useful definition of sport consumer behaviour is now offered.

Sport consumer behaviour is defined as the psychological and physical responses that occur before, during and after the use of a sport product or service. Psychological responses include perceptions, emotions and evaluations related to the sport experience; physical responses can involve physiological reactions of arousal and stress related to the sport experience. These psychological and physical responses can occur when searching, selecting, using and disposing of sport products and services (Funk, 2008). A fundamental principle of sport consumer behaviour is the desire to seek out and engage in sport experiences that provide benefits and satisfy needs and wants. This principle is illustrated by observing how sport consumers spend available resources of *time*, *money* and *effort* on sport experiences. A key point to remember in the study of sport consumer behaviour is that time, money and effort are finite resources. In other words, a sport consumer only has so much of each to devote to sport products and services.

- *Time* resources relate to the actual usage hours of sport that occurs in daily activities. The sport researcher can calculate the number of hours watching either a live sport event in person or via TV, radio, internet or mobile devices; participating in various sport and recreation activities, competitions and events; participating in fantasy leagues or tipping competitions; using the internet to follow a sport or using sport as a topic of conversation at work or at social gatherings. In addition, the time devoted to sport, recreation and event-related usage can affect other sport and non-sport activities. For example, being a professional football fan can reduce the amount of time devoted to active recreational sport participation or taking a child to the zoo. Similarly, training for a marathon event may require not playing golf on the weekends for a few months and giving up late night social entertainment. The level of attention devoted to sport also often impacts consumption behaviour not traditionally sport related. For example, individuals may decide on sport-related home decorating, food and dining, movies, clothing, education, automobiles and office supplies. Sport lifestyle purchases often occur among committed cyclists, rock climbers, as well as die-hard sport fans.
- *Money* resources reflect the financial commitment required to purchase and use the sport product or service. This can include the purchase of tickets to sporting events, club memberships, attending the sporting event, licensed merchandise, registration fees, sport equipment and subscriptions. However, decisions related to the individual's budgeting capabilities need to be taken into consideration by the sport researcher as a consumer's financial situation will impact his/her ability to use a sport product or service. For example, a sport consumer's ability to purchase a team membership, season tickets or travel to a FIFA World Cup game will be determined by his/her amount of disposable income. Collecting financial information from sport consumers can provide researchers with purchase and usage levels in order to determine supply and demand of various sport products and services.
- *Effort* resources reflect both physical and mental requirements in order to use a sport product or service. Effort is particularly applicable in the context of participatory sports. For example, training for a marathon, participating in group exercise classes at a fitness club and playing tennis are examples of activities that require physical effort. The participatory requirements of each sport activity, in terms of the level of difficulty and the physical effort required, are factors which influence sport consumer decision-making and represent personal characteristics of the sport consumer (e.g. age, fitness level, skills). For a spectator, effort is also required. For example, waking up on Saturday at 8:00am and travelling to a sport venue to begin pre-game tailgating and festivities for a live soccer match at 8:00pm requires considerable effort and stamina. For both spectator and participant, mental effort is required in pursuit of using the sport product or service. This includes the amount of cognitive activity devoted toward thinking about purchase or using the sport product or service. Regardless of

the context, the resource elements of *time, money* and *effort* are key indicators of what is important to a sport consumer, and help to understand how consumption decisions are made.

1.3 A SPORT CONSUMER DECISION-MAKING MODEL

As previously noted, consumer behaviour research aims to answer the how, when, where and why in relation to sport experiences. A typical consumer decision-making model includes the study of both external and internal forces, and how they influence consumer choices and evaluations. Figure 1.1 presents a simplistic view of how a sport con sumer decision-making sequence occurs within three major decision-making phases: inputs; internal processing; and outputs. As Figure 1.1 illustrates, the inputs phase consists of external forces that serve as inputs into the internal processing phase, which in turn leads to the outputs phase. The three phases are depicted in Figure 1.1, followed by a detailed explanation for each.

1.3.1 Inputs phase

The first phase of the sport consumer decision-making sequence is inputs, which describes how external forces influence an individual's recognition of whether purchasing and using a sport product or service helps achieve a desirable outcome. The inputs phase relates to external forces that are generally environmentally based and include a sport organization's marketing activities and socio-cultural influences. As a result, these external forces represent two information categories – marketing activities and socio-cultural factors – which are primary sources of information that help a sport consumer determine whether using a sport product or service will satisfy needs and wants. The first information category is a sport organization's marketing activities and relates to the marketing mix comprised of seven P's: product; price; promotion; place; people; physical evidence; and process. However, a discussion of the seven Ps of the marketing mix is outside the scope of this book, which is focused on the consumer perspective. For further information on the marketing mix, various sport marketing publications can be sourced including: Mullin, Hardy & Sutton, 2014; Shank & Lyberger, 2015; Shilbury, Westerbeek, Quick, Funk & Karg, 2014.

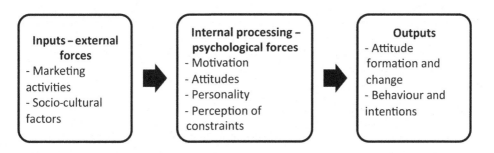

FIGURE 1.1 Sport consumer decision-making sequence

The second informational category relates to the socio-cultural factors that help a sport consumer determine whether a sport experience will provide desirable outcomes. Socio-cultural influences consist of information obtained from family, friends, colleagues, age cohorts and social and cultural groups. The inputs phase highlights the importance of understanding how such external forces shape the sport consumer decision-making process. For example, formal communication strategies such as an advertisement from a health club usually have less impact than informal communication such as word-of-mouth. The socio-cultural factors that influence sport consumer decision-making are therefore critical in developing effective marketing activities, and are further discussed in Chapter 4.

1.3.2 Internal processing phase

The internal processing phase relates to unobservable psychological mechanisms that govern the manner in which sport consumers evaluate inputs, external stimuli and actual experiences. The manner in which inputs are evaluated by a sport consumer is based on psychological forces that exist within each consumer, including motivation, personality, attitudes and perceptions that shape the search, selection, usage and disposal process.

The second phase of the sport consumer decision-making sequence relates to the psychological processing of information, stimuli and experiences. The internal processing phase encompasses a number of cognitive activities, including recognition of a need, pre-purchase searching, evaluation of alternatives and post-evaluation of the sport experience. The internal processing phase contains many unobservable psychological forces at work in the sport consumer's mind as he/she evaluate inputs.

The internal processing of inputs that occur is based on the sport consumer using psychological resources, including motivation (to initiate, direct and sustain usage), attitudes (beliefs and feelings about usage), personality (psychological traits that influence usage and determine individual characteristics) and perceptions (perceived constraints that influence formation of sport usage preferences and limit usage). When considering both the inputs and internal processing phases together, the sport consumer decision-making model represents the combination or interaction of environmental and psychological factors. The internal processing phase activates psychological mechanisms that determine whether inputs are evaluated from a cognitive process or affective process, or both. For example, the influence of psychological forces determines whether the sport consumer uses emotion to evaluate information about a sport product or service versus a more rational approach.

There are numerous psychological factors within the internal processing phase, and this book has focused on four key factors, which are further discussed in the following chapters: motivation in Chapter 5; constraints in Chapter 6; attitudes in Chapter 7; and personality in Chapter 8.

1.3.3 Outputs phase

The final stage of the sport consumer decision-making sequence, as illustrated in Figure 1.1, is the outputs phase. The outputs phase relates to both attitudinal and behavioural outcomes. Attitudinal outcomes indicate that subsequent attitude formation and change has occurred based on the sport experience. Behavioural outcomes determine the frequency and complexity of actual usage behaviour, as well as intentions to behave.

Attitudinal outcomes are unobservable responses in the form of new beliefs and feelings created as a result of evaluating or engaging in the sport experience. In other words, a new attitude has formed or a previously held attitude has changed as a result of the internal processing phase. Beliefs are cognitive outcomes and represent thoughts or opinions a sport consumer has about using a sport product or service. These outcomes provide a knowledge base in order to determine whether a sport experience fulfils needs and provides benefits. Feelings are affective outcomes and represent emotional reactions and mood states that individuals encounter in relation to the sport experience. Affective outcomes are generally pleasant or unpleasant sensations, situationally relevant, temporal and can range from stable to unstable. A strong example of an attitudinal outcome in the outputs phase is a new attitude toward a sport experience, created as the result of the post-experience evaluation.

As a sport consumer spends more time, money and effort in a specific sport context, the attitudinal outcomes can take on different characteristics. These characteristics are related to the formation of psychological connection, involvement, identification and satisfaction, representing attitudinal outcomes that can progressively develop and can range from weak to strong. Subsequent chapters in this book are devoted to main attitudinal outcomes: Chapters 9 and 10 discuss the stage-based development of psychological connections; Chapter 11 presents the construct of sport involvement; Chapter 12 examines sport team identification; and Chapter 13 discusses service quality and customer satisfaction.

Behavioural outcomes represent observable and unobservable responses with respect to a given sport product or service. Observable outcomes include actual behaviour whether it occurs before, during or after a sport experience. The terms 'frequency' and 'complexity' are used to describe how often a behaviour occurs in a given period, and the vast number of behaviour types that occur. In terms of frequency, an individual could attend 12 baseball games during a season and watch 22 games on television. Complexity reflects the breadth of behaviours available and can range from simple (a single behaviour) to complex (many different behaviours). For example, a basketball consumer can attend live games, watch game broadcasts via television or internet at home or in a pub, purchase merchandise at the sport venue or online, use social media to follow the team, join a fan forum, talk to friends about the team, attend special team events, volunteer or purchase club memberships. In contrast, unobservable behaviour relates to future intentions towards purchasing or using a sport produce or service and reflects an individual's readiness to engage in the sport experience.

1.3.4 The feedback loop

The sport consumer decision-making model highlights how decisions are made through a sequence of inputs, internal processing and outputs. In Figure 1.1, an additional arrow could be drawn between the outputs and internal processing phases to indicate a feedback loop that occurs in the sequence. This feedback loop often occurs because the evaluation of the sport experience influences future internal processing. That is, the knowledge gained from direct experience and the subsequent attitudes created help the sport consumer make future decisions. For example, the experience of registering and competing in a 5 km road race would likely influence future decisions regarding registering for another road race, such as what distance.

Knowledge from and direct experience play an important role in subsequent evaluations of external inputs, and guide future decisions regarding sport products and services. As a result, sport managers should seek to not only identify what external inputs are most effective in generating favourable internal processing, but also how to design and deliver sport experiences that generate positive attitudinal and behavioural outputs.

1.4 SPORT CONSUMER BEHAVIOUR: SPORT MARKETING ACTIONS

A comprehensive understanding of the sport consumer is critical for developing marketing actions. There are a number of techniques that sport managers can use to acquire such information about their consumers to better understand their decision making. A good place to start is to ask some simple questions of existing consumers. Examples of typical, standard questions are listed in Table 1.1.

These questions can provide information to create sport consumer profiles and personas. For example, a marketer may want to determine what type of individual purchases a specific running shoe for recreation, for fitness, for competition or for fashion. Not all consumers buy a pair of running shoes for the same reason. Hence, collecting information on who, what, where, when, how and why can provide valuable insight into different consumer and market segments.

TABLE 1.1 Sport marketing action questions
1. What product or service do our consumers mainly use?
2. How often do they use it?
3. Where do our consumers live?
4. When do our consumers use the product/service?
5. How do our consumer use the product/service?
6. Who does the consumer use it with?
7. How does the product/service make the consumer feel physically?
8. How does the product/service make the consumer feel emotionally?
9. Why do consumers buy or use our product/service?
10. What does the consumer like about the product/service?
11. Where do our consumers find out about our product/service?
12. What obstacles prevent our consumers from using our product/service?
13. Who makes the actual decision to use our product/service?

In terms of the overall sport experience, answering such questions is also beneficial for gaining consumer need insights; however, it may not provide all the necessary information to fully understand decision-making behaviour. Therefore, another useful technique is to examine the interactions that occur between the sport consumer and the sport context.

1.5 SPORT EXPERIENCE INTERACTIONS

The sport experience involves the physical and psychological responses that occur before, during and after use of the sport product or service. As a result, there are a number of interactions that can occur between the sport consumer and the physical/virtual environment delivered by management. For example, how many interactions would likely occur to an individual attending a live sporting event? These interactions could range from purchasing the ticket online, travelling to the game, enjoying pre-game activities, watching the game, receiving concessions, participating in rituals and returning home. As such, interactions between the consumer and the team's website, venue employees, team personal, volunteers and other spectators would likely occur.

The various sport experience interactions that could occur are often described as 'touchpoints', which are identifiable via the sport consumer journey mapping technique as illustrated in Table 1.2. This mapping technique can be used by sport organizations management to create a service blueprint in order to evaluate how well each touchpoint has been designed and delivered. To better understand the sport consumer's perspective, this approach is valuable to help understand the decision-making sequence through the creation of a sport consumer experience blueprint.

The sport consumer experience blueprint is a simple and instructive way to gain valuable information about consumers by treating the sport experience as a journey including pre-, during and post-consumption activities. A sport consumer's journey can be mapped in segments using a chronological step-by-step approach, with a description of activities or behaviours that may or may not be associated with management functions. An example of a sport consumer experience blueprint for a 10 km running race is presented in Table 1.2.

In this table, a sport consumer (i.e. race participant) describes the various aspects of the journey that occurred from the initial event registration, attending the race exposition, running the event, to what happened after the event. Once the sport consumer experience blueprint has been developed, the consumer can then be asked to evaluate a specific journey segment in terms of thoughts and feelings. For example, in Table 1.2 under pre-event, the consumer may respond that the website was difficult to navigate and that they were frustrated with the registration process; or that they enjoyed training with friends during the weeks leading up to the event. Another example under race day in Table 1.2 is that the consumer liked the number of water stations placed along the course for hydration purposes, which helped them achieve a preferable race time.

The benefit of this mapping technique is that the sport consumer experience is deconstructed into journey segments in order to gain better insight from the consumer. This deconstruction shifts the evaluation of the sport experience from a holistic evaluation to a series of evaluations of multiple segment experiences. For example, asking a consumer whether they were satisfied with a 10 km race is different from asking them about specific

TABLE 1.2 Sport consumer journey blueprint

Pre-event

Register for the event	Purchase new running shoes	Join a running club	Train for event	Receive event updates via email	Use website for information

Day before event

Arrive at race expo	Pick up race packet	Visit vendor/ sponsor tables	Purchase running hat	Put race number on shirt	Eat pre-race dinner

Race day

Arrive at event	Wait in line for restroom	Line up in time corral	Navigate the course	Drink fluids at various stops	Monitor race pace
Eat and drink after race	Talk to other race participants	Listen to music and announcements	Visit vendor/ sponsor tables	Get a massage	Watch award ceremony

Post-event

Check website for results	Recover from race	Wear race T-shirt to gym	Look for other races to do	Attend running club	Eat healthier

journey segments, such as whether they enjoyed training for the event, liked the registration process, felt the number of portable restrooms was enough, whether the event enabled them to make new friends, the helpfulness of course volunteers or the amount of food and drink after the event. Deconstructing the sport consumer experience into multiple journey segments can provide more detailed information on psychological and physical responses.

In addition, a specific segment of the journey (i.e. a single cell in Table 1.2) can be further deconstructed to explore related experiences, to gain an in-depth understanding of the sport consumer's beliefs and feelings in relation to that deconstructed segment. For example, within the pre-event segment in Table 1.2 under train for event, the consumer could be asked to describe how training for the event affected her/his health or other aspects of their life.

Overall, the sport consumer experience blueprint serves two informational purposes: 1) insights into the consumer's overall journey; and 2) based on this insight provide knowledge to develop marketing actions. The first purpose must embrace the consumer's perspective of the sport experience without consideration of the management perspective. In other words, there will be aspects of the journey that a sport organization is unable to manage and without considering the sport consumer experience holistically could limit understanding of the sport consumer. For example, eating at a local restaurant or spending the night in a hotel the night before the 10 km race are generally outside the control of the sport manager. The second purpose is to examine the sport consumer experience blueprint from an organizational perspective, to identify journey segment touchpoints that could potentially be managed. For example, the online registration process or the number of bathrooms provided at the start line is within the control of the sport manager. Once identified, each of these touchpoints should be evaluated in terms of service delivery. This information in relation to touchpoints will inform the type of marketing actions required to enhance customer engagement, and improve the interactions between the customer and the delivery of the sport product or service.

1.6 CHAPTER SUMMARY

This introductory chapter highlights the importance of adopting a consumer perspective to examine sport consumer behaviour as an experience. The sport experience represents the use and pleasure created from the interactions that occur between the customer and the delivery of the sport product or service. Three key factors have been discussed that influence these interactions: the sport user/consumer; the sport context; and the sport management system.

In addition, a definition of sport consumer behaviour was provided that emphasizes the psychological and physical responses that occur before, during and after the sport experience. This definition helps understand why individuals make decisions to spend available resources of time, money and effort on sport experiences.

A sport consumer decision-making sequence was also introduced with three major phases – inputs, internal processing and outputs – which also serves as a general decision-making framework for subsequent chapters in this book. Two beneficial research techniques were also provided, to help sport managers better understand the sport consumer decision-making sequence – asking relevant questions and creating a sport consumer experience blueprint to develop marketing actions.

1.7 DISCUSSION QUESTIONS

The discussion questions presented below are designed to help students review what is important in the chapter. You can answer them on your own, but they are also suitable for discussion work in small groups.

1   Why is it important to examine sport experiences from a consumer behaviour perspective versus a management perspective?
2   Which of the three factors that influence the sport experience design is least controllable and which is the most controllable?
3   Which external factor is more influential on internal processing in the sport consumer decision-making sequence?
4   What is the difference between attitudes in the internal processing phase and attitudinal outcomes in the outputs phase?
5   How does social media or a mobile device app influence the sport consumer experience?

1.8 CLASS ACTIVITY: THE CUSTOMER JOURNEY

The class activity is designed to use information learned in this chapter to develop a sport consumer experience blueprint. The sport consumer experience blueprint maps a customer's journey including pre, during and post-consumption usage to identify key touchpoints. Your task is to create your own sport experience blueprint as follows:

- First, select one of the following sport consumer experiences: a) attending a professional sport team home game or b) working out at a fitness gym in which you regularly use. Please make sure that you are familiar with the sport context chosen and map your own journey. Use a grid format similar to Table 1.2 in this chapter to create your own sport consumer experience blueprint.
- Second, identify any interactions (i.e. touchpoints) that you encountered during your journey that were managed or delivered by the sport team or fitness gym, including both physical and virtual aspects. Discuss with another student each touchpoint from a service delivery perspective. Finally, rate the performance on a three-point scale: 1 = did not meet expectations; 2 = met expectations and 3 = exceeded expectations.
- Please share your results with a classmate. Discuss each cell in your blueprint in terms of feelings and thoughts as you experienced the touchpoint and your evaluations.

REFERENCES

Funk, D.C. (2008). *Consumer Behaviour for Sport & Events: Marketing Action*. Elsevier: Jordon Hill, Oxford UK.

Kaan Turnali in his five part series on the Fan Experience Matters: Design Elements (www.forbes.com/sites/sap/2014/05/04/the-fan-experience-matters-design-elements/) Retrieved October 29, 2015.

Mullin, B., Hardy, S. & Sutton, W. (2014). *Sport Marketing* (4th Ed). Human Kinetics: Champaign IL, USA.

Schiffman, L.G. & Kanuk, L.L. (2010). *Consumer Behavior* (10th Ed). Prentice Hall: Englewood Cliffs, NJ.

Shank, M.D. & Lyberger, M.R. (2015). *Sports Marketing: A Strategic Perspective* 5th Ed. Routledge: New York, USA.

Shilbury, D., Westerbeek, H, Quick, S, Funk, D.C. & Karg, A. (2014). *Strategic Sport Marketing*, 4th Ed Allen & Unwin Academic: Crow Nest, NSW Australia.

CHAPTER 2

Sport consumer segmentation

This chapter's objectives are to:

- discuss how segmentation analysis can lead sport marketing strategy
- discuss the main consumer segmentation criteria
- present segmentation examples in the sport market
- review consumer segmentation studies in various sport contexts.

2.0 INTRODUCTION

Market segmentation is defined as 'the process of dividing a market into distinct subsets of consumers with common needs or characteristics, and selecting one or more segments to target with a distinct marketing mix' (Schiffman & Kanuk, 2004, p. 33). Segmenting consumers is an essential task for marketers, in their effort to understand their needs and characteristics, and develop targeted marketing strategies (Tapp & Clowes, 2000). Market segmentation can also benefit consumers, as products and services are then designed to satisfy their specific needs. As a result, consumers will receive better quality of services and will realize higher satisfaction levels. Schiffman and Kanuk (2004) identified three main steps in the market segmentation process: 1) segmenting a market into homogeneous subgroups; 2) selecting one or more segments to market; and 3) positioning the product or service to achieve a competitive advantage in the market.

2.1 BASIS FOR SEGMENTATION

There are two market segmentation methods: 1) a priori, which is generally conceptual and based on past research; 2) and a posteriori, which is data-driven by current research (Liu, Taylor & Shibli, 2010). In the a priori method, market groups are formed based on the researcher's prior knowledge and experience; while in the a posteriori method, market groups are formed based on primary research. Cluster analysis is often applied, in the latter case, to identify market groups with common characteristics. The most common segmentation variables are: demographic (e.g. age, gender and family type); socio-cultural (e.g. social class, race and ethnicity); geographic (e.g. urban and rural); behavioural (e.g. frequency of service use and quantity of product purchased); and psychographic (e.g. attitudes, benefits, motivation and personality) (Figure 2.1). A combination of various market segmentation variables can also be used. For instance socioeconomic and demographic variables are used to understand who the consumers are, psychographic variables further define the consumer's decision-making process (Tap & Clowes, 2000).

2.1.1 Demographic and socio-cultural segmentation

These relate to segmenting consumers according to demographic and socio-cultural variables (e.g. gender, age, family type, social class and race and ethnicity). Demographic segmentation is probably the easiest method for segmenting consumers, as demographic data are generally accessible to marketers via publications from national agencies (e.g. census, national statistical agencies, etc.).

The following sections illustrate some common socio-demographic variables, which are used for consumer segmentation.

Gender segmentation

Gender is one of the most common variables used for market segmentation. In the sport-marketing context, an interesting development has been the growing consumer power of females. Globally, it has recently been estimated that women control $28 trillion in

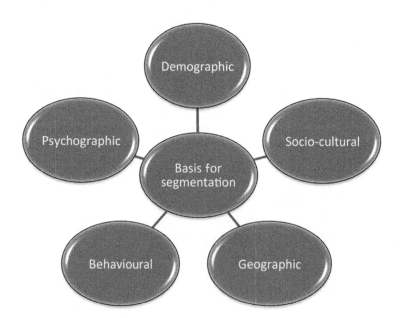

FIGURE 2.1 Segmentation variables

consumer spending and more than 70% of all consumer-related decisions (Silverstein & Sayre, 2009). As a result, the majority of sport sectors are now invested in the female consumer market. Some relevant examples of this investment include female athletic gear (e.g. shoes and clothing), female health clubs, female fitness programmes (e.g. dance classes) and female sports leagues (e.g. WNBA – www.wnba.com/). Nike, for example, has predicted that its newest line of athletic gear for women will add $2 billion to annual sales by 2017. Its main objective is to combine athletic performance with style, so that women look fashionable while the gear functions well (Kell, 2014).

There is also a wide range of brand campaigns in the sporting goods sector targeted at women, such as Nike's *Nike and Women* (2013), Under Armour's *Women. Protect This House. I will* (2010), and Adidas's *All Adidas Women* (2011).

In the sport spectator market, the power of women as a sport consumer has also been realized in recent times. The US NFL is a good example of this recognition, where it has been proposed that the future of the league depends on female fans (Chemi, 2014). The female market has grown faster than the already mature male market that has its own set of challenges for further development. The NFL seeks to further increase involvement among women in order to create committed fans; if it succeeds, this strategy will be associated with higher revenue for the league. A number of positive indicators of continual growth in the female spectator market have already emerged for the NFL (Chemi, 2014; Dosh, 2012):

- From 2012 to 2013, male audiences dropped 2.0%, while female audiences grew 3.0%.
- There were more than 80 million female NFL fans in 2013.
- NFL merchandise sold to women is continuously increasing – a 125% increase in 2011 over 2010.
- The number of US women participating in fantasy football doubled in 2011 over 2010.
- From 2009 to 2013, female NFL viewership increased 26.0% compared to an 18.0% rise for men.
- During the 2013 Super Bowl event, female viewership rose 15.0% compared to 10.0% for men.
- Eight NFL teams have female-affinity clubs, which create communities for female fans to share their love of the game.

In addition, on recognizing the economic benefits of the female market, the NFL opened a new website section just for women (www.nfl.com/women) in 2011.

Similar statistics (Nooyi, 2013; Schrotenboer, 2015) in relation to the growth of the female sport consumer market have also been reported by other US sport leagues, including:

- Half of the NBA online store shoppers are women.
- Across eight major US sport leagues, females spent nearly $1.3 billion more on sports logo apparel in 2012 over 2011.
- The number of women watching the Super Bowl from 2000 to 2011 increased by more than 34.0%.

- US female fans make up 36% of NASCAR and 43% of baseball fans.
- Among the major US sports leagues, women make up 36% of Twitter followers and 43% of Facebook fans.

In line with these telling statistics, there are several examples of sport brand campaigns that have been developed to specifically target female fans, including the WNBA's 2013 season on the NBATV commercial (2013), and the NFL's *Women's Apparel* commercial (2015).

The increasing power of the female market is also evident in the sport participation sector worldwide. Previously there was a clear lengthy gap between sport and women in terms of participation, which has considerably shortened. For instance, in the 2014 Special Eurobarometer it was reported that in Belgium, France, Greece, Latvia, Lithuania, Slovakia, Spain and the UK, men were more likely to report being regularly active in sport than women. However, in Denmark, Finland, Sweden and the Netherlands these patterns have been reversed; that is, higher sport participation rates for women over men (Van Tuyckom & Scheerder, 2010).

In respect to health club memberships, the proportion of US male and female members is almost identical – 20% and 19% respectively (IHRSA Trend Report, 2014). Also in the USA, female participation in recreational distance running events has grown substantially. According to Running USA, 90% of marathon participants were men in 1980. Yet by 2012, the participation rates for full marathon events (i.e. 42.2 km) were 58% men and 42% women. In relation to the half marathon distance (13.1 miles), women now outnumber men in terms of participation, increasing from 49% females in 2002 to 59% in 2012 (Wegner, Ridinger, Jordan & Funk, 2014).

Identifying the needs of the female sport consumer is a key topic for further developing the female sport market. Previous marketing approaches that have solely defined female sport consumers through family relationships (e.g. watching sport because the husband or son does, or attending the game to spend time with the family) are no longer appropriate. Women are now viewed as distinct and real sport consumers, whether as fans, active participants, coaches or athletes. Female-affinity clubs, for example, as created by several NFL teams, support this new trend, providing not only educational experiences, but also opportunities for networking, enhanced game experience and women being treated like genuine football fans (Brennan, 2013).

Age segmentation

On a global scale, different age groups generally have varying consumer needs and expectations. Most marketers subsequently study the influence of aging on consumer needs, to develop appropriate products/services and communication strategies. In the USA one of the most important demographic trends of its population is the changing age structure. Some clear patterns in terms of age have been observed (Shrestha & Heisler, 2011). For instance, in comparison with 1950, Americans are living notably longer. Older Americans (65+ years) represented 8.1% of the total population in 1950, which had increased to 12.8% in 2009, and is projected to reach 20.2% in 2050. In summary, one in five persons in 2050 will be aged 65 or older in the USA (Gibson, Cabler, Cance, Beck & Santos, 2013).

This trend of living longer, which is particularly common in Western countries, has important implications for sport marketers. As the number of older adults continues to grow, their needs and expectations cannot be overlooked by sport marketers. As an example, in the US fitness industry, the power of the middle-aged and elderly segments is reflected in club memberships, which increased 411% between 1990 and 2007 among 55+-year-olds (Stone, 2011).

Yet even though the growth in the 55+ segment is well documented, it has not been given considerable attention by sport marketers. Some public bodies and authorities in Western nations have initiated campaigns that target elderly sport participants, such as the US Department of Health and Human Services *New Go4Life* campaign, which focuses on fitness for older adults, organized by the National Institute of Health (Cire, 2011); as well as the Fit for the Future Programme by Age UK (Wigfield, Kispeter, Alden, Turner, 2015) and the *Walking for Health* initiative (www.walkingforhealth.org.uk/). However, commercial sport campaigns that specifically target seniors are limited – one of the most relevant examples would be Nike's *Magic Soccer Night – What do old men really do at night* (2012).

In the sport participation market, specific sports that are often defined as 'lifetime sports' (e.g. tennis, golf, walking, hiking) are traditionally popular among the older aged segments. It seems, however, that sport organizations have not effectively promoted sport participation among the 55+ market. For example, even though tennis is deemed suitable for all ages and therefore considered a life-long sport, a report by Stone (2011) shows that participation data do not fit with the aging of the population. There were 27.8 million tennis players in the USA in 2010 (9% of the overall population), yet only 12% of these participants (about 3.42 million) were aged 50+, and only 2% of all new players (about 101,000) were in the 50+ age category. This is despite 50+-year-olds being recognized as the second most loyal participant group (most frequent players) after 35–49-year-olds. Stone (2011) concluded that tennis club marketers need to develop strategies that specifically target older consumers, as this is one of their future main markets.

It is clear that an understanding of the needs and expectations of the elderly is necessary to build an effective brand communication strategy. Building trust, focusing on the 'feel' age rather than the real age, and selecting the right communication channel are important considerations. In addition, it has been proven that direct and personalized brand campaigns work better than mass and impersonal ones (Beesly, 2015). Despite the general belief that social and internet media are for young people, surveys have shown that many 60+-year-olds in the USA use blogs, videos, podcasts, forums and other internet sources before making consumer choices (Beesly, 2015). Subsequently, these media sources should not be overlooked in relation to sport marketing targeted at older consumers (Beesley, 2015).

Family type segmentation

Most marketers try to segment families in an effort to study their consumer behaviour in more depth. Yet there is a range of different family types that need to be considered, dependent on the amount and age range of the members. One of the main ways to define families is to use the traditional family life cycle, which includes a series of stages that describe the development of an individual over their lifespan, and in relation to demographic and psychographic factors (Schiffman & Kanuk, 2004). The five most common development stages within this family life cycle are: 1) bachelorhood; 2) honeymooners; 3) parenthood; 4) post-parenthood; and 5) dissolution.

Stage 1) Bachelorhood: It consists of young, single men and women who live separately from their parents, with full- or part-time jobs. The individuals who belong to this group mostly live in large urban settings and cities, and are among the prime target groups of health and fitness organizations. Socialization is a key reason why these individuals engage in sport consumption behaviour.

Stage 2) Honeymooners: This stage starts immediately after the marriage of a couple, and it continues until the birth or adoption of the first child. It includes families where both members work, who usually have considerable start-up expenses to establish their new home.

Stage 3) Parenthood: This stage starts with the birth or adoption of the first child. As it can extend for more than 20 years, until the child leaves the family home (e.g. attends college), it is generally a long, temporal stage that includes many diverse family types. Examples include young families with children less than six years old, young families with children more than six years old and older couples with children and adolescents. Many sport teams and clubs target families with young children by offering specific ticket types (family tickets), places within the stadium (family seating area), specialized services for them (e.g. parties) and sections on their website (e.g. NFL Party). In the same way, health and fitness clubs often develop family exercise programmes, so that both the kids and parents can exercise at the same time in the same facility. Organizers of city marathons also often target families with young children by implementing short races (e.g. 1 km). In addition, families with young children are often deemed a dynamic group for sport camps, which is a fast developing area in the sport market. Examples of sport brand campaigns that target families include Nike's *What Parents Say at Nike Sport Camp* (2010), and its *Parents Perspective at Nike Sports Camps* (2013).

Stage 4) Post-parenthood: This relates to families where the child has left home. The family might be more comfortable financially, with more leisure time and discretionary income available. This is also generally a long, temporal stage, which can be further divided into families whose members are still working and families whose members are in retirement. In particular, families in this stage are often a good target group for leisure, travelling and event sport tourism, as many have more time and money to travel, and to engage in leisure and recreation activities.

Stage 5) Dissolution: This stage occurs with the death of a spouse or partner in the family. Companionship is a key issue at this life cycle stage, often leveraged by rehabilitation centres and health clubs with specialized programs that target these older individuals.

It should be noted that these five main development stages cannot be applied to all consumers' life cycles – unexpected events such as divorces, temporary retirement and deaths can change the flow of the stages. Thus, while this concept of the family life cycle is useful to marketing, it is somewhat generic and needs to evolve with the ever-changing dynamics of society's families. This means that further information is often required for marketers to be able to develop accurately targeted marketing strategies (e.g. socio-cultural and demographic information).

Social class segmentation

The three most common variables that define social class are: 1) income; 2) education; and 3) occupation. These three variables are most often deemed as correlated, and there are several examples in the sport market of how social class can be used for segmentation. For example, some sport marketers target fans and spectators belonging to higher socio-economic groups to sell premium seating (Lawrence, Contorno & Steffek, 2013). In addition, there are numerous upscale fitness clubs (e.g. within luxury hotels) that target individuals from higher socioeconomic groups.

Some individual sports have traditionally been linked with specific social classes. For example, in England soccer and rugby have their origins among the working class, while golf, tennis and skiing are traditionally perceived as middle and upper class sports. Skiing is a strong example of a sport that appeals to higher socioeconomic groups. According to the US National Ski Areas Association's 2007/08 National Demographic Study, 29% of US skiers had incomes of $100,000 to $199,999 (vs. 16% of US households), and 19% of skiers had incomes of $200,000+ (vs. 3% of US households). Furthermore, skiers spent about $3 billion on their sport during this period, including $835 million on equipment, $1.6 billion on apparel and almost $1 billion on accessories. This is a typical market, which spends on travel, hobbies and leisure activities (Formichelli, 2009).

Race and ethnicity segmentation

As will be further discussed in Chapter 4, ethnic and racial subgroups have unique characteristics that should be considered by marketers, as they often influence lifestyle and consumer decision-making. As Stodolska and Shinew (2014) reported, recent US demographics have revealed a rapid increase of ethnic minority groups in the USA, indicating new and emerging markets that should be considered. In the USA, the main four race and ethnicity groups are: 1) non-Hispanic whites; 2) non-Hispanic Asians; 3) non-Hispanic-African-Americans; and 4) Hispanics. The fastest-growing group is Hispanics, which is projected to reach as high as 29% of the population by 2050 (Taylor & Cohn, 2012).

There are several examples of sport organizations, which have studied these cultural trends and have started to develop marketing initiatives to increase their consumer base among race and ethnic groups. The US NFL was one of the first to recognize the growing power of the Hispanic population as a potential fan market. Several strategies were therefore developed by the NFL to grow its Hispanic base. Examples are the development of media access (televising games in Spanish) and media partnerships across a range of channels to promote its games to the Hispanic population. These partnerships include programming with ESPN Deportes, Telemundo, Univision and the NFL Network. As an outcome, it has recently been estimated that 25 million Hispanics in the USA identify themselves as NFL fans (Alicia, 2013).

The NBA is another US sport organization that has successfully targeted ethnic and race groups, especially the fast-growing Hispanic population. Based on only 15% of the NBA's fan base being Hispanic in 2009, the NBA launched a range of marketing campaigns involving television, radio and online advertising, a website, special events, grass-roots programmes and unique consumer products to increase its Hispanic following. As Saskia Sorrosa, Senior Director of Marketing at the NBA, explained in an interview with Carter (2010), they emphasized the use of social and digital media to promote the league among race and ethnic minority groups. They also developed a website specific for Hispanic and Latino fans, where the games are delivered in a way that celebrates fans' identity and the ethnic diversity of the players (www.NBA.com/enebea). In addition, they concentrated on the development of emotional links with multicultural fans by building fans' emotional connections with Hispanic players. As a result of these marketing initiatives, Hispanic fans made up 12% of the NBA's regular season total viewership in 2011/12 – an increase of 20% over the 2010/11 season (Nielsen Sport Report Insights, 2012).

Hispanics have also grown in number within the National Collegiate Athletic Association (NCAA) fan base. The Neilson Sport Insights (2012) reported that 6.9 million viewers of Hispanic origin watched at least a portion of the NCAA Tournament on CBS and Turner in 2012. Hispanic fans are younger in age in comparison with African-American and white viewers. The average age of the Hispanic viewer during the 2012 NCAA Tournament was 39 years – lower than both African-American and white viewers who had a median age of 44 and 48 years respectively (Nielsen Sport Report Insights, 2012).

Although it should be noted that Hispanics is not the only racial group that has important marketing implications for US sport organizations. Stadler, Kristi and Rhema (2014), for example, emphasized African-Americans (accounting for about 13% of the US population) as an under-represented but promising consumer group for professional sport leagues in the USA. Lack of exposure and access to sports (e.g. limited access to certain sports, lack of marketing actions targeting them), the cost of attending games and other commitments (e.g. family, social) were reported by Stadler *et al.* (2104) to be among the main constraints for African-Americans attending professional sporting events in the USA. In contrast, performance and entertainment (e.g. quality of the team, level of competition), game atmosphere (experience during the game), comfort and convenience (e.g. accessibility, game schedule, weather), image (of the organization), identity (e.g. with athletes and teams), the social nature of sports (spending time with friends/family) and value (e.g. pride of attending) are among their main motivators for attending sporting contests in the USA.

In the sport and recreation sector, studies among different ethnic minority groups have shown that subculture influences sport participation and choices of individual activities (Stodolska & Alexandris, 2004, Stodolska & Shinew, 2014, Stodolska & Jouyeon, 2003). As a general trend, sport participation is lower among the racial and ethnic group members in the US. For instance, Vásquez, Shaw, Gensburg, Okorodudu and Corsino (2013) reported that physical activity is lower among non-Hispanic black men (48%) than non-Hispanic white (61%) and Hispanic men (59%). Similarly, physical activity is lower among non-Hispanic black women (32%) than among Hispanic women (35%) and non-Hispanic white women (49%). Non-Hispanic white men (41.8%) and Hispanic men (41.5%) are also more likely to participate in higher levels of physical activity than non-Hispanic black men (32.7%).

Similar trends have been reported among youths in the USA. For example, white non-Hispanic students reported significantly higher levels of moderate physical activity than African-American and Hispanic students (Shores & Shinew, 2014). In terms of preferences for individual sport activities, Hispanics prefer participation in more family and social-oriented activities, which generally take place in community parks. Hispanic women are one of the groups with the lowest participation rates in active sports and fitness activities (Stodolska & Shinew, 2014).

These different sport activity patterns reflect not only cultural differences; they also relate to health problems, marital status, employment status and the socioeconomic characteristics of the individuals who belong to the different ethnic groups (Shores & Shinew, 2014).

2.1.2 Geographic segmentation

In geographic segmentation, the market is divided according to the location where consumers live, which can be based on regions (urban vs. rural area), cities (different sizes) or countries (international markets). The common perception is that individuals who live in different locations have different opportunities and consumer behaviour patterns, based on the influence of where they live. As an example of geographic segmentation, the IHRSA Trend Report (2014) studies club membership in different regions across the USA. As shown in Figure 2.2, the West region has the highest percentage of club members (25%), followed by the North East (18%). In contrast, the South Central has the lowest percentage of club members (17%).

Geographic segmentation is also often applied when sport organizations select specific communications channels (e.g. local vs. national TV channels, radio stations, newspapers, magazines and direct mail-outs). Geographic segmentation, for example, is widely used by sport organizations, which have a local profile, such as state/public park and recreation

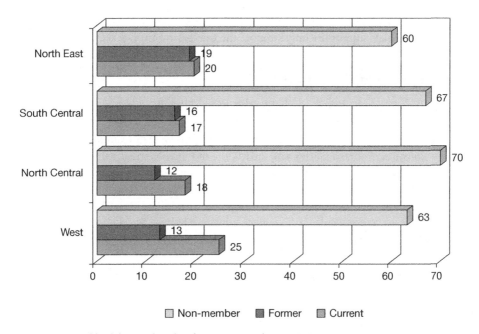

FIGURE 2.2 Health club membership by region in the US (%)

Source: IHRSA (2014)

departments, which target local communities. Sport event organizers also often use geographic segmentation in terms of targeting national or international visitors (participants or spectators); while franchised sport organizations (e.g. health clubs) also use it to decide on their catchment area (i.e. the boundaries of a geographic area where sport organizations attract customers). The use of the internet and social media as communication tools has made it easier for sport marketers to target geographically distant consumers.

Sport organizations with international profiles (e.g. European professional soccer teams and NBA teams) often develop specific targeted marketing strategies for the different continents, where their sports are more relevant, to increase their fan base. For example, to further penetrate the Chinese market, in 2015 the NBA signed its largest international digital partnership with China's internet Tencent Holdings Ltd. As part of this five-year arrangement, the NBA committed to delivering live games, original programming and highlights via Tencent's range of personal computer and mobile services. The Nike *Globalization* campaign (2011) is also an example of an international campaign promoting the global appeal of sports.

2.1.3 Behavioural segmentation

In behavioural segmentation, the consumer market is divided according to the quantity of product buying, frequency of using a service and brand loyalty. It can be based on simple indicators such as how many games an individual attends per year or how many times members visit a health club per week. It can also be based on a more sophisticated approach, such as using multiple criteria to categorize consumers, according to loyalty levels. Examples of behavioural segmentation variables in sports include the percentage of total games attended per season, the propensity to renew support in successive seasons and the extent to which supporters only support the one team (Tapp & Clowes, 2000).

2.1.4 Psychographic segmentation

Psychographic segmentation is probably the most difficult segmentation approach for marketers, as it is generally based on the intrinsic, subjective characteristics of each consumer, such as personal attitudes, interests and opinions. For example, it might relate to sport consumers' personalities and attitudes and involvement with their favourite team/sport activity. Psychological constructs such as motivation, attitudes, satisfaction and fan involvement are among the most common used by marketers.

Socio-cultural variables can also be used in combination with psychographics. Snowboarders are an example of a consumer group that can be defined by both socio-demographic and psychographic variables. It has been reported that 73.0% of the population of snowboarders are under the age of 25, and that 51.7% are under the age of 17, and that the vast majority are male (74.2%). In addition, their personality profile shows that they tend to be bold, daring and seek adventure; that their fashion style is unique and trendy; and that they are often outgoing and carefree (The Burton Company, 2011).

2.2 ACADEMIC SEGMENTATION STUDIES IN SPORTS

Previous academic research in relation to sport segmentation is not extensive, due to its emphasis on theoretical rather than applied research. However, there are some published studies which have used a combination of segmentation variables to profile sport consumers, which confirm the value of segmentation research for sport marketing theory and practice.

2.2.1 Segmentation studies in the context of sport spectatorship

Most of the segmentation studies on sport spectatorship have used a combination of variables, which include demographic (e.g. gender, age and life stage), geographic (e.g. city, county, state) behavioural (e.g. frequency of attendance) and psychographic (e.g. team commitment, attachment and brand associations, fan motives and attitudes and perceived benefits). These studies have mainly been conducted in the context of professional and college sports in the USA, as well as English professional soccer. A review of some of the most representative of these studies as follows.

Conceptual segmentation of sport fans

Hunt, Bristol and Bashaw (1999) aimed to conceptually (with no primary research) classify professional sport fans in the USA using a combination of segmentation criteria. The authors proposed five segments:

- Temporary sport fans: This relates to fans of a specific, time-bound event, which can last from a few hours to a few years – there is an end point where a temporary fan will stop being a fan. This is because most temporary fans do not identify themselves as true fans; that is, they do not use the football team to express their identities. The authors used Michal Jordan and some of the Chicago Bulls fans as an example of temporary fans. In this case, after the retirement of Michael Jordan, some fans lost their interest in professional basketball.
- Local sport fans: These sport fans are bound by geographical constraints and they are identified with a geographic area (e.g. a specific city or town football team). However, if a local fan moves to another area, it is likely that they will stop being a committed fan of the previous local area football team.
- Devoted sport fan: These fans are not as influenced by time and geographical factors as the temporary and local fan. They are instead loyal fans who have developed a strong identity with the team. These fans are a very good target group for football team marketers, because they are more willing to spend money on tickets, merchandise, team events and anything else related to their favourite team.
- Fanatical sport fans: Most of these fans are even more committed than the devoted fans. They feel strongly identified with the team and its activities. For these fans, the team has a central role in their life; they exhibit strong attitudinal and behavioural

loyalty. Most fanatical fans regularly attend games and express strong support for their favourite team via various means such as wearing the team's T-Shirt, carrying scarves and painting their body.

- Dysfunctional sport fans: Within this group, fan status is used as a means for self-identification. For these fans, winning is the most important aspect of the game; they are sometimes engaged in behaviours that disrupt the event and even cause problems. Such 'hooligans' often express anti-social behaviour before, during and after the game. These five segments and their characteristics are presented in Table 2.1.

These authors also proposed some useful marketing and promotional strategies to target and reach each of these fan groups:

- Temporary sport fans: Timing of communications is essential to targeting these fans, with promotions involving the social and entertainment aspect of the game.
- Local sport fans: Organizing local community events (e.g. school visits), including using team players, will help to target local fans.
- Devoted sport fans: Providing information about the team, players and club activities via the internet is an important strategy for targeting these fans.
- Fanatic sport fans: Leveraging their feelings and experiences via relevant information on the internet, including letting them express their devotion via team merchandise, would be beneficial.
- Dysfunctional sport fans: Most of these fans should be de-marketed. Sport managers and marketers should find ways to limit their anti-social behaviour.

Segmentation of English Premier League soccer fans

Soccer is the largest sport sector in Europe. As Deloitte's (2015a) reported, the top leagues according to their revenues are: 1) The English Premier League (*www.premierleague.com*); 2) The German Bundesliga (*www.bundesliga.com*); 3) The Spanish Primera Division

TABLE 2.1 Cluster groups of professional sport fans in the USA (a conceptual classification)

Temporary Fans	Local Fans	Devoted Fans	Fanatical Fans	Dysfunctional Fans
•Time bound •Lack of identification with the sport team	•Geographically bound •Lack of commitment with the sport team	•Loyal fans •Strongly identified with the sport team	•Devoted fans (with the sport team) •Committed fans (with the sport team)	•Disrupting behavior •Anti-social behavior

Source: Hunt, K.A., Bristol, T. & Bashaw, R.E. (1999). A conceptual approach to classifying sports fans. *Journal of Services Marketing*, 13(6), 439–452.

(www.lfp.es); 4) The Italian Serie A (www.legaseriea.it); and 5) The French Ligue (www.ligue1.com). According to a recent Deloitte report (2015b), the top 20 European soccer clubs increased their revenues by 14% in the 2013/14 year (6.2 billion euro), in comparison with 2012/13. Real Madrid (549.5 million euro), Manchester United (518.0 million euro) and Bayern Munich (487.4 million euro) were the three top European soccer clubs (Deloitte report, 2015b).

Despite these statistics, there have been limited attempts in academic literature to segment soccer fans in Europe, based on primary research. One of the most detailed qualitive studies, focused on a sample of English Premier League soccer fans, was conducted by Tapp and Clowes (2000). The authors used a combination of demographic, geographic and psychographic and behavioural variables to profile fans. Their study produced some clear patterns (as summarized in Table 2.2):

a) Demographic variables: In terms of gender, the vast majority (about 80%) of fans were males. Within the sample there was a wide range of occupations, and the age profile was also very diverse. Security was one of the main constraints for female attendance, particularly without male company.

b) Geographic variables: A segment was identified within this variable, termed 'professional wanderers', consisting of fans with managerial or professional job status, who despite their busy job commitments, maintained relationships with their local teams. These individuals, however, were not very committed fans.

c) Psychographic and behavioural variables:

• Benefit segmentation: This was used to categorize fans based on the winning vs. entertainment dichotomy. It was found that more than half of these fans (55%) preferred an entertaining game, even if their team lost. However, a high percentage (39%) perceived winning as the most important aspect of the game. Based on this segmentation, fans can be classified as either football fans (i.e. value the entertainment factor more, including the skills of the players and the technical aspects of the game) or team fans (i.e. value winning more than entertainment, and often perceive the team as a way of expressing themselves).

• Value to the club (measured by number of games attended): Fans were classified into casual (attending 1–9 home games), regular (attending 8–18 home games) and fanatics (attending all 18 home games plus some away games)

– Fanatics: These were highly involved fans, so were the most important target group for the club. They lived and breathed football, and were season ticket holders.

– Regular: These were committed fans, although not as devoted as fanatics. Most were season ticket holders.

– Casual: Most did not have close links with the local community/city. While genuine followers of the club, they also prioritized other non-football leisure and entertainment activities – deemed more as 'consumers' than 'fans'. They were not season ticket holders.

d) Behavioural variables: The authors used loyalty as a variable of behavioural segmentation. Noting that fans are more loyal than a typical consumer, it was identified that team success is an important factor for behavioural loyalty. About one-third of fans

TABLE 2.2 Segmentation variables of the English Premier League soccer fans

Demographic variables	Geographic variables	Benefit variables	"Value to the sport team" related variables	Behavioural variables
Males (80%)	Local fans	Prefer entertaining games (55%)	Fanatics	Loyal with the sport team
Females (20%)	'Professional wanderers'	Expect team winning (39%)	Regular fans	Loyal with soccer (repertoire fans)
			Casual fans	

Source: Tapp, A. & Clowes, J. (2000). From "carefree casuals" to "professional wanderers": Segmentation possibilities for football supporters. *European Journal of Marketing, 36*(11/12), 1248–1269. Segmentation of US college sport fans.

also watched other teams' games (Premier League or local games) – defined in the study as 'repertoire fans'. These repertoire fans were the least loyal toward their team, and many of them were young, educated, with higher income and status jobs. They generally favoured entertainment over winning. A summary of the main results of Tapp and Clowes' (2000) study are presented in Table 2.2.

Mahony, Madrigal, and Howard (2000) used the construct of psychological commitment in relation to a behavioural variable (attendance frequency) to segment fans of a US college sport team. The authors proposed the following four segments:

1) High in commitment and high in attendance frequency: This segment related to the true loyal fans who have developed strong psychological connections with the team. Continuous targeting of this segment was deemed essential among sport marketers; otherwise, they may gradually lose interest in the team. Reinforcement marketing strategies such as economic incentives and interactive communications should be used.

2) High in commitment and low in attendance frequency (latent loyalty): Although they attended games as frequently as the loyal fan, they had not developed a strong commitment toward the team. They generally attended games because their friends did or due to geographical proximity (e.g. living in the college city) – they can drop out any time. This segment should be targeted with promotional strategies that emphasize the cognitive component of attitudes (e.g. product information), and the social benefits of attending games.

3) Low in commitment and high in behavioural loyalty (spurious loyalty): This segment related to fans who had developed commitment toward their team, but never attended games. A number of constraints such as cost and lack of friends to attend with were likely to influence their attendance behaviour (a detailed discussion of constraints will be made in Chapter 6). These fans often preferred to stay home and watch sports on TV. Removing the constraints that many of these fans face, through marketing campaigns, is essential to encouraging them to attend games.

4) Low in commitment and low on behavioural loyalty: This segment related to fans who had not expressed a commitment toward the team and did not frequently attend games. As this is a challenging fan group, marketers need to make an upfront decision on whether to target them or to define them as a non-demand group. If they choose to target them, they will need to develop strategies focused on changing their attitudes (a detailed discussion on changing attitudes is made in Chapter 7).

The four cluster groups are presented in Figure 2.3.

More examples of psychographic variables, which have been used to segment sport fans, include team attachment (Alexandris & Tsiotsiou, 2012), fan identity and consumer motivation (Giulianotti, 2002; Hunt *et al.*, 1999) and attitudinal loyalty and brand associations (Funk, 2002; Funk & Pastore, 2000).

In summary, studies in relation to spectatorship sports have shown that psychographic variables are a useful method for segmenting fans, especially when used in combination with behavioural and demographic variables. Sport marketers should work closely with researchers to profile their fans, based on the use of primary data. Both qualitative and quantitative research can be used for identifying fans' psychographic and behavioural patterns, which will help the development of marketing strategy.

2.2.2 Segmentation studies in the context of participatory sports

Most segmentation studies in relation to active sport participation have used demographic (e.g. age, gender and family life cycle), behavioural (e.g. frequency, duration and length of participation) and psychographic (e.g. motivation, constraints, involvement and attitudes) variables. As active participation involves a wide range of sport and recreation activities (e.g. outdoor and indoor, general fitness and competitive), common patterns cannot usually be identified within segmentation studies.

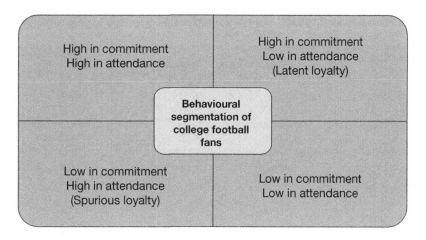

FIGURE 2.3 Cluster groups of college football fans in the USA

Source: Mahony et al. (2000)

Outdoor running sector

The outdoor runners market is one of the fastest developing in the sport industry, both in terms of recreational running and participating in organized running events such as marathons. Scheerder and Breedveld (2015) reported that in Europe, it is estimated that 50 million people run on a regular basis. Their spending in running-related expenses is estimated at 9.6 billion annually. Globally, the number of marathons finishers worldwide increased from 400,000 in 2000 to more than 1.6 million in 2013 (Scheerder & Breedveld, 2015). In the USA alone, it is estimated that the number of runners had increased from 45.84 million in 2008 to 60.48 million in 2015 (Statista, http://statista.com/statistics/227423/number-of-joggers-and-runners-usa/).

Rohm, Milne and McDonald (2006), who conducted their study in the USA, aimed to segment runners via psychographic and demographic variables, and proposed the following:

- Healthy runners: They ran the least amount of miles per week (21 miles) of all the segments. Most were in the 40–49 age group and were male (56%). They were generally motivated by fitness and mental health-related reasons.
- Social competitors: They ran the most miles per week (29 miles), and ran on average five days per week. Defined as 'serious leisure runners', they also participated in competitive marathons and were the most experienced runners. The majority was male (63%) and this segment had the highest amount of runners aged over 50. They were often motivated by physical and mental health-related reasons; however, strong competition and social-related motives differentiated them from the other segments.
- Actualized runners: This was the least experienced running segment, with the highest amount of younger runners. On average, they ran about 25 miles per week, and this segment was the only one that contained more females than males. Most were motivated by self-esteem and fitness-related reasons.

TABLE 2.3 Clusters of outdoor runners

Healthy joggers	Social competitors	Actualized runners	Devotees
• 40-49 years old • Males • Prime motives: fitness and health	• Serious leisure runners • Marathon runners • Prime motive: competition	• The least experienced runners • The youngest cluster • Prime motives: self-esteem and fitness	• 25-50 years old • Long races - marathon runners • Prime motive: addiction

Source: Rohm, A.J., Milne, G.R. & McDonald, M.A. (2006). Proven top-rate qualitative analysis and mixed methods research. *Sport Marketing Quarterly*, 15, 29–39.

- Devotees: They ran about 28 miles per week, with many preferring to participate in longer marathon-type events – more so than the other segments. Most were aged between 25 and 50, and there were more males than females. Addiction was the main reason that they ran; running was an essential part of their lives. The four running clusters are presented in Table 2.3.

Fitness sector (indoor sport/health clubs)

The fitness industry is another sport sector that continues to grow. The 2013 IHRSA report (Ablondi, 2013) revealed that internationally there was a 4.7% increase in the number of health clubs between 2012 and 2013, a 4.0% increase in revenue and a 1.8% increase in the number of memberships. These international results also revealed that in 2013 there were 153,160 health clubs, 132 million members and a total revenue of $77,747 million. The USA had the largest amount of these members (almost 56,000), while Europe had the largest amount of clubs (46,396) and overall revenue ($32,022 million).

One of the few studies that have used a national sample of health club members, in the context of public (not private) indoor sport centres in England, was Liu *et al.* (2010). This study used performance data in combination with socio-demographic variables including measuring specific service quality dimensions based on how important they were to customers: staff, catering, quality of wet facilities (swimming pools), accessibility, quality of dry facilities and cleanliness. Based on a cluster analysis, the authors proposed four customer segments:

1) Cluster 1 – physical evidence, wet focused: This was the largest segment, including customers concerned about the quality of facilities, especially the wet facilities (swimming pools) and the cleanliness. They were not overly concerned about the quality of staff and services within the club. In terms of demographics, this segment was strongly represented by older customers.
2) Cluster 2 – physical evidence, dry focused: This segment was deemed the most demanding, giving high scores across all the service quality dimensions. In particular, they expected high-quality dry facilities and catering, as well as good accessibility. The segment mainly consisted of customers aged between 25 and 44. Older and younger individuals were under-represented.
3) Cluster 3 – physical evidence, wet and catering focused: This was the second largest segment. They had high expectations of the catering within facilities, and did not seem overly concerned about dry facilities. This segment mainly consisted of young customers (aged 16–24 and students).
4) Cluster 4 – Non-physical evidence focused: This was the smallest segment with the least amount of expectations. They mostly valued the non-physical aspect of the facilities, such as catering services, accessibility and staff; the quality of the dry and wet facilities was the least important factor. Young customers aged <16 and 16–24 were strongly represented in this segment.

It should be reiterated that this study was conducted among members of public indoor sport clubs in England. Consequently, the segmentation in this study is not applicable to private sport/health clubs, which often have customers with a different socioeconomic profile.

Winter skiing sector

The winter sport market (mountain skiing and snowboarding) is one of the most prominent within the sport industry. It has recently been estimated that there are about 115 million skiers worldwide, in a market that is slowly but steadily growing. The Alps is the main skiing destination (45% market share), followed by North America (21%), Asia-Pacific (14%), Western Europe (11%) and Eastern Europe and Central Asia (9%). Most skiers are from Western Europe (27%), followed by Asia-Pacific (19%) and North America (19%) (Vanat, 2014). Despite the strong global presence of this sport sector, there have been few studies that have focused on using psychographic and behavioural variables to segment recreational skiers.

One such study is that of Alexandris, Kouthouris, Funk and Giovani (2009), conducted in Greece, which aimed to segment recreational skiers. Using motivation as a segmentation criterion and in combination with loyalty and involvement, and with the use of a cluster analysis, the authors proposed four recreational skier segments:

1) Novices: This segment included non-experienced skiers, motivated by the desire to improve their skills and abilities. They had low involvement and loyalty levels.
2) Multi-interests: While this segment was motivated by several factors, social recognition was their primary reason for skiing. They perceived skiing as a trendy activity that creates a positive image that somewhat improves or fits with their society status. This segment was the least loyal, after Novices.
3) Naturalists: This segment was mainly motivated by incentives related to enjoying nature. In contrast, they were the least motivated by the social recognition, excitement and achievement dimensions. These individuals preferred relaxing, non-crowded environments, aiming to enjoy the beauty of nature as an experience.
4) Enthusiasts: This was the segment with the highest motivation to do skiing. They were the most experienced skiers, and were generally activity oriented. As a result, they were the most involved and loyal skiers. The four skiing clusters are presented in Table 2.4.

TABLE 2.4 Clusters of mountain skiers

Novice	Multi-interest	Naturalists	Enthusiasts
• Non-experienced skiers • Motivated by the opportunity to improve their skiing skills and abilities	• Motivated by the opportunity to: • Achieve social recognition • Improve personal image	• Motivated by the opportunity to: • Enjoy the nature • Ski in relaxing environments	• The highest motivated cluster • The most involved with skiing cluster

Source: Alexandris, K., Kouthouris, C., Funk, D. & Giovani, K. (2009). Segmenting winter sport tourists by motivation: The case of recreational skiers. *Journal of Hospitality Marketing and Management, 18,* 480–500.

Golf sector

Golf is one of the several sports linked to sport tourism. It generates almost $70 billion per year for the US economy, and employs almost 2 million US citizens (Darren, 2015). According to HSBC's (2012) report, it is estimated that 80 million golfers play about 40,000 courses worldwide. Golf events are worth close to $2 billion per year, and the golf tourism market is worth more than $1 billion (HSBC, 2012).

In a recent study by Kim and Ritche (2014), based on a sample of Korean golf tourists, the following three customer segments were proposed:

1) Companion golfers: This segment included golfers who valued the social experience of playing golf. They often viewed golf as an opportunity to spend time with friends and family.
2) Intensive golfers: This segment's decision making was mainly influenced by the opportunity to combine golf with vacations. They were often price sensitive (golf and vacations) and motivated by the desire to improve their golf skills and abilities.
3) Multi-motivated golfers: This was the most motivated golfing segment, influenced by almost all motivation dimensions, including business opportunities, which is unique within the sport participant market. The business opportunities dimension is based on the motivation to play golf to spend time with corporate customers, achieve business goals and expand professional networks.

Profiling golfers with psychometric variables can guide the development of appropriate marketing and communication strategies. For example, among those motivated by social needs, a social environment should be created (e.g. group and family activities); while for those motivated by achievement/competition needs, opportunities should be provided to compete (e.g. sport tournaments). The above example of multi-motivated golfers driven by business opportunities shows how segmentation research can reveal unique consumer needs, which should not be overlooked by sport marketers (e.g. creation of opportunities for business networking). The three golf clusters are presented in Table 2.5.

TABLE 2.5 Clusters of golfers

Companion Golfers	Intensive Golfers	Multi-motivated Golfers
• Motivated by: • The Social experience of golf • Socialization	• Combine playing golf with vacations • Motivated by the opportunity to improve golf-related skills and abilities	• Driven by multiple motives • Making business contacts is among their main motives

Source: Kim, H.H. & Ritche, W.B. (2014). Motivation-based typology: An empirical study of golf tourists. *Journal of Hospitality & Tourism Research*, 36(2), 251–280.

2.2.3 Segmentation studies in the context of sport events (spectators and participants)

In their detailed review of the published segmentation literature on sport and leisure events, Tkaczynski and Rundle-Thiele (2011) summarized as the most common criteria used for market segmentation: age; gender; education and income; place of residence; motivation; trip purposes; experience; expenditure; and length of stay. All of these criteria fall under the four main segmentation bases: 1) geographic; 2) socio-demographic; 3) psychographic; and 4) behavioural. The authors therefore concluded that multiple segmentation criteria should be used when aiming to segment sport and leisure event spectators, also incorporating the travel dimension (i.e. visiting a place to attend an event). This is because segmentation based on a single variable may not represent all participants and spectators. For example, demographic groups might have different psychographic profiles (e.g. different motivations and attitudes), and geographic groups might have different socio-demographic profiles. It was also proposed by these authors that motivation should be one of the main segmentation criteria in sport and leisure event studies, including the travel element, as the general reason for visiting an event and its location is a key indicator for marketers.

An example of segmentation analysis in the context of sport events can be found in the French study of Bouchet, Bodet, Bernache-Assollant and Kada (2010). These authors used two samples of spectators at two French sport events: 1) Roland Garros tennis (live attendance); and 2) 2008 French Football Cup final (TV viewers). They categorized spectator segments via the sport event experience construct, and proposed these four spectator segments:

1) Opportunists: This segment related to spectators who attended sport events for personal benefits and rewards, such as important political or social contacts or because they deemed it an important event with high sport status.
2) Aesthetes: This segment consisted of spectators who were attracted by the entertainment aspect of the sport event and the experience of attending it. The quality of the event and achieving personal satisfaction were also important to these spectators.
3) Supporters: This segment related to spectators who attended games or watched them on TV; not so much for the event itself, but to support their favourite players or teams. They were perceived as the team (not the event) fans.
4) Interactive: This segment related to spectators who enjoyed the overall experience of game attendance, including the interaction with the environment and the event happenings. This segment was more likely to include families with children. The four event attendees' clusters are presented in Table 2.6.

Based on the above, it is clear that the segmentation of spectators attending a sport event is somewhat different from the segmentation of sport teams, as discussed earlier. Although spectators of a sport event can also be fans (of the team or the event), the vast majority of them appreciate also the entertaining aspect of the event and the sport event experience. In addition, the travel dimension of a sport event, including the motives associated with it (as will be discussed in Chapter 5), should not be overlooked, especially in relation to international sport events.

TABLE 2.6 Cluster groups of sport event spectators (Roland Garros tennis and 2008 French Football Cup final)

Opportunists	Aesthete	Supporters	Interactive
•Driven by: •Personal benefits •Personal rewards • Making political and social contacts	•Driven by: •Entertainment motives •Opportunity to live the experience of attending the event •Achieving personal satisfaction	•They are fans of the sport team •Driven by the opportunity to: •Support their team •Support their favorite athletes	•Enjoy social interaction •Enjoy happenings during the event •Total experience is important •Want to to be involved with the event

Source: Bouchet, P., Bodet, G., Bernache-Assollant, I. & Kada, F. (2011). Segmenting sport spectators: Construction and preliminary validation of the Sporting Event Experience Search (SEES) scale. *Sport Management Review, 14*(1), 42–53.

A second example of segmentation in the context of a sport event can be found in the study of Prayag and Grivel (2014) who applied segmentation analysis to young athletes (and not to spectators), who competed in a Junior Handball World Cup championship. Four segment groups were revealed:

1) Indifferent athletes: This was the least motivated segment, mainly influenced by socialization motives. The hedonistic aspect of participation was not important for them. This segment mainly consisted of female participants and those from Northern Europe.
2) Enthusiast athletes: This was the most motivated segment, influenced by several motivational dimensions including escape, excitement, competing, learning and discovery, participation, prestige and socialization. The segment mainly consisted of participants from Eastern Europe.
3) Socializers: This segment mainly related to those who wanted to participate in the event to socialize with their co-athletes and build social networks.
4) Competitive athletes: This segment related to participants driven by the competition aspects of the event and the prestige of winning. This cluster mainly consisted of male participants, from both Western Europe and North Africa.

2.3 CHAPTER SUMMARY

Patterns of sport consumer segmentation are difficult to generalize across the whole sport market, mainly due to its diversity. In this chapter, the main segmentation criteria were discussed, including several relevant examples from the sport industry. It has been made clear here that segmentation using combined variables including demographics, behavioural usage and psychographic information is an important but also challenging undertaking for sport marketers. Thus, cooperation between practitioners and researchers will likely improve the quality of market research, both in terms of the research design (e.g. more conceptual studies) and the analysis (e.g. identification of cluster groups with common behavioural patterns).

2.4 DISCUSSION QUESTIONS

The discussion questions presented below are designed to help students review what is important in the chapter. You can answer them on your own, but they are also suitable for discussion work in small groups.

1) Discuss the most common segmentation criteria, by presenting examples from the sport market.
2) Present examples to show how demographic and socioeconomic segmentation analysis can be applied in the sport market.
3) Present examples to show how socio-cultural segmentation can be applied in the sport market.
4) Present examples to show why and how trends in demographics and ethnic/racial groups should be considered by sport marketers.
5) Present examples of strategies that can be used by sport marketers (both participant and spectator sectors) in order to target: a) women; b) elderly; and c) Hispanic populations.

2.5 CLASS ACTIVITY: CONSUMER SEGMENTATION IN SPORTS

The class activity is designed to use information learned in this chapter to understand and apply the principles of sport market segmentation.

For a US or European professional sport league of your choice:

1) Profile the fans and spectators with the use of specific segmentation criteria (via internet searches).
2) Select three clear target groups and: a) discuss their unique consumer characteristics (e.g. needs, expectations, motivation, culture); b) develop a marketing strategy plan on how these groups can be specifically targeted.

REFERENCES

Ablondi, J. (2013). IHRSA Global Report: Global Fitness Industry Overview. http://ihrsa.org/research-reports

Alexandris, K., Kouthouris, C., Funk, D. & Giovani, K. (2009). Segmenting winter sport tourists by motivation: The case of recreational skiers. *Journal of Hospitality Marketing and Management*, 18, 480–500.

Alexandris, K. & Tsiotsou, R. (2012). Sport fans attachment segments: A psychographic profile based on team self-expression and involvement. *European Sport Management Quarterly, 12*(1), 65–81.

Alicia, J. (2013). *How the NFL Built a 25 Million Person Hispanic Fan Base*. Retrieved from www.forbes. com/sites/aliciajessop/2013/09/26/how-the-nfl-built-a-25-million-person-hispanic-fan-base

Beesley, C. (2015). Retrieved from www.allbusiness.com/marketing-to-seniors-and-baby-boomers-have-you-13940100–1.html

Bouchet, P., Bodet, G., Bernache-Assollant, I. & Kada, F. (2011). Segmenting sport spectators: Construction and preliminary validation of the Sporting Event Experience Search (SEES) scale. *Sport Management Review, 14*(1), 42–53.

Brennan, B. (2013). *NFL Raises Its Game with Women Consumers*. Retrieved from www.forbes.com/sites/bridgetbrennan/2013/09/04/nfl-raises-its-game-with-women-consumers

Carter J.F. (2010). *8 Social Media Strategies to Engage Multicultural Consumers*. Retrieved from www.mashable.com/2010/04/21/social-media-multicultural

Chemi, E. (2014). *The NFL Is Growing Only Because of Women*. Retrieved from www.bloomberg.com/bw/articles/2014-09-26/the-nfl-is-growing-only-because-of-female-fans

Cire, B. (2011). New Go4Life campaign focuses on fitness for older adults. Retrieved from www.nih.gov/news/health/oct2011/nia-19.html

Darren, H. (2015). The State of the Golf Industry in 2015. Retrieved from www.forbes.com/sites/darrenheitner/2015/04/04/the-state-of-the-golf-industry-in-2015/

Deloitte. (2015a). *Annual review of football finance*, by Sport Business Group, Retrieved from www2.deloitte.com/uk/en/pages/sports-business-group/articles/annual-review-of-football-finance.html

Deloitte. (2015b). *Commercial Breaks Football Money League* by Sport Business Group. Retrieved from www2.deloitte.com/uk/en/pages/sports-business-group/articles/deloitte-football-money-league.html

Dosh, K. (2012). *NFL may be hitting stride with female fans*. Retrieved from http://espn.go.com/espnw/news-commentary/article/7536295/nfl-finding-success-targeting-women-fans-merchandise-fashion

Formichelli, L. (2009). Market Focus – Skiers: Hitting the Slopes, *Target Marketing, the Secret to Marketing Success*. Retrieved from www.targetmarketingmag.com/article/hitting-slopes-401426/1

Funk, D. & Pastore, D. (2000). Equating attitudes to allegiance: The usefulness of selected attitudinal information in segmenting loyalty to professional sports teams. *Sport Marketing Quarterly, 9*(4), 175–184.

Funk, D. (2002). Consumer-based marketing: The use of micro-segmentation strategies for understanding sport consumption. *International Journal of Sports Marketing and Sponsorship, September/October*, 231–255.

Gibson, K., Cabler, T., Cance, K., Beck, J. & Santos, J. (2013). Generation Z: The next generation of college students, NIRSA. Retrieved from www.jmu.edu/recreation/_files/presentations/gen-z-social-media.pdf

Giulianotti, R. (2002). Supporters, followers, fans, and flâneurs. *Journal of Sport and Social Issues, 26*(1), 25–46.

HSBC. (2012). *Golf's 2020 Vision: The HSBC Report*. Retrieved from http://thefuturescompany.com/wp-content/uploads/2012/09/The_Future_of_Golf.pdf

Hunt, K.A., Bristol, T. & Bashaw, R.E. (1999). A conceptual approach to classifying sports fans. *Journal of Services Marketing, 13*(6), 439–452.

IHRSA (2014). Trend report: focus on gender, generation and region, 3(3). www.ihrsa.org/research-reports

Kell, J. (2014). *Nike makes a big push into the fast-growing women's segment*. Retrieved from www.fortune.com/2014/10/22/nike-women-business/

Kim, H.H. & Ritche, W.B. (2014). Motivation-based typology: An empirical study of golf tourists. *Journal of Hospitality & Tourism Research, 36*(2), 251–280.

Lawrence, H., Contorno, R.T. & Steffek, B. (2013). Selling premium seating in today's sport marketplace. *Sport Marketing Quarterly, 22*(1), 9–19.

Liu, Yi-De, Taylor, P. & Shibli, S. (2010). Utilizing importance data to identify customer segments for English public sport facilities. In K. Alexandris (ed.), *Performance Measurement and Leisure Management.* London: Routledge.

Mahony, D.F., Madrigal, R. & Howard, D. (2000). Using the psychological commitment to team (PCT) scale to segment sport consumers based on loyalty. *Sport Marketing Quarterly, 6*(1), 15–25.

Nielsen Sport Insights. (2012). *Nielsen Sports Newsletter.* The Nielsen Company. Retreived from www.nielsen.com/gr/en.html

Nooyi, I. (2013). *Sports: By Women and For Women.* Retrieved from www.huffingtonpost.com/indra-nooyi/post_5638_b_3920443.html

Prayag, G. & Grivel, E. (2014). Motivation, Satisfaction, and Behavioral Intentions: Segmenting Youth Participants at the Interamnia World Cup 2012. *Sport Marketing Quarterly, 23,* 148–160.

Rohm, A.J., Milne, G.R. & McDonald, M.A. (2006). Proven Top-rate Qualitative Analysis and Mixed Methods Research. *Sport Marketing Quarterly, 15,* 29–39.

Scheerder J. & Breedveld, K. (2015). *Running Across Europe.* NY: Palgrave MacMillan.

Schiffman, L. & Kanuk, L. (2004). *Consumer Behavior.* NJ: Prentice Hall.

Schrotenboer, B. (2015). *Fantasy sports games see more women in the future.* Retrieved from www.usatoday.com/story/sports/nfl/2015/01/22/fantasy-sports-daily-games-women-customers/22198493/

Shores, K. & Shinew, K. (2014). Race, ethnicity and physical activity. In M. Stodoloska, K. Shinew, M. Floyd & Walker (eds), *Race, Ethnicity and Leisure.* Champaign, IL: Human Kinetics.

Shrestha, L.B. & Heisler, E.J. (2011). *The changing demographic profile of the United States* [electronic version]. Washington, DC: Congressional Research Service.

Silverstein, M. & Sayre, K. (2009). *The Female Economy.* Retrieved from https://hbr.org/2009/09/the-female-economy

Special Eurobarometer. (2014). *Sport and Physical Activity (412).* Directorate-General for Education and Culture, Brussels, European Commission.

Stadler, B.A., Kristi, S. & Rhema, F. (2014). Room for growth in professional sport: An examination of the factors affecting African-American attendance. *Sport Marketing Quarterly, 23*(4), 225–243.

Statista (The Statistics Portal). Number of joggers/runners: Number of people who went jogging or running within the last 12 months in the United States (USA) from spring 2008 to spring 2015 (in millions). Retrieved from www.statista.com/statistics/227423/number-of-joggers-and-runners-usa/

Stodolska, M. & Jouyeon, Y. (2003). Impacts of immigration on ethnic identity and leisure behavior of adolescent immigrants from Korea, Mexico and Poland, *Journal of Leisure Research, 35*(1), 49–79.

Stodolska, M. & Alexandris, K. (2004). The role of recreational sport in the adaptation of first generation immigrants in the United States, *Journal of Leisure Research, 36,* 379–413.

Stodolska, M. & Shinew, K. (2014). Leisure among Latino Americans. In M. Stodoloska, K. Shinew, M. Floyd & Walker (eds), *Race, Ethnicity and Leisure.* Champaign, IL: Human Kinetics.

Stone, M. (2011). *The 'New' Older Market.* Retrieved from www.tennisindustrymag.com/articles/2011/08/19_the_new_older_market.html

Tapp, A. & Clowes, J. (2000). From 'carefree casuals' to 'professional wanderers': Segmentation possibilities for football supporters. *European Journal of Marketing, 36*(11/12), 1248–1269.

Taylor, P. & Cohen, D. (2012). *A Milestone En Route to a Majority Minority Nation.* PewResearch Centre, Social and Demographic Trends, Retrieved from www.pewsocialtrends.org/2012/11/07/a-milestone-en-route-to-a-majority-minority-nation/

The Burton Company. (2011). *Psychographics and Behavioral.* Retrieved from https://eatsleepshred.word press.com/category/marketing-background/target-markets/

Tkaczynski, A. & Rundle-Thiele, S.R. (2011). Event segmentation: A review and research agenda. *Tourism Management, 32,* 426–434.

Vanat. (2014). *International Report on Snow & Mountain Tourism* [overview of the key industry figures for ski resorts]. Retrieved from www.vanat.ch

Van Tuyckom, C. & Scheerder, J. (2010). A multi-level analysis of social stratification patterns of leisure time physical activity among Europeans. *Science and Sports, 25,* 304–311.

Vásquez, E., Shaw, B.A., Gensburg, L., Okorodudu, D. & Corsino, L. (2013). Racial and ethnic differences in physical activity and bone density: National Health and Nutrition Examination Survey, 2007–2008. *Prev Chronic Dis, 10*:130–183. Retrieved from http://dx.doi.org/10.5888/pcd10.130183

Wegner, C.E., Ridinger, L.L., Jordan, J.S. & Funk, D.C. (2014). Get Serious: Gender and Constraints to Long-Distance Running. *Journal of Leisure Research, 47*(3), 305.

Wigfield, A., Kispeter, E., Alden, S. & Turner, R. (2015). *Age UK's fit for the future Project Evaluation Report.* Centre for International Research on Care, Labour and Equalities. University of Leeds. Retrieved from www.ageuk.org.uk/health-wellbeing/fit-as-a-fiddle/fit-for-the-future/

VIDEO FILES

Adidas. (2011). *All Adidas Women* campaign [Video file]. Retrieved from www.youtube.com/watch?v=NIsvor0ID_U

NFL. (2015). *Women's Apparel Collection* commercial [Video file]. Retrieved from www.youtube.com/watch?v=tDV0pUQ8LbA

Nike. (2013). *Parents Perspective at Nike Sports Camps* campaign [Video file]. Retrieved from www.youtube.com/watch?v=kNsqlF8XgcM

Nike. (2013). *Nike and Women* campaign [Video file]. Retrieved from www.youtube.com/watch?v=oHbFSZdQikI

Nike. (2012). *Magic Soccer Night – Still doing it* campaign [Video file]. Retrieved from www.youtube.com/watch?v=dAB6o_7hQBE

Nike. (2011). *Globalization* campaign [Video file]. Retrieved from www.youtube.com/watch?v=8A0NTWjoaiY

Nike. (2010). *What Parents Say at Nike Sports Camp* campaign [Video file]. Retrieved from www.youtube.com/watch?v=M3UTwM_GnBU

WNBA. (2013). The WNBA's 2013 season [Video file]. Retrieved from www.youtube.com/watch?v=UTVISaGZ-zI

Under Armour. (2010). *Women. Protect This House. I will* campaign [Video file]. Retrieved from www.youtube.com/watch?v=Wkt0Q6p33fo

PART 2

Inputs: external forces and branding

CHAPTER 3

The sport product and the sport consumer

This chapter's objectives are to:

- introduce the sport industry
- define the sport consumer
- outline the difficulties in marketing the sport product
- discuss branding theory in the context of sport
- define brand equity
- analyse brand associations and their importance in sport consumer behaviour
- discuss brand associations and their measurement in the context of sport.

3.0 INTRODUCTION: THE SPORT INDUSTRY

The sport industry is not homogeneous. While predominately a service-oriented industry, there are also sporting goods manufacturers and retailers that produce and sell tangible sport products. According to a Plunkett Research report (Sport Industry Overview, 2015), the estimated size of the entire global sport industry in 2015 was $1.5 trillion, with the USA at around $498.4 billion. The types of organizations that produce sport products and services include:

a) sport organizations and leagues that 'produce' spectatorship sport services (e.g. Boston Celtics, Manchester United, NBA League, NCAA League, The English Premier League);

b) sport organizations that deliver participatory sport services or create opportunities for sport participation and development (e.g. voluntary sport associations/clubs, local authority/public sport departments, college/university sport programmes, private health clubs, sport camps);

c) sport event organizers that create opportunities for either participation or spectatorship – usually linked with sport tourism (e.g. New York Marathon, Athens Classic Marathon, Super Bowl);

d) sport manufacturers that produce sport goods (e.g. Adidas, Nike, Puma, Under Armour);

e) sport retail stores, sport team boutiques and online sport stores (e.g. the NBA store, the Nike store);
f) printed and electronic sport media (e.g. ESPN, Euro sport), covering sport news and broadcasting of sport games and events;
g) sport sponsors; while they do not 'produce' a sport product, they contribute to the 'production' (and game experience) via financial support;
h) individual athletes, especially professionals (e.g. LeBron James, Lionel Mesi).

3.1 THE SPORT CONSUMER

There are four types of sport consumers: a) active sport consumer; b) passive sport consumer; c) consumer of tangible sport products; and d) consumer of sport events (see Figure 3.1).

3.1.1 The active sport consumer

The active sport market relates to individuals that participate in sport and recreation activities. This participation can be indoor or outdoor. Indoor sport participation generally takes place in sport centres, which can be public (municipal, local authority, state), private (e.g. health clubs), college/university (e.g. university fitness centres) or not-for-profit sport clubs (e.g. a climbing association). In contrast, outdoor sport participation relates to a

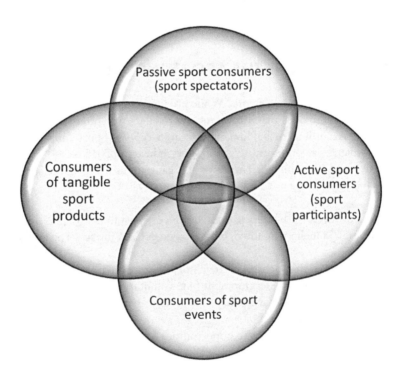

FIGURE 3.1 The sport consumer

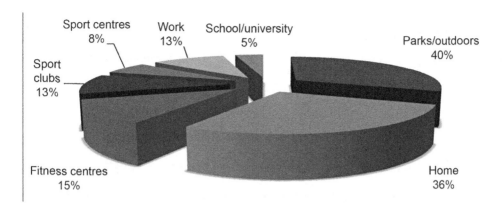

FIGURE 3.2 Places of sport participation in Europe

range of external settings, such as parks, trails, mountains, seaside locations and can be in the form of organized or unorganized sports.

Organized sport programmes are generally provided by local authorities, state recreation departments, non-profit sport clubs, schools and universities, as well as private sport organizations such as health clubs, private fitness instructors (e.g. personal trainers) and private sport clubs (e.g. tennis clubs, water sport clubs, extreme sport clubs). Unorganized sport participation mainly takes place outdoors (e.g. walking, running, mountain biking), but can also occur in indoor sport facilities (e.g. basketball courts) and at home (e.g. home fitness). According to a recent report by Special Eurobarometer (2014), among sport participants in Europe, most activity takes place in informal settings, such as parks and outdoors (40%), and at home (36%). However, activity also takes place in organized settings such as health or fitness centres (15%), sport clubs (13%) and sport centres (8%), as well as at work (13%), and at school or university (5%) (see Figure 3.2).

The private health club sector has continued to grow, despite the negative worldwide economic environment. According to Plunkett Research's report (2015), the health club sector revenue was about $22.4 billion in the USA in 2013, and $78.1 billion worldwide. According to the IHRA, at the end of June 2013, 20% of Americans were members of health clubs, which is the highest amount ever (IHRSA Trend Report, 2014).

In contrast to the high membership numbers in the private health club sector, a recent report by the US Physical Activity Council (2015) revealed that 28.3% of Americans were physically inactive in 2014, the largest percentage of inactivity over the last six years (2015, Participation Report). The corresponding inactivity rate of 2013 was 27.6%. In terms of sport activities participation rates, 61% participated in fitness, 48.4% in outdoor sports and 35.4% in individual sports, 13.9% in water sports and 13.5% in racquet sports (see Figure 3.3).

According to the Special Eurobarometer (2014), most European citizens (59%) are non-sport participants or seldom participate in sport activities. Of the 41% who participated in sport activities at least once a week, only 8% participated five times a week or more. From 2009 to 2014, the amount of Europeans that never exercised or played sport

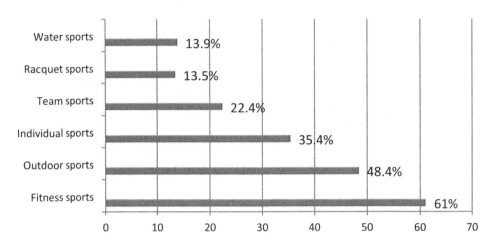

FIGURE 3.3 Participation rates in sports in the USA (%)

increased 3.0% (from 39% to 42%), while those that participated on a seldom basis decreased 4.0% (from 21% to 17%).

As also identified in the Special Eurobarometer (2014), there are substantial variations among the European countries in relation to sport participation. Sweden (9%), Denmark (14%) and Finland (15%) recorded the lowest amounts of non-participants (i.e. never exercise or partake in sports (see Figure 3.4), while Bulgaria (78%), Malta (75%) and Portugal (64%) had the highest (see Figure 3.5). The three Nordic countries (Sweden, 70%, Denmark 68% and Finland, 66%) had the highest amounts of regular (weekly) sport participants.

In terms of the most popular sport/physical activity by European country, swimming was recorded as most prevalent in four countries (France, the Netherlands, Northern Ireland and Spain), cycling in three (Germany, Poland and Switzerland) and walking in Denmark and Finland. In addition, fitness-related activities were identified as most popular in England and Italy (see Table 3.1 for further detail) (Scheerder *et al.*, 2011).

3.1.2 The passive sport consumer

The passive sport market is in relation to individuals who are spectators of sport contests. However, a distinction needs to be made here between those who attend live sport games (spectators in the stadium) and those who watch them on TV or online. A distinction also needs to be made between the terms 'sport spectator' and 'sport team fan' – two terms often used interchangeably. A sport team fan is someone who expresses positive emotion toward a specific sport team (e.g. a Manchester United fan); these feelings can vary from weak (expression of a preference) to strong (an enhanced psychological connection). A sport team fan is always a sport consumer; someone who watches their favourite team's games, utilizes various forms of media to follow the team and often purchases team merchandise. In contrast, a sport spectator may not have a preference for a specific sport team; they may simply enjoy watching the sporting contest.

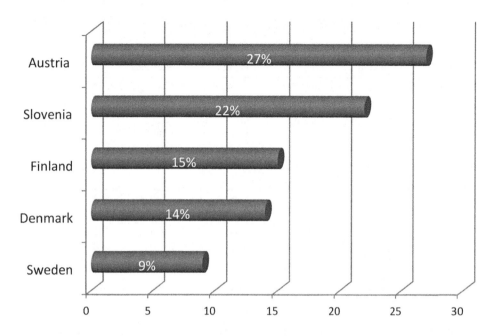

FIGURE 3.4 Percentage of respondents who NEVER exercise or participate in sports

Source: Special Eurobarometer (2014)

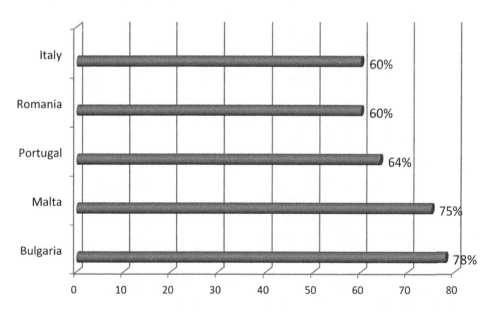

FIGURE 3.5 Percentage of respondents who NEVER exercise or participate in sports (Top 5)

Source: Special Eurobarometer (2014)

TABLE 3.1 Most popular sport activities by country (European)

	1	2	3	4	5
Denmark	Walking	Running	Fitness	Aerobics	Swimming
England (UK)	Gym	Swimming	Football	Cycling	Athletics/running
Finland	Walking	Cycling	Gym/weight exercise	Cross country/skiing	Jogging
Flanders	Running	Recreational cycling	Swimming	Fitness	Walking
France	Swimming	Cycling	Petanque/bowling	Walking and trekking	Running/jogging
Germany	Cycling	Running	Fitness	Swimming	Gymnastics
Italy	Fitness/aerobics/gymnastics	Football	Swimming	Cycling	Running/jogging
The Netherlands	Swimming	Cycling	Fitness/aerobic	Running	Walking
Northern Ireland (UK)	Swimming/diving	Walking	Exercise bike/running machine/spinning class	Jogging	Dance
Poland	Cycling	Jogging/walking	Swimming	Football	Volleyball
Spain	Swimming	Football	Cycling	Fitness	Mountaineering
Switzerland	Cycling	Hiking/walking	Swimming	Downhill skiing	Running/jogging

Source: Scheerder, J., Vandermeerschen, H., Van Tuyckom, C., Hoekman, R., Breedveld, K. & Vos, S. (2011). *SPM 10, Understanding the Game: Sport Participation in Europe.* KU Leuven, Research Unit of Social Kinesiology and Sport Management, Belgium.

In terms of the economic size of US professional sport leagues, the NFL recorded the highest revenue in 2013–14 ($9.6 billion), followed by the MLB ($7.9 billion) and then the NBA ($4.8 billion) (Plunkett Research, 2015, see Table 3.2).

In Europe, soccer is the largest sport spectatorship market. Its overall revenue in 2012/13 was 19.9 billion euro, with the 'big five' European leagues earning half of this (9.8 billion euro), including: English Premier League at 2.5 billion euro (www.premier league.com); German Bundesliga at 1.7 billion euro (www.bundesliga.com); and Spanish Primera Division at 1.6 billion euro (www.lfp.es) (Deloitte, 2014, see Table 3.2).

In terms of attendance, the NFL had the highest average attendance per game in the 2013/14 season (68.775 spectators), followed by MLB (30,450) (see Figure 3.6 (Plunkett Research, Sports Industry Overview, 2015).

In terms of European soccer sport club attendance, Germany's Borussia Dortmund (www.bvb.de/eng) had the highest average attendance in the 2013/14 season (80,295). In the 2013/14 season, six out of the top ten European football clubs in relation to attendance were German (see Table 3.3) (Top 100 European Football Clubs Ranked by Average Attendance, 2014).

TABLE 3.2 Economic size of sport leagues in the USA and Europe

Economic Size of Sport Leagues in USA revenue)[a]	Economic Size of Professional Soccer Leagues in Europe[b]
1. NFL: $ 9.6 billion	The English Premier League: 2.5 billion euros
2. MLB: $ 7.9 billion	The German Bundesliga: 1.7 billion euros
3. NBA: $ 4.8 billion	The Spanish Primera Division: 1.6 billion euros
4. NHL: $ 3.7 billion	The Italian Serie A: 1.4 billion euros
5. NCAA sports revenue: $ 989 million (including Divisions I, II, III)	The French Ligue: 1.1 billion euros
6. MLS: $600 million	

Sources: a. Plunkett Research: Sports Industry Overview (2015). b. Deloitte: Annual Review of Football Finance (2014).

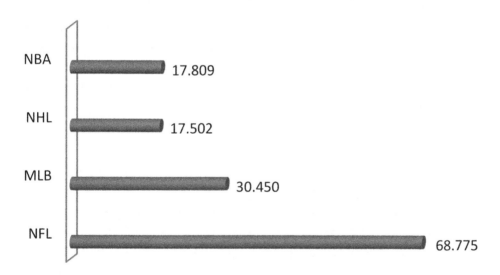

FIGURE 3.6 Average per game attendance of the five major sport leagues in North America (2013–14)

Source: Plunkett Research, Sport Industry Overview (2015)

TABLE 3.3 Top 10 European soccer teams in terms of attendance (2013–14)

1.	Borussia Dortmund	80,295	Germany
2.	Manchester Utd	75,205	England
3.	Barcelona	72,115	Spain
4.	Real Madrid	71,565	Spain
5.	Bayern Munich	71,000	Germany
6.	Schalke	61,570	Germany
7.	Arsenal	60,015	England
8.	Borussia Munchengladbach	52,240	Germany
9.	Hertha BSC	51,890	Germany
10.	Hamburg SV	51,825	Germany

Source: Top 100 European football clubs ranked by average attendance, 2014. http://footballeconomy. com/content/top-100-european-football-clubs-ranked-average-attendance-2014.

3.1.3 The consumer of tangible sport products

This market relates to those who buy sport-related equipment and clothing for sport, exercise, leisure and lifestyle purposes. Such sport equipment and apparel is generally produced by national or international sport businesses (e.g. Adidas, ASICS, North Face, Under Armour), and consumed in sport retail stores, sport team boutiques and online shops. This is the only sport consumer category where the tangible aspect of the sport product is stronger than the intangible (service aspect). It is estimated that in 2014 US consumers purchased sporting goods at a total value of USD$63,64 billion, compared with USD$62,07 billion in 2013 (Statista: The Statistics Portal, Consumer purchases of sporting goods in the US from 2002 to 2015).

3.1.4 The consumer of sport events

Individuals who either participated or attended sport events have been categorized in this book as a separate market because they offer unique characteristics, including a combination of sport with tourism. This is despite no previous sport marketing literature defining the consumer of sport events as a separate category (Shank & Lyberger, 2015). It has been identified as an individual category here because of: a) its link with tourism (sport tourism), and b) global recognition that sport tourism is one of the fastest developing forms of travel, with important financial, social and political impacts for communities, regions, cities and some countries in regard to international sport events (Alexandris & Kaplanidou, 2014).

Active sport event consumers can be professional or amateur athletes who compete in sport events, as well as leisure participants who take part in sport events. Most of the latter can be termed 'serious leisure participants', as they often invest a considerable amount of time and effort in training, and a considerable amount of money on specialized sport equipment and travelling to participate in sport events.

TABLE 3.4 World marathon majors participants (2007–14)

	2007	2014	% change
Berlin	32.497	36.755	13%
Boston	23.869	35.755	50%
Chicago	25.522	40.802	60%
London	36.396	36.621	<1%
New York	39.265	55.000*	40%
Tokyo	30.870	36.030	17%

*Entrance cap

Source: Stewart, C. & Dwiarmein, G. (2014). Rising participation, significant economic impact, and community engagement: Major marathons and their contribution to host cities. Sportcal.

The international outdoor sport event market has emerged as one of the fastest growing over the past few years, which has attracted considerable attention from academics (Alexandris & Kaplanidou, 2014). Examples of outdoor sport events that are taking off include 5 km, 10 km, half and full marathon running events, road and mountain bike races, triathlons, obstacle events and several extreme sport events. In a recent publication by Scheerder, Vandermeerschen, Van Tuyckom, Hoekman and Breedveld (2015), it was estimated that 50 million European citizens run on a regular basis, and spend around 9.6 billion euro annually. In the USA, a 10.5% growth in outdoor sport event consumption was reported between 2010 and 2012 (Schumacher, 2012).

In relation to outdoor running events, at least 80 major international marathons and thousands of smaller ones occurred during 2013 (Stewart & Dwiarmein, 2013). As shown in Table 3.4, the New York marathon is the largest in terms of participants – it recorded its highest amount of participants in 2013 (50,740) (Stewart & Dwiarmein, 2013). Other marathons that have notably increased in participant numbers include the Boston (50% increase in 2014 over 2013) and Chicago marathons (60% increase between 2007 and 2014).

A unique aspect of the sport event consumer is that they usually combine the sport competition aspect with the tourism destination dimension. These participants are often motivated by both competition and tourism-related factors.

3.2 THE SPORT PRODUCT: UNIQUE CHARACTERISTICS

The sport industry is made up of a combination of intangible services and tangible products. It includes sport organizations that provide pure services (e.g. a sport consultancy), others that produce tangible products (e.g. sport manufacturers) and others that deliver a combination of services and products (e.g. sport retail stores). A helpful way to better understand the nature of the sport product is to use the tangibility spectrum, as proposed by Zeithaml and Bitner (2003, see Figure 3.7).

FIGURE 3.7 The tangibility spectrum

As the sport industry is largely made up of services (or at least a combination of services and products), the main differentiators between this and the sport product have been listed below:

1) Sport services are intangible; therefore, they are difficult to be clearly defined and communicated. For example, it is often challenging to decipher what the core sport products are in the context of a professional basketball club, a city marathon or a health club. Such core product identification often needs to be drawn from consumer expectations and experiences. A beneficial method for analysing a sport service is to apply Zeithaml and Bitner's (2003) three service level analysis: 1) the core product; 2) the tangible product; 3) and the augmented product (also see Figure 3.8):

   a) The core product: This captures consumers' main reasons for using the sport service and their expected benefits. To decipher what its core products are, such as for a football club, health club or city marathon, the main needs that drive individuals to watch a football match, join a health club or run a marathon (for example) first need to be identified. As examples, entertainment could be the core product of a football team, health and exercise for a fitness club and competition for a running marathon. Sport marketers should first identify what their core product(s) is, and then develop the marketing philosophy and subsequent marketing strategy around it. Using the above professional basketball team example, the marketing department could design strategies that improve fans' experiences during the game, and to somewhat separate the outcome of the game (e.g. winning or losing) from their spectacle experience (i.e. positive and irrelevant of the outcome of the game).

   b) The tangible product: This relates to the elements that customers can see and touch, such as facilities (e.g. the stadium), equipment (e.g. treadmills) and the internet (e.g. website), as well as players, coaches and employees (e.g. fitness instructors). In regard to outdoor sport events (e.g. mountain and city running marathons), the physical environment and the competition route are also part of the tangible factor. The tangible elements of sport services create a visual image and contribute to brand development. Examples can be the colour and design of the facility, the atmospherics and the dressing code of employees, the logo, the communication materials and the website.

c)   The augmented product: This relates to the supportive product and services that are provided to improve the overall consumer experience, such as parking areas, coffee shops/health bars/restaurants (e.g. in a stadium), playgrounds (e.g. in a health club), half-time competitions (e.g. at a basketball game) and the support team (e.g. provision of isotonic drinks during marathons). The augmented product is often perceived as an essential component of the sport product – in a highly competitive sport market, it can create a competitive advantage. The core product of many sport organizations can be the same (e.g. skiing in a ski resort), but the supporting services are those that often create unique experiences and influence consumer decision-making (e.g. supporting services in a ski resort).

2)   Sport services cannot be standardized; therefore, guaranteeing the consistency of their quality is difficult. There are a number of difficult-to-control factors that influence the quality and consistency of sport service delivery. For example, there is no guarantee that an aerobics session at a health club will be of the same quality every day. Even if

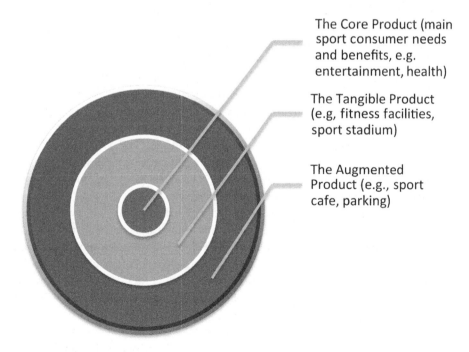

The Core Product (main sport consumer needs and benefits, e.g. entertainment, health)

The Tangible Product (e.g, fitness facilities, sport stadium)

The Augmented Product (e.g., sport cafe, parking)

FIGURE 3.8 The three levels of the sport product

the knowledge and skills of the instructors can, in a large degree, be standardized, there are difficult-to-control factors such as the instructor's mood, the behaviour of participants and the conditions within the facility (e.g. a crowded session) that can influence the consumer experience.

3) The evaluation of sport service quality is mostly subjective. While products are evaluated based on specific criteria (e.g. sport shoes are assessed by weight, cushioning, motion control and support), which provide a somewhat objective evaluation, sport services are most often affected by the personal stakeholder experience and expectations. It is therefore often difficult to identify what is a good Pilate's programme, what is a good mountain marathon or what is a good basketball game. Everything is dependent on personal experiences and expectations, which can generally only be measured by primary data collection (marketing research).

4) Most sport services are produced and consumed at the same time; in contrast, an industrial product is manufactured in a factory and consumed in a retail store. Subsequently, the industrial production process is methodologically tested and controlled, which is not always feasible for sport services. As an example, a city marathon is 'produced' and consumed in the city at the same time; making it difficult to actively monitor its progression. This can also create negative consumer experiences, as anything that could go wrong during a marathon (e.g. an accident) will be immediately seen by spectators and media. Consider the Olympic Games, which is the most complicated sport event worldwide – risks include accidents, terrorism actions and organizational mistakes. If something goes wrong at the Olympic Games, it cannot be 'hidden' by organizers, which is why its committee strategically implements numerous operational plans, in an effort to predict and curtail risky situations. A task that is all but impossible.

5) There are many instances where sport league competitors need to cooperate to enable the sport product to be appealingly delivered. It's a case of sport leagues needing their competing sport teams to 'get along' for the sake of the brand. However, to a large degree, the intensity of the competition determines the sport event consumer's experience. Strong rivalries are one of the most appealing aspects of sport leagues, such as Manchester City vs. Manchester United, Green Bay Packers vs. Chicago Bears and Real Madrid vs. Atletico Madrid. The NBA is a relevant example of a sport league, which strives to maintain its competitive reputation, such as by setting criteria for new franchisees/teams (e.g. financial indicators, market/fan size) and strengthening weaker teams with first draft picks.

6) The social phenomenon of sport should be focused on. This is because there are many sport organizations which are non-profit establishments (e.g. state, park and district sport organizations; local authority sport clubs and voluntary sport associations). Subsequently, policymakers and marketers need to develop marketing plans that achieve both social (e.g. promoting sport in local communities and improving communities' members' quality of life) and financial objectives (e.g. balancing state/local authority sport departments' budgets).

Examples of unique characteristics of the sport services are presented in Table 3.5.

TABLE 3.5 Examples of unique characteristics of sport services

	Examples
They are intangible	What is the product of a football team?
They are difficult to be standardized	How can the delivery of an exercise session be standardized?
Quality evaluation is subjective	What is a good basketball game?
They are produced and consumed at the same time	A city-running marathon is 'produced' and 'consumed' at the same time
Sport league competitors need to cooperate	Sport leagues needing their competing sport teams to 'get along' for the sake of the brand
Sport is a social phenomenon	Public sport and recreation programs should contribute to citizens' quality of life

3.2.1 The unique characteristics of the sport product: marketing challenges

The unique characteristics of the sport product create certain challenges for sport marketers, which can be summarized as follows (also see Table 3.6):

1) Communication with prospective customers about product sales is a more challenging process, due to the intangible aspect of the sport service. For example, it is not always easy to decide which tangible aspects of a sport service should be included in promotional leaflets (e.g. stadium, sport facilities, employees, tennis court) or what tangible dimensions should be presented in a 30-second TV commercial.

2) Pricing of the sport service is often a complex process; there are often several factors that need to be individually priced and also added into the final cost. For example, the price to travel to and attend a marathon event in another country needs to include transportation, accommodation, participation fees and associated leisure trips. All of these would need to be considered when organizing, packaging and marketing the whole sport product.

3) Sport organization personnel are a key part of the sport product and service, which can positively or negatively influence the consumer's overall experience. For example, previous research has revealed that fitness instructors are one of the main factors that influence the health club members' experience; they are sometimes more important than the tangible elements (e.g. facilities) (Alexandris, Zahariadis, Tsorbatzoudis & Grouios, 2004). Other relevant examples of where the personnel play an important role are sport services targeting children (e.g. sport camps and sport academies), outdoor sport programmes (e.g. leaders and guides) and personal training programmes (e.g. personal trainers).

4) There are several unpredictable natural factors that can influence customers' service quality perceptions but are often difficult for sport management to control. Weather, for example, is an unpredictable factor in many outdoor sports including marathons,

football matches and skiing. In these situations, it is not always easy for sport managers and marketers to deliver on their promises.

5) In addition to personnel, other customers and participants can also influence the sport consumer experience. For instance, the atmosphere that fans create within a stadium can impact on other spectators' experiences, either positively (e.g. celebratory atmosphere) or negatively (e.g. violence, hooliganism). Similarly, co-exercisers in organized sport programmes can influence the sport consumer experience either positively (e.g. a social atmosphere) or negatively (e.g. not following the rules in an exercise programme).

6) Another potential issue with sport services is that they cannot be returned, particularly when the consumer is dissatisfied with their experience. This often creates challenges for marketers, as sport service *consumer perceived risk* is particularly high (i.e. cannot try before they buy, and no product quality guarantees); they therefore need to develop marketing strategies that reduce perceived risks (Zeithaml & Bitner, 2003). Perceived risk is often defined as consumers' cognitive dissonance due to the uncertainty that they face before buying a service/product (Schiffman & Kanuk, 2004). Such risks can be financial (e.g. is the product worth the money I am paying?), quality related (e.g. is the product of good quality) or psychological, such as in relation to social acceptance (e.g. will my friends approve of my purchase?). In relation to sport services, psychological perceived risk is highly prevalent, for example, among middle-aged and elderly women deciding whether to participate in organized sport programmes.

7) Social objectives of sport provision (e.g. improving community members' quality of life) are often difficult to define and measure, as they do not include financial goals. Yet they should be part of marketing plans, preferably tested with both quantitative and qualitative indicators, especially in relation to public, local authority and park recreational sport programmes.

TABLE 3.6 The unique characteristics of sport services: marketing challenges

	Examples
Communication with perspective sport customers about sport product sales might be challenging	Design of promotional leaflets (e.g. a health club)
Pricing sport services can be a complex process	Pricing a package for participating in an international running marathon
Personnel is an essential part of sport services	Fitness instructors, Basketball players, sport coaches, etc.
Unpredictable natural factors might influence customers' sport service quality perceptions	Weather in an outdoor sport event
Sport services cannot be returned	Dissatisfying sport participation/sport event spectatorship experience
Social objectives of sport services are difficult to be quantified	Improve citizens' quality of life

Based on the above unique characteristics of sport services, some basic marketing strategies are proposed as follows (also see Table 3.7):

1) Efforts should be made to 'tangibilize' the sport service with the use of tangible cues. Such tangible cues will contribute to the building of the image and development of brand associations of the sport organization, such as via its logo, business cards, brand colouring or employee dress code.

2) Word-of-mouth communication strategies should be developed for the sport organization, as this more informal mode has been proven to be a highly effective communication channel for sport services; it can also help decrease customers' perceived risks. Social and digital media influence largely the development of word-of-mouth communications (e.g. Trip Advisor for booking leisure trips and services), with customer satisfaction the prerequisite for positive word-of-mouth.

3) Marketing strategies should be designed that create strong brand associations for the sport service. Branding a service is usually more difficult than branding a product, due to its intangibility (see the section on Branding the Sport Product below for further discussion in this area).

4) Implement marketing initiatives that personalize and customize the sport service and the corresponding consumer experience. This will help to overcome obstacles related to the subjectivity of evaluating sport service quality. Personal training is a highly relevant example of how a sport service can be personalized and customized.

5) Control sport service quality via the implementation of industry norms and well-defined standards, based on market research that applies valid service quality models. Examples include mystery shoppers, used by franchised organizations to test the operation of their franchised outlets, or well-established service quality models such as SERVQUAL (Parasuraman, Zeithaml & Berry (1988), as adjusted in sport settings (Alexandris *et al.*, 2004).

TABLE 3.7 Sport services: examples of strategies to address marketing challenges

	Examples
Tangibilize sport services	Use tangible cues (e.g. brand colouring, employee dress codes)
Develop positive word-of-mouth communication	Invest on customer satisfaction
Build strong sport brands	Create strong sport brand associations
Personalize and customize sport services and consumer experience	Build the *Empathy* dimension of sport service quality
Develop norms and standards for sport service quality	Use established sport service quality models (e.g. GAP and SERVQUAL models)
Use marketing research to measure customer experience	Collect quantitative or qualitative data to measure sport consumer experience
'Train' customers of sport services	Use 'codes of behaviour' for sport consumers (sport participants and game spectators)

6) Use market research so that marketers can define their core sport product and identify their customers' corresponding expectations. Both quantitative (surveys) and qualitative (e.g. focus groups and observation) research should be used.

7) In addition to employees, customers should also in some way be 'trained' by the management, based on their considerable impact on the consumer experience. However, this can obviously be a challenging task for marketers, managers and policymakers, especially in the case of unruly sport fans (e.g. reduce fans' anti-social behaviour, hooliganism).

3.3 BRANDING THE SPORT PRODUCT

A brand has been defined as 'a name, terms, sign, symbol, or design, or a combination of them, intended to identify the goods and services of one seller or group of sellers and differentiate them from those of competition' (AMA, cited in Keller, 2008, p. 2). In terms of sport brands, this can relate to an apparel sport business (e.g. Under Armour), a sport event (e.g. Super Bowl), a health club (e.g. Gold's Gym), a retail outlet (e.g. NBA store), a sport team (e.g. Chicago Bulls), an athlete (e.g. LeBron James), a sport media (e.g. ESPN) or a sport league or association (UEFA Champions League or US tennis association). Each brand should have its own specific attributes that help to differentiate it from competitors, while also satisfying consumer needs. As Keller (2008) pointed out, these differences can be rational (e.g. sport shoes with good technology), tangible (e.g. sport facilities), symbolic (e.g. 'tough sport', 'honest' sport team) or emotional (e.g. 'my' college football team).

There are many benefits for building branded sport products. Strong brands inspire consumer trust and confidence; they can reduce consumer risk (e.g. functional, financial and psychological risk), and create consumer loyalty (Gladden & Funk, 2002; Keller, 1993, 2003; Low & Lamb, 2000). Due to the specific characteristics of the sport product (as discussed in section 3.3.1), branding sport services is a more challenging task for marketers than branding tangible products.

3.3.1 Customer-based brand equity

The best approach to understand how the power of a brand is developed and the factors that influence brand building is to introduce the construct of customer-based brand equity. Keller (1993) defined brand equity in terms of the 'marketing effect uniquely attributable to the brand, when different outcomes result for a product or a service because of its brand name as compared to if the same products or service did not have that name' (p. 1). That is, brand equity explains why different outcomes are derived from the same marketing strategies when applied to branded vs. non-branded products.

Customer-based brand equity occurs when a consumer is familiar with a product and has positive brand associations toward it. In this regard, Keller (1993) proposed that brand equity is determined by brand knowledge (see Figure 3.9). Brand knowledge is a two-dimensional construct, consisting of brand awareness and brand image. Brand awareness relates to a consumer's ability to recognize the name of a brand they have previously seen or heard about (e.g. do you recognize the names of AC Milan, Boston Celtics and

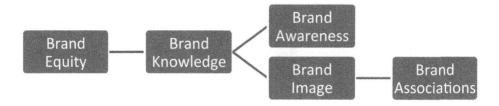

FIGURE 3.9 Brand equity dimensions

Source: Keller (1993)

NASCAR if you see them in an article?), or recall the brand from memory when given the product category (e.g. can you name an English Premier League or an MLS soccer team?). Brand image is based on brand associations, which are defined as thoughts and ideas held by individuals in their memory relating to a specific service or product (Aaker, 1991; Keller, 1993).

3.3.2 Brand associations

Keller (1993) defined brand associations as 'informational nodes linked to the brand node in memory and contain the meaning of the brand for the consumers' (p. 3). Marketers use brand associations to develop positive consumer attitudes, promote positive product attributes, explain consumer benefits and differentiate from the competition. In contrast, consumers use brand associations to help them organize, process and retrieve product information from their memory to facilitate purchase decision-making (Aaker, 1991). Keller (1993) classified brand associations into three categories: 1) attributes; 2) benefits 3); and attitudes (Figure 3.10).

Attributes: These represent specific features of each product/service (e.g. light shoes, clean facility and reliable team) and are classified by Keller (1993) into product and non-product-related attributes (see Table 3.8). Product-related attributes are those that 'relate to a product's physical composition or a service requirement' (Keller, 1993, p. 4); they are developed based on the functional attributes of each product, which are evaluated against their performance. In a sport context, product-related attribute associations of a sport stadium, for example, are related to the tangible stadium elements that determine its quality, such as design, security, seating comfort, restaurants, parking, lighting, etc. Non-product-related associations could be pricing information, package or product appearance, user imagery (e.g. who uses the product) and usage imagery (e.g. when the product is used) (Keller, 1993); they do not relate to the product's performance. In a sport context examples of non-product-related associations include the 'name' and history of a sport stadium (e.g. Old Trafford, Staples Centre), or the logo/symbol of a sport team (e.g. LA Lakers, AC Milan), as well as perceptions about the price of a sport product (e.g. tennis is an expensive sport) and the image of a sport product (e.g. modern, conservative,trendy). These perceptions can also be influenced by socioeconomic and psychographic factors.

Price is often a strong determinant of how consumers perceive brands (e.g. higher status is associated with higher prices). A higher priced product is expected to convey a positive

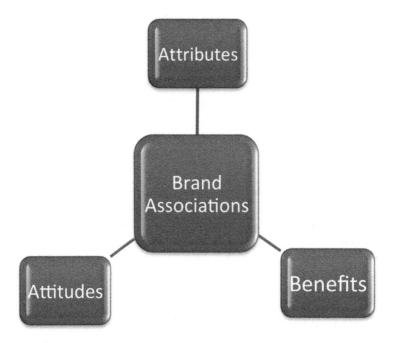

FIGURE 3.10 Categories of brand associations

Source: Keller (1993)

TABLE 3.8 Sport brand associations: attributes

Examples of product-related attributes	Examples of non product-related attributes
Design of a sport facility	Price of a sport service
Safety/Security in a sport stadium	Packaging of a sport product
Seating comfort in a sport stadium	Name of a sport stadium
Parking of a sport facility	History of a sport stadium
Audio-visual equipment in a sport facility	Logo of a sport team/sport product
Lighting in a sport facility	Symbol of a sport team
Executive suites in a sport stadium	Image of a sport team

or a negative image (Wu & Chalip, 2013), and influence the development of non-product-related brand associations. User and usage imagery are perceptions that are often formed either directly through consumer experience (i.e. when they use the product) or indirectly through formal and informal marketing communication focused on each product's target group.

The logo, brand name and commercial slogans are some of the elements of non-product-related associations that Keller (2003) emphasized – influencers of the brand recall and recognition process. Keller (2003) put forward criteria to apply when deciding on a brand name or logo, including simplicity, familiarity and distinction. For example, the brand name should be easy to comprehend, pronounce and spell – vivid, familiar and distinctive words will improve consumer recognition of the brand and logo, attract attention and reduce confusion with competitor brands.

Many sport organizations understand the essentiality of creating impactful logos and effective slogans. For example, Hilary Shaev (2013), Vice President of Marketing of the WNBA, recalled their brand-building effort to create a logo and build a communication message reflecting the athleticism and cultural diversity of their players, while conveying a contemporary image (www.WNBA.com). Well-known commercial slogans include Nike's *Just do it*, Adidas's *Impossible is Nothing*, North Face's *Never stop exploring*, and the NBA's *Where amazing happens*. These are examples of sport organizations that have clear, well-designed and highly recognizable logos and slogans (see www.nike.com, www.adidas.com, www.thenorthface.com, and www.NBA.com for further information).

Benefits: These are related to consumers' expectations of the value of using a product/service. Keller (2003, 2008) categorized benefits as follows (Figure 3.11):

a) Functional: This corresponds with the product-related attributes – these benefits are linked with consumers' expectations to satisfy consumption-related needs, such as becoming a member of a health club to achieve social and psychological well-being, or buying a pair of sport shoes to prevent a knee injury when running.
b) Experiential: These are related to consumers' experiential needs, such as participating or watching sport to feel pleasure, excitement and stimulation.

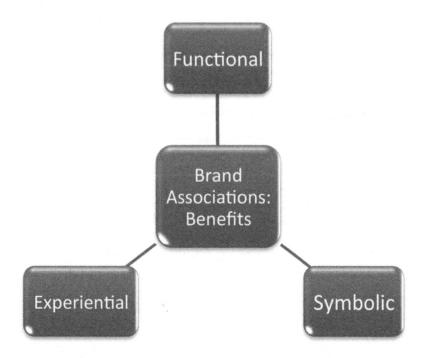

FIGURE 3.11 Brand associations: benefits

Source: Keller (2003)

c) Symbolic: These are external expected benefits, which relate to satisfying the needs of social approval and recognition when using a service (e.g. prestige, status). For example, a student who attends college games for social approval (because their college mates do it), or an individual who is a member of a health club because such behaviour fits with their social status and norms.

Attitudes: These have been defined as 'consumers' overall evaluation about the brand' (Keller, 1993, p. 4); and are formed based on consumers' beliefs and feelings toward a product. The development of beliefs is a result of a cognitive process, as consumers evaluate the degree to which a product possesses certain attributes and benefits (e.g. quality brand, safe stadium, reliable sport camp). In contrast, feelings and emotions are developed based on the degree to which a consumer likes or dislikes a sport product (as an emotional reaction). Attitude theory is further discussed in Chapter 7.

3.3.3 Measurement of brand associations in sport

There are several studies that have used Keller's (1993) brand association model and developed scales to measure sport brand associations in the context of professional sport teams, sport leagues, sport clubs and athletes. In each of these studies, the researchers have developed the factorial structure of measurement scales to include the three brand association dimensions defined by Keller (1993): attributes; benefits and attitudes.

However, there have been limitations in terms of the number and nature of dimensions included (e.g. weak representation of the benefits and attitude dimensions), and the types of measurement scales included (e.g. Likert scales vs. bipolar scales vs. semantic differential scales). More research is required in this area to establish more valid and reliable brand association scales that can be used by sport marketers as part of evaluating the brand equity of their businesses. The most representative of these studies are discussed in further detail in the subsections below.

3.3.4 Sport team brand associations

In the context of professional sport, Gladden and Funk (2002) defined brand associations as attributes, benefits and attitudes linked in the consumers' mind with a specific sport team. Based on this, they developed the sport team association model, which involves 16 associations. Similarly, Ross, Russell and Bang (2008) introduced a team brand association framework with 13 associations. Both of these models are presented in Table 3.9.

As shown in Table 3.9, the sport team associations have many similarities as well as some differences. It should, however, be pointed out that both of these measurement scales of sport team associations were developed for US professional sport teams. In contrast, when Ross et al.'s (2008) scale was validated among fans in the Portuguese professional soccer league (see Biscaia et al., 2013), some differences in the factorial structure of the scale were revealed. Because of these differences, the non-player personnel dimension was replaced by the management and head coach dimensions, while the identification and rivalry dimensions were dropped.

Such research-changing differences confirm the common difficulty in applying measurement scales developed in the USA to other geographical areas (e.g. European professional sport leagues). It is feasible to conceive that the importance of each brand association dimension will be influenced by fans' cultural differences (e.g. North American, European, Asians and Australians) and the organizational model of the different sport leagues.

TABLE 3.9 Sport team brand associations

Star player: related to the star players of the sport team	Brand mark: related to the logo, symbol and colours of the sport team
Product delivery: related to how exciting and entertaining are the sport games	Rivalry: related to the competitive nature of the sport and the competition among the sport teams
Nostalgia: related to memories that the sport team brings	Concessions: related to eating and consuming beverages in the sport stadium
Tradition: related to the history of the sport team	Social interaction: related to opportunities for social interaction when watching a game
Logo design: related to the colours and the logo of the sport team	Commitment: related to fans' enduring affiliation to a particular sport team
Affective reaction: related to the development of fans 'positive feelings'	Team history: related to the history of the sport team (e.g. years competing, trophies etc.)
Success: related to the performance and winning record of the sport team	Organizational attributes: related to management actions
Knowledge: related to the degree to which fans know a lot about the sport team	Team success: related to the competitiveness and the quality of the team
Head Coach: related to the reputation and quality of the head coach	Team play characteristics: relate to the style of play and the sport game strategy
Importance: related to the degree to which the sport team is important for the fan	Non-player personnel: related to coaches, trainers, team management and owners
Pride in place: related to the degree to which the sport club brings prestige in the community/neighbourhood	Stadium: related to the home stadium and its surrounding community
Stadium: related to the architecture of the stadium and its contribution to the sport game experience	Identification: related to the degree to which fans see themselves psychologically connected with their sport team
Management: related to the way that the management runs the sport team	Internalization: related to fans' psychological attachment with their team
Fan identification: related to the degree to which fans see themselves psychologically connected with their sport team	
Escape: related to the degree to which opportunities for escape from the daily routine are developed	
Peer group acceptance: related to the degree to which the friends approve and support being a fan of the sport team	
Source: Gladden and Funk (2002).	Source: Ross et al. (2008).

3.3.5 Sport league brand associations

Brand associations can also be measured for sport leagues. Kunkel, Funk and King (2014) introduced a sport brand architecture framework and identified 17 league brand associations for four sport leagues in Australia, as presented in Table 3.10.

3.3.6 Sport/fitness club brand association

In the context of participatory sports, Alexandris, Douka, Papadopoulos and Kaltsatou (2008) proposed an eight-dimensional brand association scale (see Table 3.11). This scale is an extension of Filo, Funk and Alexandris' (2008), and was developed in the context of private health/fitness clubs.

3.3.7 Athlete brand associations/image

As noted earlier in this chapter, individual athletes can also be considered independent sport products, as well-known sportspeople often have their own brands and attract sponsorship investments. Arai, Ko and Kaplanidou (2013) therefore developed a scale to measure the brand image of individual athletes, with 10 brand association dimensions as shown in Table 3.12.

TABLE 3.10 Sport league brand associations	
Association	*Related to*
Atmosphere	The atmosphere in the sport stadium
Community Pride	The degree to which the league brings pride to the national football community
Competition	The competition in the league between sport teams
Diversion	The degree to which day to everyday problems are forgot (as a result of watching football in the league)
Education	Opportunities to increase knowledge about football
Excitement	The degree to which the league is perceived as excited
Game representation	The degree to which the league represents the game of football
Logo	The logo of the league
Management	The way that the league is managed
Nostalgia	The degree to which the league brings back good memories
Performance	The level of football played
Player development	Opportunities for young players to be developed
Rivalry	The competition between teams
Socialization	Opportunities for socialization
Star player	The degree to which the league has star players
Specific Team	The presence in the league of a team that a fan follows
Tradition	The history and tradition of the league

Source: Kunkel, T., Funk, D. & King, C. (2014). Developing a conceptual understanding of consumer-based league brand associations. *Journal of Sport Management*, 28(1), 49–67.3.3.6 Sport/fitness club brand associations.

TABLE 3.11 Sport/fitness club brand associations

Brand Associations	Related to
Popularity	The image of the fitness club
Nostalgia	Memories of exercising in the fitness club
Logo design	The logo, symbol and colours of the fitness club
Escape	The degree to which escape-related needs are satisfied
Vicarious achievement	The degree to which club membership brings social recognition
Management	The quality of the organization (fitness club management)
Pride in place	The degree to which the fitness club brings prestige in the community/neighbourhood
Affect	Positive feelings developed when participating in exercise programmes in the health club

Source: Alexandris, K., Douka, S., Papadopoulos, P. & Kaltsatou, A. (2008). Testing the role of service quality on the development of brand associations and brand loyalty. *Managing Service Quality, 18*, 239–255.

TABLE 3.12 Athletes' brand associations

Brand Associations	Defined by
Athletic expertise	An athlete's knowledge and skills related to the sport
Competition style	The degree to which the competition style is exciting, distinct and attractive
Sportsmanship	The degree to which the athlete respects fair play and his/her opponents when competing
Rivalry	The degree to which the match is exciting and dramatic
Physical attractiveness	The physical appearance of the athlete
Symbol	The athlete's fashion style
Body fitness	The athlete's fitness condition
Life story	The athlete's personal history and lifestyle
Role model	The degree to which the athlete is a role model and good leader in the community
Relationship effort	The degree to which the athlete communicates with his/her fans and is open to their request

Source: Arai, A., Ko, Y.J. & Kaplanidou, K. (2013). Athlete's brand image: Scale developing and model test. *European Sport Management Quarterly, 13*(4), 383–403.

3.3.8 The Forbes List of the most valuable sport brands

In the sport industry, there are lists published annually that measure the strength or value of sport brands; the most wellknown is Forbes. In the 2014 Forbes List, sport brands are categorized into businesses, events, athletes and teams. In 2014, Nike was listed as the top sport brand in the business category, with an estimated value of $15 billion, Super Bowl was the top sport event with an estimated value of $500 million, the New York Yankees were the most valuable team brand in sports with an estimated value of $521 million, and LeBron James was the top athlete with estimated brand value of $37 million.

It should be noted that the methodology for calculating these brand values depends on the category. For example, the event brand value is calculated based on the revenue from media, sponsorships, tickets and licensed merchandise per-event-day of competition, while the athlete's brand value is calculated based on their endorsement income, less the average endorsement income of top 10 athletes in the same sport. However, there has been some criticism of the criteria and indicators used to calculate the value of the sport brands in the Forbes List. It has been argued that the rankings possess a degree of subjectivity including a US bias (Casanova, 2014). Such backlash only confirms the common difficulties encountered when measuring the strength of a sport brand, especially when primary consumer behaviour research is not facilitated.

3.4 CHAPTER SUMMARY

In summary, branding the sport product is an essential but also challenging element in sport marketing, especially in relation to sport services. Marketers need to design strategies, which build brand equity, including increasing brand familiarity among sport consumers and helping them to develop positive associations toward their brand. Fantasy football is a strong example of a beneficial brand-building strategy, with Dwyer (2013) confirming that this activity has been highly successful for the NFL. The use of social media has also been put forward as a key brand-building strategy for sport organizations (Walsh, Calvio, Lovell & Blaszka, 2013).

Market research in relation to sport brand equity and brand associations is still developing. The measurement of brand associations and the empirical investigation of the antecedents and consequences of brand equity are topics that require more research, especially in different sport contexts (e.g. spectatorship sports, and participatory sports and events).

3.5 DISCUSSION QUESTIONS

The discussion questions presented below are designed to help students review what is important in the chapter. You can answer them on your own, but they are also suitable for discussion work in small groups.

1) What are the unique characteristics of the sport product? Present examples to support your answer.

2) What challenges do the unique characteristics of sport products create for sport marketers? Present examples to support your answer.
3) What are basic strategies that can be developed to address the unique characteristics of the sport product?
4) Define brand equity in compliance with Keller's (1993) model.
5) Discuss the three dimensions of brand associations as proposed by Keller (1993). Present sport-related examples of brand associations to support your answer.
6) Explain how brand associations can be measured in relation to spectatorship sport (e.g. a football team) and participatory sport (e.g. a health club).

3.6 CLASS ACTIVITY: SPORT PRODUCT AND SPORT CONSUMER

The class activity is designed to use information learned in this chapter to understand the unique characteristics of the branded sport product/service.

Choose each of the following: a) an MLB team; b) an NCAA football team; c) an apparel sport company; and d) a private health club. Conduct your own sport brand image research as follows:

1) Develop a questionnaire to measure their brand associations.
2) Critically discuss whether a single questionnaire (with the same brand association dimensions) is applicable to all of the sport contexts.
3) Have your classmates complete the questionnaires.
4) Analyse the data and assess whether the brand associations are the same or different across the sport contexts.
5) Critically discuss the factors that have influenced the development of the brand associations across the sport contexts.

REFERENCES

Aaker, D. (1991). *Managing Brand Equity*. New York: The Free Press.

Alexandris, K., Douka, S., Papadopoulos, P. & Kaltsatou, A. (2008). Testing the role of service quality on the development of brand associations and brand loyalty. *Managing Service Quality*, 18, 239–255.

Alexandris, K. & Kaplanidou, K. (2014). Marketing sport event tourism: Sport tourist behaviors and destination provisions. *Sport Marketing Quarterly*, 23(3), 125–126.

Alexandris, K., Zahariadis, P., Tsorbatzoudis, C. & Grouios, G. (2004). An empirical investigation of the relationships among service quality, customer satisfaction and psychological commitment in a health club context. *European Sport Management Quarterly*, 4, 36–52.

Arai, A., Ko, Y.J. & Kaplanidou, K. (2013). Athlete's brand image: Scale developing and model test. *European Sport Management Quarterly*, 13(4), 383–403.

Biscaia, R., Correia, A., Ross, S., Rosado, A. & Maroco, J. (2013). Spectator-based brand equity in professional soccer. *Sport Marketing Quarterly*, 22(1), 20–32.

Casanova, M. (2014). *Rated ranking: The Forbes Fab 40 – The World's most valuable sports brands 2014*. Retrieved from www.branding-institute.com/rated-rankings/the-forbes-fab-40-the-worlds-most-valuable-sports-brands-2014

Deloitte. (2014). Annual Review of Football Finance. Retrieved from www.footballeconomy.com/content/premiership-revenues-top-%C2%A325bn

Dwyer, B. (2013). The impact of game outcomes on fantasy football participation and national football league's media consumption. *Sport Marketing Quarterly, 22*(1) 20–33.

Filo, K., Funk, D. & Alexandris, K. (2008). Exploring the role of brand trust in the relationship between brand associations and brand loyalty in sport and fitness *International Journal of Sport Management and Marketing, 3*, 39–57.

Forbes. (2014). The Forbes Fab 40: The World's Most Valuable Sports Brands. Retrieved from www.forbes.com/pictures/mlm45jemm/the-most-valuable-company-brands/

Gladden, J.M. & Funk, D.C. (2002). Developing an understanding of brand associations in team sport: Empirical evidence from consumers of professional sport. *Journal of Sport Management, 16*(1), 54–81.

IHRSA (2014). Trend Report: Focus on Gender, Generation and Region, 3(3).

Keller, K. (1993). Conceptualizing, measuring, and managing customer-based brand equity. *Journal of Marketing, 57*(1), 1–22.

Keller, K. (2003). Brand synthesis: The multidimensionality of brand knowledge. *Journal of Consumer Research, 29*(March), 595–600.

Keller, K. (2008). *Strategic Brand Management*. NJ: Prentice Hall.

Kunkel, T., Funk, D. & King, C. (2014). Developing a conceptual understanding of consumer-based league brand associations. *Journal of Sport Management, 28*(1), 49–67.

Low, G. & Lamb, G. C. (2000). The measurement and dimensionality of brand associations. *Journal of Product & Brand Management, 9*(6), 350–370.

Parasuraman, A., Zeithaml, V. & Berry, L. (1988). SERVQUAL: Multiple-item scale for measuring consumer perceptions of service quality. *Journal of Retailing, 64*, 12–40.

Physical Activity Council. (2015). *Participation Report*. Retrieved from www.physicalactivitycouncil.com/

Plunkett Research ® Ltd. (2015*). Sport Industry Overview*. Retrieved from www.plunkettresearchonline.com/researchcenter/statistics/display.aspx?industry=30&keywords=sport+industry

Ross, S.D., Russell, K.C. & Bang, H. (2008). An empirical assessment of spectator-based brand equity. *Journal of Sport Management, 22*(3), 322–337.

Scheerder, J. & Breedveld, K. (2015). *Running across Europe*. London: Palgrave and MacMillan.

Scheerder, J., Vandermeerschen, H., Van Tuyckom, C., Hoekman, R., Breedveld, K. & Vos, S. (2011). *SPM 10, Understanding the Game: Sport Participation in Europe*. KU Leuven, Research Unit of Social Kinesiology and Sport Management, Belgium.

Schiffman, L. & Kanuk, L. (2004). *Consumer Behavior*. NJ: Prentice Hall.

Schumacher, D.G. (2012). *Report on the Sports Travel Industry*. National Associations of Sport Commissions (NASC). Retrieved from www.sportscommissions.org/Portals/sportscommissions/Documents/About/NASC%20Sports%20Travel%20Industry%20Whitepaper.pdf

Shaev, H. (2013). Industry insider: WNBA Brand Pyramid. *Sport Marketing Quarterly, 22*, 121–122.

Shank, M. & Lyberger, M. (2015). *Sports Marketing: A strategic perspective*. London-New York: Routledge.

Special Eurobarometer (2014). *Sport and Physical Activity (412)*. Directorate – General for Education and Culture, Brussels, European Commission.

Statista: The Statistics Portal (2015). Consumer purchases of sporting goods in the U.S. from 2002 to 2015 (in billion U.S. dollars). Retrieved from www.statista.com/statistics/200773/sporting-goods-consumer-purchases-in-the-us-since-2004/

Stewart, C. & Dwiarmein, G. (2013). Rising participation, significant economic impact, and community engagement: Major marathons and their contribution to host cities. Sportcal Insight (Sport Marketing Agency).

Top 100 European Football Clubs Ranked by Average Attendance 2014 (2014). Retrieved from www. footballeconomy.com/content/top-100-european-football-clubs-ranked-average-attendance-2014

Walsh, P., Calvio, G., Lovell, M.D. & Blaszka, M. (2013). Difference in event brand personality between social media users and non-users. *Sports Marketing Quarterly, 22*(4), 214–223.

Wu, D.G. & Chalip, L. (2013). Expected price and user image for branded and co-branded sports apparel. *Sport Marketing Quarterly, 22*(3), 138–152.

Zeithaml, V.A. & Bitner, M.J. (2003). *Services Marketing: Integrating customer focus across the firm.* New York: McGraw-Hill.

CHAPTER 4

Sport consumer behaviour and the influence of the socio-cultural environment

This chapter's objectives are to:

- discuss the influence of the socio-cultural environment on sport consumer behaviour
- discuss the main changes in demographics
- analyse the role of family on sport consumer socialization
- discuss the main age cohorts and their relevance for sport consumer behaviour
- discuss the relationship between social class and sport consumption
- analyse how cultures and subcultures influence sport consumer behaviour
- identify the growth of ethnic and racial groups, and discuss their perspective as sport consumers.

4.0 INTRODUCTION

The social environment in which we live creates a number of 'reference groups' that influence an individual's decisions related to personal life, work and leisure. A reference group is any person or group that serves as a point of comparison for an individual, including influencing the formation of consumer values, attitudes, and behaviour (Schiffman & Kanuk, 2004). Reference groups can take the form of symbolic groups, and can include family, friends and colleagues, as well as sport fan clubs, running and golf clubs and sport communities.

In this chapter, the main focus is on the family, age cohorts, social, culture and sub-culture reference groups, and their influence on sport consumer behaviour. These groups will be discussed with reference to changes in the socio-demographic and cultural environment, to analyse how these changes influence sport consumption. Some of the more prominent changes, such as an aging population and an increase in ethnic groups, are already having a major influence on the sport consumer market.

4.1 FAMILY AS A REFERENCE GROUP

A family is defined as two or more persons who are related by blood, marriage or adoption, and who live together (Schiffman & Kanuk, 2004). Although families are also often referred to as 'households', households are not always families, as they might include unmarried couples, friends and roommates.

There have been some clear demographic changes in the structure and dynamics of families in Western countries. For example, the role of the Western woman in the family has changed; an increasing number of women are now employed and career-oriented, which has changed the traditional stereotype of women at home. As a result of their household income contributions, many Western women now have more power in the family including in relation to consumer decision-making. As reported by the Female Factor (www.thefemalefactor.com), it is estimated today that more than 70% of consumer decisions in Western countries are now made by women. Furthermore, 75% of women identified themselves as the primary shoppers for their households. Finally, many Western families are now made up of unmarried couples – nearly 12% of all couples living together were unmarried in the USA in 2011 (Family Facts.org, 2011).

The changed role of woman in society and within families, including their increasing influence on family consumer decision-making, has implications for the sport market. This is a new and fast-developing market (the female consumer) for sport organizations. Traditional male sport activities such as fathers attending sport games with their children (e.g. football, basketball) have started to become attractive to females. The power of the female consumer market and its influence on families' sport-related decisions has been realized by numerous professional leagues in the USA (e.g. NBA, NFL), health and fitness organizations internationally, as well as international sport goods companies. Refer back to Chapter 2 for further discussion on the female consumer market.

4.1.1 Families and consumer socialization of children

Consumer socialization is the process that helps children to learn and imitate their parents' and other relatives' consumption behaviour, in order to acquire values, habits and attitudes related to their consumer behaviour (Ward, 1981).

The family plays an important role in children's consumer-related decisions, especially during primary and secondary school years. Parents influence the consumer behaviour of their children in various ways, including direct teaching of consumer-related skills, and indirect influencing such as co-shopping where they are consumer role models and supervise their children's purchases. The family's media consumption behaviour also has a notable impact on children's consumer socialization. As Neeley (2005) observed, inter-personal communication within the family is a main influencer on children's consumption behaviour, as it nurtures the development of children's values and attitudes toward life (e.g. active lifestyle), including their consumer behaviour.

Prior research indicates that most children are introduced to sport (active participation or a sport team's fan) during their pre-school years by their parents (Funk & James, 2001). A common trend is for the father to influence boys' attitudes and preferences toward specific sport activities and teams, while the mother generally influences girls' attitudes toward sport. For example, parents who watch and cheer for a specific basketball team on TV will positively influence their children's attitudes toward this team (to become a sport team fan) (Kolbe & James, 2000).

In Europe, the influence of fathers on their sons' sport socialization is particularly prominent with regard to soccer. As discussed by The Social Issues Research Centre (2008), many older fans have fond memories of attending a soccer game during their early years with their father – a soccer fandom that is generally inherited within the family (including mothers and grandmothers) and passed down through the generations. This process plays an important role in maintaining traditions and values within the family, and creating a sense of belonging for family members (The Social Issues Research Centre, 2008).

In a study conducted in Portugal, De Carvallo, Scheerder, Boen and Sarmento (2014) reported that more than half of sport consumers in Portugal became soccer fans at six years old, and 90% before 12 years old. This was often because of family tradition and the presence of the professional club in their region. Furthermore, children who grew up in families with a sport history (e.g. parents who were athletes) were more likely to be involved in sport – the parents acted as role models for their children.

Fredricks and Eccles (2004) believed there are several reasons why families play such an important role in children's sport involvement:

1) Children spend a large amount of time during their pre-school and school years at home with the family, which creates opportunities for learning, interaction and imitation.
2) Parents are usually involved in their children's sport education, including decisions about what sport to learn during their leisure time or what game to attend or watch on TV.
3) Some parents provide valuable feedback about their children's sport performance (e.g. from interacting with their coaches), and subsequently influence their experience of sport participation.

4.2 AGE COHORTS AS A REFERENCE GROUP

Individuals from the same age cohort often have common characteristics in their social, leisure and consumer behaviour. The main age cohorts are as follows:

• *Baby boomers:* This cohort was born during the post-World War II era. They are further categorized as: a) leading-edge baby boomers (born 1946–1954); and b) trailing-edge baby boomers (born from 1955–1965) (Colby & Ortman, 2014). Baby boomers are in the age range of 50–69 in 2016. They are a major consumer target group since US demographic trends show that more than 20% of the total US population will be over 65 years by 2029, and that one in five will be aged 65+ by 2050 (Coly & Ortman, 2014). Similar demographic trends have been predicted for Canada, Australia and Europe. For instance, in Australia the 65+ cohort is forecast to increase from 12% in 1999 to between 24% and 26% by 2051.

These demographic trends are significant for the sport and leisure industry. Baby boomers are a highly relevant target consumer group for sport organizations, as they have both time and money (it is estimated that they spend $400 billion per year), they are healthier than their predecessors and they are often well-educated (Kelly, 2015).

A relevant example of the size and importance of the baby boomer cohort is in relation to tourism and especially to adventure and sport tourism. Patterson and Pegg (2009) reported that while in 1999 alone, over 593 million international travellers were aged 60 years, this figure was projected to be greater than 2 billion trips annually by 2015. According to Ianniello (2006), there is a market today among older individuals for adventure tourism. More and older individuals today express a preference to participate in physically challenging leisure activities while on vacations. They prefer authentic leisure activities, which help them escape the stress of their everyday routine and socialize.

Patterson and Pegg (2009) proposed that promotional campaigns targeting older individuals for adventure and sport tourism should use metaphors such as doing, touching and seeing, rather than just seeing. Furthermore, such campaigns should emphasize the sense of adventure, escapism, the challenge of actual involvement and the feeling of freedom, while also addressing intrinsic motivations such as fun, escape and socialization. All of these should be associated with images of the elderly participating in adventure and sport tourism. It has, however, to be noted that despite these revealing statistics, this age cohort is often overlooked by the sport industry, mostly due to the stereotype that sports are not for the elderly. Up to now, there have been minimal commercial sport campaigns that target baby boomers (Fidelman, 2014).

- *Generation X (1965–1980):* Also referred to as 'baby busters', this cohort consists of about 65.7 million people in the US (Hymowitz, 2015). It is a highly diverse cohort in the US that includes many foreign immigrants; as a result, they are generally more tolerant of racial differences. In terms of their consumer behaviour, many are preoccupied with material possessions – largely driven by the desire to make money and buy products (James & Manolis, 2000). They are also often frequent TV viewers, exposed to a large amount of commercials. Heavily exposed to TV, mobile devices and the internet, this is the first true consumer-oriented, consumer-savvy generation (Carlson, 2009).
- *Generation Y (1980–1995):* Also referred to as 'millenians' or 'echo boomers', recent research revealed that about 56 million US citizens belong to this cohort (Valentine & Powers, 2013). They are largely influenced by technology and the internet, and are generally well-educated, and better travelled than their parents. In addition, this cohort is often perceived as individualistic, technologically savvy and sophisticated (Wallop, 2014). In terms of their consumer behaviour, they often desire distinctive brands as a means of self-expression; shopping also has an entertainment value, as there is an experiential expectation from their consumerism (Schawbel, 2015). Their materialistic culture is largely influenced by technology; traditional media are less influential to them. For instance, they watch less TV than previous generations. Most of this cohort prefer online advertising and interact with brands online. Many companies therefore use social and digital media to attract this consumer group (Valentine & Powers, 2013).

This cohort has no doubt become a key target consumer group for many professional sport leagues worldwide. For example, it has been reported that millenians are now the prime market for MLS (with an estimated 70 million fans in USA), because most of them grew up with soccer and understand the game (Birkner, 2014). In an interview reported in *Marketing News Weekly* (Bickner, 2014), Dan Courtemanche, who is the executive vice president of communications for New York-based Major League Soccer and Soccer United Marketing, emphasized on their extensive use of technology for marketing purposes; MLS launched an independent YouTube channel called 'KickTV', which promotes soccer on Generation Y and focuses on soccer globally. Furthermore, MLS (through its MLS Plus division), in cooperation with NBC Sports Network, introduced YouTube short shows and movies designed to show the personalities of their players off the field in a pleasant/funny way, to develop psychological links with these younger fans (Birkner, 2014).

- *Generation Z (born since 1995):* They are about 23 million in the US today (Schroer, 2014). This latest cohort is growing under the strong influence of technology – they have never lived without mobile devices or the internet. This cohort often place value on social acceptance, and trust their friends more than advertisements. More of them value authenticity and are prone to think creatively. In terms of their consumer behaviour, music, fashion, cosmetics and videogames are heavily used to obtain peer acceptance. They also often spend considerable time indoors, watching TV, playing videogames and using the internet; consequently, they are likely to be perceived as the overweight generation that does not pursue as healthy a lifestyle as the earlier cohort (Williams & Page, 2011). This is, therefore, a generation that represents a very worthy target consumer group for active sport and recreation participation, if they are convinced to lead healthier lifestyles.

A good example of how social and digital media can be used to promote sports among Generation Z is the use of fantasy football on digital applications. As stated by Mark Waller (NFL executive vice president international), in an interview with Perlberg (2014), fantasy football is used by NFL as a marketing tool for Generation Z, because it is fun and educational, and increases children's involvement with the game. Furthermore, in addition to watching games on TV and online, the NFL has invested in the use of mobile applications that provide football-related content, in cooperation with an education game company (Jump Start). It has been reported that two million US children now engage with the NFL online, including via its *Child's Play: NFL targeting kids, young fans with new initiatives* campaign (*Sports Business Daily*, 2010). According to Mark Waller, these digital platforms speak to their youngest generation of fans in their language, on their terms and in their environment of laptops, tablets and mobile phones. These mobile applications combine entertainment with education into a form of 'edutainment' (Perlberg, 2014).

In a recent report, the IHRSA (2014) provided results on why the age cohorts should be used for designing targeted marketing strategy in the USA. For instance, the IHRSA reported Generation Y as having the highest amount of health club members (23%), and Generation Z as the lowest (8%). Furthermore, a notable 16% of Generation X and 11% of baby boomers were recorded as current members of health clubs (see Graph 4.1).

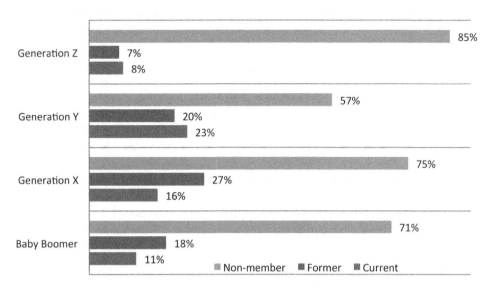

FIGURE 4.1 Health club membership (% of the population) by generations in the USA

Source: IHRSA (2014)

Based on these findings, it was recommended that health clubs focus on younger members (Generation Y), while also developing marketing strategies and in-club activities both to maintain and attract Generation X and baby boomers. Furthermore, it was suggested that health clubs organize family-friendly fitness programmes (e.g. childcare, youth training, family health programmes) for current and prospective Generation X members, and wellness programmes to attract Generation X and baby boomers (as shown in Figure 4.1).

4.3 SOCIAL CLASS AS A REFERENCE GROUP

Social class is defined as a homogeneous group of people who have common values, lifestyles and behaviour (Schiffman & Kanuk, 2004). Wealth, power and social status are three elements that are highly relevant to this definition. Power relates to the ability of an individual to influence his or her own aspects of social and professional lives, while social status mostly relates to social recognition.

However, the measurement of social class is not straightforward; there is no general agreement on how it can be measured and what variables should be included. Williams (2002) believed that occupation is the optimum predictor of social class in Western societies. This is because different occupations have different statuses – the nature of the job affects the behaviour and attitudes of consumers. Higher status jobs are those that have control over the business ownership; that is, the means of production including the labour force. Individual personalities, values, attitudes and motivations usually differ based on the type of job and status; all of which influence the individual's consumer behaviour.

Education is another variable that is often perceived as influencing social status. In many Western countries, education is strongly correlated with work status and social mobility; although there are cases where these relationships are not as strong. More educated individuals tend to read more, be more informed and spend more time on the internet, and also be more demanding customers – they generally spend more time searching for product information. They also tend to have healthier lifestyles and are more likely to be physically active. In addition, most of them have a better understanding of the benefits of active recreation, and spend less time watching TV. In terms of sport, more educated individuals have been identified as more likely to participate in active forms of recreation than their less educated counterparts (Alexandris & Carroll, 1998). This is probably due to their increased knowledge of the benefits of exercise.

Income is another factor that can determine social class, although it has been reported that the correlation between social class and income is often minimal (Downward, Lera-Lopez & Rasciute, 2014). While it is generally considered that income will determine the purchase of specific products and services (e.g. low, expensive or strong brands), Williams (2002) contended that it can also influence the information-seeking process. He argued that individuals with higher income generally spend more time searching for information, and often use utilitarian evaluative criteria before buying a product, such as quality, reliability or authenticity.

The categorization of a population into social classes is not always an easy task – in some countries, there are no clear subdivisions. In this context, several social class systems have been proposed for the US population. For example, Thompson and Hickey (2005, see Table 4.1) proposed the following categorization: 1) upper class – 1% of the population, including wealthy Americans with incomes of more than USD$500,000; 2) upper middle class – 15% of the population, including highly educated executives and managers with household incomes of more than USD$100,000; 3) lower middle class – 33% of the population, including semi-professionals with household incomes between USD$35,000 and USD$75,000; 4) working class – 32% of the population, including pink- and blue-collar workers with incomes in the range of USD$16,000 to USD$30,000; and 5) lower class –14%–20% of the population, where the majority live below the poverty line with income less than USD$18,000.

TABLE 4.1 Social stratification in the USA

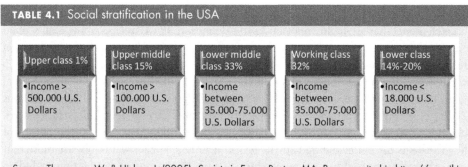

Source: Thompson, W. & Hickey, J. (2005). *Society in Focus*. Boston, MA: Pearson, cited in https://en.wiki pedia.org/wiki/Social_class_in_the_United_States.

Social class and sport consumer behaviour

It is now widely understood that social class influences consumer choices, based on common values, attitudes and lifestyles. However, in the area of sport, the influence of socioeconomic status on active sport participation and sport spectatorship needs reviewing further. In regard to the active sport participation sector, it has been suggested that both the level of participation and the selection of specific sport activities are influenced by social class. The Special Eurobarometer (2014) reported an influence of socioprofessional categories on physical activity participation; for example, 87% of managers participate in some form of physical activity, which dropped to 75% among other white-collar professions. In this study, the highest amounts of non-participation in sport were reported for 'housepersons' such as housewives (45%) and the unemployed (35%) (as shown in Figure 4.2).

Furthermore, other research has indicated that higher social class members tend to engage more in individual sport activities such as golf, tennis and skiing, while those of lower socioeconomic standing generally engage more in team sports such as basketball, football, volleyball and softball (Eitzen & Sage, 2003). Eitzen and Sage (2003) put forward four reasons for the influence of social class on sport participation: 1) the high cost of participation in individual activities such as sailing, skiing, golf and tennis; 2) the limited opportunities for participation in individual sports in community/public sport environments – these activities are usually provided by private sport clubs, which are in favour of individual sports; 3) the conspicuous consumption nature that sport participation creates for affluent individuals – those who prefer to participate in individual sports that showcase their spending capabilities; and 4) the differences in the amounts of free time between higher and lower level employees – those who work on shifts (lower level employees) are generally free to engage in team activities within specific time schedules, while higher level employees (e.g. executives) do not always finish work at a specific time each day, making it easier for them to participate in individual sports.

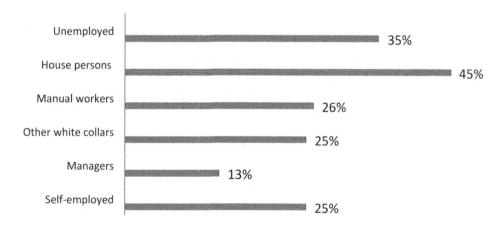

FIGURE 4.2 Physical activity non-participation (%) by socio-professional groups

Source: Eurobarometer (2014)

Among the variables that determine social class, it has been argued that education has the strongest influence on sport participation (Beenackers *et al.*, 2012; Scheerder *et al.*, 2011) – that more educated individuals are more likely to participate in sport. This is based on the perception that education creates a better understanding of the benefits of sport and the value of an active lifestyle, influencing a more positive attitude toward sport. It was reported by the Special Eurobarometer (2014) that the percentage of individuals who never engage in physical activities falls from around 50% of those who finished education by the age of 15, to 30% of those who finished at 16–19 years, which drops further to 19% of those who finished studying at the age of 20+.

Similar statistics have been revealed in studies, which investigated the influence of social class on youth sports. A study conducted by The Aspen Institute (2005) in the USA reported that children of families with an annual household income of more than $100,000 (20% of all USA households) are more likely to participate in organized sports than those from families with lower incomes. The lowest participation rates were found among children of families with the lowest income ($25,000). It was concluded by The Aspen Institute (2005) that sporting opportunities provided by school and community groups, and financial and time-related problems are responsible for these inequalities.

It should be noted, however, that the image of sport in society is continuously changing. For example, the former stereotype that sport is only for higher socioeconomic classes barely exists today. Another stereotype reversal is in relation to English football, which was traditionally associated with working class individuals. Today's average English football fan is far more socioeconomically diversified – there are now more middle class fans at football stadiums, including women, children and individuals of ethnic minority groups. As Bradshaw (2014) reported, this socioeconomic shift is mostly due to the inception of the English Premiership League in 1992, which improved the physical environment of the stadiums and services offered. Even the salaries of the league's players (on average around £25,000 to £30,00 per week for the Premier League, and £1,500 per week for League Two, which is about three times the national average) confirm that English football is no longer a working class sport – if anything, it is now more of a middle class sport (Bradshaw, 2014).

Tennis is another example of a sport where social perceptions are changing. Formerly perceived as an upscale sport, linked with high and middle socioeconomic groups, there has been criticism that this image has hindered its development in England (Barford, 2008). As a result, a number of strategies have been developed by the English Tennis Foundation in cooperation with the Tennis for Free charity to change the image of the sport. These strategies have included partnerships with schools and local authorities to promote the game and deliver tennis sessions in public sport venues (not only private clubs), training of coaches, promotional messages emphasizing the benefits of tennis as a sport activity (a sport played by all ages) and reduced prices for tennis courts and teaching sessions (Barford, 2008).

A particularly powerful example of the changing image of sport in society is in relation to action or extreme sports, which have commonly been considered alternative lifestyle sports. These include risky and individualistic sports and activities, such as BMX riding, street sports and long-boarding, skateboarding and snowboarding. The popularity of these sports in relation to participating and watching has been on the rise in recent times, mostly due to the changing economic lifestyle in Western communities and increased media coverage. It has therefore been proposed that sport marketers research these action sports on a global scale to analyse the direction that future sports will likely take and how they can enter into different socio-demographic groups and international markets (Ratten & Ratten, 2011).

When considering the influence of social class on sport consumption, it needs to be emphasized that this is a two-way relationship. In addition to socioeconomics affecting the popularity of a sport, sport can also be used to reduce social inequalities and promote social integration (Stodoloska & Alexandris, 2004). This is particularly relevant to public sport provision, such as via community centres and 'sport for all' programmes. That is, achieving social objectives related to increasing sport participation among disadvantaged groups of the general population (e.g. lower socioeconomic, ethnic minority and disabled individuals) is the most important task for sport marketers and managers in the area of public sport provision.

In regard to sport spectatorship, the influence of social class should be distinguished between attending and watching a game (e.g. on TV at home). In terms of attending games, income and education are variables that influence game attendance in North American sports (professional sport leagues) – the cost of attending a game clearly has an impact (Eitzen & Sage, 2003). In terms of watching games, it is the type of sports that differentiates between social class group members. As an example, affluent individuals are more likely to watch sport activities such as tennis and golf, college educated are more likely to watch college sports, while lower educated individuals are more likely to watch activities such as wrestling, tractor pulls and bowling (Eitzen & Sage, 2003).

As a final note it should be considered that the economic crises in many countries have had an influence on social stratification and sport consumer demand. Although it is not still clear how such financial crises influence demand across the various sport sectors. It has recently been contended, for example, by the fitness industry in Europe that economic crises have limited impact on market growth – this sector has continued to develop despite many European countries suffering financially.

4.4 CULTURES AND SUBCULTURES AS A REFERENCE GROUP

Culture is defined by the set of values, beliefs and traditions that are developed from childhood and transferred from generation to generation (Schiffman & Kanuk, 2004). The concept of values is central in the definition of culture, and includes family, religion, friendship and charity. Such values are generally relatively stable, few in number, not tied to specific objects or situations, accepted by members of society and guide human and consumer behaviour (Schiffman & Kanuk, 2004). An individual's values system is generally developed on a national level (e.g. national culture), regional level and family level. Thus, values generally differ across different countries, as well as regions and places within a country. Achievement and success, efficiency and practicality, progress, material comfort, individualism, humanitarianism, youthfulness and fitness and health are among the core US values (Schiffman & Kanuk, 2004).

Culture is a high-impact consideration in most business marketing, as personal values and beliefs generally influence consumer-related decisions. At an international sport level, a simple way to understand the role of culture in sport behaviour is to study the popularity of individual sports in different countries. For example, football, baseball, basketball, ice hockey and soccer are the most popular sports in the USA; football, cricket, rugby, badminton and tennis are the top five in England; football, rugby, soccer, tennis and cricket are the top five in Australia; and basketball, football, badminton, table tennis and baseball are the top five in China (Mughal, 2014; Sporteology, http://mostpopular sports.net/) (Table 4.2). The popularity of different sports varies across most countries due to their cultural differences (values and traditions).

In terms of active sport participation, the Special Eurobarometer (2014) reported that citizens in Northern Europe are typically the most physically active, while the lowest levels of participation are in the Southern Europe countries. While these differentiations possibly reflect each country's sport policy, such as investments in sport participation promotions, they are also no doubt related to cultural differences.

4.4.1 Subcultures: race and ethnicity

Subcultures consist of individuals who possess common values, beliefs and traditions that differentiate them from other members of the same culture. Individuals with the same race and ethnicity constitute subculture groups, which also often have different sport consumption patterns. Subcultures are particularly notable in countries that have a large amount of groups with different ethnic origins. For instance, shifting US demographics clearly demonstrate the importance of understanding the cultures of different ethnic and racial minority groups for sport marketing.

Stodolska, Shinew, Floyd and Walker (2014) identified that between 2000 and 2010, racial and ethnic minorities accounted for 91.7% of the US population growth, mostly Hispanics. Their projections indicate that whites will not ever be a majority by 2050 (there

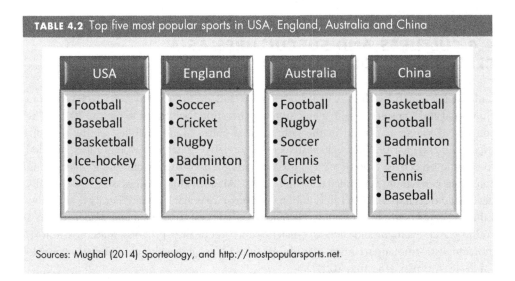

TABLE 4.2 Top five most popular sports in USA, England, Australia and China

USA	England	Australia	China
• Football	• Soccer	• Football	• Basketball
• Baseball	• Cricket	• Rugby	• Football
• Basketball	• Rugby	• Soccer	• Badminton
• Ice-hockey	• Badminton	• Tennis	• Table Tennis
• Soccer	• Tennis	• Cricket	• Baseball

Sources: Mughal (2014) Sporteology, and http://mostpopularsports.net.

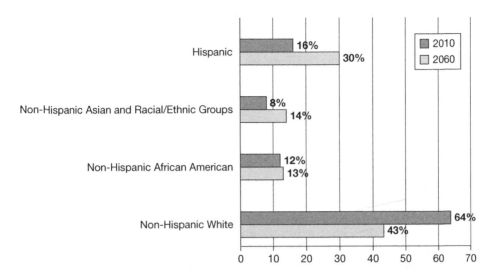

FIGURE 4.3 Percentage of racial and ethnic groups in 2000 and 2060 (projected)

Source: Murdock (2014)

will be the 47% of the total population). Other research (Murdock, 2014) has also forecasted that by 2060 (in a population of 420 million people), the US population will be 43% non-Hispanic whites (compared with 64% in 2010), 13% non-Hispanic African-Americans (compared with 12% in 2010), 14% non-Hispanic Asians and members of other racial and ethnic groups (compared with 8% in 2010) and 30% Hispanics (compared with 16% in 2010), as shown in Figure 4.3.

Subsequently, these data indicate that more than 50% of all US citizens less than 18 years of age will belong to minority ethnic groups by 2023. Hispanics, as the fastest-growing group, is an important consumer target market for the sport industry.

Such demographic shifts emphasize that ethnic and racial minority groups should not be overlooked by sport marketers. Some professional sport leagues such as the NBA, NFL and MLS have already realized the growth potential of these ethnic groups and have started marketing and advertising campaigns to increase their fan base among these cultural groups, especially Hispanics. A more detailed discussion about how ethnic minority groups are targeted by sport organizations was made in Chapter 2 (section 2.1.1).

These changing demographics also have implications for the development of 'new' sports in different countries, such as recreational soccer and MLS in the USA. Soccer is a relatively new sport in the USA, compared with the more traditional sports of baseball, basketball and football. Yet its rapid increase in popularity, mainly due to changing demographics, indicates that it might soon be a strong competitor of traditional US sports. Recent research has revealed that young citizens and particularly Hispanics are the most avid soccer fans – 26% of Hispanics nominated soccer as their favourite sport to watch, followed by football (22%), basketball (14%) and baseball (13%). In contrast, only 3% of non-Hispanic whites preferred soccer over other sports in the USA (Cox, 2014).

When factoring in how fast the Hispanic population is increasing, it becomes abundantly clear that the soccer fan base in the USA will also continue to grow. A trend that will be further strengthened by the young profile of soccer fans in the USA. A recent ESPN sports poll, as reported by Cox (2014), found that in addition, the recruitment of star European players, such as England's David Beckham, is also helping to popularize the game in the USA (Cox, 2014).

4.5 CHAPTER SUMMARY

This chapter has discussed the influence of socio-cultural and demographic factors that influence consumer decision-making in relation to sport products and services. National demographics are constantly shifting, and as a result of the changing economic climate (e.g. social stratification), lifestyle (e.g. family structures, improved health care systems (e.g. increase in life expectancy) and globalization (e.g. immigration), sport marketers need to be more aware than ever of demographic trends when devising marketing strategies. It is essential for sport marketers to understand the culture of the different age, socio-economic and socio-cultural groups, including their values, motivations and expectations, to better understand their sport consumer behaviour.

Specific promotional strategies should be developed for each of these target groups, in terms of the language used, communication and branding messages and chosen media, as well as what sport services will be provided. Social media, partnerships with multicultural media, informal communication channels through local communities and professional players in promotional campaigns are some of the main strategies that should be considered, based on the different cultures and subcultures.

4.6 DISCUSSION QUESTIONS

The discussion questions presented below are designed to help students review what is important in the chapter. You can answer them on your own, but they are also suitable for discussion work in small groups.

1) What are the main reference groups that influence sport consumer behaviour? Present examples to support your answer.
2) What are the main demographic changes that influence (or will influence) sport consumer behaviour?
3) What is the role of family on sport consumer socialization?
4) What are the main age cohorts in the USA and what are their characteristics?
5) What is the influence of social class on active sport participation and sport spectatorship?
6) What are the main changes in the patterns of race and ethnic groups? Will these changes influence the sport market?

4.7 CLASS ACTIVITY: INFLUENCE OF SOCIO-CULTURAL ENVIRONMENT ON SPORT CONSUMER BEHAVIOUR

The class activity is designed to use information learned in this chapter to understand the influence of the socio-cultural environment on sport consumer behaviour.

a) Using the latest census statistics, make a graphical presentation of the USA population, based on demographic, socioeconomic and cultural (ethnic and racial groups) information.
b) Select two professional sport leagues in the USA and make a graphical presentation of the spectators (i.e. those who attend games), based on demographic, socioeconomic and cultural (ethnic and racial groups) information.
c) Compare the census information and the profile of the fans of the leagues. Can you see any demographic, socioeconomic or cultural groups that are not well-represented among the fans of the two leagues? Can you interpret these findings?

REFERENCES

Alexandris, K. & Carroll, B. (1998). The relationship between selected demographic variables and recreational sport participation in Greece. *International Review for the Sociology of Sports, 33*(3), 291–297.

Barford, V. (2008). Can tennis be made less middle class? Retrieved from http://news.bbc.co.uk/2/hi/uk_news/magazine/7519914.stm

Beenackers, M., Kamphuis, C., Giskes, K., Brug, J., Kunst, A., Burdorf, A. & van Lenthe, F. (2012). Socioeconomic inequalities in occupational, leisure-time, and transport related physical activity among European adults: A systematic review. *International Journal of Behavioral Nutrition and Physical Activity, 9,* 116.

Birkner, C. (2014). Major league soccer sets big marketing goals. *Marketing News Weekly.* Retrieved from www.sportmarketingassociation.com/s/Wendling_Elodie.pdf

Blackwell, R., Miniard, P. & Engel, G. (2007). *Consumer Behavior.* Cincinnati, OH: Thomson Learning.

Bradshaw, L. (2014). *Is football a working class sport?* Retrieved from http://exclusivesportsmedia.tv/is-football-still-a-working-class-sport/

Carlson, E. (2009). Twentieth-century US. generations. *Population Bulletin, 64,* 1.

Colby, S. & Ortman, J. (2014). The baby boom cohort in the United States: 2012 to 2060 population estimates and projections. *Current Population Reports,* May, 1–16. www.census.gov/prod/2014pubs/p25-1141.pdf.

Cox, D. (2014). *Is Soccer Destined to Become America's National Pastime?* Retrieved from www.huffingtonpost.com/daniel-cox/soccer-in-america_b_4740668.html

De Carvallo, M., Scheerder J., Boen, F. & Sarmento, J.P. (2014). SPM19, *What brings people into the soccer stadium? (Part 2): The case of Portugal from a marketing perspective.* Belgium: KU Leuven, Research Unit of Social Kinesiology and Sport Management.

Downward, P., Lera-Lopez, F. & Rasciute, S. (2014). The correlates of sport participation in Europe. *Journal of Sport Science, 14*(6), 592–602.

Eitzen, D.S. & Sage, G.H. (2003). *Sociology of North American Sport* (7th ed.). Boulder CO: Paradigm Publishers.

Family Facts.org. (2011). *Nearly 12 percent of couples living together are unmarried.* Retrieved from www.familyfacts.org/charts/110/nearly-12-percent-of-couples-living-together-are-unmarried

Fidelman, M. (2014). *Six Powerful Sports Marketing Promotions That Are Better Than Google.* Retrieved from www.forbes.com/sites/markfidelman/2014/02/19/6-powerful-sports-marketing-promotions-that-are-better-than-google/

Fredricks, J.A. & Eccles, J.S. (2004). Parental influences on youth involvement in sports. In M. Weiss (ed.), *Developmental Sport and Exercise Psychology: A Lifespan Perspective.* Morgantown, WV: Fitness Information Technology.

Funk, D.C. & James, J.D. (2001). The psychological continuum model: A conceptual framework for understanding an individual's psychological connection to sport. *Sport Management Review, 4*(2), 119–150.

Hymowitz, C. (2015). Gen X was right: Reality really does bite, *Bloomberg Business.* Retrieved from www.bloomberg.com/news/articles/2015–06–10/millennials-think-they-have-it-bad-generation-x-has-it-worse

Ianniello, J. (2006). *Baby boomers – A lucrative market for the Pacific Asia region.* Paper presented at the 55th Pacific Asia Travel Association Annual Conference, Pattaya, Thailand.

IHRSA (2014). *Trend Report: Focus on Gender, Generation and Region, 3*(3).

James, A.R. & Manolis, C. (2000). Baby boomers and busters: An exploratory investigation of attitudes toward marketing, advertising and consumerism. *Journal of Consumer Marketing, 17,* 481–497.

Kelly, D. (2015) Demographics: the last baby boomer just turned 5, *Bunzel Media,* Retrieved from www.bunzelmedia.com/Demographics-The-Last-Baby-Boomer-Just-Turned-50/20695567

Kolbe, R.H. & James, J.D. (2000). An identification and examination of influences that shape the creation of a professional team fan. *International Journal of Sports Marketing and Sponsorship, 2*(1), 23–37.

Mughal, K.U. (2014.). *Top 10 most popular sports in America.* Sporteology retrieved from http://sporteology.com/top-10-most-popular-sports-in-america/

Murdock, S. (2014). Forward. In Stodoloska, M., Shinew, K., Floyd, M., Walker, G. (eds), *Race, Ethnicity and Leisure.* Champaign, IL: Human Kinetics.

Neeley, S. (2005). Influences on consumer socialization. *Young Consumers, 6*(2), 63–69.

Patterson, I. & Pegg, S. (2009). Marketing the leisure experience to baby boomers and older tourists. *Journal of Hospitality Marketing & Management, 18,* 254–272.

Perlberg, S. (2014). How the NFL is marketing itself to children. *CMO Today,* Retrieved from http://blogs.wsj.com/cmo/2014/08/27/nfl-cmo-mark-waller-interview/

Ratten, V. & Ratten, H. (2011) Guest editorial on international sports marketing. *Journal of Business & Industrial Marketing, 26*(8), 555–556.

Schawbel, D. (2015) Ten new findings about the millennial consumer, *Forbes.* Retrieved from www.forbes.com/sites/danschawbel/2015/01/20/10-new-findings-about-the-millennial-consumer/

Scheerder, J., Vandermeerschen, H., Van Tuyckom, C., Hoekman, R., Breedveld, K. & Vos, S. (2011). *SPM 10, Understanding the Game: Sport Participation in Europe.* Belgium: KU Leuven, Research Unit of Social Kinesiology and Sport Management.

Schiffman, L. & Kanuk, L. (2004). *Consumer Behavior.* NJ: Prentice Hall.

Schroer, W. (2014). Generations X, Y, Z and the others. *The Social Librarian. Bringing the power of social marketing to librarians.* Retrieved from www.socialmarketing.org/newsletter/features/generation3.htm

Special Eurobarometer (2014). Sport and Physical Activity (412). Directorate – General for Education and Culture, Brussels, European Commission.

Sports Business Daily (2010). Child's Play: NFL targeting kids, young fans with new initiatives, Issue 11. Retrieved from www.sportsbusinessdaily.com/Daily/Issues/2010/09/Issue-11/Leagues-Governing-Bodies/Childs-Play-NFL-Targeting-Kids-Young-Fans-With-New-Initiatives.aspx

Sporteology: It's all about Sports (n.d.). *Most popular sports in the world.* Retrieved from http://mostpopularsports.net/

Stodolska, M. & Alexandris, K. (2004). The role of recreational sport in the adaptation of first generation immigrants in the United States. *Journal of Leisure Research, 36,* 379–413.

Stodolska, M., Shinew, K., Floyd, M. & Walker, G. (2014). Treatment of race and ethnicity in leisure research. In Stodoloska, M., Shinew, K., Floyd, M., Walker (eds), *Race, Ethnicity and Leisure.* Champaign, IL: Human Kinetics.

The Aspen Institute (2005). *Project Play: Reimagining Youth Sports in America.* Retrieved from www.aspenprojectplay.org/

The Female Factor (n.d.). Women in the Economy. Retrieved from www.thefemalefactor.com/statistics/statistics_about_women.html

The Social Issues Research Centre (2008). Football Passions. Retrieved from www.sirc.org/football/football_passions.shtml

Thompson, W. & Hickey, J. (2005). *Society in Focus.* Boston, MA: Pearson. Cited in https://en.wikipedia.org/wiki/Social_class_in_the_United_States

Valentine, D. & Powers, T. (2013). Generation Y values and lifestyle segments. *Journal of Consumer Marketing, 30*(7), 597–606.

Wallop, H. (2014). Gen Z, Gen Y, baby boomers – a guide to the generations. *The Telegraph.* Retrieved from www.telegraph.co.uk/news/features/11002767/Gen-Z-Gen-Y-baby-boomers-a-guide-to-the-generations.html

Ward, S. (1981). Consumer socialization. In Kassarjian, H. & Robertson, T. (eds), *Perspectives in Consumer Behaviour* (3rd ed.). Glenview, IL: Scott Foresman, 380–396.

Williams, T. (2002). Social class influences on purchase evaluation criteria. *Journal of Consumer Marketing, 19*(3), 249–276.

Williams, K.C. & Page, R.A. (2011). Marketing to generations. *Journal of Behavioral Studies in Business, 3,* 1–17.

PART 3

Processes: internal psychological components

CHAPTER 5

Sport consumer motivation

This chapter's objectives are to:

- show the relevance of motivation theory for sport marketing and communication
- discuss the value of sport motivation research on understanding aspects of sport consumers' decision-making
- discuss different motivation types, based on the self-determination theory
- discuss the personal investment theory in the context of sport
- present examples of how motives in the contexts of sport participation, sport spectatorship and sport event tourism can be measured.

5.0 INTRODUCTION

The concept of motivation refers to the forces that initiate, direct and sustain human behaviour (Iso-Ahola, 1999). That is, it reflects the desire of an individual to satisfy personal needs and achieve personal goals. Motivation is an important psychological construct because it is often associated with positive behavioural outcomes. According to Vallerand (2001), such outcomes can be categorized into three types: 1) cognitive; 2) affective; and 3) behavioural. Learning, concentration and attention are examples of cognitive outcomes. In such cases in a sporting context, motivated individuals are prone to seeking information that complements their favourite sport behaviour (e.g. spend time on the internet, participate in sport blogs or read magazines and newspapers). They are also more likely to be focused when trying to learn a sport activity (e.g. participating in tennis classes). Affective outcomes include increased interest, satisfaction and enjoyment, improved mood and reduced anxiety. Also in relation to sport, highly motivated individuals are more likely to feel the psychological benefits of sport and leisure consumption than the less motivated ones (e.g. improved mood after watching a sport game, or reduced anxiety after attending a yoga class). Behavioural consequences relate to the development of consumer loyalty, which can be expressed as either current sport consumption (e.g. attending many games, participating in sports often, spending a lot of time on the internet or becoming a specialized sport consumer), or future sport consumption (i.e. intending to attend sport games, participate in sports, become a member of a health club etc.). The development of positive word-of-mouth is also a part of positive behavioural consequences.

Motivation research provides valuable information to sport marketers and practitioners, such as answering the questions of 'why' and 'how' with respect to sport consumer behaviour. For example:

- Why do fans attend their favourite team's games?
- What are fans' expectations when attending a sport game?
- Why do individuals become members of health/fitness clubs?
- Why do individuals participate in running marathons?
- How do leisure runners make decisions on which city marathon to participate in?
- How do individuals make decisions on which sport activities to participate in during their leisure time (e.g. fitness vs. outdoor sports)?
- Why do motives for attending a sport game or participating in sports vary among individuals of different socio-demographic groups (e.g. age, social class, ethnicity)?
- How can sport consumer motivation be measured via valid and reliable question-naires?
- How can sport motivation data be used by sport marketers to develop marketing strategy?

Based on such questions, the study of sport consumers' motivations helps marketers to:

- segment sport consumers according to their motives, needs and expectations – based on psychographic segmentation data of their current and prospective customers;
- design effective communication strategies to address sport consumer needs and expectations;
- satisfy sport consumer needs and expectations with customized sport and recreation services;
- build customer behavioural and attitudinal loyalty, by satisfying their needs and expectations.

Targeting sport consumers' motivations has already been used as a marketing strategy by some well-known sport brands, such as Nike's *What's your Motivation* (2011) and *Girls – Sport Motivation* (2013) campaigns, the NBA's *Motivation – What's Your Excuse* (2013) and ASICS's *Better Your Best* (2013).

5.1 DEFINITION AND THE NEED RECOGNITION PROCESS

The motivation process begins with a need recognition stage, where an individual realizes they have a specific need that is unfilled (see Figure 5.1). This need is recognized when a discrepancy exists between the individual's present state and an ideal state. For example, consider an individual who feels stressed about a hectic daily routine and desires a change (e.g. need for escape). As a result, they may decide to attend a basketball game or go jogging after work, to address their escape need.

The discrepancy between the present and ideal state often creates a feeling of tension – an unpleasant condition or feeling when a need remains unfulfilled. Tension can develop from many types of needs, and the magnitude or level of tension determines the urgency that engages the 'drive state'. The drive state occurs when an individual is aroused to reduce or eliminate an unpleasant situation and restore balance. Within the drive state, the degree of pressure exerted on the individual to restore balance creates a 'push' and reflects the strength of motivation.

The strength of motivation within the drive state is what pushes the individual toward choosing the pathway that will best restore balance. Strength of sport motivation is a construct that has been used in several studies in the context of sport and leisure, and has aptly explained some aspects of sport behaviour (e.g. Carroll & Alexandris, 1997; Alexandris, Funk & Pritchard, 2011). In such studies, the strength of sport motivation is measured by five motivational signs or facets: 1) guilt sensitivity – defined by an individual's feelings of guilt about not engaging in the sport behaviour (e.g. not participating in sport activities or attending a sport game); 2) persistence – defined by an individual's determination to continue pursuing the sport behaviour despite the presence of constraints (e.g. running in a marathon despite the bad weather); 3) defensive fluency – defined by an individual's ability to list the benefits that result from engaging in sport behaviour (e.g. exercise improves physical and psychological health); 4) preferences – defined by an individual's readiness to present themselves with specific preferences for sport behaviour (e.g. cricket is my favourite sport to watch); 5) activity – defined by the time spent in sport behaviour (e.g. time spent on their favourite team's website) (Carroll & Alexandris, 1997; Cattel & Child, 1975).

Following on from the need recognition stage, the want stage represents the pathway toward a specific form of consumption that an individual chooses to reduce tension. Such consumer needs and wants can be satisfied in numerous individualistic ways, and the chosen path is often based on a unique set of personal experiences.

The subsequent goal state represents the final stage in the motivation process – the acquisition of the need (see Figure 5.1). Such goal attainment occurs through a consumption activity that fulfils the need and reduces the tension. This motivation process is highly relevant to sport marketing, where the objective is to communicate to consumers that the pathway or experience offered (i.e. product, event, service, brand) will help them attain their goal and restore balance.

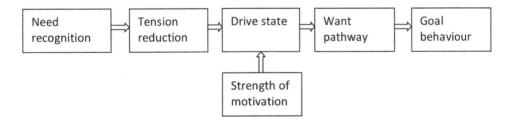

FIGURE 5.1 Sport and consumer motivation process

5.2 BIOLOGICAL AND PSYCHOLOGICAL NEEDS

There are a number of biological and psychological needs most individuals are able to self-identify that initiate the recognition stage. Based on this and as shown in Figure 5.2, psychologist Abraham Maslow (1943) proposed a well-known hierarchy of needs, which motivate people to action. These include physiological needs (e.g. water, air, sleep, food); safety needs (e.g. security, shelter, protection); belonging needs (e.g. friendship, acceptance by others); esteem needs (e.g. prestige, asserting one's individual identity, personal accomplishment and achievement); and self-actualization needs (e.g. self-fulfilment, skill mastery, enriching experience). The lack of these needs creates a discrepancy and creates tension.

Based on Maslow's hierarchy of needs, sports marketers can segment sport consumers according to their needs and subsequently target them. In general, different sport services appeal to different need categories. For example, research has shown (Funk *et al.*, 2009) that socialization is a major motivating factor for individuals to attend sport games or participate in group sport activities (i.e. fulfils need for belonging). The Cross Fit's *It's a way of life* (2011) commercial is a worthy example of how social and belonging needs can be targeted. Furthermore, there are sport services that appeal to specific ego needs. Marathon recreational runners, for example, compete with themselves by setting personal goals (e.g. to finish the marathon or achieve a specific time), which helps them satisfy ego-related needs. There are also sport services that appeal to self-actualization needs. It has been suggested that learning and skill development are major motivating factors for many individuals to engage in sports, such as tennis, skiing and snowboarding. The *Never*

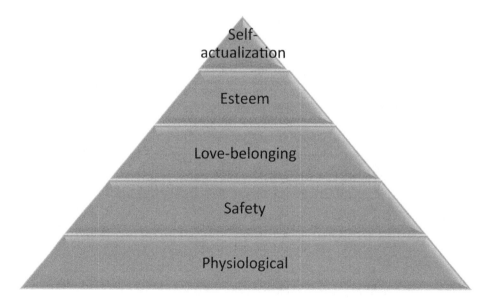

FIGURE 5.2 Maslow's hierarchy of needs

Stop Exploring (2014) campaign by North Face is an example of how a commercial can target learning, exploring and self-actualization needs.

5.3 GOAL BEHAVIOUR IN SPORTS

As previously noted, goal behaviour represents the acquisition of the individual's needs. Hence, sport marketers should concern themselves with communicating the positive attributes and benefits of their products and services that can direct or pull the consumer along a specific consumption pathway. Such benefits include improved physical health (e.g. from exercise participation), improved psychological health (e.g. improved mood, relaxation), skill development (e.g. in youth sport programmes) and social development (e.g. networking in marathons). As an example, according to the IHRSA's trend report (2014) the main goals for becoming a member of a health club are: staying healthy (61%), feeling better about myself (49%) and staying in shape (49%) (see Figure 5.3).

While sport marketers generally have limited ability to influence the initial internal push forces operating within the motivation process, most can provide pathways that pull and direct sport behaviour.

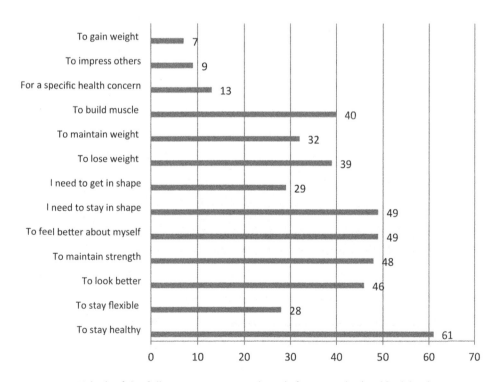

FIGURE 5.3 Which of the following are personal goals for using the health clubs that you currently belong to? (%)

Source: IHRSA (2014)

5.4 TYPES OF MOTIVATION AND THE SELF-DETERMINATION THEORY

Motivation not only varies with respect to its extent (i.e. how much), but also its orientation (Ryan & Deci, 2000). According to the self-determination theory (www.self determinationtheory.org/theory/), there are two types of motivation: 1) intrinsic motivation and 2) extrinsic motivation (Deci & Ryan, 1985; Ryan & Deci, 2000) (see Table 5.1). In addition, there is a final stage of 'amotivation'. These motivation types run along a continuum from intrinsic to extrinsic motivation, and then to amotivation (Deci & Ryan, 1985). That is, the level of self-determination and motivation decreases as an individual moves from intrinsic motivation to amotivation (see Figure 5.4).

5.4.1 Intrinsic motivation

Intrinsic motivation relates to engaging in an activity for the sake of engagement. In such instances, individuals are motivated by the desire to feel pleasure and satisfaction, derived simply from performing the activity (Deci & Ryan, 1985; Vallerand & Fortier, 1998). Many forms of sport and recreation behaviour are intrinsically motivated, as individuals usually choose their leisure activities freely – in the absence of external pressures – expecting pleasure and excitement from participation (Weissinger & Bandalos, 1995). For instance, an individual who chooses to watch a football game during his/her free time because he/she believes it will be an entertaining experience is an intrinsically motivated spectator. In addition, an individual who participates in a city marathon to experience running in that

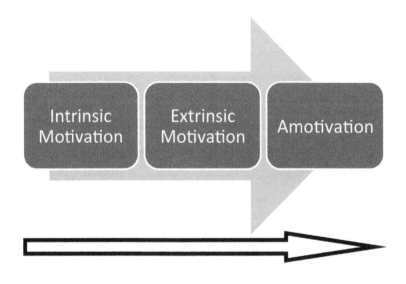

High Self-Determination   Low Self-Determination

FIGURE 5.4 The self-determination motivation theory

other city (e.g. New York), and not for the competition, is intrinsically motivated. Intrinsic motivation often leads to positive behavioural outcomes – in a sport context, intrinsically motivated consumers are those more likely to develop sport commitment and loyalty. There have been many sport marketing campaigns that use intrinsic motivation to promote the sport consumption experience, such as the NBA's *I Love This Game* (2011), the US Open's *It Must Be Love* (2012) and FIFA 15's *Feel the Game* (2014).

In addition to the three main motivation types discussed previously, it was further proposed by Deci and Ryan (1985) that there are several types of motives that occur at different points along a self-determination continuum. When including these other motive types, the continuum will run from high to low levels of self-determination, as the individual moves from intrinsic to extrinsic motivation, and finally to amotivation. In this scenario, intrinsic and extrinsic motivation each consists of three sub-dimensions (Pelletier *et al.*, 1995; Pelletier, Vallerand & Sarrazin, 2007).

In terms of intrinsic motivation, the three sub-dimensions are:

* intrinsic motivation to know
* intrinsic motivation toward accomplishment
* intrinsic motivation to experience stimulation.

Intrinsic motivation to know: This is engaging in an activity to satisfy needs related to learning, exploring and personal development (Vallerand, 2001). Examples in a sport context are individuals who start attending tennis classes to improve their tennis skills, individuals who participate in international city marathons to explore local culture and individuals who attend yoga classes to better understand their body. Intrinsic motivation to know needs can also relate to sport spectatorship, such as individuals who watch a football game to learn the rules and understand the game strategy, or who attend a basketball game to feel the atmosphere in the stadium (exploring needs). The North Face's *Never Stop Exploring* (2014) commercial is an example of how such learning and exploring needs can be targeted.

Intrinsic motivation toward accomplishment: This is engaging in an activity to achieve personal goals and create accomplishments (Vallerand & Losier, 1999). Setting personal goals is a common self-motivating strategy among recreational sport participants. For example, an individual who aims to complete the Classical Athens marathon (55 km) is likely to feel internal satisfaction when he/she does so. Such personal goals can be set by sport leaders (e.g. a group instructor) in organized sport activities, or by an individual sport participant (e.g. a recreational runner). ASICS's *Made of Sport* (2012) commercial is a relevant example of how intrinsic motivation toward accomplishment needs can be targeted.

Intrinsic motivation to experience stimulation: This relates to satisfying sensation seeking, fun and excitement needs (Vallerand, 2001). This type of motivation is applicable to most sport consumption types, including fun sport games (e.g. those with strong competition and nice game atmosphere) that entertain spectators and satisfy the need for sensation seeking. Outdoor (e.g. snowboarding) and extreme (e.g. freestyle skiing) sports also are examples of activities that satisfy the need for sensation seeking. Examples of sport commercials that target sensation-seeking-related needs can be found in Salomon's *SkyRun 2014* (2014) and Nike's *My Time is Now* (2012) advertising campaigns.

5.4.2 Extrinsic motivation

Extrinsic motivation relates to engaging in a behaviour as a 'means to an end' – not just for the sake of it (Ryan & Deci, 2000). This is where individuals are motivated by the desire to achieve external rewards. There are many examples of extrinsically motivated sport behaviour, such as exercising to lose weight (i.e. external reward). However, it is common practice for youth sport coaches to avoid using such external rewards – including an emphasis on winning – when teaching youth sports (e.g. in youth sport camps), to avoid extrinsically motivated behaviour. It is not generally considered an effective marketing strategy to promote and target extrinsically motivated behaviour, as while extrinsic motivation can lead to sport engagement, it is unlikely it will lead to the development of loyalty and long-term behaviour.

In terms of extrinsic motivation, the three proposed sub-dimensions are (Vallerand & Losier, 1999):

- identified regulation
- introjected regulation
- external regulation.

Identified regulation: This is where an individual engages in a behaviour because he/she feels it is significant for him/her. This is where the individual anticipates specific self-indulgent outcomes from engaging in the behaviour, but does not necessarily expect to experience excitement and pleasure. For example, some individuals participate in exercise programmes because of the associated health benefits, but it does not necessarily mean such behaviour is entertaining for them.

Introjected regulation: This refers to engaging in behaviours that are regulated by internally controlled imperatives (Blais, Sabourin, Boucher & Vallerand, 1990). In such instances, internal pressure often causes an individual to engage in a behaviour, possibly to avoid feelings of guilt or anxiety. Introjected reasons for engaging in a sport activity are usually in compliance with 'should' and 'must' (Vallerand & Losier, 1999). Examples in relation to sport behaviour include engaging to avoid feelings of guilt (e.g. running is an activity I should do during my leisure time), or because it 'fits' with an individual's self-esteem (e.g. I must do weight training because it improves my appearance, or I should attend a tennis game because it reflects my social status).

External regulation: This is the least self-determined form of extrinsic motivation. Here an individual engages in a behaviour purely for external rewards (e.g. social recognition) or to avoid punishment (e.g. rejection within their social group). For instance, an individual may participate in exercise to achieve social recognition (i.e. socially acceptable behaviour). In addition, a college student who attends basketball matches only because their friends do – to avoid social exclusion – is displaying externally regulated behaviour.

5.4.3 Amotivation

The last stage in the motivation process is amotivation. This is where there is an absence of motivation – the individual has no reason to continue to engage in the sport behaviour, he/she is neither intrinsically or extrinsically motivated (Deci & Ryan, 1985). In a sport

TABLE 5.1 Types of motivation according to the self-determination theory	
Types of motivation	Definitions and examples
a) Intrinsic motivation	Engaging in a sport behaviour for the sake of enjoyment
To know	Learn and Explore (e.g. learn how to climb)
Toward accomplishment	Achieve Personal Goals (e.g. finish the marathon)
To experience stimulation	Have fun and experience excitement (e.g. enjoy the football game)
b) Extrinsic motivation	Engaging in a sport behaviour motivated by external factors and rewards
Identified regulation	Expect specific outcomes from sport engagement (e.g. lose weight)
Introjected regulation	Participate to avoid feelings of guilt and anxiety (e.g. should not miss my sport training session)
External regulation	Expect external rewards or avoid punishment (e.g. should start exercising in order to avoid rejection from my friends)
c) Amotivation	Absence of motivation. No reason to continue sport engagement.

context, amotivated individuals are those who will eventually stop engaging in sport activities (Fortier, Vallerand, Briere & Provencher, 1995).

A synopsis of the different types of motivation, as proposed by the self-determination theory, is presented in Table 5.1.

5.5 OUTCOMES OF MOTIVATION

Different types of motivation lead to different outcomes (Vallerand, 2001) – such outcomes are often decreased in positivity across the continuum from intrinsic motivation to amotivation. Based on this, individuals with high intrinsic motivation are more likely to achieve positive outcomes (e.g. continue taking part in the activity, and become loyal and committed consumers); amotivated individuals are more prone to negative outcomes for themselves (e.g. stop engaging in the behaviour). Extrinsic motivation can be associated with both positive (e.g. identified regulation) and negative ones (e.g. external regulation).

5.6 TYPES OF MOTIVATION AND SPORT FANS

The simultaneous presence of both intrinsic and extrinsic motivations was identified in a study by marketing agency Octagon, as reported in *Sports Business Journal* by King (2010). In this study, the motives of fans of four USA professional sport leagues were investigated. As shown in Table 5.2 most of the motives were intrinsic (e.g. nostalgia, love of the game, player excitement, active appreciation, team devotion). However, there were

TABLE 5.2 What fuels fans' passion for sports

NFL	MLB	NBA	NHL
•Team devotion •Personal indulgence •All consuming •Love of the game •Talk and socializing •TV preference •Nostalgia •Sense of belonging •Gloating	•Nostalgia •Team devotion •Talk and socialization •Personal indulgence •Player excitement •All consuming •Sense of belonging •Love of the game •Gloating •TV preference • Active appreciation •Player affinity	•All consuming •Team devotion •Nostalgia •Personal indulgence •Talk and socializing •Active appreciation •Player excitement •Gloating •Sense of belonging •Love of the game •Player affinity	•Team devotion • All consuming •Talk and socialization •Personal indulgence •Sense of belonging •Nostalgia •Gloating •Player excitement •Love of the game

Source: King, B. (2010). What makes fans crazy about Sports? http://sportsbusinessdaily.com/Journal/Issues/2010/04/20100419/SBJ-In-Depth/What-Makes-Fans-Crazy-About-Sports.aspx.

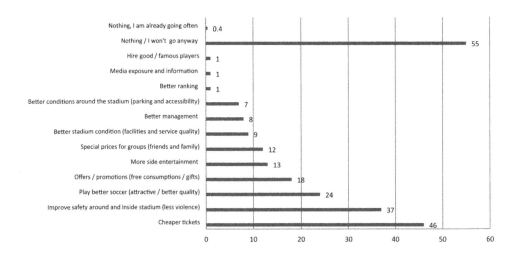

FIGURE 5.5 What can the club improve to make you attend more?

Source: da Carvallo, M., Scheerder, J., Boen, F., & Sarmento, J. P. (2014).

also extrinsic motives such as all-consuming, talking and socializing. In addition, the relative importance of specific motives differed among the sport league fans in the study. These results confirm the significance of sport marketers studying fan motivation in specific contexts (see Table 5.2 for further detail).

Another study that substantiated the relevance of the motivation stages among sport fans was conducted in the Portuguese professional football league (de Carvallo, Scheerder, Boen & Sarmento, 2014). As shown in Figure 5.5, 55% of these fans believed that the club could not do anything more to motivate them to attend more games. These fans were closer to the amotivation stage of the motivation continuum. Other factors that were reported to motivate these fans to attend more games were related to a combination of internal (e.g. more entertainment, better quality of football) and external (rewards on behalf of the club such as offers, promotions and special prices for groups) incentives.

5.7 MOTIVATION AND PERSONAL INVESTMENT

One of the theoretical frameworks that has been used extensively to explain motivation is the Personal Investment Theory (Maehr & Braskamp, 1986; Maher, 1984). This framework does not focus on the types of motives as in the self-determination theory; it places more emphasis on the role of the social and cultural contexts in determining motivational patterns (see Teixeira, Carraca, Markland, Silva & Ryan, 2012 for further detail). As the socio-cultural environment's influence on sport engagement and consumption has already been discussed in this book, this theoretical framework has also been used to help obtain a better understanding of sport consumer behaviour. Using this framework in a sport consumer context, an individual invests his/her time and effort in activities that are

FIGURE 5.6 Personal investment theory: components of meaning

chosen based on their perceived social value and personal meaning. The three main components of personal meaning that were proposed in the personal investment theory are (see Figure 5.6):

- beliefs about self
- perceived options and alternatives
- personal goals.

5.7.1 Beliefs about self

This has been defined as 'the more or less organized collection of perceptions, beliefs, and feelings related to who one is' (Maher, 1984, p. 126). One of the main components of the beliefs about self is personal competence, which refers to the perceptions an individual has about his/her abilities to perform an action effectively and successfully. This sense of personal competence is often considered a powerful determinant of an individual's decision to invest in a specific activity. An individual's perceptions about self-competence are subjective, and are generally based on personal evaluations – they usually guide preferences and choices. That is, individuals usually do whatever they think they can do, while they avoid engaging in activities in which they feel incompetent. Perceptions about competence also influence continuing engagement in specific behaviours (e.g. development of commitment). In this context, individuals are more likely to continue with an activity where they feel they are improving their skills and abilities. Encouragement within their social environment (e.g. friends, family) can also heavily impact on an individual's self-perceived competence and ability to build their personal self.

Perceived personal competence is highly applicable to the context of sport behaviour. Individuals who believe they lack the abilities and skills to participate in a specific sport activity (e.g. playing football) will likely avoid participation. Research has shown that personal perceptions related to a lack of skills and abilities are the most influential in an individual's decision not to participate in sports (Alexandris *et al.*, 2009, 2011). Nike's *Believe in Yourself* (2009) and *I Can* (2006), as well as the 2014 FIFA World Cup's *I Believe* (2014) are examples of sport marketing campaigns that aim to motivate individuals to feel competent and capable of performing specific sport activities.

Another belief applicable to most sport settings is the construct of *identity* (Wann, Melnick, Russell & Pease, 2001), which is defined as the way an 'individual perceives himself/herself as associated with certain groups and holds selected others to be significant' (Maehr & Braskamp, 1986, p. 59). In the context of sport spectatorship, team identity is a key construct included in motivation research that aims to further understand fan behaviour (Lock, Taylor, Funk & Darcy, 2012).

There are many examples of commercials that aim to make sport consumers feel part of teams, groups and sport societies, including ASIC's *We are Marathoners* (2014), Cross Fit's *It's a Way of Life* (2011) and Puma's *Hard Chorus* (2010).

5.7.2 Perceived options and alternatives

This is where individuals make behavioural choices based on opportunity, including what is available to do (e.g. which sport events can be attended on Saturday afternoons), what is realistic to do (e.g. is it realistic to run in a mountain marathon), as well as what is acceptable to do (e.g. whether it is socially acceptable for a woman to play football). The limited availability of choices can be real (e.g. lack of financial resources to go skiing) as well as perceived (e.g. lack of knowledge about where they can participate in aerobic classes).

The sport industry is part of the entertainment industry. Most individuals have a range of options on how they can spend their leisure time, including active sports (e.g. participation in sport activities), passive sports (e.g. attending a sport game), as well as other leisure choices such as going to a movie or to a coffee shop. Most of these decisions are made based on an individual's needs, as well as an evaluation of the cost (e.g. money, time, effort spent) vs. the benefits (e.g. positive physical and psychological outcomes) of consuming a specific activity.

The personal investment theory contends that an individual's perceived choices are also influenced by what is deemed socially acceptable. Personal values (e.g. healthy lifestyle) and socio-cultural norms (e.g. spending time with the family) often influence the perceived availability and uptake of options. Encouragement or discouragement by significant others and reference groups can positively or negatively impact on an individual's behavioural choices and actions. For example, personal values and/or social stereotypes related to family roles might influence a woman's participation in sport activities or their attendance at sport games. *Empowering Women & Girls Through Sports* (2012), developed by the US Bureau of Educational and Cultural Affairs, is a relevant example of a campaign that aimed to overcome societal stereotypes and encourage females to participate in sports.

When introducing the personal investment theory, Maehr (1984) used elite athletes as an example of how the availability of opportunities, based on the social environment, can explain sport behaviour. Many elite athletes are born into 'sport families'. Such families' positive sport values often 'create' opportunities for their children to participate in sport, including encouraging more specialized sport participation such as via more time and money invested in training. In the context of sport spectatorship, it has also been suggested that most children become fans of a specific team based on the influence of their family and friends (de Carvallo *et al.*, 2014).

Within sport and recreation literature, an individual's perceived options to participate in sports have often been examined based on two main elements: 1) programme compatibility and 2) perceived constraints (Raedeke & Burton, 1997). Programme compatibility relates to an individual's belief that participation in specific sport activities will enable him/her to achieve desired benefits (e.g. improved health, entertainment). Many sport promotions highlight such benefits from consuming their products or services, such as *Fitness in 100 Words (2014)* by Cross Fit. Perceived constraints (see Chapter 6 for further information) relate to the presence of external and internal factors that can inhibit an individual's participation in sport activities, such as those shown in Table 5.3.

5.7.3 Personal goals

Personal goals relate to sought-after outcomes or results that individuals expect from engaging in a specific behaviour. In a sport context, examples of these personal goals are to improve physical fitness (e.g. exercise), to increase self-discipline (e.g. martial arts), to reduce tension and anxiety (e.g. attend a sport event with friends) or to feel part of a sport network (e.g. member of a sport blog). Personal goals generally motivate individuals and guide their

TABLE 5.3 Factors that influence the perceived availability of options and alternatives

	Examples
Personal values	Health
	Success
	Well-being
	Achievement
	Power
	Team work
Socio-cultural environment	Family roles
	Gender roles
	Religion
	Social approval
	Image of sports in society
Perceived constraints	Perceived skills
	Health concerns
	Body image
	Negative past experiences
	Fitness levels

TABLE 5.4 The personal investment theory (Maehr & Braskamp, 1986)

Factors that influence an individual's motivation to invest his/her time and effort on a specific sport behaviour	Definitions and examples
a) **Beliefs about self influenced by:**	Defined as: feelings related to who one is
• Personal competence	Ability to perform a sport behaviour effectively
• Identity	How an individual perceives himself/herself in association with certain sport groups
b) **Perceived options and alternatives influenced by:**	Defined as: perceptions of what opportunities for sport engagement are available
• Personal values	Beliefs or ideals shared by members of a culture
• Socio-cultural environment	Social and cultural groups who influence perception about sport choices
• Perceived constraints	Factors that limit engagement in a behaviour
c) **Personal goals**	Defined as: the outcomes that individuals expect when engaging in sports (e.g. fan and enjoyment)

decisions to invest their time, effort and energy into pursuing a specific activity – they are often developed to satisfy the individual's personal needs. Two of ASIC's sport marketing campaigns are notable examples of commercials that specifically target sport consumers' personal goals: 1) *Next* (2013); and 2) and *Effort is Beautiful* (2012).

While most behaviour is goal-oriented, there are situations where an individual does not pursue specific actions and plans based on true personal goals (e.g. I am watching a basketball match because I have nothing else to do). In such instances, their behaviour is largely amotivated.

A synopsis of the main components of the personal investment theory is presented in Table 5.4.

5.8 THE MEASUREMENT OF SPORT MOTIVES

A number of sport motives have been identified that drive individuals toward sport consumption, involving a range of research tools such as scales (i.e. questionnaires) used by researchers and sport marketers. However, some of these published scales are highly detailed, which can make them difficult for sport marketers to use. In the following sections, the main sport motive dimensions that have been proposed and empirically tested in the literature are discussed, specifically in the contexts of active sport participation, sport spectatorship and sport event tourism.

5.8.1 Sport motives in the context of active sport participation

In the context of active sport participation, such as climbing, running and skiing, the Recreation Experience Preference (REP) scale (Manfredo, Driver & Tarant, 1996) is the most widely applied. Based on this scale, sport and recreation experience is interpreted as 'the package or bundle of psychological outcomes desired from a recreation engagement' (p. 189); that is, engaging in sport activities to achieve certain psychological outcomes (e.g. outdoor running for stress relief).

Manfredo *et al.* (1996) conducted a meta-analysis of published studies that had used the REP questionnaire between 1976 and 1986, and found evidence of the scale's validity and reliability. However, since the REP includes a large number of motive sub-scales, they recommended that researchers should determine which are most applicable in the context of their studies (e.g. indoor or outdoor sport) and use shortened versions of the questionnaire. Some published studies have since used shorter versions of the REP scale (e.g. Alexandris, Kouthouris, Funk & Giovani, 2009; Kyle, Absher, Hammitt & Cavin, 2006), based on the context of their study (e.g. outdoor recreation, exercise, etc.).

The main motive sub-scales that were proposed by Manfredo *et al.* (1996) are presented in Table 5.5.

5.8.2 Motives in the context of sport spectatorship

Due to the diversity of sport consumers and sport event contexts, a large number of survey tools have also emerged for measuring motivation to attend sport events. These involve multiple questions to measure specific motives, which can further explain sport consumer behaviour.

TABLE 5.5 Motives for sport participation (recreational experience preference scale) (Manfredo et al., 1996)

Motive dimension	Examples of individual items
I participate in sports for:	
Achievement and social recognition	Build my self-confidence
Stimulation	Experience excitement
Autonomy	Feel free
Risk taking	Take risks
Sport equipment	Use my sport equipment
Family/friends togetherness	Spend time with my family
New people	Meet new people
Learning	Learn new skills
Enjoy nature	Spend time in the nature
Introspection	Think about my personal values
Creativity	Be creative
Nostalgia	Bring back pleasant memories
Physical fitness/health	To keep fit
Escape personal/social/physical pressures	Reduce stress
Teaching/leading others	Teach my outdoor skills to others

Funk, Filo, Beaton and Pritchard (2009) developed the SPEED scale to assess the 'Big 5' motives for sport spectatorship regardless of sport event context: 1) socialization; 2) performance; 3) excitement; 4) esteem; and 5) diversion (SPEED).

Further explanation on each of these SPEED motives is listed in Table 5.6.

It has been suggested that these five sport motives represent a core set of psychological needs that explain the individual's desire to attend sport events. As these SPEED motives have been identified across a range of prior and existing scales in sport literature, they are both theoretically supported and practically useful across various sport experiences. As a result, the SPEED scale can facilitate future work in sport consumer behaviour by providing the ability to examine and compare 'core' motives across numerous sport contexts. These motives also represent a platform from which to build and identify additional contextual motives (e.g. utilitarian motives) for attending specific sporting events. In addition, the SPEED scale provides sport managers with a concise and basic research tool, using only 10 questions with sound psychometric properties.

5.8.3 Motives in the context of sport event tourism

Iso-Ahola (1992) defined tourism motivation as 'a meaningful state of mind which adequately disposes an actor or a group of actors to travel' (p. 257). The majority of studies in both mainstream tourism and sport event tourism have adopted a push-pull categorization of motivation (Baloglou & Uysal, 1996; Crompton & McKay, 1997; Hanquin & Lam, 1999). Push motivation relates to an internal desire to eliminate an unpleasant state and reduce tension, which generally initiates motivation. It represents the recognition of internal/psychological needs, such as excitement, education, relaxation, enjoyment and escape (Yoon & Uysal, 2005). Pull motivation mainly involves external forces related to the attributes of the destination, the design and condition of facilities, the

TABLE 5.6 SPEED motives in sport consumer behaviour (Funk, Filo, Beaton and Pritchard, 2009)

SPEED	Description
Socialization	Represents a desire for social interaction. Individuals are motivated to seek a sport event experience due to opportunities for the enhancement of human relationships through external interaction with other spectators, participants, friends and family.
	Items:
	The chance to socialize with others
	The opportunity to interact with other people
Performance	Represents a desire for aesthetic and physical pleasure. Individuals are motivated to seek a sport experience due to opportunities to enjoy the grace, skill and artistry of athletic movement and physiological movement.
	Items:
	The gracefulness associated with the game
	The natural elegance of the game
Excitement	Represents a desire for intellectual stimulation. Individuals are motivated to seek a sport event experience due to opportunities for mental action and exploration from the atmospheric conditions created by the uncertainty of participation and competition and the spectacle of associated activities.
	Items:
	I enjoy the excitement associated with the games
	I find the games very exciting
Esteem	Represents a desire for competency. Individuals are motivated to seek a sport event experience due to opportunities for achievement and challenge that produce a sense of mastery and heighten a sense of personal and collective self-esteem.
	Items:
	I feel like I have won when the team wins
	I get a sense of accomplishment when the team wins
Diversion	Represents a desire for mental well-being. Individuals are motivated to seek a sport event experience due to opportunities to escape and remove themselves from daily work and life routines that create stress.
	Items:
	I can get away from the tension in my life
	It provides me with a break from my daily routine

atmosphere, the scenery, the local culture and the local cuisine (Yoon & Uysal, 2005). Push factors relate to the desire to actually travel; pull factors explain why individuals are attracted to a particular travel destination.

Depending on the context of the sport consumer behaviour study (e.g. participating in a city marathon), some of the active sport participation dimension motives can be applied to sport tourism (e.g. competition, fitness), in addition to tourism-related motives. The most common sport event motive dimensions that have been proposed in sport tourism literature include (Funk & Bruun, 2007; Getz & McConnell, 2011; Gibson, Kaplanidou & Kang, 2012; Hanquin & Lam, 1999; Kozak, 2002; McGehee, Loker-Murphy & Uysal, 1996):

- fun and excitement
- achievement and challenge
- competition
- improving athletic abilities/getting fit/staying healthy
- participating in a famous event/city
- escape and relaxation
- social interaction
- prestige and social recognition
- experience of the local culture
- learning and exploration of the destination.

5.9 CHAPTER SUMMARY

Sport motivation, including the motivation process, the two main theories of motivation (i.e. self-determination theory and personal investment theory) and the various sport motives identified in literature, has been discussed in this chapter. It would appear that it is difficult to identify one theory that can used to interpret all sport consumer behaviour types, mainly due to the unique characteristics of differing sport consumer contexts (e.g. active vs. passive sport consumption).

The self-determination and personal investment theories were focused on to highlight the need to understand sport consumer behaviour within the main existing theoretical frameworks of human motivation. To date, most sport consumer behaviour studies have been atheoretical and limited in their abilities to adequately identify specific sport motives rather than overall sport consumer behaviour.

As noted earlier in this chapter, motivation research is significant for sport marketers in their efforts to understand why and how sport consumers make specific decisions. Such research can guide the development of appropriate sport marketing and communication strategies. However, it should also be emphasized that additional primary research is essential for adequately measuring sport consumer motives; that is, data collected via quantitative surveys or qualitative methodologies (e.g. interviews or focus groups). In addition, as the design and implementation of most studies require the use of valid and reliable scales and/or the development of dependable interview guides, followed by appropriate statistical or qualitative analysis, cooperation between academics/researchers and sport practitioners is imperative.

5.10 DISCUSSION QUESTIONS

The discussion questions presented below are designed to help students review what is important in the chapter. You can answer them on your own, but they are also suitable for discussion work in small groups.

1) How can Maslow's hierarchy of needs theory be applied by sport marketers?
2) Discuss the two types of motivation, as proposed by the self-determination theory, and find examples for each of the two types in relation to motivation and their sub-dimensions.
3) What are the main outcomes of motivation? How do the three main motivation dimensions (i.e. intrinsic, extrinsic and amotivation) relate to outcomes?
4) What are the three components of meaning in the personal investment theory?
5) Show the relevance of personal investment theory for sport marketing, by providing specific examples.
6) What are the main motive dimensions as proposed by the REP scale?
7) What are the main motive dimensions as proposed by the SPEED scale?
8) What are the differences in the measurement of motives between spectatorship sport (e.g. watch a game) and sport event tourism (participate in a city marathon)?

5.11 CLASS ACTIVITY: MOTIVATIONS OF THE SPORT CONSUMER

The class activity is designed to use information learned in this chapter to understand sport consumer motivation.

a) Design a study to measure: 1) college students' motives for becoming members of their college's sport and recreation centre; and 2) college students' motivation for attending their college team's basketball games:

- Design the methodology of the two studies (data collection method, sample and sampling process).
- Develop two scales to measure college students' motives (one for becoming members and one for attending the games).
- Collect 100 questionnaires for each study.
- Analyse the data.
- Discuss the marketing implications of the results.

b) Search on the internet (e.g. YouTube) and find sport commercials:

- developed for participatory sports (e.g. fitness clubs);
- developed for spectatorship sports (e.g. NCAA or other professional sport leagues);
- developed for sport events (e.g. a city marathon);
- developed for sport goods (e.g. Nike, Adidas, ASIC).

Critically review these commercials and discuss which consumer motives they are targeting, using the self-determination and personal investment theories for interpretation.

REFERENCES

Alexandris, K., Funk, D. & Pritchard, M. (2011). The impact of constraints on motivation, activity attachment and skier intentions to continue. *Journal of Leisure Research, 43,* 56–79.

Alexandris, K., Kouthouris, C., Funk, D. & Giovani, K. (2009). Segmenting winter sport tourists by motivation: The case of recreational skiers. *Journal of Hospitality Marketing and Management, 18,* 480–500.

Baloglu, S. & Uysal, M. (1996). Market segments of push and pull motivations: A canonical correlation approach. *International Journal of Contemporary Hospitality Management, 8,* 32–38.

Blais, M., Sabourin, S., Boucher, C. & Vallerand, R. (1990). Toward a motivational model of couple happiness. *Journal of Personality and Social Psychology, 59*(5), 1021–1031.

Carroll, B. & Alexandris, K. (1997). Perception of constraints and strength of motivation: Their relation to recreational sport participation. *Journal of Leisure Research, 29,* 279–299.

Cattel, R.B. & Child, D. (1975). *Motivation and Dynamic Structure.* London: Holt, Rinehart and Winston.

Crompton, J. & McKay, S.L. (1997). Motives of visitors attending festival events. *Annals of Tourism Research, 24,* 425–439.

de Carvallo, M., Scheerder J., Boen, F. & Sarmento, J.P. (2014). What brings people into the soccer stadium? (Part 2). The case of Portugal from a marketing perspective. www.kennisbanksporten bewegen.nt/?file=26858&m=14228832068action=file.download

KU Leuven, Research Unit of Social Kinesiology and Sport Management, Belgium.

Deci, L. & Ryan, M. (1985). *Intrinsic Motivation and Self-determination in Human Behavior.* New York: Plenum Press.

Fortier, M., Vallerand, R., Briere, N. & Provencher, P. (1995). Competitive and recreational sport structures and gender: A test of their relationship with sport motivation. *International Journal of Sport Psychology, 26,* 24–39.

Funk, D. & Bruun, T. (2007). The role of socio-psychological and culture-education motives in marketing international sport tourism: A cross-cultural perspective. *Tourism Management, 28,* 806–819.

Funk, D.C., Filo, K., Beaton, A. & Pritchard, M. (2009). Measuring motives for sport event attendance: Bridging the academic-practitioner divide. *Sport Marketing Quarterly, 18,* 126–138.

Getz, D. & McConnell, A. (2011). Serious sport tourism and event travel careers. *Journal of Sport Management, 25,* 326–338.

Gibson, H., Kaplanidou, K. & Kang, S.J. (2012). Small scale event sport tourism: A case study in sustainable tourism. *Sport Management Review, 15,* 160–170.

Hanquin, Z.Q. & Lam, T. (1999). An analysis of mainland Chinese visitors' motivation to visit Hong Kong. *Tourism Management, 20,* 587–594.

IHRSA. (2014). *Trend Report: Focus on Gender, Generation and Region, 3*(3).

Iso-Ahola, S.E. (1982). Toward a social psychological theory of tourism motivation: A rejoinder. *Annals of Tourism Research, 12,* 256–262.

Iso-Ahola, S. (1999) Motivational foundations of leisure. In E.L. Jackson & T.L. Burton (eds), *Leisure Studies: Prospects for the Twenty-First Century* (pp. 35–51). State College, PA: Venture Publishing.

King, B. (2010). What makes fans crazy about Sports? Retrieved from www.sportsbusinessdaily.com/Journal/Issues/2010/04/20100419/SBJ-In-Depth/What-Makes-Fans-Crazy-About-Sports.aspx

Kozak, N. (2002). Comparative analysis of tourist motivations by nationality and destination. *Tourism Management, 23*, 221–232.

Kyle, G., Absher, J., Hammitt, W. & Cavin, J. (2006). An examination of the motivation–involvement relationship. *Leisure Sciences, 28*, 467–485.

Lock, D., Taylor, T., Funk, D. & Darcy, S. (2012). Exploring the development of team identification. *Journal of Sport Management, 26*, 283–294.

Maehr, M.L. & Braskamp, L.A. (1986). *The Motivation Factor: A Theory of Personal Investment*. Lexington, MA: D.C. Heath.

Maehr, M.L. (1984). Meaning and motivation: Toward a theory of Personal Investment. In R.E.C. Ames (ed.). *Motivation in Education: Student motivation, 1* (pp. 115–144). San Diego: Academic Press.

Manfredo, M., Driver, B. & Tarrant, M. (1996). Measuring leisure motivation: A meta-analysis of the recreation experience preference scales. *Journal of Leisure Research, 28*, 188–213.

Maslow, A. (1943). A theory of human motivation. *Psychological Review, 50*, 370–396.

McGehee, N.G., Loker-Murphy, L. & Uysal, M. (1996) The Australian international pleasure travel market: Motivations from a gender perspective. *The Journal of Tourism Studies, 7*(1), 45–47.

Pelletier, L., Fortier, M., Vallerand, R., Tuson, K., Briere, N. & Blais, M. (1995). Toward a new measure of intrinsic motivation, extrinsic motivation, and amotivation in sports: The sport motivation scale (SMS). *Journal of Sport and Exercise Psychology, 17*, 35–53.

Pelletier, L., Vallerand, R. & Sarrazin, P. (2007). The revised six-factor Sport Motivation Scale (Mallett, Kawabata, Newcombe, Otero-Forero & Jackson, 2007): Something old, something new, and something borrowed. *Psychology of Sport and Exercise, 8*, 615–621.

Raedeke, T. & Burton, D. (1997). Personal investment perspective on leisure-time physical activity participation: Role of incentives, program compatibility, and constraints. *Leisure Sciences, 19*(3), 209–228.

Ryan, R. & Deci, E. (2000). Self-determination theory and the facilitation of intrinsic motivation, social development and well-being. *American Psychologist, 55*(1), 68–78.

Scheerder, J., Vandermeerschen, H., Van Tuyckom, C., Hoekman, R., Breedveld, K. & Vos, S. (2011). *SPM 10, Understanding the Game: Sport Participation in Europe*. Belgium: KU Leuven, Research Unit of Social Kinesiology and Sport Management.

Teixeira, P., Carraca, E., Markland, D., Silva, N. & Ryan, M. (2012). Exercise, physical activity, and self-determination theory: A systematic review. *International Journal of Behavioral Nutrition and Physical Activity, 9*(78), 1–30.

Vallerand, R. (2001). A hierarchical model of intrinsic and extrinsic motivation in sport and exercise settings. In G. Roberts (ed.), *Advances in Motivation in Sport and Exercise, Champaign* (pp. 321–357). Champaign, IL: Human Kinetics.

Vallerand, R.J. & Fortier, M.S. (1998). Measures of intrinsic and extrinsic motivation in sport and physical activity: A review and critique. In J.L. Duda (ed.), *Advancements in Sport and Exercise Psychology Measurement* (pp. 81–101). Morgantown, WV: Fitness Information Technology.

Vallerand, R. & Losier, G. (1999). An integrative analysis of intrinsic and extrinsic motivation in sport. *Journal of Applied Sport Psychology, 11*, 142–169.

Wann, D., Melnick, M., Russell, G. & Pease, D. (2001). *Sport Fans: The psychology and social impact of spectators*. London: Routledge.

Weissinger, E. & Bandalos, D. (1995). Development, reliability and validity of a scale to measure intrinsic motivation in leisure. *Journal of Leisure Research, 27*, 379–400.

Yoon, Y. & Uysal, M., (2005). An examination of the effects of motivation and satisfaction on destination loyalty: A structural model. *Tourism Management, 26*, 45–56.

VIDEO FILES

ASICS. (2013). *Better Your Best* campaign [Video File]. Retrieved from www.youtube.com/watch?v= OsA27ueSODY

ASICS. (2013). *Next* campaign [Video File]. Retrieved from www.youtube.com/watch?v=A6wHtxKwILM

ASICS. (2012). *Effort is Beautiful* campaign [Video File]. Retrieved from www.youtube.com/watch?v= IRMcMQ0rWsw

ASICS. (2014). *We are Marathoners* campaign [Video File]. Retrieved from www.youtube.com/watch?v= iuAN3UI_LOg.

ASICS. (2012). *Made of Sport* [Video File]. Retrieved from www.youtube.com/watch?v=bu60n_v5IZI

Bureau of Educational and Cultural Affairs. (2012). *Empowering Women & Girls through Sports* [Video File]. Retrieved from www.youtube.com/watch?v=CpgAcQmIw8k

Cross Fit. (2011). *It's a Way of Life* [Video File]. Retrieved from www.youtube.com/watch?v=LHTi-Dd1mD4

Cross Fit. (2014). *Fitness in 100 Words* [Video File]. Retrieved from www.youtube.com/watch?v= K5fg7VcrJ70

FIFA 2014. World Cup. (2014). *I Believe* [Video File]. Retrieved from www.youtube.com/watch?v= 6pjliE37ENY

FIFA 2015. (2014). *Feel the Game* [Video File]. Retrieved from www.youtube.com/watch?v=Q21bznzy_ HY

NBA. (2013). *Motivation – What's Your Excuse* [Video File]. Retrieved from www.youtube.com/ watch?v=olLCokQl9rs

NBA. (2011). *I Love This Game* [Video File]. Retrieved from www.youtube.com/watch?v=MARyIn7 zpZs and

Nike. (2011). *What's Your Motivation* [Video File]. Retrieved from www.youtube.com/watch?v= 6uhCxBk6cQE.

Nike. (2013). *Girls – Sport Motivation* [Video File]. Retrieved from www.youtube.com/watch?v= Aq_QCwikOgw

Nike. (2012). *My Time is Now* [Video File]. Retrieved from www.youtube.com/watch?v=U4qUfOMMCgc

Nike. (2009). *Believe in Yourself* [Video File]. Retrieved from www.youtube.com/watch?v=N3U5411 JzbM

Nike. (2006). *I can* [Video File]. Retrieved from www.youtube.com/watch?v=iZxQDAyFY6s

North Face. (2014). *Never Stop Exploring* [Video File]. Retrieved from http://adage.com/article/cmo-strategy/north-face-s-emotional-push-people-outdoors/295629/

Puma. (2010). *Hard Chorus* [Video File]. Retrieved from www.youtube.com/watch?v=uiskWM1hzL8

Salomon. (2014) Sky Run [Video File]. Retrieved from www.youtube.com/watch?v=yYlOyvWUgvg

US Open. (2012). *It Must Be Love* [Video File]. Retrieved from www.youtube.com/watch?v=CTU4-L7gQyg

CHAPTER 6

Constraints in sport engagement

This chapter's objectives are to:

- discuss the factors that limit sport game attendance
- discuss the factors that limit sport participation
- explain how intrapersonal, interpersonal and structural constraints influence sport engagement
- explain how individuals use negotiation strategies to overcome constraints to sport engagement
- discuss the interaction between sport motivation and perception of constraints on sport engagement
- propose marketing and policy strategies for reducing the negative effects of constraints on sport engagement.

6.0 INTRODUCTION

Cohen (2014) in an article in *The Wall Street Journal* reported that student attendance at college football games in the USA fell 7.1% from 2009 to 2013. It was also reported that home attendance for the majority of teams in the South East Conference (includes 14 universities located primarily in the southern part of the US), which has dominated college football in recent years, also declined (Tuttle, 2014). Such decreases in sport event attendance highlight one of the challenges US college sport marketers face in encouraging students to attend football games (Koba, 2013; Tuttle, 2014). Similar declining trends in live game attendance have also been reported in the USA professional sport leagues, such as MLB, NBA and motor sports (Koba, 2013). For example, total game attendance for the MLB declined by 417,192 people between 2012 and 2013 (baseball-reference.com).

Sport and recreation participation is also declining across many developed countries. Hallal *et al.* (2012) reported that 31% of the adult population worldwide is physically inactive. According to the Special Eurobarometer (2014), 59% of Europe's citizens never or seldom exercise, while only 41% exercise at least once a week – an increase in non-participation from 39% (2009) to 41% (2013).

The downward trend of sport participation and spectatorship highlights a pressing challenge for private and public organizations involved in the delivery of sport and recreation products and services. The previous chapter on sport motivation listed a number of reasons why individuals engage in goal-directed behaviour, but motivation represents only one side of the equation. That is, while motivation is important, there are other factors that prevent or constrain sport behaviour that need to be considered. For instance, addressing why fans do not attend games, why fans stay at home and why people do not exercise are relevant questions for sport marketers and policymakers. This is where leisure constraints theory and research can help.

Extensive research on leisure constraints has been conducted over the past 20 years (for a detailed review, see Godbey, Crawford and Shen, 2010). This is mostly due to its added value in understanding an individual's decision making in relation to sport consumption (active or passive sport participation). The volitional nature of sport as a leisure activity makes the study of leisure constraints highly relevant for helping to understand whether individuals freely choose to participate in sport activities or attend sport games, or whether other factors influence their decisions (Alexandris & Carroll, 1997a; Pritchard, Funk & Alexandris, 2009).

Research on leisure constraints can therefore benefit marketing and management practice as it can provide:

- a better understanding of an individual's decision-making in relation to sport consumption (i.e. active participation, sport spectatorship, sport tourism events);
- an understanding of what the internal and external factors are that inhibit sport consumption;
- a determination of the latent demand for sport consumption (e.g. genuine lack of interest vs. lack of interest due to perceived constraints);
- identification of disadvantaged groups in terms of accessing sport and recreation services, which is particularly relevant to public sport provision, where sport services are often seen as social welfare;
- a better understanding of how constraints interact with other personal (e.g. motivation) and environmental factors (e.g. technology), and determine the final outcome (e.g. sport participation, sport specialization and sport attachment);
- the segmentation of sport consumers, based on how and which constraints are perceived as influential in their decision to consume sport services and products;
- the design of marketing and communication strategies to alleviate the effects of leisure constraints.

Most leisure constraint research has been conducted in North America, although there have also been studies in the United Kingdom, Greece, Holland, Australia, Germany, Korea and China – confirming its global attention. In addition, while leisure constraint theory has primarily been developed via academic research, it is worth noting that several applied/consultancy projects across different studies have utilized leisure constraint theory, aiming to understand the factors that limit engagement with sports. Examples of such research include Sport England's *Active People Survey* (2012) and *Market Segmentation* (2010), the Australian Bureau of Statistics' *Multi-Purpose Household Survey Participation in Sports and Physical Recreation* (2015) and the *Why Don't People Participate* study (n.d.)

by the BC Recreation and Parks Association and the Heart and Stroke Foundation of BC & Yukon, Canada.

There have also been professional published articles and reports discussing factors that limit attendance at spectator sports, including *Why Students Aren't Going to College Football Games* (Tuttle, 2014), *Where Did All the College Football Fans Go* (Kramer, 2013) and *Why Rising Ticket Prices and Technology Lead NFL Fans to Stay Home* (Green, 2012). While these reports have all identified sport engagement limitations, a more in-depth approach is required to ascertain a better understanding of constraint theory.

6.1 DEFINITIONS

Constraints have been defined as 'factors that are assumed by researchers and perceived or experienced by individuals to limit the formation of leisure preferences and to inhibit or prohibit participation in leisure activities' (Jackson, 1991, p. 279). This definition indicates that constraints can be both real and perceived, and represent a subjective evaluation of how individuals view everyday factors that might prohibit or limit their sport consumption. The 'perceived' aspect of constraints justified the decision in this book to include constraints (regardless of constraint type) as individual factors that shape sport and recreation behaviour.

One of the first most significant developments in leisure constraint research has been the grouping of constraints into three major categories, according to the level that they are perceived (internally vs. externally). Crawford and Godbey (1987) classified constraints into intrapersonal, interpersonal and structural (Table 6.1).

6.1.1 Intrapersonal constraints

Intrapersonal constraints are internal individualized factors, such as self-perceptions and beliefs about personal skills and abilities, body image, cultural issues and religion-related aspects; they can also be perceptions relating to safety and personal interests. Consider, for example, an overweight individual who is contemplating exercise. It is highly likely that

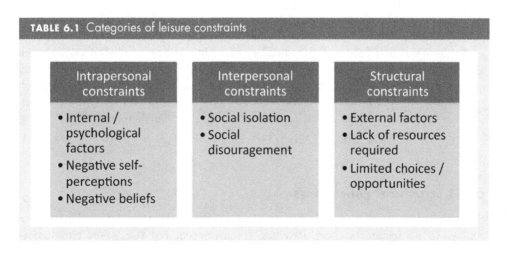

TABLE 6.1 Categories of leisure constraints

Intrapersonal constraints	Interpersonal constraints	Structural constraints
• Internal / psychological factors • Negative self-perceptions • Negative beliefs	• Social isolation • Social disouragement	• External factors • Lack of resources required • Limited choices / opportunities

due to his/her negative body image, he/she will avoid participating in an organized group exercise programme. Likewise, a family (particularly with young children) will often evaluate the benefits versus costs of attending a football game. Due to concerns about safety issues (e.g. fans' anti-social behaviour, hooliganism), for instance, they might decide not to invest in going to the game, and alternatively choose to watch the game on TV.

In an interview with Mike Golub (2014), Chief Operating Officer and President of the MLS's Portland Timbers, it was emphasized that when people attend a sporting event, they expect a safe, secure environment; but many professional sport leagues around the world cannot guarantee this. Caruso and Di Domizio (2012), who investigated the factors that led to decreased fan attendance in the Italian professional soccer league (Serie A), reported that football hooliganism was one of the main reasons that discouraged families from attending – soccer is frequently associated with a violent and risky environment.

As intrapersonal constraints relate to internal perceptions of an activity, they are present in almost all individual sport consumption-related decisions. It is therefore a matter of how an individual negotiates and overcomes these negative perceptions that determine whether he/she engage in a specific sport behaviour. Thus, negotiation of perceived constraints is a key topic in the decision-making process for sport participation; it will be further discussed in section 6.5.

The negative influence of intrapersonal constraints on sport consumption has been considered by many sport organizations around the world. Several examples of campaigns and actions used to overcome these constraints include the NBA's *Motivation – What's Your Excuse* (2013); the 'So All Kids can Play' programme (2015), which is a Canadian (Nova Scotia) charitable organization that helps disadvantaged kids overcome the barriers preventing or limiting their participation in organized sport; and Sport England's *This Girl Can* (2015), which encourages sport engagement among women and particularly girls.

6.1.2 Interpersonal constraints

Interpersonal constraints can relate to an individual's inability to find partners to engage in sport and recreation behaviour, social isolation and social discouragement. Most sport engagement takes place in social environments. In an English study, for example, it was reported that 34% of people participate in sports with their friends; another 23% with their spouse, partner or other family member; 11% are members of clubs; and only 33% participate in sport alone (Jones, Millward & Buraimo, 2011).

As discussed in Chapter 4 the social element in most sport-related consumption activities is strong. Social interaction is a key motive for engaging in sport activities (e.g. attending a game with friends, skiing with family and friends, participating in an obstacle run with friends). Certain sport activities are group focused and specifically require partners to interact with (e.g. playing football or baseball). Furthermore, as discussed in Chapter 5, social acceptance and support are key motivators in an individual's decision to engage in sport activities.

6.1.3 Structural constraints

Structural constraints are mainly external and relate to perceptions of available oppor-tunities to participate in sport activities, resources required (e.g. sport equipment), financial issues, time-related restrictions and the quality of the facilities/stadium (e.g. parking, experience during game attendance). It should be noted that while structural constraints are mostly deemed as external, some of them are individual self-perceptions (e.g. perceived availability of free time). As an example of a structural constraint, consider a fan who wants to buy a ticket for his/her favourite professional football team, but cannot afford the price of the ticket.

The escalating price of tickets to attend inmost US professional sport leagues has already been identified as an issue (Green, 2012). It has been reported that NFL games are the most expensive to attend, with an Adult Cost Index of US \$113.42; the National Hockey League (NHL) is next (\$84.05), followed by the NBA (\$74.67) (Gaines, 2014). The Adult Cost Index calculates the overall price for a single fan to purchase an average-priced ticket, one beer, one soft drink, one hot dog and half the cost of parking at the stadium. In a similar study among MLB teams, it was reported that a family of four can expect to pay approximately \$212 on average to attend a game (Wiles, 2014). The increased cost for live attendance at professional sports highlights that even when an individual may be motivated to attend a game, the amount of money required may constrain or alter this goal-directed behaviour.

Structural constraints can also relate to external problems associated with sport facilities and services, such as limited availability and accessibility, a limited range of sport programmes, as well as the quality of the overall game or participation experience. Previous research, for example, has shown that the experience of attending a game is no longer as differentiated from watching it at home, due to technological advancements that have improved the home experience, as well as the difficulties that some sport teams face to improve the live experience (Kramer, 2013). Stadium upgrades such as WiFi systems, more comfortable seating and areas for students/fans to gather before games are examples of facility-related aspects that should be considered for college sports in particular.

6.1.4 Dimensions of leisure constraints

While these three broad leisure constraint categories (intrapersonal, interpersonal and structural) are useful for theory testing and development, a more detailed approach definition of leisure constraints is required, for making constraints research more useful for practitioners. A number of constraint dimensions within each of three constraints were proposed in the literature (e.g. Alexandris, Tsorbatzoudis & Grouios, 2002; Alexandris, Funk & Pritchard, 2011; Casper, Bocarro & Kanters, 2011; Damali & McGuire, 2013; Galen & Yu Kyoum, 2011). These dimensions and examples of individual constraint items within each dimension are presented in Table 6.2.

6.1.5 Applications of leisure constraints: the IHRSA's study

Applied research conducted by professional sport organizations has identified a number of constraints to sport participation and sport spectatorship. The IHRSA (2014), in its annual study on health club membership, identified cost (55%) as the main constraint for becoming a health club member, followed by alternative cost-free exercise places (28%) and lack of time to exercise (22%). These three constraints are primarily structural; although intrapersonal constraints such as feeling out of place (19%) and feeling too out

Constraint categories and dimensions	Individual constraints
TABLE 6.2 Constraint categories, constraint dimensions and individual constraint items	
Intrapersonal constraints	
Individual/psychological constraints	Low self-esteem
	Body image
	Low perceived skills
	Fear of getting hurt
	Feel tired
	Do not like exercising in social situations
	Do not like exercising in crowded areas
Alternatives for sport participation/ spectatorship	Prefer other sport activities
	Prefer other leisure activities
	Prefer watching a game at home
Cultural issues	Family roles
	Social status
	Religion
	Social discouragement
Limited interest/negative past experiences	Limited interest
	Negative past experience
	Do not like sports
Lack of time	Do not have time because of family/social commitments
	Do not have time because of work commitments
	Scheduling problems (game or exercise classes)
Interpersonal constraints	
Lack of partners/social isolation	No friends to participate with or to attend with
	My friends/family do not like sports
	My friends do not encourage sport participation
Lack of knowledge	Lack of information on what activity to participate (or which sport event to attend)
	Lack of information about places to exercise
	Structural constraints
Sport product (game, event, facilities, sport services)	Limited recreation/exercise places
	Low quality of sport facilities
	Low quality of sport services

TABLE 6.2 Continued		
	Low game quality	
	Low event quality	
	Total experience is not satisfying	
	No parking	
Financial problems	Cannot afford the expenses required (e.g. tickets, subscription, equipment, cost of travel etc.)	
Accessibility problems	Do not have transportation	
	Takes time to reach the sport places	

of shape to even think about it (10%), as well as interpersonal constraints such as not knowing anybody who goes to a health club (11%) were also reported in the study. These results are presented in Figure 6.1.

In a second applied study conducted by Sport Octagon (cited by King, 2010), in the context of sport spectatorship, perception of constraints was compared between NBA and NFL fans (see Table 6.3). Here, cost of tickets, cost of attendance and comfort (e.g. seating, rest rooms, crowds) were identified as the three main constraints that kept fans at home (i.e. watching the game on TV instead of attending). The cost of attending a game varies considerably among different professional US sport leagues and teams, with the NFL being the most expensive, followed by NHL and NBA (Gaines, 2014). Thus, it is worth highlighting that attendance constraints were reported more frequently by NFL fans than by NBA fans (Table 6.3).

6.2 A DECISION-MAKING MODEL OF LEISURE CONSTRAINTS

Crawford, Jackson and Godbey (1991) first introduced the hierarchical model of leisure constraints. In this framework, intrapersonal, interpersonal and structural constraints were ordered within a decision-making model, starting from the formation of a preference to engage in a sport-related behaviour, and moving toward actual engagement and specialization.

In this model, it was proposed that the three categories of leisure constraints are experienced progressively, with intrapersonal constraints encountered first, based on their influence on the formation of an interest or preference to engage in a behaviour. For example, an individual who has a negative perception about a sport activity (e.g. I don't have the skills required to play golf, running is not accepted in my culture or I don't feel comfortable playing tennis in social situations) is likely to refrain or feel blocked from any form of participation. Similarly, if somebody does not have the skills to play football, it is unlikely they will express a desire (preference) to participate in this activity. Intrapersonal constraints would appear to be the most influential on sport engagement, as they have the ability to block participation.

Interpersonal constraints come after intrapersonal in Crawford *et al.*'s model, based on their influence on both the initial preference and the actual engagement (consumption).

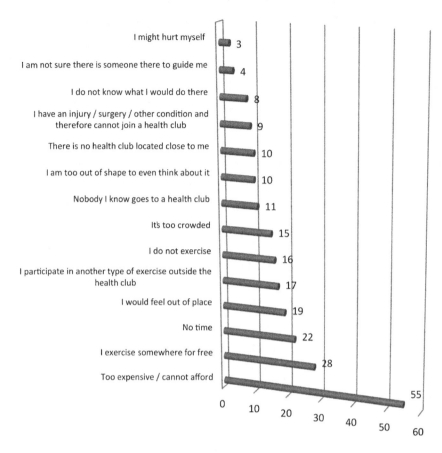

I might hurt myself — 3
I am not sure there is someone there to guide me — 4
I do not know what I would do there — 8
I have an injury / surgery / other condition and therefore cannot join a health club — 9
There is no health club located close to me — 10
I am too out of shape to even think about it — 10
Nobody I know goes to a health club — 11
It's too crowded — 15
I do not exercise — 16
I participate in another type of exercise outside the health club — 17
I would feel out of place — 19
No time — 22
I exercise somewhere for free — 28
Too expensive / cannot afford — 55

0 10 20 30 40 50 60

FIGURE 6.1 What keeps you from joining a health club? (%)

Source: IHRSA (2014)

TABLE 6.3 The influence of constraints on sport game attendance

Why stay at home?

What are the most relevant factors when deciding to watch a game on TV, rather than attend it in person?

	NFL (%)	NBA (%)
Cost of tickets	84	72
Overall cost of attendance	80	65
Comfort (seating, rest rooms, crowds, etc.)	57	39
Home viewing experience is superior (replays, commentary, viewing angles, HD, etc.)	54	41
Hassle/time commitment necessary for attending	52	42
Can watch several games/flip between channels	45	34

Source: King (2010) http://sportsbusinessdaily.com/Journal/Issues/2010/04/20100419/SBJ-In-Depth/What-Makes-Fans-Crazy-About-Sports.aspx.

Consider, for example, an individual who expresses a desire to play football (i.e. preference to participate in the activity); he/she might not get to participate in the end, because of lack of partners. Interpersonal constraints can also influence the preference or desire for participation. For example, it is less likely that an individual will express a desire to play football if none of their friends do so.

Lastly, the structural constraints are experienced after the intrapersonal and interpersonal constraints, based on this model. These constraints generally intervene between existing leisure preferences and actual engagement (consumption). Thus, even if a preference has been expressed and partners have been found, the lack of a playing venue might limit participation. Structural constraints are deemed the least influential, as while they usually limit and alter engagement, they do not necessarily block participation. That is, individuals who face structural constraints may still experience some form of sport engagement, even if it involves adjusted behaviour (e.g. participate less time, engage in a different sport, attend a different game) – they have already developed a preference for sport engagement. For example, if a swimming pool is not easily accessible, an individual might choose to go running instead; or if a season ticket is perceived as too expensive, an individual might buy a single game admission instead.

The three categories of constraints and their main influence on sport preference and sport participation/consumption are presented in Figure 6.2.

While this hierarchical model of leisure constraints has been supported in the context of sport participation, its applicability in the context of sport spectatorship is still questionable. Therefore, a discussion of some indicative published studies in the context of sport spectatorship follows.

6.3 CONSTRAINTS IN THE CONTEXT OF SPORT SPECTATORSHIP

Research in the context of sport spectatorship is limited, yet understanding why spectators choose not to attend live sport games is important for sport marketers and practitioners. Kim and Trail (2010) pointed out that identifying such constraints gives sport marketers and managers the opportunity to more effectively serve existing fans and design effective strategies to attract new ones. As already noted in this chapter, attendance remains a key issue for most sport teams and continues to be a challenging issue for sport marketers.

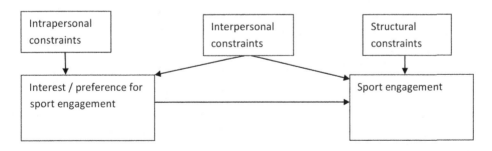

FIGURE 6.2 A hierarchical model of leisure constraints

Source: adjusted from Crawford *et al.* (1991)

In one of the few relevant studies, Pritchard *et al.* (2009) utilized a content analysis of perceived constraints from a sample of baseball (MLB) spectators and identified a number of internal and external factors including the following:

a)   external constraints

   • financial (cost of tickets and concessions)
   • schedule conflicts with personal schedule
   • stadium accessibility and transportation problems
   • diminishing appeal (due to weather and the visiting team).

b)   internal constraints

   • low priority, due to family/personal/other commitments
   • alternative leisure choices (e.g. going to a movie)
   • physical limitations (e.g. health issues or feeling tired).

In terms of the importance of the two types of constraints on predicting attendance, Pritchard *et al.* (2009) reported that extrinsic constraints had the strongest influence.

A similar but more detailed constraint structure was presented in the study of Kim and Trail (2010), which was based on a sample of fans of a women's professional basketball team in the USA. Based on Crawford *et al.*'s (1991) hierarchical model of leisure constraints, the following internal and external constraints were proposed:

a)   internal (intrapersonal and interpersonal) constraints

   • lack of knowledge, such as lack of understanding of the rules and the technical/strategic aspects of the game (intrapersonal constraints);
   • lack of success, as measured by the winning record and position in the league (intrapersonal constraints);
   • lack of someone to attend with such as friends or family members (interpersonal constraints);
   • no interest from others such as family, friends and significant others (interpersonal constraints).

b)   external constraints

   • parking problems;
   • location, defined by limited accessibility to the stadium area;
   • commitments such as work, family, friends and study;
   • financial costs, related to the price of single or season tickets, and the cost of attending a game;
   • leisure alternatives such as attending movies or going to a restaurant/bar;
   • sport alternatives such as active recreation (e.g. exercising, fitness);
   • other sport entertainment such as watching other sports on TV or attending local sport events.

In terms of the importance of the constraint dimensions to predict attendance, Kim and Trail (2010) reported that lack of success (internal constraint) and leisure alternatives (external constraint) were the two most influential. However, the hierarchical model of leisure constraints (Jackson, Crawford & Godbey, 1993) was not entirely supported in this study.

It is also worth noting that in Kim and Trail's study, the team's poor performance and the outcome of the game (i.e. losing vs. winning), although perceived as discouraging factors for attending games, were not identified as highly influential factors. This indicates that at least in some professional sport leagues, sport marketers should separate the fan game experience from the outcome of the game.

In summary, while the hierarchical model of leisure constraints was used in sport spectatorship studies, there are some unique aspects that make this model not entirely applicable in the context of sport spectatorship. First, the hierarchy of importance of constraints is questionable, based on the study findings by Pritchard *et al.* (2009) and Kim and Trail (2010). This is because structural constraints (e.g. stadium location, financials) can be just as important as intrapersonal and interpersonal constraints. Second, there is a lack of stability of constraint dimensions. For example, the performance of the team can vary from season to season or within a season, acting as both a constraint (unsuccessful season) and a motivator (successful season). In addition, the contextual and cultural aspects influencing fans' perception of constraints should be considered. For example, both professional and college sports in North America differ in many aspects in comparison to sport leagues in Europe, Australia and Asia. These include variations in the organization of the leagues, the quality of sport facilities/services, the game atmosphere, the entertainment nature of the games and the characteristics/profiles of fans (e.g. socioeconomic, demographic and psychographic). Subsequently, while constraint dimensions, as defined by the hierarchical model of leisure constraints, can be applied to cross-cultural studies, the relative importance of each of them on predicting game attendance can differ from country to country.

6.4 CONSTRAINTS IN THE CONTEXT OF SPORT EVENTS/TOURISM

Leisure constraint theory has often been used in sport tourism research, aiming for a better understanding of an individual's decision making in relation to participating in or attending a sport event. For example, Funk, Alexandris and Ping (2009) investigated which types of perceived constraints prohibited attending the 2008 Beijing Olympic Games, and revealed the following:

- intrapersonal constraints relating to limited knowledge of the destination, language problems and perceived difficulties in travelling within China;
- interpersonal constraints reflecting difficulties in finding co-travellers, often due to perceived concerns over communism in China, security and terrorism at a high-profile event and conditions of the country's public facilities;
- structural constraints reflecting perceived concerns over the cost of travelling to Beijing, the long distance required to travel and the amount of time required.

The above results indicate that organizers and marketers of international sport events particularly in non-Western countries should design effective communication strategies to change negative visitor perceptions of issues that include safety and security, a country's political conditions and often negative local residents' attitudes toward visitors. Creating an image of a safe and friendly country, and promoting local hospitality, culture and traditions can help achieve this.

6.5 NEGOTIATING CONSTRAINTS FOR SPORT ENGAGEMENT

The inclusion of the negotiation proposition by Jackson *et al.* (1993) within the hierarchical model of leisure constraints has been an extension of the original framework. It was proposed that leisure participation 'is dependent not on the absence of constraints (although this may be true for some people) but on negotiation through them. Such negotiations may modify rather than foreclose participation' (Jackson *et al.*, 1993, p. 4).

This proposition insinuates that all individuals perceive some type of constraint; thus, the final decision (engagement or not) is not always inclusive. In addition, constraints might lead to modified engagement (e.g. less time, or selection of an alternative activity). Consider, for example, an individual who wants to use a fitness facility such as a private health club to get into shape. However, due to their inability to afford the membership fees, he/she might instead become a member of a public or community recreation club with lower fees. In such a situation, he/she is still a sport participant despite the presence of structural constraints (financial issues).

6.5.1 Internal negotiation strategies

Individuals use internal negotiation strategies to overcome constraints. These negotiation strategies relate to the context of each activity (e.g. indoor, outdoor recreation, spectatorship) and the study population (e.g. gender and age). A review of the literature shows that a basic categorization of the negotiation strategies is: 1) cognitive and 2) behavioural. This categorization was originally proposed by Jackson and Rucks (1995) and Hubbard and Mannell (2001), and has since been adopted in other studies.

Cognitive strategies relate to actions developed by an individual so he/she can cope with the requirements of the specific sport activity, such as skill acquisition, sport education and collection of sport-related information. For example, an individual might choose to register for swimming classes to learn techniques and participate in this activity his/her their leisure time (i.e. cognitive strategy to overcome constraints related to lack of skills). In addition, the individual might start reading information in blogs and professional websites to find information and increase his/her knowledge about this specific sport activity (e.g. technical aspects, strategy and equipment). Cognitive strategies can also relate to actions in an individual's everyday life, such as time management, or socialization to overcome interpersonal constraints. An example in relation to socialization is an individual who becomes a member of a sport fan club to mingle and find like-minded fans to attend his/her favourite team's games with.

In contrast, behavioural strategies relate to actions designed by an individual to change or strengthen positive attitudes toward sport and recreation, such as understanding the benefits of sport engagement (e.g. physical, social and psychological benefits). Behavioural strategies can relate to the provision of sport education via seminars, information about sport participation programmes and opportunities and advertising campaigns, including targeted marketing and effective communication of the benefits of sport engagement, can increase positive attitudes toward a particular sport. As part of these sport marketing campaigns, informal communications (e.g. blogs), community networks (e.g. church), educational institutions (e.g. schools) and opinion leaders (e.g. sport celebrities) can be used.

The use of specific internal negotiation strategies is often related to the context of the sport behaviour (e.g. type of sport) and the socio-demographic characteristics of the population (e.g. females). For example, in a study by James (2000) among female recreational swimmers, body image constraints were often overcome via strategies including receiving support from friends and avoiding attracting attention. Body image was also identified as the main leisure constraint among females in Frederick and Shaw's (1995) study, where women often used cognitive strategies to minimize concerns about their physical appearance.

Several multidimensional scales have been developed to measure the internal constraint negotiation strategies. Examples of these constraint negotiation dimensions and individual items that can be used to measure them are presented in Table 6.4.

TABLE 6.4 Internal leisure constraint negotiation strategies

Negotiation dimensions	Negotiation items
Skill acquisition/physical fitness improvement	Improve skills
	Learn skills
	Improve physical fitness
Improve knowledge	Understand the game strategy
	Understand the technical skills
	Improve knowledge about sport equipment
	Learn about opportunities to engage in sport behaviour
Find partners	Find friends to participate with
	Become a member of social groups
	Become a member of blogs
	Become a member of a sport club
Time management	Prioritize sport engagement
	Organize daily schedule
Self-motivate	Read sport-related material
	Buy sport equipment
	Become sport educated
	Set personal goals
Adjust lifestyle	Eat healthily
	Reduce unhealthy habits

6.6 CONSTRAINTS AND MOTIVATION FOR SPORT ENGAGEMENT

One of the main areas of contention sport managers often have to tackle is understanding why some individuals overcome sport engagement constraints, while others remain 'blocked' by them. Attitudes and motivation have been identified as factors that often interact with constraints and determine the final outcome (Jackson *et al.*, 1993). The following quote by basketball legend Michael Jordan clearly conveys this internal negotiation process:

'And should you face any obstacles along the way, don't let them blur your focus: Obstacles don't have to stop you. If you run into a wall, don't turn around and give up. Figure out how to climb it, go through it, or work around it. And by all means: "If you quit once it becomes a habit. Never quit!!!"' (Pauwels Consulting, 2013)

This quote relates to an internal negotiation process between perceived constraints and motivation to engage in goal-directed behaviour. In the sport context, motivation positively influences the expression of a preference for sport engagement, and can interact with one or more of the constraint categories (i.e. intrapersonal, interpersonal and structural). If motivation is stronger than perception of constraints, the outcome might be positive (i.e. sport engagement); but if the constraints are stronger than motivation, the outcome might be negative. For example, when an individual strongly believes in the physical and psychological benefits of active sport participation (strong motivation to participate), he/she is more likely to prioritize his/her everyday obligations to allow time for sport participation. However, if that same individual does not perceive positive outcomes from sport participation (low motivation to participate), he/she is more likely to report time-related constraints as a reason for non-participation. Several studies have provided support for the internal negotiation proposition in relation to sport engagement, such as Alexandris, Kouthouris and Grouios (2007); Frederick and Shaw (1995); Kennelly, Moyle and Lamont (2013); and Lyu and Chi (2014).

The relationship between sport motivation and perception of constraints can be viewed as interrelated. The studies of Alexandris *et al.* (2002) and Alexandris *et al.* (2007) suggested that perception of constraints can influence the development of motivation, as seen in Figure 6.3. For example, consider an individual who wants to adopt an active lifestyle via exercise. In this instance, if he/she faces strong intrapersonal constraints (e.g. negative body image, health problems or injuries) or interpersonal constraints (e.g. social discouragement), his/her level of motivation will probably be low. These studies reported that intrapersonal constraints often negatively influence the development of intrinsic motivation and make individuals amotivated to participate in sports. That is, individuals who strongly perceive intrapersonal constraints (e.g. lack of skills, low fitness levels) are less likely to be intrinsically motivated and more likely to be amotivated (Figure 6.3).

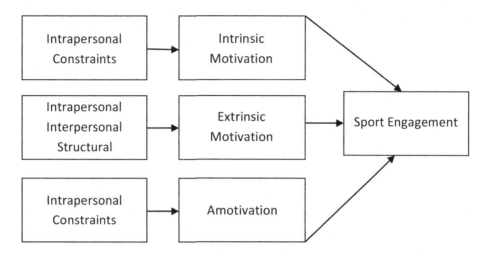

FIGURE 6.3 The influence of constraints on motivation

6.7 SOCIO-CULTURAL DIFFERENCES IN THE PERCEPTION OF LEISURE CONSTRAINTS

Perception of constraints among different socio-demographic groups has become increasingly important to sport managers, who need to identify how disadvantaged groups perceive constraints in relation to access to sport and recreation services. Most studies that have investigated the perception of constraints in relation to socio-demographic variables have been done in the context of active sport participation. Particularly, the roles of age, gender, socioeconomic status and family size have been studied in relation to the perception of constraints in the context of active sport participation (e.g. Alexandris & Carroll, 1997b; Henderson & Gibson, 2013).

6.7.1 Age and perception of leisure constraints

Previous research has frequently shown that the patterns of perceived leisure constraints differ among different age groups. It is generally identified that psychological leisure constraints increase with advancing age (Searle & Jackson, 1985; Jackson, 1993). Intrapersonal leisure constraints related to lack of partners, lack of knowledge and lack of opportunities are often perceived more intensely by older than middle-aged individuals (McGuire, Dottavio & O'Leary, 1986; Jackson, 1993). In contrast, lack of time constraints often exhibit an inverted U relationship with advancing age – their relevance to sport engagement increases from youth to middle-aged, but declines thereafter (Searle & Jackson, 1985; McGuire et al., 1986; Jackson, 1993). In addition, financial constraints on sport engagement often diminish with advancing age, due to the discretionary income of middle-aged and older individuals (Searle & Jackson, 1985; McGuire et al., 1986; Jackson, 1993).

6.7.2 Gender and perception of leisure constraints

Females generally perceive more leisure constraints than males. Several studies have focused solely on leisure constraints among female individuals (for a review, see Henderson & Gibson, 2013), with results suggesting females perceived more intensively intrapersonal constraints than men, such as body image, limited skills, low self-esteem, safety issues, family roles and cultural expectations. In particular, safety issues are a common constraint for women, such as in relation to their inability to find partners to participate with (e.g. I don't have somebody to go jogging with and I'm afraid to go alone).

Some of the cultural-related constraints, such as family expectations, social stereotypes and religious issues, are also particularly strong among women, especially in Muslim communities. In a recent study in Saudi Arabia (Caroll, 2014), family roles, Islamic interpretation, government policy, culture stereotypes, education and other personal leisure constraints were identified as prominent among women. The author proposed that the Saudi Arabia government needs to educate the country that Islam encourages sport for women, so that the cultural norms in relation to women can be changed; and also emphasized the significance of schools in promoting female sport participation.

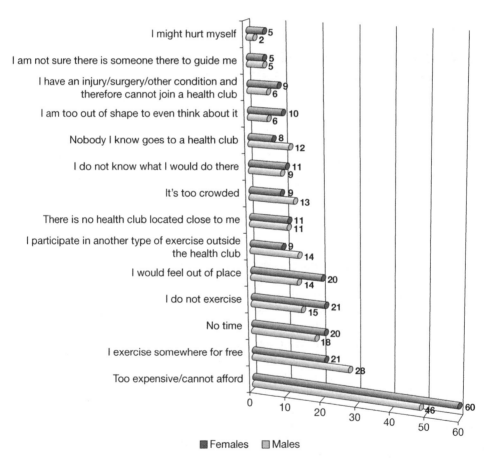

FIGURE 6.4 What keeps you from joining a health club by gender? (%)

Source: IHRSA (2014)

Similar gender-specific results were reported in the IHRSA (2014) study in relation to factors that kept individuals from joining a health club. In this study, more females than males reported structural constraints such as financial issues (e.g. too expensive or cannot afford), and intrapersonal constraints (e.g. lack of time, I don't exercise, I would feel out of place, I am too out of shape to even think about it, I have an injury/surgery/other condition and cannot join a health club). Although it is worth highlighting that men in this study more frequently reported interpersonal constraints (e.g. nobody I know goes to a health club), and participation in alternative forms of exercise (e.g. outdoors, in cost-free places). The relevant gender-defined results from this study are presented in Figure 6.4.

6.7.3 Education and perception of leisure constraints

Previous research indicates that the level of education often negatively correlates with the perception of leisure constraints, especially in the context of active participation (Alexandris & Carroll, 1997a; Alexandris & Carroll, 1997b). That is, less-educated individuals have higher perception of leisure constraints and are less likely to get involved in active sport participation. It has been suggested that the influence of education on the perception of leisure constraints relates to the deeper understanding of the benefits that can be obtained among more educated individuals (Alexandris & Carroll, 1997a; Alexandris & Carroll, 1997b). In addition, given that education is closely related to socio-economic status, differences in the standard of living, lifestyle and financial resources between groups with different education levels can often influence the opportunity and ability to participate in sports.

6.8 CHAPTER SUMMARY

Perceived constraints are deemed as highly influential factors affecting an individual's motivation and decision making in relation to both active sport participation and sport spectatorship. The original hierarchical model of leisure constraints and its extensions represent a theoretical framework that can be utilized to study the importance of the different types of constraints in different sport contexts. Corresponding surveys and/or qualitative research, designed to measure sport consumer constraints, should be used by sport marketers and practitioners as tools to guide the development of effective sport policy, marketing and communication strategy.

6.9 DISCUSSION QUESTIONS

The discussion questions presented below are designed to help students review what is important in the chapter. You can answer them on your own, but they are also suitable for discussion work in small groups.

1) Discuss the three categories of leisure constraints and find applications for each of them.

2) Critically discuss the hierarchical model of leisure constraints, with reference to active sport participation and spectatorship behaviour.
3) Propose strategies to alleviate the effects of leisure constraints, by discussing all the dimensions proposed in the literature.
4) Critically discuss the relationship between socio-demographic variables and perception of leisure constraints. Find examples from different sport contexts to support your arguments.
5) Critically discuss the internal negotiation proposition by providing examples of different sport contexts.
6) Critically discuss the main internal negotiation dimensions that have been reported in the literature. Provide examples to support your discussion.
7) Compare and contrast the structure of leisure constraint dimensions between active sport participation and sport spectatorship (e.g. game attendance and sport event attendance).

6.10 CLASS ACTIVITY: CONSTRAINTS IN SPORT ENGAGEMENT

The class activity is designed to use information learned in this chapter to understand the influence of perceived constraints on sport engagement.

a) Design a survey using your classmates as a sample to investigate:

- the factors that limit their participation in the campus sport and recreation programmes
- the factors that limit their attendance in two college sports (e.g. football and baseball).

Then apply the hierarchical model of leisure constraints in your effort to interpret the results. Based on the analysis of the data, provide suggestions on how these constraints can be removed.

b) For a sport event that is going to be organized by your college, conduct a survey among the local community to examine if they are willing to attend the event and what the factors are that might inhibit their attendance. Apply the hierarchical model of leisure constraints to interpret the results.
c) Select a convenient sample of five classmates who are committed members of the college fitness club. Design a qualitative study, by interviewing them, with the aim to understand the internal negotiation strategies they use to overcome everyday leisure constraints and exercise frequently.

REFERENCES

Alexandris, K. & Carroll, B. (1997a). An analysis of leisure constraints based on different recreational sport participation levels: A study from Greece. *Leisure Sciences, 19*, 1–15.

Alexandris, K. & Carroll, B. (1997b). Demographic differences in the perception of constraints on recreational sport participation: Results from a study in Greece. *Leisure Studies, 16*, 107–125.

Alexandris, K. & Carroll, B. (1999). Constraints on recreational sport participation within the adult population in Greece: Implications for the provision and management of sport services. *Journal of Sport Management, 13*(4), 317–332.

Alexandris, K., Funk, D. & Pritchard, M. (2011). The impact of constraints on motivation, activity attachment and skier intentions to continue. *Journal of Leisure Research, 43*, 56–79.

Alexandris, K., Kouthouris, C. & Girgolas (2007). Investigating the relationships among motivation, negotiation, and alpine skiing participation. *Journal of Leisure Research, 39*(4), 648–668.

Alexandris, K., Tsorbatzoudis, C. & Grouios, G. (2002). Perceived constraints on recreational sport participation: Investigating their relationship with intrinsic motivation, extrinsic motivation and amotivation. *Journal of Leisure Research, 34*, 233–252.

Australian Bureau of Statistics. (2015). *The Multi-Purpose Household Survey Participation in Sports and Physical Recreation.* Retrieved from www.abs.gov.au/ausstats/abs@.nsf/mf/4177.0

BC Recreation and Parks Association & Heart and Stroke Foundation of BC & Yukon. (n.d.). *Why Don't People Participate?* Retrieved from www.physicalactivitystrategy.ca/pdfs/Why_Dont_People_Participate.pdf

Canada-Nova Scotia (2015). 'So All Kids can Play'. Retrieved from www.kidsportcanada.ca/nova-scotia/

Caroll, M. (2014). *Barriers to Women's Sports Participation in Saudi Arabia.* Retrieved from http://informa australia.wordpress.com/2014/09/02/barriers-to-womens-sports-participation-in-saudi-arabia/

Caruso, R. & Di Domizio, M. (2012). *Counter-hooliganism Strategy and Stadium Attendance: The Italian experience.* Retrieved from http://footballperspectives.org/counter-hooliganism-strategy-and-stadium-attendance-italian-experience

Casper, J.M., Bocarro, J. & Kanters, M. (2011). Measurement properties of constraints to sport participation: A psychometric examination with adolescents, *Leisure Sciences: An Interdisciplinary Journal, 33*(2), 127–146.

Cohen, B. (2014). At college football games, student sections likely to have empty seats: Declining attendance reflects soaring ticket prices, increase in televised games, The Wall Street Journal. Retrieved from http://time.com/money/3208397/college-football-student-tickets-fans/

Crawford, D. & Godbey, G. (1987). Reconceptualizing barriers to family leisure. *Leisure Sciences, 9*, 119–127.

Crawford, D., Jackson, E. & Godbey, G. (1991) A hierarchical model of leisure constraints. *Leisure Sciences, 13*, 309–320.

Damali, B.A. & McGuire, F. (2013). The enabling potential of constraints. *Journal of Leisure Research, 45*(2), 136–149.

Frederick, C. & Shaw, S.M. (1995). Body image as a leisure constraint: Examining the experience of aerobic exercise classes for young women. *Leisure Sciences, 11*, 57–73.

Funk, D., Alexandris, K. & Ping, Y. (2009). To go or stay home and watch: Exploring motives and perceived constraints for the 2008 Beijing Olympic Games. *International Journal of Tourism Research, 11*, 41–53.

Funk, D.C. & James, J.D. (2001). The Psychological Continuum Model: A conceptual framework for understanding an individual's psychological connection to sport. *Sport Management Review, 4*(2), 119–150.

Gaines, C. (2014). *This is How Much it Costs to Go See all 122 Major North American Pro Sports Teams in Person.* Retrieved from www.businessinsider.com/nfl-mlb-nba-nhl-cost-2014-1

Galen, T. & Yu Kyoum, K. (2011). Factors influencing spectator sports consumption: NCAA women's college basketball. *International Journal of Sports Marketing & Sponsorship, 13*, 1.

Godbey, G., Crawford, D. & Shen, S. (2010). Assessing hierarchical leisure constraints theory after two decades. *Journal of Leisure Research, 42*(1), 111–134.

Golub, M. (2014). Industry insider: Interview with M. Golub, Chief Operating Officer and President of Major League Soccer's Portland Timbers. *Sport Marketing Quarterly*, 184–186.

Green, M. (2012). Why Rising Ticket Prices and Technology Lead NFL Fans to Stay Home. Retrieved from www.thedailybeast.com/articles/2012/12/23/why-rising-ticket-prices-and-technology-are-leading-nfl-fans-to-stay-home.html

Hallal, P., Andersen, L., Bull, F., Guthold, R., Haskell, W. & Ekelund, U. (2012). Global physical activity levels: Surveillance progress, pitfalls, and prospects. *Lancet, 380*, 247–257.

Henderson, K. & Gibson, H. (2013). An integrative review of women, gender, and leisure: Increasing complexities. *Journal of Leisure Research, 45*(2), 115–136.

Hubbard, J. & Mannell, R. (2001). Testing competing models of the leisure constraint negotiation process in a corporate employee recreation setting. *Leisure Sciences, 2*, 145–163.

IHRSA (2014). Trend Report: Focus on Gender, Generation and Region, 3(3).

Jackson, E. (1991). Special issue, introduction. Leisure constraints/constrained leisure. *Leisure Sciences, 13*, 273–278.

Jackson, E. (1993). Recognising patterns of leisure constraints: Results from alternative analyses. *Journal of Leisure Research, 25*, 129–149.

Jackson, E., Crawford, D. & Godbey, G. (1993). Negotiation of leisure constraints. *Leisure Sciences, 15*, 1–11.

Jackson, E. & Rucks, V. (1995) Negotiation of leisure constraints by junior-high and high school students: An exploratory study. *Journal of Leisure Research, 27*, 85–105.

James, K. (2000). You can feel them looking at you: The experience of adolescent girls at swimming pools. *Journal of leisure Research, 32*, 262–228.

Jones, H., Millward, P. & Buraimo, B. (2011). Adult participation in sports: Analysis of the Taking Part Survey. Retrieved from http://repository.liv.ac.uk/id/eprint/1725170

Kennelly, M., Moyle, B. & Lamont, M. (2013). Constraint negotiation in serious leisure: A study of amateur triathletes. *Journal of Leisure Research, 45*(4).

Kim, Y. & Trail, G. (2010). Constraints and motivators: A new model to explain sport consumer behavior. *Journal of Sport Management, 24*, 190–210.

King, B. (2010). What makes fans crazy about sports? Retrieved from www.sportsbusinessdaily.com/Journal/Issues/2010/04/20100419/SBJ-In-Depth/What-Makes-Fans-Crazy-About-Sports.aspx

Koba, M. (2013). Keeping fans in the stands is getting harder to do. Retrieved from http://sports.yahoo.com/news/nba-keeping-fans-in-the-stands-is-getting-harder-to-do-005355696.html

Kramer, A. (2013). Where Did All the College Football Fans Go? Retrieved from http://bleacherreport.com/articles/1814887-where-did-all-the-college-football-fans-go

Little, D. (2002). Women and adventure recreation: Reconstructing leisure constraints and adventure experiences to negotiation continuing participation. *Journal of Leisure Research, 34*, 157–177.

Lyu, S.O. & Chi, O. (2014). Recreationists' constraints negotiation process for continual leisure engagement. *Leisure Sciences: An Interdisciplinary Journal, 36*(5), 479–497.

McGuire, A., Dottavio, D. & O'Leary, J. (1986). Constraints to participation in outdoor recreation across the life span: A nation-wide study of limitors and prohibitors. *The Gerontologist, 26*, 538–544.

Pauwels Consulting. (2013). What job seekers can learn from Michael Jordan. Retrieved from www.pauwelsconsulting.com/job-application-tips/michael-jordan-quotes-job-seekers/

Pritchard, M., Funk, D. & Alexandris, K. (2009). Barriers to consumption: The impact of perceived constraints. *European Journal of Marketing, 43*, 169–187.

Prochaska, J.O. & Velicer, W.F. (1997). The transtheoretical model of health behaviour change. *American Journal of Health Promotion, 12*, 38–48.

Raymore, L., Godbey, G., Crawford, D. & von Eye, A. (1993). Nature and process of leisure constraints: An empirical test. *Leisure Sciences, 15*, 99–113.

Ridinger, L., Funk, D.C., Jordan, L. & Kaplanidou, K. (2012). Marathons for the masses: Exploring the role of negotiation-efficacy and involvement on running commitment. *Journal of Leisure Research, 44*, 155–178.

Searle, M. & Jackson, E. (1985). Socio-economic variations in perceived barriers to recreation participation among would-be participants. *Leisure Sciences, 7*, 227–249.

Special Eurobarometer (2014). Sport and Physical Activity (412). Directorate – General for Education and Culture, Brussels, European Commission.

Sport England. (2012). *Active People Survey*. Retrieved from http://archive.sportengland.org/research/active_people_survey.aspx

Sport England. (2010). *Market Segmentation*. Retrieved from http://archive.sportengland.org/research/market_segmentation.aspx

Sport England (2015). This Girl Can [Video File]. Retrieved from www.youtube.com/watch?v=SyAXv4mmGhc (Also see http://thisgirlcan.co.uk/)

Tuttle, B. (2014). Why Students Aren't Going to College Football Games. Retrieved from http://time.com/money/3208397/college-football-student-tickets-fans/

Wiles, R. (2014). *How much it will cost to attend a MLB game?* Retrieved from www.azcentral.com/story/money/business/consumer/2014/07/12/cost-attend-majorleague-baseball-game/12578975/

VIDEO FILE

NBA. (2013). *Motivation – What's Your Excuse* [Video File]. Retrieved from www.youtube.com/watch?v=olLCokQl9rs

CHAPTER 7

Sport consumer attitudes

This chapter's objectives are to:

- explain the nature of sport consumer attitudes and their relationship with sport behaviour
- show the value of attitude theory for sport marketing
- discuss the tri-component model of attitudes and its marketing implications
- explain the sources of consumer attitude formation
- discuss the Theory of Planned Behaviour (TPB)
- show the value of attitude research in evaluating sport sponsorship programmes.

7.1 DEFINITIONS

An attitude in the sport context has been defined as representing an individual's general thoughts and feelings of favourableness towards a sport or recreation object that is often learned from our socio-cultural environment (Ajzen, 1988). Given that an individual's attitude is unobserved and abstract in nature, it is normally examined as a consumer behaviour construct that is useful for marketers based on its ability to predict intentions and actual behaviour. Consumers have developed specific attitudes toward products and services they like or dislike, which often determine their consumer behaviour such as information search, brand preference and purchase of a product/service. Attitude research is therefore beneficial for developing a sport marketing strategy, since this information can provide a better understanding of consumer decision-making. Examples of attitude research topics that are important for sport marketing include:

- measuring consumer attitudes toward a new product/service (e.g. a new fitness programme in a health club);
- determining the risk of a new product/service being unsuccessful (e.g. collecting data on fans' attitudes toward a new line of the team's merchandising);
- measuring the attitudes of specific target groups toward a new product, and then selecting the right marketing strategy (e.g. testing how attractive a new exercise programme is for the elderly);

- measuring consumer attitudes in relation to an advertising spot/commercial (e.g. testing fans' attitudes toward a promotional campaign about season ticket sales);
- measuring consumer attitudes toward a specific sport brand (e.g. image of a professional sport team);
- designing effective communication strategies to transform consumer attitudes (e.g. public authority's marketing campaign to change local attitudes toward a healthy lifestyle);
- evaluating sponsorship programmes (e.g. measuring fans' attitudes toward the sponsoring of their favourite team);
- evaluating corporate social responsibility actions (e.g. measuring fans' attitudes).

As noted already, attitudes can predict intensions and actual behaviour. However, for such a prediction to eventually occur, it has been suggested that four elements must be taken into consideration: 1) the presence of an attitude object, such as whether one likes baseball or running events; 2) the actual behaviour (e.g. attending a baseball game or running a marathon); 3) the context in which the behaviour takes place (e.g. the stadium where the game is held, or the city that hosts the marathon); and 4) the situation element, meaning the specific circumstances that, at a particular point of time, influence the relationship between attitudes and behaviour (e.g. the weather might be too wet to attend a baseball game, or fitness level might not yet be high enough to run that marathon) (Funk, Haugtvedt & Howard, 2000).

A number of theories and frameworks have been developed to analyse the attitude construct and its relationship with actual behaviour, including the tri-component model of attitudes and the Theory of Planned Behaviour, which are further discussed below.

7.2 THE TRI-COMPONENT MODEL OF ATTITUDES

In general, scholars and researchers consider attitude as a multidimensional construct. Based on this common perspective, a structural model of attitude was proposed (Schiffman & Kanuk 2004) to help understand the relationship between attitudes and behaviour, using three components that form an individual's evaluations of the 'attitude object': 1) affective component; 2) cognitive component; and 3) conative – behavioural component (as shown in Figure 7.1).

7.2.1 The affective component

The affective component includes feelings and emotional reactions toward a specific object within a given context. Feelings and emotions play a significant role in sport consumer decision-making, especially sport spectator behaviour where many consumer-related decisions such as attending a game and buying merchandise, equipment and souvenirs are made based on positive feelings and favourable emotions that occur before, during or after a game. For example, consider the attitudes of a fan toward his/her favourite football team. His/her positive feelings toward the team (affective component) will likely motivate him/her to attend a game (conative/behavioural component). As Funk and Pastore (2000) revealed in their study among professional sport fans in the US, positive feelings often arise

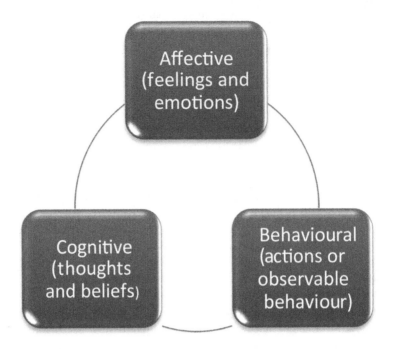

FIGURE 7.1 The tri-component attitude model

when sport fans develop psychological connections with their favourite sport teams, including feelings of fun, entertainment, social inclusion and excitement. The majority of sport commercials targeting specific sport fans aim to influence the affective component of their attitudes, such as the 2012 US Open's *It Must Be Love* (2012), FIFA's 15 *Feel the Game* (2014) and the NBA's *I Love This Game* (2011).

An individual's affective response toward a specific object can also be influenced by his/her mood at the moment of purchase decision making (e.g. if they are feeling happy when purchasing). For this reason, many sport marketers aim to influence the emotions of sport consumers not only via the core product (e.g. the game between two teams, or the gym facility) but also through the design of attractive and tangible environments (e.g. use of colours and music in sport stadiums and health clubs).

Sport marketers generally treat consumer feelings as evaluative in nature and often use pairs of opposing adjectives for consumers to rate their attitude toward the attitude object. Examples of adjectives used to describe a consumer's feelings toward a professional sport team are pleasant versus unpleasant, awful versus nice, angry versus happy and favourable versus unfavourable. Such opposing adjective pairs can be used in various sport and recreation contexts, such as by asking a consumer to consider a gym, running event or article of clothing, and rating these feelings on semantic differential scales.

7.2.2 The cognitive component

In a sport context, the cognitive component involves thoughts and beliefs toward sport and recreation products and services. In general, beliefs are developed based on the knowledge an individual has collected about the attributes and benefits of the object. This knowledge can result from personal experience or from information received via formal (e.g. sport commercials) and informal (word of mouth) communication channels. Cognitive-based attitudes are developed when consumers search for product/service information, or evaluate the attributes and benefits of the product, or consider alternatives to make a rationale decision. The role of knowledge that cultivates beliefs in sport consumer behaviour is often equally important with feelings and emotions.

As an example of the impact of knowledge, an individual who wants to start exercising is likely to search health clubs available in the area, and select the one that best satisfies his/her needs (e.g. evaluation of attributes and benefits such as accessibility, quality of facilities, exercise programmes, value for money, social interaction). In another example, consider a parent who wishes to register his/her six-year-old daughter in a karate class at the local dojo. Knowledge related to the benefits of learning karate (e.g. self-discipline and self-protection) can play an important role in the development of positive beliefs about the specific activity, and motivate him/her to engage in the behaviour (e.g. register their daughter in the karate club). In a further example, consider an individual who wants to join a tennis club. If there are many tennis clubs and facilities in the area, the individual is likely to research information about each club related to personally important attributes (e.g. price, number of tennis courts, coaches' qualifications, facility opening times), which can lead to the development of positive thoughts about a specific tennis club, and help in the selection process.

Consumers today are often experienced consumers with a wide range of sport products/services available to choose from (e.g. sport brands, games, sport clubs, children camps, outdoor sport events, skiing resorts). Technology advancements have also meant that most of this information is easily accessible via the internet, social media and online consumer reviews (e.g. blogs, TripAdvisor website). Thus, the evaluation of a sport product's or service's attributes has become a key component in the sport consumer's decision-making process.

There are several examples of sport commercials, which have targeted the cognitive component of sport consumers, by presenting detailed information about the brand. These include Cross Fit's *What is Cross Fit?* (2012) and *Fitness in 100 Words* (2014), ASICS's *ASICS® GEL-Kayano® 19* (2013) and Adidas's *Process: The Adidas Ultra Boost AKA* (2015).

As with the affective component, sport marketers often use opposing adjective pairs to enable consumers to rate their beliefs (cognitive component) about a specific sport or recreation object. Examples of opposing adjectives used to describe feelings toward a professional sport team include productive versus unproductive, good versus bad, worthless versus useful and weak versus strong. In addition, sport marketers often measure the cognitive components of an attitude by using associations linked to a sport brand, as previously discussed in Chapter 3. As an example of this approach, the consumer could rate the importance of brand attributes (e.g. logo, stadium, star player) or benefits (e.g. socialization, escape, peer group acceptance) associated with a professional sport team.

7.2.3 The behavioural component

The behavioural component of the attitude consists of actions or observable behaviour that occurs in relation to an object. The behavioural component often relates to the outcome of the consumer decision-making process (e.g. whether to purchase a brand T-shirt, number of brand T-shirts purchased over a season). Within sport marketing research, sport consumer behaviour is often measured using objective observable data such as from actual game attendance. Researchers can also measure an individual's behavioural intentions to consume a sport product or service (e.g. intention to attend favourite team's game on Saturday, or intention to buy a hat of favourite team's main sponsor). Word-of-mouth communications is also a common behavioural variable that is used in sport marketing research (e.g. intention to say good things about the sport camp to friends).

7.3 SOURCES OF ATTITUDE FORMATION

There are numerous external factors that can influence the formation of personal attitudes. As shown in Table 7.1, the most common are personal direct experiences, the social environment, formal communication channels and direct marketing; these sources of attitude formation are discussed below:

a) *Personal direct experience* is the primary source of attitude formation. In the sport context, an individual who has a pleasant experience when using a sport product or service, such as attending a 45-minute spin class at a gym, will likely develop positive thoughts and feelings toward it. Recognizing the importance of personal direct experience for initial attitude formation, sport marketers often try to stimulate product/service trials to influence consumer attitudes. For example, health clubs regularly use free coupons or single-visit promotions to attract new members to their facility and programmes. Such a visit can lead to positive effects (e.g. enjoyable class) and thoughts (e.g. nice facilities) toward the health club. On the other hand, negative experiences can lead to the development of negative attitudes. Consider the negative impact of hooliganism on the experience of soccer spectators. In countries where safety at soccer games is an issue, parents are often reluctant to attend football games with their children.

b) *The social environment* is also an important source of influence on attitude formation. Individuals interact every day with friends, family and significant others who can influence the development of beliefs and personal values. Sport research has shown that a child becomes aware of a specific sport activity and its subculture from various socialization agents and information sources, such as family members, direct contact (e.g. participating in a sport camp), friends and the media (Funk & James, 2001). Such research has also suggested that children born into 'sport educated' families are more likely to adopt an active lifestyle later in life, and even become professionally competitive in sports (e.g. athletes). Community sport programmes developed by local authorities are often successfully used to promote positive sport and recreation involvement. In contrast, societies that place less value on sport, either due to culture or religious teachings, can have a negative influence on the development of sport attitudes.

c) *Formal communication channels* can represent traditional as well as new/social media. Mass media campaigns (e.g. internet, magazines, newspapers, TV, radio) generally aim to increase consumers' awareness about specific products and services, which can influence attitude formation and stimulate purchase decisions. It has been recognized that advertising is usually more effective on consumers who have no or limited direct experience with a specific product or service, where they are relying on the information received from formal communications (Schiffman & Kanuk, 2004).

While traditional media is an established marketing strategy to influence attitudes, the use of social media has changed the way in which companies communicate with current and prospective consumers. For example, advertising via social media (e.g. Facebook, Twitter, blogs) is an effective marketing strategy for companies targeting young and educated individuals. In the sport sector, the use of social media has become particularly influential. According to the 2013 Sports Media Consumption Report (cited in Pollitt, 2013), 63% of fans went online to access sport-related content, which represented a 56% increase from 2011.

For social media to be successful in a sport marketing context, it is important to engage both spectators and the sport team members in the use of the social media. Thus, the use of 'emotional' images that capture the game experience in developing social media content can help increase sport fan involvement (Pollitt, 2013). The NHL, for example, turned to digital and social media to reach and engage new fans – its social media accounts subsequently recorded 3 million followers on Twitter, 3.7 million Facebook followers and another 753,000 on Instagram. These are particularly impressive results when you consider that they do not even include the thousands or millions of other fans who follow individual team social media accounts (Pollitt, 2013).

d) *Direct marketing* remains a useful strategy for influencing consumer attitudes. It generally involves a company communicating with a targeted individual or group segmented from a larger population based on psychographic and behavioural characteristics. Direct marketing is a particularly effective strategy because it enables the personalization of communications and messages to promote branded products and services. An example in the sport context is the targeting of a 'community' of scuba divers – a niche market with specific socioeconomic, psychographic and behavioural characteristics. According to a recent report by the US Diving Equipment and Marketing Association (2014), there are approximately 2.7 to 3.5 million active scuba divers in the USA, and about 6 million active scuba divers worldwide. This report also revealed that the mean age of a US scuba diver is 33 years old; in addition, 65% are males, 64% have an annual household income of between US $100,000 and US

TABLE 7.1 Sources of attitude formation

	Examples
Personal experience	Degree of satisfaction when attending a football game
The social environment	Families as consumer socialization agents
Traditional and new/social media	Mass media, blogs, Facebook, Twitter
Direct marketing	e-communication

$150,000, 59% are university graduates (undergraduate or postgraduate) and 24% have children aged between 11 and 17. Based on such specific socioeconomic, psychographic and behavioural characteristics, many international relevant resorts and hotels target their marketing and offerings toward scuba diving individuals and groups that fit these criteria. Their communications with the scuba diving community are often direct, such as via emails, blogs and newsletters that aim to directly influence positive attitudes toward their hotel as an ideal destination for scuba diving.

7.4 MULTI-ATTRIBUTE ATTITUDE MODELS: THE THEORY OF PLANNED BEHAVIOUR

As previously discussed, an individual's behaviour is largely determined by their attitudes toward an object. The Theory of Planned Behaviour (TPB) is one of the multi-attribute attitude models that has been used extensively by sport and consumer psychologists.

The TPB proposes that all behaviour is determined by a person's intentions, which are based on three key factors: 1) beliefs; 2) subjective norms; and 3) perceived behavioural control. The TPB (Ajzen, 1985, 1988, 1991) is an extension of the Theory of Reasoned Action (Ajzen & Fishbein, 1980), and includes the following variables (as also shown in Figure 7.2):

- actual behaviour
- intention to engage in a behaviour
- attitude toward the behaviour (beliefs)
- subjective norms
- perceived behavioural control.

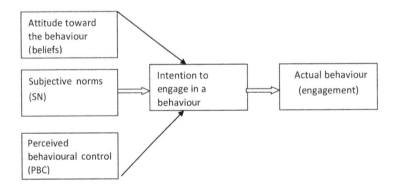

FIGURE 7.2 The theory of planned behaviour

Source: Aijen, I. people.umass.edu/aizen/tpb.diag.html

The TPB as illustrated in Figure 7.2 indicates that an individual's actual sport behaviour (e.g. participation in a morning yoga class, attending a professional basketball game) is predicted by their intention to engage in a specific behaviour. These positive or negative intentions to engage in the behaviour are influenced by attitudes, subjective norms and perceived behavioural control.

The *attitude variable* is determined by an individual's beliefs concerning the consequences of performing an action and a personal evaluation of the desirability of such consequences. Consider a recreational runner who expresses an intention to run a half marathon event in New York City. The development of positive attitudes will be dependent on his/her beliefs about the consequences of running in the event. For example, if he/she thinks the event will help him explore a new city, socialize with other runners and have an exercise goal, he/she is likely to develop positive attitudes toward the event.

Subjective norms represent what is considered acceptable within the socio-cultural environment such as significant others (e.g. friends, family and work colleagues). That is, the subjective norm component relates to opinions of significant others about the specific behaviour and the extent to which an individual is motivated to comply with the opinions of others (i.e. motivation to comply). Again in regard to running in the New York City half marathon, if the family and friends support and encourage him/her, it is likely that he/she will develop positive attitudes toward the event. In contrast, if his/her family and friends do not support his/her intentions and discourage participation in the event, this will create a negative attitude.

Perceived Behaviour Control (PBC) relates to an individual's perceptions of his/her ability to successfully perform the specific behavioural action. Perceived behavioural control can be negatively influenced by existing internal and external constraints that the individual faces when trying to participate in sports (Ajzen & Driver, 1991; Kimiecik, 1992). So, PBC is influenced by the availability of resources (e.g. time, money), range of choices (e.g. programmes, facilities) and perceived skills required to engage in the sport behaviour. As explained by Ajzen and Madden (1986, p. 455), 'a behavior may be said to be completely under a person's control, if the person can decide at will to perform it or not to perform it'. The issue of volitional control is highly applicable to the context of sport and recreation, with some research showing that relevant individuals face both real and perceived constraints. In the case of the runner, the financial cost, work and family commitments and ability to complete 22.1 kilometres will influence his/her intentions to participate in the New York City half marathon.

Continuing with the sport context, perceived behavioural control is a particularly influential factor for specific groups within many societies, such as females and ethnic groups influenced by social and cultural norms, as well as the elderly with chronic illnesses. Such groups are often influenced by negative internal psychological perceptions and stereotypes about their ability and suitability to engage in sport behaviours. Thus, sport marketing and communications with groups like these often require a motivational approach, to convey to them that they have control over their decisions regarding sport engagement. Indicative examples of such motivational sport campaigns include the Bureau of Educational and Cultural Affairs *The Empowering of Women & Girls through Sports* (2012), ASICS's *Effort is Beautiful* (2012) and Nike's *Believe in Yourself* (2009) and *I Can* (2006).

As a final note on TBP, it should be emphasized that not all consumer-related decisions are planned. Impulsive behaviour is common in relation to product and service consumption, especially in the context of sport. It has previously been reported that impulsive buying behaviour accounts for up to 80% of all purchases in certain sport product categories (Chen, Lin & Chang, 2013). In line with this, several factors have been identified as influencing compulsive consumer behaviour in sports; some of them are external such as price promotions, store atmosphere, store design and game experience, while others are internal such as personality traits, user product involvement and demographic and socio-cultural characteristics (Chen *et al.*, 2013).

7.4.1 Measuring the components of the theory of planned behaviour

The utility of the TPB to predict sport and recreation behaviour has been well recognized in the academic literature. Previous sport research has revealed strong correlations between intention and behaviour, as well as between attitudes and intention (Sheppard, Hartwick & Warshaw, 1988). In line with this, there are several valid and reliable scales that marketers can use to measure consumer attitudes, subjective norms and perceived behavioural control, and consequently predict actual behaviour with a relative degree of accuracy.

Attitudes are often measured in sport consumer behaviour research via semantic or bipolar adjective scales. Based on such measurements, consider the example of a fitness centre manager who wants to assess members' attitudes toward a potential new sport (e.g. squash) and the building of two relevant facilities. Examples of opposing adjectives that could be used to measure members' attitudes toward these squash plans include:

Squash as a sport activity is:

Dull	1	2	3	4	5	Exciting
Boring	1	2	3	4	5	Fun
Conservative	1	2	3	4	5	Modern
Useless	1	2	3	4	5	Useful
Difficult	1	2	3	4	5	Easy
Harmful	1	2	3	4	5	Beneficial
Slow	1	2	3	4	5	Fast

The first three pairs of adjectives measure the affective component of attitudes toward squash, while the last four measure the cognitive component. In a similar example, consider that a sport event organizer of a city marathon wishes to measure participants' attitudes toward the city, as a tourism destination. Opposing adjectives that could be included in the scale are as follows:

As the host of the marathon, the city is:

Dull	1	2	3	4	5	Exciting
Traditional	1	2	3	4	5	Modern
Unfriendly	1	2	3	4	5	Friendly

Dirty	1	2	3	4	5	Clean
Boring	1	2	3	4	5	Interesting
Dangerous	1	2	3	4	5	Safe
Noisy	1	2	3	4	5	Quite

In addition to these adjective scales, survey questions that use Likert scale items have been developed by researchers to measure the subjective norm component in sport contexts. Such questions generally assess the approval of significant others on a decision to engage in sport behaviour (e.g. my friends encourage me to play tennis, my friends discourage me from attending soccer games). Other questions have also been developed by researchers to measure an individual's control over sport behaviour (perceived behavioural control), including the following: If I want, I can play tennis once a week for a month; For me, playing tennis weekly is easy; or I will play tennis weekly each month, even if I face difficulties in doing so.

Lower scores in the perceived behavioural control measure indicate that an individual is highly constrained and subsequently unlikely to engage in a sport behaviour. These individuals need to be motivated (with targeted communication strategies) to overcome perceived constraints. In contrast, lower scores in the subjective norm measure indicate that an individual does not have the support to engage in sport behaviour. Although societal values are difficult to change, they can be influenced with appropriate marketing and communication strategies (e.g. targeted campaigns about the physiological, psychological and social benefits of engaging in sport, education programmes for ethnic groups, sport teaching programmes for children, promotion of fair play values in competitive sports). The US Tennis Association's *Sportsmanship* campaign (2014) was developed to adapt societal values – it is an example of how the benefits of sport engagement and the positive values of sport in society can be promoted.

It should be noted here that changing an individual's attitudes towards sports can be a challenging task for any sport marketer. Attitude change strategies are therefore discussed in the next section.

7.5 ATTITUDE CHANGE

In a sport context, there have already been instances where marketers have strived to change consumers' attitudes toward a sport product or service from negative to positive. Thus, Schiffman and Kanuk (2004) proposed five strategies for altering consumer attitudes:

1) Changing the basic motivational function: This is where sport marketers aim to make consumers aware of their needs, or help them understand their needs. For example, giving consumers information about the utility of a specific product (e.g. becoming a member of a health club to improve your psychological health), facilitating their increased knowledge (e.g. trekking on Mount Olympus creates an opportunity for exploring Greek mythology) and reflecting consumer values and lifestyles (e.g. run in

the Boston marathon to express your personal values about an active lifestyle and the health benefits).

2) Associating the product with an admired group or event: This is a highly applicable strategy in the sport context, where companies often implement corporate social responsibility actions to establish a positive society image. For example, donations to charity organizations constitute a common social responsibility strategy. Furthermore, many companies aim to associate their brands with city marathons (as events with a positive image) through sponsorship. Sport sponsorship is often perceived as a corporate social responsibility activity, particularly where the sponsored organization is a non-profit one (e.g. an amateur sport club). In reality, all sport sponsorships are commercial programmes, but they can be positioned as social responsibility actions to create a positive image of the sponsor in society.

3) Changing consumer beliefs about the sport brand. Perceptions about brand beliefs can be influenced by emphasizing the utility of existing brand attributes (e.g. children should attend sport camps because it helps them socialize) and by adding new ones (e.g. a hotel extends its services by introducing a spa centre for its customers).

4) Changing consumer beliefs about competitors' sport brands: This strategy relates to marketers concentrating on negatively influencing consumer attitudes toward their competitors' brands, rather than solely focusing on positively influencing consumer attitudes toward their own products or services.

The above five strategies assume that attitudes can be changed; but there might also be instances where attitudes automatically change as a result of the actual behaviour (Aronson, Wilson & Akert, 2007). According to the cognitive dissonance theory (Festinger, 1957), individuals develop dissonance because of cognitive inconsistencies, such as in situations when their self-image is threatened. Cognitive dissonance often produces discomfort, causing individuals to try to reduce such uneasiness by changing their behaviour, or trying to justify their behaviour.

The cognitive dissonance theory is highly applicable in the context of consumer behaviour in the form of post-behaviour dissonance. For example, buying an expensive branded product is often associated with doubts whether the choice was the right one and if the product was worth the money. Consumers try to reduce this dissonance by rationalizing their decision (e.g. look for information about the product, read reviews), seeking the encouragement or approval of their friends and looking for testimonials about the quality of the product. To reduce such dissonance among consumers, marketers should develop strategies to reinforce their choice, such as offering product and best price guarantees, after-sales services and testimonials through advertisements.

Consider, for example, an individual who purchases an annual membership to a health club. Cognitive dissonance can develop when the individual begins to question whether the selection of the club was the right decision, if the annual membership was worth the money and if he/ she is likely to continue exercising (and visiting the club) for the whole 12-month period and not drop out during the first couple of months. In such instances, the health club manager could reduce consumer dissonance by reinforcing the decision to become a member (e.g. include within the annual package extra services and vouchers, and refund coupons and promote socialization to build the social support of other club members).

7.6 APPLICATION OF ATTITUDE RESEARCH: SPORT SPONSORSHIP EVALUATION

Sponsorship evaluation is an area where attitude theory and research is highly relevant in a sport context – sponsorship is a prominent marketing and communication strategy in the sport industry. Sponsorship spending in the sport and leisure industry continues to grow. According to the 2014 IEG report (IEGSR, 2014), sponsorship spending in North America increased from US $18.9 billion in 2012 to $19.8 billion in 2013 (4.5% increase). This increase was higher than for both marketing and promotion (4.3%) and advertising (1.8%), as shown in Figure 7.3.

Similar figures have been reported for global sponsorship spending, with increases from US $51.1 billion in 2012 to US $53.1 billion in 2013 recorded (3.9% increase) (see Figure 7.4). Excluding North America, sponsors from all other parts of the world spent USD$33.4 billion in 2013, representing a 3.9% increase from the previous year. In 2014, Europe was the second biggest market in sponsorship globally (USD$14.8 billion), followed by Asia-Pacific (USD$3.3 billion) which experienced the highest increase across the regions (5.6%), as shown in Table 7.2.

Sport sponsorship covers approximately 70% of the total 2014 sponsorship spending, followed by entertainment (10%), arts (4%), festival/fairs/annual events (4%) and associations/membership organizations (3%).

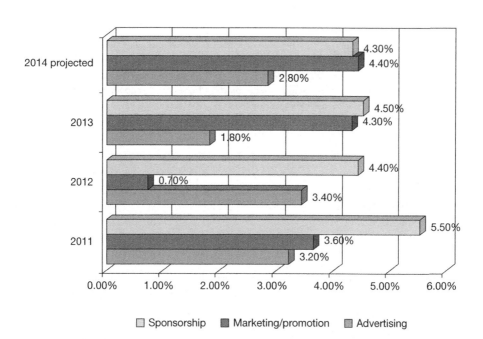

FIGURE 7.3 Annual growth of advertising, marketing/promotion and sponsorship in North America

Source: 2014 IEG report, LLC.

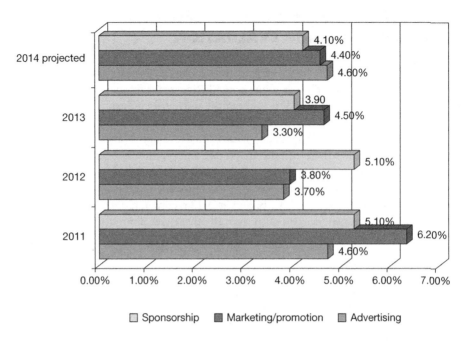

FIGURE 7.4 Total global sponsorship spending

Source: 2014 IEG report, LLC.

TABLE 7.2 Global sponsorship spending by region (in US$)					
	2012 spending (billion)	2013 spending (billion)	Increase from 2012 (%)	2014 spending (%)	Increase from 2013 (projected %)
Europe	14.1	14.5	2.8	14.8	2.1
Asia-Pacific	12	12.6	5	13.3	5.6
Central/South America	3.9	4	2.6	4.2	5
All other countries	2.2	2.3	4.5	2.4	4.3
Source: 2014 IEG, LLC.					

Attitude research is often used in sport sponsorship research to measure the effectiveness of sponsorship programmes. A number of theoretical models have been developed, which include several behavioural and attitudinal variables in the form of positive sponsorship outcomes (consequences) and antecedents of sport sponsorship. These positive sponsorship outcomes and antecedents of sport sponsorship are discussed below.

7.6.1 Positive attitudinal sport sponsorship outcomes

Measuring the effectiveness of sport sponsorship with sales figures is not always providing marketing insights, because sales are also influenced by other marketing and communication activities and macro environmental factors (e.g. economic climate, changes in consumer spending). This can make it difficult to isolate a sponsorship programme and test its unique influence on sponsorship-related sales. As a result, the success of a sponsorship programme is mostly evaluated via communication data (e.g. presence of the sponsor brand in a broadcast, printed, electronic or digital media) and consumer information data (qualitative or quantitative surveys), which evaluate the development of positive behavioural and attitudinal outcomes for the sponsor.

The most common of these behavioural and attitudinal variables are the following (also see Figure 7.5):

a) Brand awareness: This measures the percentage of sport consumers who recognize the sponsor of a sport team/association, event or athlete.
b) Brand recall: This measures the percentage of sport consumers who can remember (recall) the sponsor after an event took place.
c) Sponsor brand image: This is based on the associations that sport consumers develop with respect to the sponsor brand. As discussed in Chapter 3, these brand associations consist of three main dimensions: 1) attributes, related to the characteristics of the brand (e.g. light sport shoes); 2) benefits, related to consumers' expectations of

FIGURE 7.5 Sport sponsorship outcomes

using the brand (e.g. these vitamins will help my health); and 3) attitudes, related to consumers' affective and cognitive evaluations of the brand (e.g. nice-looking and technologically advanced sport shoes). Building the image of a sponsor is one of the main sponsorship objectives.

d) Consumer purchase intentions: Since the influence of sponsorship on real sales is difficult to determine, sport consumer intentions to buy sponsors' products is the most common attitudinal variable used in sport sponsorship studies (Alexandris, Tsaousi & James, 2007; Gwinner & Swanson, 2003; Harvey, 2001; Lee, Sandler & Shani, 1997; Madrigal, 2001). While consumer purchase intentions do not always predict actual buying behaviour, they are a strong indicator, as noted in section 7.4 in relation to the tri-component and planned behaviour theories.

e) Word-of-mouth communications: Developing positive word-of-mouth for the sponsor brand is a highly desirable outcome for sponsors (Alexandris *et al.*, 2007; Harvey, 2001). Although the development of positive word-of-mouth usually requires product experience and customer satisfaction, sport consumers (especially fans with high identification levels) are usually willing to say good things about the sponsor brand of their favourite team, and help build sponsor brand awareness and sponsor brand image (Alexandris *et al.*, 2007).

7.6.2 Attitudinal variables as antecedents of sport sponsorship

There are certain attitudinal variables that have been found to positively influence the effectiveness of a sponsorship programme. These attitudinal factors often act as antecedents of positive sponsorship outcomes, and can be summarized as follows (also see Figure 7.6):

a) Fans' attachment level with the team (or team identification): It is defined as the psychological connection that fans develop with their favourite sport teams. Fans with high attachment levels have a strong degree of identification with their team and its values, which is associated with positive behavioural outcomes, such as attending more games and being informed about the team and its activities (e.g. reading news, spending time on social media, using mobile applications). Sponsors that invest in teams with high fan attachment levels are more likely to achieve successful sponsorship programmes (Gwinner & Swanson, 2003; Madrigal, 2001). That is, highly identified fans are more likely to be aware of the team sponsor (sponsorship awareness), develop positive attitudes toward the sponsor, look for information about the sponsor and potentially buy its products. It is therefore important for sport marketers to develop strategies for increasing their fans' identity with the team, to create an attractive environment for sponsorship investment.

b) Sport activity/fan involvement: Sport activity involvement has been defined as 'an unobservable state of motivation, arousal or interest toward a recreation activity or associated product' (Havitz & Dimanche, 1997, p. 246). This refers to the degree to which a specific sport activity or a specific sport team has a central role in an individual's life (e.g. learning about it and talking about it with friends), it is perceived as attractive (e.g. fun and exciting), and it is identified with personal values (e.g. protect the environment in outdoor recreation).

Individuals who are highly involved in a sport activity (e.g. runners or cyclists or a specific sport team fans) are more likely to develop positive attitudes toward the sponsor of an event in which they participate (e.g. a marathon) or of their favourite sport team. This is underpinned by their higher motivation to be knowledgeable about issues related to their favourite sport activity/team, including its associated products and sponsors. Positive behavioural outcomes include increased sponsorship awareness, positive attitudes toward the sponsor brand, willingness to search for information about the sponsor products and intentions to buy the sponsor products.

Several studies in different sport settings have provided evidence on the positive relationship between sport involvement and sponsorship outcomes. Lascu *et al.* (1995), for example, reported that individuals in their study who rated themselves highly in relation to golf commitment were more likely to remember the sponsors of an event than those who rated themselves as low. Similarly, Alexandris *et al.* (1997) recognized that fans who were highly involved in basketball were more likely to recognize the sponsors of a basketball event and develop positive attitudes towards them.

c) Attitudes toward a sport event: In the context of sport events, spectators' attitudes toward the event can be a significant predictor of sponsorship outcomes. Research conducted in relation to sponsorship of the winter and summer Olympic Games and World Cup Football (Lee *et al.*, 1997) indicated a positive relationship between event image and sponsorship outcomes. Spectators' attitude toward a sport event is a useful measure for sport marketers, because it is a relatively stable characteristic for some established events (Lee *et al.*, 1997). Most sport spectators' attitudes are formed based on: 1) the expected benefits from attending the event (e.g. pleasure and entertainment); 2) the attributes of the event relevant to the participants' competition (e.g. event with strong teams or prestigious athletes); 3) its image and status (e.g. European Champions League); 4) the media impact (e.g. broadcasted via national or international media); and 5) tangible aspects of the event (e.g. stadium or city destination) (Gwinner, 1997; Lee, Sandler & Shani, 1997; Speed & Thompson, 2000).

Sport spectators who perceive an event to be attractive, entertaining, interesting and prestigious are more likely to be aware of the sponsors of the event and develop favourable attitudes toward them (Alexandris, Tsiotsou & James, 2012; D'Astous & Bitz, 1995; Poon & Prendergast, 2006; Speed & Thomson, 2000). Therefore, sport marketers should develop strategies to build the brand of an event (e.g. increase brand awareness and develop positive event associations), to create a favourable environment for sponsorship investment. This is particularly relevant, as well as particularly challenging, in relation to new or non-established sport events.

d) Attitudes toward sport sponsorship: Sport consumers can develop positive or even negative in some cases beliefs about sport sponsorship (Bennett, 1999; Harvey, 2001; Meenaghan, 2001). The effectiveness of sponsorship, as an alternative communication strategy to advertising, is often based on the 'goodwill' factor, which refers to the positive attitude that consumers have about sponsorship as an action of corporate social responsibility. Sport sponsorship research has indicated (Alexandris *et al.*, 2007; Speed & Thomson, 2000) that most consumers believe that sponsorship is a corporate social responsibility action (on behalf of the sponsor), aiming to help sport,

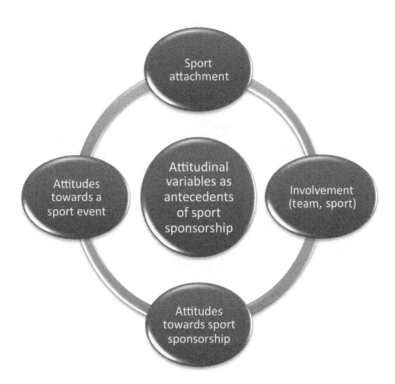

FIGURE 7.6 Attitudinal variables as antecedents of sport sponsorship

leisure and art activities that contribute to social welfare. For example, sport consumers who have strong positive attitudes toward sponsorship (e.g. sponsorship can make Olympic Games happen) might develop favourable attitudes toward the actual sponsors (Lee, Sandler & Shani, 1997). In contrast, negative attitudes toward sponsorship can arise when consumers associate sponsorship with pure commercialization. Although all sponsorship programmes have a commercial base, sport marketers should avoid creating the image of sponsorship as a pure commercialized action.

7.7 CHAPTER SUMMARY

Attitude is an important construct in sport consumer behaviour, particularly as it often predicts actual purchase behaviour. Consumers who develop favourable attitudes toward a sport object are more likely to consume it. Thus, sport marketers should aim to positively influence both the affective and cognitive components of consumer attitudes. The tri-component model and the theory of planned behaviour were both discussed in this chapter to explain the multidimensional nature of sport attitudes and the factors that influence their development.

There are several factors that have been recognized to influence sport attitude formation (e.g. direct personal experience, the social environment and significant others, formal and informal marketing communication and direct marketing). Sport marketers should study these factors in order to design appropriate strategies to create a favourable environment for positive attitude formation. In order to achieve this, primary research (surveys and qualitative research) on sport consumer attitudes is required. Research in the area of sport sponsorship evaluation provides a good example of how attitude research can help the development of sport marketing strategy; several attitude variables have been used in theoretical models to measure the positive outcomes of sport sponsorship and identify the factors that determine sponsorship effectiveness.

7.8 DISCUSSION QUESTIONS

The discussion questions presented below are designed to help students review what is important in the chapter. You can answer them on your own, but they are also suitable for discussion work in small groups.

1) Discuss the components of the tri-dimensional attitude model, by providing examples in the sport context.
2) How applicable is the planned behaviour theory for sport marketers? Present specific examples to support your arguments.
3) Compare and contrast the tri-component attitude model with the theory of planned behaviour.
4) What are the main sources of attitude development? Which sources can be considered as the most powerful ones and why?
5) What are the main strategies that can be used in order to change consumer attitudes? Present examples to support your discussion.
6) How can attitude theory be used to help sponsorship research? Provide an example of a sponsorship programme to support your argument.
7) What are the main attitudinal variables that can act as antecedents of a successful sponsorship programme? Discuss them in the contexts of a sport event (e.g. NBA all-stars game) and a professional sport team (e.g. a baseball team).

7.9 CLASS ACTIVITY: SPORT CONSUMER ATTITUDES

The class activity is designed to use information learned in this chapter to understand sport consumer attitudes.

a) Choose two sport commercials (targeting fans and sport participants) which aim to influence the affective and cognitive components of sport consumer attitudes.

- profile the target groups
- discuss the communication messages used
- critically evaluate if and how the affective and cognitive components of attitudes are influenced, justifying your answers.

b) Design a project in order to measure, via the use of quantitative primary data, students' attitudes towards the following college sports:

- baseball
- basketball
- football
- tennis
- soccer.

c) What are the main factors that have influenced the development of the attitudes, which have been identified in part (b)? Critically discuss them.

REFERENCES

Ajzen, I. (1985). From intentions to actions: A theory of planned behavior. In J. Kuhl & J. Beckmann (eds), *Action Control: From cognition to behavior* (11–39). New York: Springer.

Ajzen, I. (1985, 1988). TPB Diagram. Retrieved from http://people.umass.edu/aizen/tpb.diag.html

Ajzen, I. (1988). *Attitudes, Personality and Behavior*. Chicago, IL: Dorsey.

Ajzen, I. (1991). The theory of planned behavior. *Organizational Behavior and Human Decision Process*, *50*, 179–211.

Ajzen, I. & Driver, B. (1991). Application of the theory of planned behavior to leisure choice. *Journal of Leisure Research*, *24*, 207–224.

Ajzen, I. & Fishbein, M. (1980). *Understanding Attitudes and Predicting Social Behavior*. NJ: Prentice Hall, Englewood Cliffs.

Ajzen, I. & Madden, T. (1986). Prediction of goal-directed behavior: Attitudes, intentions, and perceived behavioral control. *Journal of Experimental Psychology*, *22*, 453–474.

Alexandris, K., Tsaousi, E. & James, J. (2007). Predicting sponsorship outcomes from attitudinal constructs: The case of a professional basketball event. *Sport Marketing Quarterly*, *16*, 13–139.

Alexandris, K., Tsiotsou, R. & James, J. (2012). Testing a hierarchy of effects model of sponsorship effectiveness: The role of team attachment and sponsor image. *Journal of Sport Management*, *26*, 363–378.

Aronson, E., Wilson, T.D. & Akert, R.M. (2007). *Social Psychology* (6th ed.). NJ: Pearson Education.

Bennet, R. (1999). Sport sponsorship spectator recall and false consensus. *European Journal of Marketing*, *33*, 291–313.

Chen, C.Y., Lin, Y.H. & Chang, W.M. (2013). Impulsive purchasing behavior for professional sports team-licensed merchandised – from the perspective of group effects. *Sport Marketing Quarterly*, *22(2)*, 71–83.

D'Astous, A. & Bitz, P. (1995). Consumer evaluations of sponsorship programmes. *European Journal of Marketing*, *29*, 6–22.

Diving Equipment and Marketing Association. (2014). Fast Facts: Recreational Scuba Diving and Snorkeling. Retrieved from http://c.ymcdn.com/sites/www.dema.org/resource/resmgr/Research_Documents/Diving_Fast_Facts-2014.pdf

Festinger, L. (1957). *A Theory of Cognitive Dissonance*. Stanford, CA: Stanford University Press.

Funk, D., Haugtvedt, C. & Howard, D. (2000). Contemporary attitude theory in sport: Theoretical considerations and implications. *Sport Management Review*, *3(2)*, 125–144.

Funk, D.C. & James, J. (2001). The psychological continuum model: A conceptual framework for understanding an individual's psychological connection to sport. *Sport Management Review*, *4(2)*, 119–125.

Funk, D. & Pastore, D. (2000). Equating attitudes to allegiance: The usefulness of selected attitudinal information in segmenting loyalty to professional sports teams. *Sport Marketing Quarterly, 9*(4), 175–184.

Gwinner, K. (1997). A model of image creation and image transfer in event sponsorship. *International Marketing Review, 14*, 145–158.

Gwinner, K. & Swanson, S. (2003). A model of fan identification: Antecedents and sponsorship outcomes. *Journal of Services Marketing, 17*, 275–294.

Harvey, B. (2001). Measuring the effects of sponsorships. *Journal of Advertising Research, 1*, 59–64.

Havitz, M. & Dimanche, F. (1997). Leisure involvement revisited: Conceptual conundrums and measurement advances. *Journal of Leisure Research, 29*, 245–278.

IEGSR. (2014). *2014 IEG Report*. Retrieved from www.sponsorship.com/iegsr/2014/01/07/Sponsor ship-Spending-Growth-Slows-In-North-America.aspx

Jhaveri, H. (2015). *Gary Bettman says social media success drives NHL growth*. Retrieved from http://ftw.usatoday.com/2015/01/gary-bettman-social-media-nhl-growth

Kimiecik, J. (1992). Predicting vigorous physical activity of corporate employees: Comparing the theories of reasoned action and planned behavior. *Journal of Sport and Exercise Psychology, 14*, 192–206.

Lascu, D.N., Giese, T.D., Toolan, C., Guehring, B. & Mercer, J. (1995). Sport involvement: A relevant individual difference factor in spectator sports, *Sport Marketing Quarterly, 4*(4), 41–62.

Lee, M., Sandler, D. & Shani, D. (1997). Attitudinal constructs towards sponsorship: Scale development using three global sporting events. *International Marketing Review, 14*(34), 159–169.

Madrigal, R. (2001). Social identity effects in a belief attitude-intentions hierarchy: Implications for corporate sponsorship. *Psychology and Marketing, 18*, 145–165.

Meenaghan, T. (2001). Understanding sponsorship effects. *Psychology and Marketing, 18*(2), 95–122.

Pollitt, C. (2013). Social Media Marketing Lessons from the NHL. Retrieved from www.huffingtonpost. com/chad-pollitt/social-media-marketing-le_b_4305135.html

Poon, D. & Prendergast, G. (2006). A new framework for evaluating sponsorship opportunities. *International Journal of Advertising, 25*(4), 471–488.

Schiffman, L & Kanuk, L. (2004). *Consumer Behavior*. NJ: Prentice Hall.

Speed, R. & Thomson, P. (2000). Determinants of sport sponsorship effects. *Journal of the Academy of Marketing Science, 28*, 226–238.

Sheppard, B., Hartwick, J. & Warshaw, P. (1988). The theory of reasoned action: A meta-analysis of past research with recommendations for modifications and future research. *Journal of Consumer Research, 15*(3), 325.

VIDEO FILES

Adidas. (2015). Process: The Adidas Ultra Boost AKA 'The World's Best Running Shoe Retrieved from www.youtube.com/watch?v=4J_kxwT9zX4

ASICS. (2013). *ASICS® GEL-Kayano® 19* [Video File]. Retrieved from www.youtube.com/watch?v= RHMkNIRRF-8

ASICS. (2012). Effort is Beautiful [Video File]. Retrieved from www.youtube.com/watch?v= IRMcMQ0rWsw

Bureau of Educational and Cultural Affairs. (2012). *The Empowering of Women & Girls through Sports* [Video File]. Retrieved from www.youtube.com/watch?v=CpgAcQmIw8k

Cross Fit. (2014). Fitness in 100 Words [Video File]. Retrieved from www.youtube.com/watch?v= K5fg7VcrJ70

Cross Fit. (2012). What is Cross Fit? [Video File]. Retrieved from www.youtube.com/watch?v= ZZdp59yyG0M

FIFA 15. (2014). Feel the Game [Video File]. Retrieved from www.youtube.com/watch?v=Q21bznzy_HY

NBA. (2011). I love this game [Video File]. Retrieved from www.youtube.com/watch?v=MARyln7zpZs;

Nike. (2009). *Believe in Yourself* [Video File]. Retrieved from www.youtube.com/watch?v=N3U 5411JzbM

Nike. (2006). I Can [Video File]. Retrieved from www.youtube.com/watch?v=iZxQDAyFY6s

US Open. (2012). It Must Be Love [Video File]. Retrieved from www.youtube.com/watch?v=CTU4-L7gQyg

US Tennis Association. (2014). US Tennis Association *Sportsmanship* [Video File]. Retrieved from www.youtube.com/watch?v=DI3SEkKufP8

CHAPTER 8

Personality and sport consumer behaviour

This chapter's objectives are to:

- define the construct of 'personality' and discuss its relevance for sport consumer behaviour
- show how personality theory can be applied in sport consumer behaviour
- present the main personality traits and their relevance for sport consumer behaviour
- define the construct of sport 'brand personality'
- present a sport brand personality model
- review sport brand personality studies and present the main brand personality models that have been developed in different sport contexts
- show the value of brand personality research for developing sport marketing strategy.

8.0 INTRODUCTION

Personality is what makes one individual different from another and relates to individual differences in the way people think, feel and behave. Similar to attitudes, personalities are often learned and can be influenced by the environment, but also have a genetic foundation. As a result, personality is considered more stable than attitudes, which are more likely to fluctuate over time. The American Psychological Association (2002) defined personality as 'the unique psychological qualities of an individual that influence a variety of characteristic behaviour patterns (both overt and covert) across different situations and over time'. These psychological qualities are often referred to as traits that have three distinct properties of personality. So, personality: a) reflects individual differences; b) is consistent and enduring; c) can change, under some circumstances and influences (Schiffman & Kanuk, 2004). Further detail on each of these properties is as follows:

a) *Personality reflects individual differences*: This is based on the theory that the traits (inner characteristics) which determine an individual's personality are unique – it is unlikely for two individuals to have the same personality. They can have similar personality traits, but they will not be exactly the same. For example, in the sport context some individuals seek risk and adventure in their leisure time (e.g. participants of extreme sports), while others seek relaxation (e.g. yoga participants). These differences in their recreation behaviour reflect, to a large degree, differences in their personality traits.

b) *Personality is consistent and enduring*: Personality is a relatively stable characteristic. It is well known among practitioners that marketing strategies do not aim to change consumer personalities. Instead, marketers aim to study and understand consumer personalities, and develop appropriate marketing strategies that can appeal to their main personality traits.

c) *Personality can, under some circumstances, change*: While it has been recognized that personality is a relatively stable characteristic, it can sometimes change due to the influence of an individual's maturing process, socio-cultural environment, as well as major life events (e.g. deaths, births of children, career changes). In addition, as societal values can also evolve over the years, it is expected that these changes can also influence an individual's personality.

These three distinct properties of personality enable the addressing of sport consumer questions such as the following:

- Why do some people like participating in individual sports, while others prefer team sports?
- Why do some people like exercising indoors, while others prefer outdoors?
- Why do some people like watching contact sports (e.g. rugby, boxing), while others prefer non-contact sport (e.g. volleyball, swimming)?

The value of personality research lies in its ability to predict actual consumer behaviour. In consumer research personality is linked with product category choice, media use, product innovation, psychographic segmentation and attitude change. Yet personality research has received limited attention in the context of sport consumer behaviour, and is an area that should be further considered to help understand sport consumer decision-making.

In the context of sport and leisure, Barnett (2013) observed that personality traits have strong predictive power in explaining why individuals choose to participate in specific recreation activities and what they expect from their participation. In the context of sport fan behaviour, personality traits have been reported to influence the development of need-affiliation motives and team identification (Donavan, Carlson & Zimmerman, 2005). Personality theory can also help to understand why individuals become fans of certain sport teams. For example, it has been suggested that fans often identify with teams that exhibit characteristics perceived to match their own personality traits (Stankovich, 2011).

Such research on the consumer personality, founded on the measurement of the individual's psychological traits, can help sport marketers to:

- segment sport consumers, according to personality traits
- develop communication messages to appeal to sport consumer segments, based on personality traits

- develop, promote and deliver sport services, adjusted to the needs of each sport consumer segment based on their specific personality profile;
- build the personality of sport products and services (e.g. sport teams, sport organizations, sport activities);
- build brand personality to develop consumer loyalty;
- identify and use brand personality as a positioning criterion and a competitive advantage strategy.

Robbins (2001) introduced the following three main sources, which he believed influence personality traits: 1) biological or genetic basis; 2) the sociocultural environment; and 3) situational conditions. This categorization by Robbins (2001) suggests that the personality is made up of three main factors: 1) heredity; 2) environment; and 3) situation. Further descriptions on these are as follows:

a) *Heredity* refers to those factors that are determined by the molecular structure of the genes, located in the chromosomes. In simpler terms, an individual's personality is influenced by both their parents and their biological, physiological and psychological make-up.

b) *Environment* relates to the socio-cultural and environmental factors that influence the development of an individual's personality. Examples of such factors are family, school, friends and social groups, as well as the values and culture of the society in which an individual grows up.

c) *Situation* moderates both the influence of heredity and environment on an individual's personality. This is based on the theory that even though personality is a relatively stable characteristic, it can change in different situations (e.g. periods of financial difficulties, family problems, health problems).

8.1 THE TRAIT PERSONALITY THEORY

Trait theories of personality imply personality is biologically based. They are based on research that has identified enduring characteristics that can be used to determine an individual's behaviour; these characteristics are referred to as 'personality traits' (Kassin, 2003). According to Schiffman and Kanuk (2004), the most prominent personality traits applicable in consumer behaviour are: 1) extraversion; 2) agreeableness; 3) conscientiousness; 4) emotional stability; and 5) openness to experience (Figure 8.1). Each of these personality traits is also discussed in further detail below.

a) *Extraversion:* This trait describes how comfortable an individual is about developing social relationships. An extraverted individual is perceived as sociable, open and good at building social relationships. In contrast, an introverted individual is usually perceived as closed, reserved and not good at developing social relationships. It has been proposed that extraversion has three core elements: 1) tendency to experience frequent positive moods; 2) sensitivity to potential rewards; and 3) tendency to attract social attention (Barnett, 2013). Extraverted behaviour satisfies the needs for belonging and affiliation, as discussed in Chapter 5.

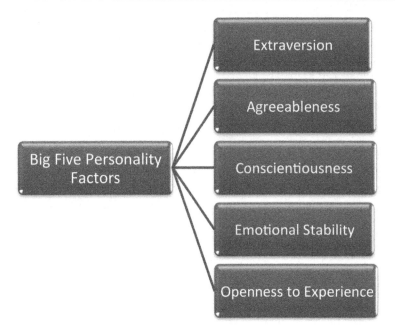

FIGURE 8.1 The Big Five personality factors

Source: Schiffman and Kanuk (2004). Consumer Behavior, NJ: Prentice Hall.

It has been suggested that the extraversion trait is relevant to the context of sport and recreation (Barnett, 2013). Extraverted individuals are more likely to choose sport activities that create opportunities for social interaction and social relationships, such as watching and playing team sports. In contrast, introverted individuals are more likely to select solitary recreational activities, such as swimming and rock climbing.

In the context of US college sport fan behaviour, Donavan *et al.* (2005) reported that extraverted college students are more likely to seek opportunities for developing affiliation with college sport teams and clubs. Socialization and the experience of the social atmosphere in the sport environment are among the prime motivators for attending college sport games.

b) *Agreeableness:* This trait defines how good an individual is at cooperating with others. A highly agreeable individual is usually perceived as cooperative, trusting, good-natured and caring, with the ability to provide emotional support to others. Research in the recreation context (Barnett, 2013) has shown that individuals with personalities high in agreeableness are more likely to achieve satisfaction from their recreation engagement. These individuals are also more likely to seek social experiences in their leisure time (Barnett, 2013). Similar results were reported in research among US college student football fans (Donavan *et al.*, 2005), where it was identified that individuals high in agreeableness often seek the satisfaction of affiliation-related needs.

c) *Conscientiousness:* This trait relates to an individual's reliability and capacity for behavioural and cognitive control. A highly conscientious individual is generally perceived as reliable, responsible, dependable and well-organized. Highly conscientious individuals are also more likely to adhere to social norms, and less likely to be engaged in risky, unhealthy or less acceptable social behaviour (e.g. risky driving, risky health behaviour, crime). They are also more likely to be committed to their family, work and friends (Barnett, 2013). As a result, these individuals are expected to avoid risky sport and leisure experiences.

Research in the context of sport and leisure has shown that most individuals who are high in conscientiousness avoid engaging in sport and leisure activities that can be judged negatively by others or not accepted by their close social groups (Barnett, 2013).

d) *Emotional stability:* This trait refers to an individual's ability to cope with stress. Individuals with high emotional stability are usually described as calm, relaxed and self-confident, while individuals with low emotional stability are usually nervous, stressed, anxious and insecure. In the context of sport and leisure, research has indicated that individuals who are low in emotional stability are less likely to experience pleasure from activities that provide opportunities for social interaction and derive less enjoyment from sport participation (Barnett, 2013). Furthermore, individuals with high anxiety levels often avoid competitive leisure activities and instead seek opportunities where they will feel more 'successful'. Similarly, individuals with high depression levels often struggle to feel enjoyment and pleasure from leisure participation (Barnett, 2013).

e) *Openness to experience:* Open individuals are often perceived as those who are creative, curious and willing to try new things and pursue new experiences. In contrast, most closed individuals have a preference for simplicity and for traditional experiences. In terms of sport and leisure behaviour, individuals who are open to new experiences are generally more willing to seek opportunities for exploring, learning and improving their personal skills and abilities. They are usually ready to try new activities, particularly those that are social, challenging, active and novel (Barnett, 2013). For example, individuals who participate in mountaineering-related activities are high on sensation seeking, and enjoy experiences which are perceived as risky and exciting.

These five personality traits are beneficial to sport marketers, as they can provide additional unique information about the differences in an individual's personality.

8.2 MARKETING RESEARCH ON THE CONSUMER PERSONALITY

There are several examples on how consumer personality research can help sport marketers. So:

• Consumer personality traits can be used as criteria for sport consumer psychographic segmentation.

• Consumer psychographic segmentation, based on personality traits, can be used as a predictor of how individuals make choices about the selection of specific sport and leisure activities. For example, individuals with strong traits of sensation seeking and openness to experience are more likely to be attracted to risky, extreme and challenging sport activities (e.g. outdoor sports).

- Personality research can be used to predict sport consumer expectations. For example, individuals with high levels of openness to experience are more likely to seek sport opportunities that offer new experiences, often participating in challenging activities, which can help to increase skills and create social interaction.
- Personality research can guide communication strategy – different advertisements and media channels appeal to different sport consumers based on their personality profiles. For example, individuals with strong extraversion and agreeableness personality traits would be more responsive to communication strategies that emphasize the social aspect of spectatorship or participation.

There are numerous examples of sport brand commercials that have targeted specific sport consumers based on their personality characteristics. For example, Jeep's Super Bowl commercial *Encourages Us to Always Have Adventure* (2014) and the East Coast Adventure Racing's *American Adventure Sports* promo (2011) both specifically target adventurists. Similarly, North Face's *Curiosity* (2014) and *The Journey is the Reward* (2014) campaigns were targeted at sport consumers seeking sensation, adventure, risky situations and new experiences. In addition, Puma's *Live Life, Don't Watch It* (2012), *Social Brings the Party to Tokyo!* (2011) and *Puma Social Party* (2011) ad series was targeted at extraverted individuals who seek the social experience of sport.

The benefits of identifying and using consumer personality traits in sport advertising and marketing are well documented. However, it has been argued that the usefulness of personality traits is reliant on the ability to explain actual consumer behaviour or preference. Engel, Blackwell and Miniard (1995) therefore suggested that for personality traits to be reliable predictors of consumer behaviour and usable in psychographic segmentation, the following criteria need to be satisfied:

1) Demographic factors (e.g. age, gender, education, income) should be combined with personality traits. If consumer groups with common personality traits are not homogeneous in terms of demographic factors, they probably have limited value for psychographic segmentation.
2) The scales used to measure personality traits should be reliable and valid, which should be checked via a detailed analysis of their psychometric characteristics. This is particularly relevant when using these personality scales for cross-cultural comparisons (e.g. different countries).
3) An adequately sized personality segment. Target groups, which are homogeneous in terms of personality traits, should be large enough to be worth targeting.

8.3 BRAND PERSONALITY

In the same way that individuals have unique personalities, a product/service can also be perceived as having personality-like traits by consumers (Schiffman & Kanuk, 2004). The term 'brand personality' is used to describe this perception, which Aaker (1997) defined as 'the set of human characteristics associated with a brand' (p. 347). In addition, Azoulay and Kapferer (2003) viewed brand personality as 'the set of human personality traits that are both applicable and relevant for brands' (p. 151).

From a brand personality perspective, consumers often attach symbolic meaning to brands and often select those with perceived personalities that best reflect or fit their own inner characteristics/traits (Austin, Siguaw & Mattila, 2003). Examples of personality traits attached to brands include modern, traditional, competitive, smart, fast, interesting, explorative, innovative and safe. In some cases, consumers have even perceived brands as representing human characters or celebrities (Aaker, 1991; 1996; Aaker, 1997).

Brand personality is a symbolic or self-expressive function rather than a utilitarian one (Aaker, 1991). So, how a consumer attaches personal meaning to a brand and identifies with that brand (symbolic meaning) is often more important than the consumer's evaluation of product-related attributes (utilitarian function). Consumers are more likely to develop psychological links with brands that are represented through emotional meanings and messages. Thus, 'storytelling' via advertisements is a common communication strategy for companies to build their own brands (Murray, 2013).

In the sport context, there is ample evidence that emotion plays a strong role in sport consumer branding. The NBA's *Where Amazing Happens* (2009) is a relevant example of a brand promotion that involves a strong emotional element. Similarly, Olympics P&G's *Thank You Mom* commercial (2014), and North Face's *Your Land* campaign (2014) focus on the emotional element in their campaigns.

Building a brand personality is an essential tool for most marketers – it has a strong impact on consumer preferences, and has been strongly associated with the development of brand trust and loyalty, due to the emotional connections that strong brands develop with their customers. Brand personality can also be used as a segmentation criterion and a tool for brand differentiation (Hosany, Ekinci & Uysal, 2007).

Academics and marketing managers have often used the brand personality approach to develop a marketing strategy for specific products. The bulk of this research has utilized measures of a brand's personality. For example, Aaker (1997) developed a five-factor brand personality measurement instrument, based on the Big Five personality framework discussed earlier in this chapter. These factors have since been used extensively in the marketing literature for different products and services (Eisend & Stokburger-Sauer, 2013). In his measurement instrument, Aaker (1997) introduced the following five brand personality traits, which she believed consumers generally perceive in a product/service (also see Figure 8.2):

1) *Sincerity*: The tendency of a brand to be perceived as down-to-earth, honest, wholesome and cheerful.
2) *Excitement*: The tendency of a brand to be perceived as daring, spirited, imaginative and up-to-date.
3) *Competence*: The degree to which a brand is perceived as reliable, intelligent and successful.
4) *Sophistication*: The degree to which a brand is perceived as upper class and charming.
5) *Ruggedness*: The tendency of a brand to be perceived as outdoorsy and masculine.

These five brand personality traits have been widely applied in the marketing literature, but have also received some criticism. For example, in a detailed review of Aaker's (1997)

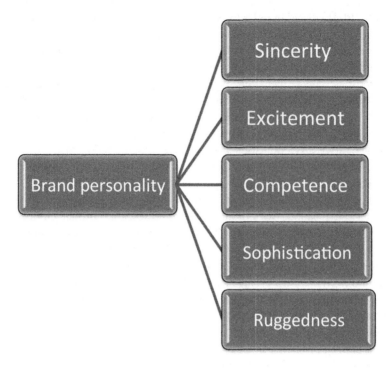

FIGURE 8.2 Aaker's brand personality model

Source: Aaker, J. L. (1997). Dimensions of brand personality. *Journal of Marketing Research, 34*(3), 347–356.

brand personality model, Avis (2012) questioned the applicability of the five traits on different consumer settings and contexts (e.g. different sectors such as sport, hospitality and banking). Other criticism includes feedback that the adjectives used in the measurement of the five sub-scales used to describe each of the five personality dimensions are not always appropriate across different products, services and sectors; they should, therefore, be customized to different product categories. For example, the adjectives used might have different meaning in different contexts, especially in services sectors such as sport and recreation (e.g. Ross, 2008; Tsiotsou, 2012; Tsiotsou, Alexandris & Cornwell, 2014).

8.4 BRAND PERSONALITY IN SPORT

In the sport consumer behaviour literature there are several examples that show the applicability of sport brand personality research on sport marketing. For example:

- Sport team brand personality is related to city brand personality (Aiken, Campbell & Koch, 2013). That is, a professional sport team is often perceived as having similar traits to the city in which it is based. For example, personality traits associated with the city of Pittsburgh such as working class and industrial are among the perceived brand personality traits of the Pittsburgh Steelers NFL team.

- A sport event's personality influences sponsorship decisions (Tsiotsou *et al.*, 2014). Using England's FA Cup as an example, it was reported by O'Reilly (2015) that the FA Cup was not able to find sponsors for the 2014–15 season because the 'FA magic' appears to have lost its sparkle and the brand is no longer deemed attractive. In this example, prospective sponsors believed there were better opportunities for sponsorship investments in other parts of the sport market.
- The personality of athletes such as NASCAR drivers, boxers and golf players align with the personality of their commercial sponsor(s); this often creates positive consumer attitudes toward the sponsor, and consumer purchase intentions (Dees, Bennett & Ferreira, 2010).
- Individual athletes can have their own brand personalities, which are often built over a career, based not only on sport performance but also on lifestyle. English footballer David Beckham is a good example of the power of an athlete's brand personality. Physical attractiveness, sex appeal, a celebrity marriage, working class roots and hard training created an image of a wholesome, clean-living, devoted family man – a role model for many fans and an attractive brand personality for sponsors (Vincent, Hill & Lee, 2009; Yu, 2005).
- A strong indicator of how successful an athlete's brand personality is relates to how much they are paid. Forbes (2015) reported the top four highest-paid athletes internationally are professional boxers Floyd Mayweather (US$300 million) and Manny Pacquaioa (US$160), followed by soccer players Christiano Ronaldo (US$79.6 million dollars) and Lionel Messi (US$73.8).
- Social media, as a marketing and communication strategy, often influences the development of brand personality. Walsh *et al.* (2013) reported that followers of NCAA Facebook page scored brand personality of NCAA events higher than those who were not followers of NCAA Facebook page.

In summary, sport brands can be perceived by consumers as possessing unique personality traits. However, attempts to develop valid and reliable scales to measure possible brand personality trait differences across various sport product and brand contexts have been mixed. Most studies have used Aaker's five traits model; however, the results have been mixed both in terms of the number of traits included and the adjectives used to describe each trait. These variations were largely due to the sport contexts, which can be categorized as: 1) sport teams; 2) sport events; and 3) sport activities. These are further discussed below.

8.4.1 Sport team brand personality

Sport teams often develop their own brand personalities when spectators and fans associate human personality traits with a specific team (e.g. a modern, successful, competitive sport team). Identifying the brand personality of sport teams can help marketers develop appropriate marketing and communication strategies. Research in the area of sport team brand personality is still limited. So far, there has been general agreement that the five personality traits proposed by Aaker (1997) are not entirely applicable in the context of sport teams, due to their unique characteristics (e.g. competing in sport leagues with rules and regulations), and their symbolic, hedonic and experiential nature, as discussed in Chapter 3.

Braunstein and Ross (2010) proposed the following seven traits in relation to sport team brand personality, which were developed and validated based on a sample of college students in the USA:

1) *Successful*: Examples of traits that define whether a team is perceived as successful are high-performance, dependable, superior, respected, reliable, mature and hard working.
2) *Sophisticated*: Based on the degree to which a team is perceived as stylish, glamorous, upper class, attractive or trendy.
3) *Sincere*: Expressed by the degree to which a team is perceived as honest.
4) *Genuine*: Relevant traits include charming, friendly and family-oriented.
5) *Rugged*: Based on whether a team is perceived as bold, daring and rugged.
6) *Community-driven*: Expressed by the degree to which the sport team is perceived as inspirational and service-oriented.
7) *Classic*: This relates to a team's traits being perceived as classic, traditional and old-fashioned.

In addition, Tsiotsou (2012) proposed the following five sport team brand personality traits (named 'SPORTEAPE'), which was based on a study of Greek and English fans and their relevant professional football leagues:

1) *Competitiveness*: This refers to fans' perceptions of a team as being capable of beating its competitors. It is associated with traits such as dynamic, proud, successful and ambitious.
2) *Prestige*: This is based on fans' perceptions of the team as being superior and well-recognized. It is associated with traits such as glorious, strong and honorary.
3) *Morality*: This relates to the degree to which a team is perceived as one that follows the codes of conduct and ethics. It is associated with traits such as principled, ethical and cultural/cultivated (often promotes the growth of cultural and educational programmes).
4) *Authenticity*: This refers to fans' perceptions of a team being unique and original.
5) *Credibility*: This expresses the degree to which a team is considered reliable and trustworthy. It is associated with traits such as wealth (financial) and influence (on the league's decision making).

The above two studies on sport brand personality have indicated that common traits exist among sport teams, such as competitiveness, successfulness, morality and sincerity. However, they have also suggested that unique brand personality traits also apply, such as community-driven and rugged, which were not revealed in both the studies. Such differences might also reflect the cultural contexts of these two specific studies (i.e. different countries), the different populations used (i.e. students vs. general population) and the different types of sport leagues (i.e. college vs. professional football league). Thus, while these studies indicate there is a general 'skeleton' for measuring the brand personality of sport teams, there are always going to be variations based on the context of each study.

8.4.2 Sport event brand personality

Established sport events can be considered as having brand personalities. Lee and Cho (2009) argued that the brand personality of a sport event is mostly developed based on spectators' interactions with team players or their performances. Furthermore, it has also been suggested that both positive and negative traits can characterize a sport event personality. For example, research by Lee and Cho (2009) on an NBA All Stars game revealed that some sport consumers perceived the event as arrogant and aggressive.

On conducting a study among US college students, Lee and Cho (2009) proposed the following five dimensions for the measurement of sport event brand personality:

1) *Diligence*: This relates to the traits of talented, determined, skilful, well-trained, dedicated and devoted. Examples of relevant sport events include the Olympic Games, the US Super Bowl, the US Open for tennis and figure skating events.
2) *Uninhibitedness*: Examples of relevant traits include daring, fearless, thrill-seeking, brave, bold, dynamic and extroverted. The X Games and snowboarding events are often associated with this brand personality dimension.
3) *Fit*: This relates to the traits of physical, athletic, muscular, be in-shape and strong. The US Super Bowl and Tour de France are most associated with these traits.
4) *Tradition*: The main traits of this dimension are traditional, classical and timeless. The Olympic Games and the British Open for golf have been linked to this brand personality dimension.
5) *Amusement*: This relates to the traits of entertainment, interesting and fun. USA's Super Bowl, NBA Playoffs and NCAA Football Championship are all associated with these traits.

A universally applicable scale to measure sport event brand personality across numerous contexts is not realistic. There is a wide range of sport events, which differ in terms of their size (e.g. local, national, mega events); nature (e.g. sport, hallmark, cultural events); and impact (local vs. national vs. international). Furthermore, there are some sport events where the brand personality is cultivated by the spectators (e.g. Super Bowl); while in others it is sourced from participants (e.g. a participant of the Boston Marathon). This is why Meenaghan (1991) proposed focus group research as most appropriate for developing brand personality traits associated with individual sport events.

8.4.3 Sport activity brand personality

The notion that a sport activity can possess brand personality traits has also been examined by some researchers. For example, Alexandris, Dub and Funk (2016) studied ski resort visitors in Greece and identified the following five brand personality traits in relation to recreational skiing:

1) *Excitement*: This refers to the degree to which the activity is perceived as appealing, interesting and enjoyable.
2) *Competence*: This relates to the personality traits of popularity, success and awareness (i.e. being well recognized).

3) *Sophistication*: This is expressed by the degree to which the activity is perceived as 'cool', glamorous and upper class.
4) *Ruggedness*: This refers to the degree to which the activity is perceived as fast, risky and physically demanding.
5) *Sincerity*: This is based on the degree to which the activity is perceived as authenticated, honest and original.

8.5 CHAPTER SUMMARY

The notion that one individual can differ from another in terms of personality is well established. Such differences are generally in the form of personality traits that can be measured to help understand the manner in which people think, feel and behave. Within the context of sport consumer behaviour, various traits that are context specific have been identified, allowing sport organizations to better serve and communicate with sport consumers.

The development of sport brand personality scales highlights the importance of understanding the link between a sport consumer's personality traits and the sport consumption context, as well as the traits of the sport event, sport activity and team. However, attention is required to enable sport marketers to maximize the use of context-specific brand personality traits through more customized measurement tools. This requires further collaboration between practitioners and academics to collect and interpret primary data on consumer personality.

8.6 DISCUSSION QUESTIONS

The discussion questions presented below are designed to help students review what is important in the chapter. You can answer them on your own, but they are also suitable for discussion work in small groups.

1) Discuss the relevance of the Trait Personality Theory for sport consumer behaviour, and use examples.
2) Examine Aaker's brand personality model by discussing its applicability to sport consumer behaviour.
3) Discuss the main criticism of Aaker's brand personality model in relation to sports.
4) How can brand personality be measured in the context of sport teams, sport events and sport activities?

8.7 CLASS ACTIVITY: SPORT BRAND PERSONALITY AND CONSUMER BEHAVIOUR

The class activity is designed to use information learned in this chapter to understand how sport brand personality influences sport consumer behaviour.

a) Select two NBA teams of your choice:

- Develop a questionnaire to measure the brand personalities of the teams.
- Have your classmates complete the questionnaire (aim to collect about 100 questionnaires).
- Analyse the data and compare the brand personality of the two teams.
- Interpret the differences found, using marketing and communication theory.

b) Find two strong sport brands that have distinct personality profiles:

- Examine and discuss how marketing and communication strategy have influenced the development of their brand personality.
- Find two of their recent commercials and analyse them with reference to how they target consumers with specific brand personality traits. Discuss the role of consumer emotions in their communication strategy.

REFERENCES

Aaker, D. (1991). *Managing Brand Equity*. NY: The Free Press.

Aaker, D. (1996). *Building Strong Brands*. NY: The Free Press.

Aaker, J.L. (1997). Dimensions of brand personality. *Journal of Marketing Research, 34*(3), 347–356.

Aiken, D., Campbell, R.M. & Koch, E.C. (2013). Exploring the relationship between team (as brand) personality and geographic personality: linking consumer perceptions of sports teams and cities. *International Journal of Sports Marketing & Sponsorship, 15*(1), October.

Alexandris, K., Dub, J. & Funk, D. (2016). The Influence of Sport Activity Personality on the Stage-Based Development of Attitude Formation: A Recreational Skiing Perspective. Submitted for publication.

American Psychological Association. (2002). Glossary of Psychological Terms. Retrieved from www.apa. org/research/action/glossary.aspx?tab=16

Austin, J.R., Siguaw, J.A. & Mattila, A.S. (2003). A re-examination of the generalizability of the Aaker brand personality measurement framework. *Journal of Strategic Marketing, 11*, 77–92.

Avis, M. (2012). Brand personality factor based models: A critical review. *Australasian Marketing Journal, 20*(1), 89–96.

Azoulay, A. & Kapferer, J.N. (2003). Do brand personality scales really measure brand personality? *The Journal of Brand Management, 11*(2), 143–155.

Barnett, L.A. (2013). What people want from their leisure: The contributions of personality facets in differentially predicting desired leisure outcomes. *Journal of Leisure Research, 45*(2), 150–191.

Braunstein, J.R. & Ross, S.D. (2010). Brand personality in sport: Dimension analysis and general scale development. *Sport Marketing Quarterly, 19*, 8–16.

Dees, W., Bennett, G. & Ferreira, M. (2010). Personality fit in NASCAR: An evaluation of driver-sponsor congruence and the impact on sponsorship effectiveness outcomes. *Sport Marketing Quarterly, 19*(1), 25–35.

Donavan, D.T., Carlson, B.D. & Zimmerman, M. (2005). The influence of personality traits on sport fan identification. *Sport Marketing Quarterly, 14*(1), 31–42.

Eisend, M. & Stokburger-Sauer, N.E. (2013). Brand personality: A meta-analytic review of antecedents and consequences. *Marketing Letters, 24*(3), 205–216.

Engel, J., Blackwell, R. & Miniard, P. (1995). *Consumer behaviour (8th edition)*. Orlando, Florida: Dryden Press.

Forbes. (2015). *The World's Highest-Paid Athletes*. Retrieved from www.forbes.com/athletes/list/#tab: overall

Hosany, S., Ekinci, Y. & Uysal, M. (2007). Destination image and destination personality. *International Journal of Culture, Tourism and Hospitality Research, 1*(1), 62–68.

Kassin, S. (2003). *Psychology*. NJ: Prentice Hall, Inc.

Lee, H-S. & Cho, C-H. (2009). The matching effect of brand and sporting event personality: Sponsorship implications. *Journal of Sport Management, 23*, 41–64.

Meenaghan, T. (1991). The role of sponsorship in the marketing communication mix. *International Journal of Advertising, 10*(1), 35–47.

Murray, P.N. (2013). *How Emotions Influence What We Buy. The emotional core of consumer decision-making*. Retrieved from www.psychologytoday.com/blog/inside-the-consumer-mind/201302/how-emotions-influence-what-we-buy

O'Reilly, L. (2015). *Why the FA Cup still has no sponsors*. Retrieved from www.businessinsider.com/fa-cup-still-has-no-sponsor-in-the-fourth-round-of-the-tournament-2015–1

Robbins, S.P. (2001). *Organizational behavior* (9th ed.). NJ: Prentice Hall.

Ross, S.D. (2008). Assessing the use of the brand personality scale in team sport. *International Journal of Sport Management and Marketing, 3*(1), 23–38.

Schiffman, L. & Kanuk, L. (2004). *Consumer Behavior (8th edition)*. NJ: Prentice Hall.

Stankovich, C. (2011). *What do your favorite sports teams say about your unique personality?* Retrieved from www.examiner.com/article/what-do-your-favorite-sports-teams-say-about-your-unique-personality

Tsiotsou, R. (2012). Developing a scale for measuring the personality of sport teams. *Journal of Services Marketing, 26*(4), 238–252.

Tsiotsou, R.H., Alexandris, K. & Cornwell, T.B. (2014). Using evaluative conditioning to explain corporate co-branding in the context of sport sponsorship. *International Journal of Advertising, 33*(2), 295–327.

Vincent, J., Hill, J. & Lee, J. (2009). The multiple brand personalities of David Beckham: A case study of the Beckham brand. *Sport Marketing Quarterly, 18*, 173–180.

Yu, C-C. (2005). Athlete endorsement in the international sports industry: A case study of David Beckham. *International Journal of Sports Marketing & Sponsorship, 6*(3), 189–199.

VIDEO FILES

East Coast Adventure Racing. (2011). *American Adventure Sports* [Video File]. Retrieved from www.youtube.com/watch?v=ZwCutPlyKcE

Jeep. (2014). Restless, Super Bowl Official Commercial www.youtube.com/watch?v=mHg9XSyd8Fo

NBA. (2009). *Where Amazing Happens* [Video File]. Retrieved from www.youtube.com/watch?v=CL8GjenvyKM

North Face. (2014). *Curiosity* [Video File]. Retrieved from www.youtube.com/watch?v=GNWkehVuO84

North Face. (2014). *The Journey is the Reward* [Video File]. Retrieved from www.youtube.com/watch?v=NnE1cau5U6I

North Face. (2014). *Your Land* [Video File]. Retrieved from www.youtube.com/watch?v=tll-4WONtg0

Olympics P&G. (2014). *Thank You Mom* [Video File]. Retrieved from www.youtube.com/watch?v=1SwFso7NeuA

Puma. (2012). *Live Life, Don't Watch It* [Video File]. Retrieved from www.youtube.com/watch?v=J4HuXzxaBIY

Puma. (2011). *Social Brings the Party to Tokyo!* [Video File]. Retrieved from www.youtube.com/watch?v=iuLn51d9AkA

Puma. (2011). *Puma Social Party* [Video File]. Retrieved from www.youtube.com/watch?v=Pcibjr5–6kY

PART 4

Outputs: sport consumer connections and satisfaction

CHAPTER 9

The Psychological Continuum Model

This chapter's objectives are to:

- introduce the Psychological Continuum Model (PCM)
- describe how movement occurs through the PCM
- describe the four stages of the PCM
- present marketing activities applicable at each stage of the PCM
- describe the correspondence between psychological and behavioural outcomes in the PCM.

9.0 INTRODUCTION

The decision to participate in a sport and recreational activity, attend a sport event as a spectator or purchase a professional sport team's T-shirt is based on a number of internal and external forces. Previous chapters of this book have discussed various internal concepts and theories such as motivation, perception, attitude and personality, as well as how the external forces related to a sport organization's marketing actions and other socio-cultural factors influence the sport experience. This chapter next presents a commonly used theoretical framework that integrates much of this information to identify how an individual forms a connection with a sport object (e.g. team, player, sport event, recreational activity), and how this connection may change over time.

Within the sport consumer decision-making sequence illustrated in Figure 1.1 in Chapter 1, this sport object connection is labelled as an 'attitudinal' outcome in the outputs phase. This connection outcome results from an individual engaging in a sport experience and forming new beliefs and feelings that alter a previously held attitude. The corresponding theoretical framework is called the 'Psychological Continuum Model' (Funk & James, 2001; 2006), which outlines a stage-based progression of sport engagement. To begin this chapter's discussion of the PCM, the following sample scenario is offered.

Mark's story is a typical account of how sport consumer behaviour is influenced and decision-making occurs. Mark's connection to basketball appears to be an element in

Mark is a college student and avid basketball fan. Each year he organizes a team of students to play in the intramural league at his university. He can be found playing pick-up games at the recreation centre most nights and weekends. During the NBA season, he hosts watch parties in his apartment or at the local pub, and attends games when he is home in Cleveland on winter break. Mark graduates next month and wants to buy himself a special gift for his upcoming graduation. While searching online for a new Cavaliers cap, he sees an advertisement for Nike basketball shoes at Dicks Sporting Goods. Mark decides that a new pair of Nikes is exactly what he wants and he clicks on the link to purchase.

his decision-making process to purchase a new pair of basketball shoes. This creates two questions. First, why does Mark's connection to basketball motivate him to purchase Nike shoes? Second, and equally as important, how did Mark become such an avid basketball fan?

Chapter 5's discussion of sport consumer motivation provided the necessary foundation to help understand why individuals choose to purchase and use sport products and services, which assists in answering the first question above on why Mark purchased the Nike shoes. However, answering the second question is more complex. Obviously Mark's connection to basketball did not happen overnight – it probably developed over time. Thus, to answer this historical type of question, a comprehensive framework is recommended to better understand why some individuals develop a stronger connection to a sport object than others. This is where the PCM introduced above (Funk & James, 2001) comes into play, as it outlines how an individual can develop a psychological connection to a sport or recreational object, and how this connection may change over time. It is important to reiterate here that the 'object' can be a sport team, player, league, event or activity.

Based on the importance of the PCM in terms of understanding sport consumer behaviour, the rest of this chapter provides an overview of the PCM, followed by Chapter 10, which provides a more detailed explanation of each stage of the PCM.

9.1 INTRODUCING THE PSYCHOLOGICAL CONTINUUM MODEL (PCM)

In the sport context, the PCM proposes that an individual forms a connection toward a sport object, and that this connection subsequently progresses along four hierarchical stages: 1) awareness; 2) attraction; 3) attachment; and 4) allegiance (Beaton, Funk & Alexandris, 2009). These four stages represent distinct psychological connections, as illustrated in Figure 9.1.

At first glance, the PCM shown in Figure 9.1 may appear complex. However, the diagram simply integrates the decision-making process previously to a horizontal manner. The boxes in the middle of the diagram represent the four hierarchical stages of awareness, attraction, attachment and allegiance. These stages represent the potential progression individuals may go through as they increase their psychological connection with a sport

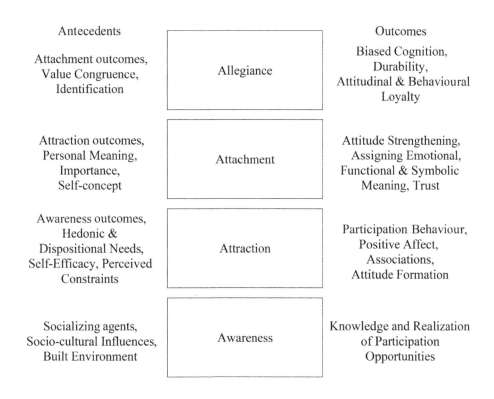

Antecedents		Outcomes
Attachment outcomes, Value Congruence, Identification	Allegiance	Biased Cognition, Durability, Attitudinal & Behavioural Loyalty
Attraction outcomes, Personal Meaning, Importance, Self-concept	Attachment	Attitude Strengthening, Assigning Emotional, Functional & Symbolic Meaning, Trust
Awareness outcomes, Hedonic & Dispositional Needs, Self-Efficacy, Perceived Constraints	Attraction	Participation Behaviour, Positive Affect, Associations, Attitude Formation
Socializing agents, Socio-cultural Influences, Built Environment	Awareness	Knowledge and Realization of Participation Opportunities

FIGURE 9.1 Psychological Continuum Model

object. The antecedents located on the left side of the diagram describe various internal and external forces that influence the stage-based progression and operate as inputs for each stage. On the right side of the diagram are outcomes that describe the connection stage in terms of attitudinal characteristics.

The PCM suggests that an individual may progress upward along the four stages via the influence of internal and external antecedents. It should be noted that outcomes from a preceding stage can also operate as antecedents in the next higher stage, which represents the feedback loop previously discussed in the decision-making sequence in Chapter 1 section 1.4.4. The PCM proposes that an individual reaches a particular stage based on the evaluation of personal, psychological and environmental inputs.

At this point, it is probably helpful to visualize a four-storey building with a lift to symbolize the PCM. In this scenario, the boxes in the middle of Figure 9.1 represent floors, and the higher up you go in the building the more connected you become. For example, the awareness stage is the ground floor where you enter the lift. The top floor, allegiance, is where you are fully committed. However, the PCM lift is unique in that the individual must visit each floor for a period of time prior to proceeding to the next floor. As a result, the individual cannot skip a floor, but the amount of time spent on each floor can vary and is dependent upon various individual and external factors. That is, vertical advancement and length of time one stays on a particular floor depends upon personal, psychological and environmental forces.

9.2 MOVEMENT WITHIN THE PCM

Continuing with the elevator analogy, movement within the PCM elevator results from a consumer consciously evaluating antecedents and outcomes. This evaluation process controls the direction and speed of movement. As a result, a consumer can move upward to a higher floor or move downward to a lower floor. That is, if you think of internal processing as gears and these gears move the elevator between floors, the speed and direction of movement depends upon the relative influence of each input and the unique psychological characteristics of the individual. The following sections provide a general description of movement in the lift context.

9.2.1 Awareness stage

The awareness stage is primarily created from external forces. In Figure 9.1, these are labelled as 'antecedents' and include socializing agents, socio-cultural influences and built environments in which the consumer lives. These are key inputs to create the initial connection. A detailed discussion of socializing agents and socio-cultural influences was made in Chapter 4 sections 4.1–4.4. In the sport context, the outcomes of awareness are characterized by knowledge and realization that a sport object exists. Returning to the story of Mark and his connection to basketball, the awareness stage outcomes can be noted by the phrase 'I know about basketball'. This level of basketball awareness subsequently feeds back, serving as an input for the attraction stage connection to develop.

9.2.2 Attraction stage

In Figure 9.1, the antecedents of the attraction stage are listed as awareness outcomes (e.g. in relation to Mark's story, knowledge and realization that basketball exists), hedonic and dispositional needs (e.g. fun playing basketball, taking a break from studying or working to play basketball, developing the skills required to play basketball), self-efficacy and perceived constraints. These antecedents represent a general level of knowledge and a desire to seek out opportunities that satisfy needs and receive benefits, as well as the ability to engage in behaviour related to the sport or recreational activity. For example, if Mark was to state 'I like basketball', this would illustrate that an attraction stage connection has formed.

9.2.3 Attachment stage

As presented in Figure 9.1, the attraction stage outcomes feedback serves as an antecedent along with other antecedents to develop attachment. Attachment forms when the sport object takes on personal meaning and importance, and becomes integrated into the self-concept. Outcomes of attachment are characterized by stronger attitudes, trust and the individual assigning emotional, functional and symbolic meaning. In the context of Mark, emotional meaning relates to joy and pleasure derived from the act of playing or watching basketball; functional meaning is when Mark uses playing or watching basketball as a means to an end, such as spending time with friends, and symbolic meaning occurs when he expresses to others an identity and self-concept related to basketball. For Mark, this connection to basketball could be represented by the phrase 'I am a basketball player'.

9.2.4 Allegiance stage

The outcomes of attachment feedback, and along with the antecedents of value congruence and identification, create the allegiance connection. Allegiance is characterized by subjective cognition in terms of how information and experiences are evaluated from, for example, a basketball perspective, such as durability and loyalty. That is, the meaning of basketball becomes more durable and has a greater impact on cognitive activities and behaviour. For Mark, this connection can be represented by the phrase 'I live for basketball'.

If we return to the example of Mark the basketball enthusiast when using the PCM stages, we can begin to understand how his connection to basketball is a critical element in his decision to purchase Nike shoes. The strength of his connection determines the impact of external and internal forces, such as the shoe advertisement from Dick's Sporting Goods, the Cleveland Cavaliers team, a star player on the team, a desire to get a graduation present, his university friends and the number of times he plays basketball each week. This helps answer our first question about why Mark's connection to basketball has influenced his purchase of Nike basketball shoes. The PCM can also help answer the second question as to how Mark became such an avid basketball fan, as we trace his progression through the PCM framework. The next chapter provides a more detailed discussion on the antecedents and outcomes at each stage of the PCM.

9.3 MARK'S DECISION-MAKING JOURNEY ALONG THE PCM

9.3.1 Mark's awareness stage

Mark's introduction to basketball occurred early, at the age of five, through a key socializing agent, his aunt Sarah. Sarah is a huge basketball fan of the Cleveland Cavaliers and when visiting on the weekends would watch the 'Cavs' play on TV. During these visits, Sarah would sit with Mark and watch the game, teaching him about the Cavs, the NBA and basketball in general. Over the next 10 years, Mark and his aunt often talked about basketball, which also provided an opportunity for the two to interact at family gatherings. Mark spent his primary school years playing basketball at school and in the neighbourhood with other children. But Mark also played football and soccer, and enjoyed many other sport and recreational activities. At the age of 15, Mark went to watch a Cavs game with his secondary school class and was impressed with the arena and atmosphere. Mark had seen many Cavs basketball games on TV; but until that moment, had never shown a desire for playing basketball competitively. Until this stage in his life, Mark knew about basketball, but did not prefer this sport activity to others. Mark's progression to the attraction stage began after his realization at the live game, when his parents bought him a pair of basketball shoes and put up a basketball goal in the driveway of his house. Over the next year, Mark began playing basketball a few times a week.

9.3.2 Mark's attraction stage

Mark began to realize that he liked playing basketball because it provided him with a number of opportunities to satisfy needs and wants. For instance, he was able to make new friends and spend time with his family because they would come and watch him play. Mark also liked the physical exertion required to play, and particularly enjoyed watching the ball go through the net. Mark also enjoyed the thrill of a close game, especially against teams in the Cavalier's NBA conference. Mark became one of the best players in the neighbourhood and during weekend recreational basketball games was usually picked first on a team when sides were chosen. In addition, playing basketball gave Mark a chance to get away from studying and weekend house chores.

9.3.3 Mark's attachment stage

Mark progressed into the attachment stage relatively quickly, and within a year began playing in community recreation basketball leagues and for his secondary school team. Basketball had become an important part of Mark's life and he attached functional, emotional and symbolic meaning to the sport. Mark would describe himself as a basketball player to friends and became a big fan of the NBA and Cleveland Cavaliers. As he entered college, he often wore basketball clothes to class, spent time playing in the recreation centre, followed basketball news and events using social media including Facebook and Twitter and joined a university intramural basketball team. Mark even joined a basketball student fan club that would attend and watch his university team's home games.

9.3.4 Mark's allegiance stage

Mark progressed into the allegiance stage sometime during college, as the strength of his connection to basketball became more durable. Mark thought of basketball and related activities daily. He always found time to play basketball and follow the NBA and his favourite team the Cavaliers regardless of university and work requirements. Mark's allegiance to basketball influenced the amount of mental effort he devoted to selecting and processing news and information related to basketball in general and the Cavs in particular. When Mark thought of leisure and recreation, this was always via a basketball perspective. As a result, it is understandable how Mark's decision to buy a pair of Nike basketball shoes for his graduation was influenced by his connection to basketball.

In general, the PCM is a stage-based framework that helps understand how a psychological connection progressively forms between an individual and a sport object. Yet, what controls movement upward and downward along the stages is often complex. The use of a lift analogy with gears and levers has therefore been used in this chapter to help illustrate how this movement occurs. However, few individuals beyond mechanical engineers really know the intricate workings of lifts. Most of us know how to use a lift and can push a button to go from the ground level to the second floor. However, the mechanical process involving simultaneous working of various parts such as pulleys, levers, cables, electric circuits and timing belts operates unseen. This is similar to sport consumption where we often only observe the type and frequency of consumption behaviour without observing the internal mechanisms that influence these behavioural outcomes. Thus, the next section provides a description of how movement generally operates within the PCM stages via the internal mechanism of an evaluation process.

9.4 THE INTERNAL MECHANISM THAT EXPLAINS STAGE MOVEMENT WITHIN THE PCM

The strength of a connection that forms within each stage of the PCM is based on an evaluation of external information and experiences created from engaging in some form of sport consumption behaviour (Funk, 2008). The evaluation shapes how external information and environmental cues from socializing agents are processed by the individual. For example, an individual can evaluate information about basketball that is communicated via mass media, advertising and friends (e.g. basketball is a fun, social activity to watch). In addition, the individual can evaluate basketball based on prior experience or expectations (e.g. I played basketball and it was fun). Although, ultimately the individual evaluates whether or not to like or dislike basketball.

9.4.1 The evaluation process

The internal process that governs movement within the PCM stages is the evaluation of inputs. This evaluation mechanism represents a collection of internal processes as previously discussed in Chapter 5 on motivation, Chapter 6 on constraints, Chapter 7 on attitudes and Chapter 8 on personality. This evaluation mechanism largely draws upon prior knowledge and experience to evaluate additional information, to determine if, and the degree to which, a sport activity provides desirable outcomes (Funk, 2008). Hence, prior knowledge and the acquisition of knowledge and experiences about a sport object largely control movement through the PCM. That is, the level of knowledge and experience increases as one moves up through the PCM stages. Influential sources in the evaluation process and stage movement are referred to as environmental and internal inputs.

Environmental inputs represent major sources of external information and consist of two main categories. In the sport context, the first environmental information category relates to a sport organization's marketing and communications. Sport marketing activities serve as inputs by communicating specific attributes and benefits of the sport product or service. For example, through advertising, Mark's aunt recognized how attending a basketball game would provide an opportunity to spend time with her nephew at a reasonable price in an entertaining environment. The second environmental information category is socio-cultural influences. Socio-cultural influences consist of information and recommendations received from family, friends, work colleagues and neighbours, TV, internet and social media that also influence movement by providing information about how a sport activity provides desirable outcomes such as fun, excitement, peer group acceptance and mastery of skill. For Mark, his desire for Nike shoes was most likely influenced by Nike commercials using a star player as well as his friends who approve of his decision to wear the shoes.

Internal inputs consist of two categories related to psychological and personal characteristics. Psychological inputs represent intrinsic factors previously discussed in Chapter 5 on motivation, Chapter 6 on constraints, Chapter 7 on attitudes and Chapter 8 on personality. Personal inputs represent individual specific socio-demographic characteristics including gender, age, education, ethnicity, family lifecycle, previous experience, income and physical characteristics of height and weight. The following sections describe the four PCM stages in relation to the internal evaluation process.

9.4.2 Awareness stage evaluation

Within the awareness stage evaluation process it is the sport consumer socialization process that describes how a sport object is introduced to an individual. In relation to sport consumption, prior research has generally attempted to examine socialization to answer two fundamental questions: 1) 'when' do people become aware of a sport object; and 2) 'how' do people become aware of a sport object (James, 2001). For example, the role of family in the story of Mark's basketball journey previously described is a significant influence on the introduction of sport to an individual. The PCM framework proposes that most individuals by the time they are adult consumers have learned skills, and possess knowledge and attitudes related to functioning as sport consumers in society. As a result, sport awareness is often created from a developmental process through which prior learning continues to shape future learning, contributing to various levels of sport awareness. For example, prior sport awareness levels as a child influence social learning as a teenager, and this level of sport awareness subsequently influences social learning as an adult.

Using the example of a sport team, the evaluation of awareness in relation to the team depends upon existing knowledge and experiences. Figure 9.2 presents an illustration of awareness toward a sport team. Each oval in the diagram represents a piece of information that a consumer is likely to know about a sport team. For example, most consumers

FIGURE 9.2 Sport team awareness

know that sport teams have coaches, players, play in a venue, cost money to attend games, win and lose matches, have a logo and mascot, play in a league and have a management structure. Yet despite this knowledge, if the information is all the consumer internally possesses toward the team, there is no emotion or positive affect.

9.4.3 Attraction stage evaluation

The second stage of attraction introduces positive affect and emotion in regards to a sport team. In the basketball context and Mark's journey previously described, he began to participate and/or watch basketball, internalize experiences, interpret and assign value and meaning to actions and construct judgements regarding various situations and people he interacted with. In the general sport context, the individual as a sport consumer has acquired more knowledge about the team and begins to develop a network of interrelated beliefs about the team. The relationship between the sport team and various beliefs held by the consumer can be illustrated as a spider web. Figure 9.3 provides an illustration of an association network for a sport consumer in the attraction stage related to a sport team.

The ovals in Figure 9.3 represent various beliefs the consumer may hold about a professional sport team. Each oval contains unique information about specific attributes

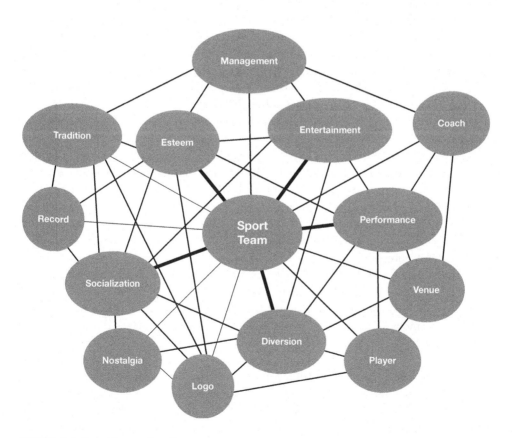

FIGURE 9.3 Sport team attraction

and benefits linked with the sport team in the consumer's memory and are similar to team brand associations previously described in Chapter 3 section 3.3.4 (Gladden & Funk, 2002). The associations can include team logo, head coach, star player, record, tradition, nostalgia, venue and management. The team associations can also include motives for sport consumption previously discussed in Chapter 5 section 4.8.2, including socialization, performance, esteem, entertainment and diversion (Funk, Filo, Beaton & Pritchard, 2009). It should be noted that each oval is evaluated by some degree of positive or negative affect, which can create a stronger link. This is illustrated through the diagram's line – the thicker lines linked to socialization, performance, entertainment, esteem and diversion indicate that a sport consumer knows and likes the opportunity to satisfy needs and receive benefits through the team-related consumption activities. This association network enables the sport consumer to use current knowledge and experience to evaluate new information and consider future consumption behaviour.

9.4.4 Attachment stage evaluation

The attachment stage represents a connection based on the emotional, functional and symbolic meaning assigned to a sport team by an individual. Attachment represents a dynamic and emotionally complex evaluation process where the influence of extrinsic situational factors is reduced. Within the PCM, movement from the attraction stage to the attachment stage indicates a fundamental change to the psychological connection. For example, socializing agents such as family are influential environmental forces in the early stages of the PCM (Funk & James, 2001). However, the connection changes because the meaning of the information and previous experiences are internalized into the self-concept; that is, the individual's image of herself/himself.

To help understand this change, it is beneficial to explore a process of connecting objects together through the technique soldering. In general terms, soldering is a process through which two metal objects are joined together by means of heating an alloy that bonds the two objects together as it cools. The soldering technique is beneficial for assessing the internal sport consumer process through which the sport attachment connection occurs in the PCM framework – it represents an internal bonding procedure that connects the different sport team associations. In the sport context, these objects can represent team brand associations (i.e. attributes and benefits) linked to a professional sport team as illustrated in Figure 9.3.

In comparison, in Figure 9.4, while the ovals and lines still represent the same associations as in Figure 9.3, the grey area indicates the introduction of the connective 'alloy' as used in the soldering process. In the sport team context, when an 'alloy' is heated, it melts and spreads among the various associations linked to the team; then as the alloy cools, it creates a bond between two or more associated links. The outcome of this process is that unique associations are bonded together – the previous unique associations are now interconnected. In this example, melting of the alloy does not damage the associated links, but they now exist in a collective bonded structure that takes on new meaning.

The attachment stage represents a connection based on the emotional, symbolic and functional meaning of the sport team more than unique associations. This bonding produces a psychological connection, which is more stable than in the attraction stage.

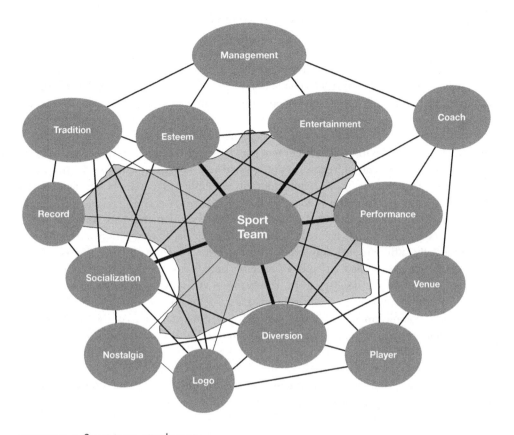

FIGURE 9.4 Sport team attachment

The enhanced connection in sport object attachment often results from internal forces such as personal values that are important to the individual, self-concept and trust in the sport organization to shape the evaluation process. These internal forces represent the alloy mixture within the soldering process. That is, personal values, self-concept and trust are the main elements of the alloy mixture that forms the bonding alloy presented in grey in Figure 9.4. In summary, the heating of the 'alloy' occurs from multiple experiences and evaluations, which, when cooled, bond the associations collectively into a stronger connection.

9.4.5 Allegiance stage evaluation

A beneficial approach to help understand the differences between the attachment and allegiance stages is to return to the process of connecting metal objects together; that is, soldering versus welding. Soldering has a lower melting point, requiring less heat to liquefy the alloy and produce the bond. In contrast, welding requires more heat and pressure to melt the alloy and bond two or more pieces of material. Another difference is that welding often damages or alters the shape of the individual pieces in the bonding process. As a result, welding joins material together similar to the process of coalescence.

Coalescence is the process by which two or more particles forge during contact. For example, when two drops of water touch they forge together to create a single drop. Think of a drop of water on a kitchen table. If another drop of water falls onto the table and touches the first drop, the two drops are forged, creating a single drop. In welding, coalescence produces an indistinguishable bond between two metal objects. For example, two pieces of metal are forged and become one continuous solid object. The two metal pieces are also altered during the welding process due to the heat and pressure to create the weld pool. In the sport context, coalescence accounts for the internal fusion of the structure created within the attachment stage to create a more continuous permanent structure. As more heat and pressure are applied (i.e. sport consumer evaluations and experiences), the psychological connection will strengthen. Hence, the allegiance stage connection is created from the welding process.

This welding analogy and description of coalescence demonstrates how the sport allegiance connection forms. Figure 9.5 illustrates the allegiance connection and represents a substantially different structure when compared to attachment stage connection in Figure 9.4. The unique association ovals have become fused together into more complex ovals related to values and self-concept. For example, the sport team is perceived as being linked to important values of self-respect, trust, belonging, warm relationships, self-fulfilment, accomplishment and security, as well as various definitions of the self. It should be noted that ovals representing associations linked to the team, such as SPEED motives and service attributes, are still present in Figure 9.5, but have forged with other ovals.

As described in the welding process above, the spatial boundaries around the unique ovals have become unrecognizable due to the bonding process. The integrated structure created within the attachment stage has changed into a more continuous, permanent structure. As more heat and pressure are applied (i.e. experiences and evaluations), the psychological connection strengthens, becoming more durable and impactful as the sport team becomes woven into the fabric of everyday life.

FIGURE 9.5 Sport team allegiance

The above discussions of the PCM and its four stages have laid the conceptual foundation to help answer the two questions put forward earlier in this chapter. First, why does Mark's connection to basketball motivate him to purchase Nike shoes? Second, and equally as important, how did Mark become such an avid basketball fan? The next section provides general information on sport marketing activities that can be utilized by sport managers at each stage of the PCM.

9.5 SPORT MARKETING ACTIVITIES IN THE PCM

9.5.1 Sport marketing in the awareness stage

Sport marketing activities within the awareness stage should attempt to position the sport product or service to accomplish two outcomes: 1) entice an individual to enter the PCM 'elevator' by knowing that a sport object exists; and 2) increase the level of awareness and incrementally build momentum en route to the attraction stage. At this stage, marketing strategies should focus primarily on marketing activities in relation to socializing agents. The primary focus at this stage/level should be on mass media outlets such as TV and the internet, as well as social media and word-of-mouth. For instance, marketing actions can involve proactively fostering sport object awareness by managing media relations within the local community, as the role of the media is an important element of brand introduction. The primary role is to use socializing agents such as family, mass media, community and friends to help create awareness of the sport object.

9.5.2 Sport marketing in the attraction stage

Sport marketing activities within the attraction stage should attempt to position the sport product or service to accomplish three outcomes: 1) attract new customers; 2) do more business with existing customers; and 3) reduce the loss or churn of existing customers. The following strategies are provided as examples:

• Traditional forms of marketing such as advertising and direct communication are useful in creating attraction, as this stage commonly involves search and trial behaviour. Traditional techniques can communicate specific attributes and benefits of the sport product to influence socializing agents as well as the sport consumer. Marketers can also utilize a range of traditional promotions such as discounts (e.g. two for one ticket), the win-loss record of the opposing team, T-shirt give-aways, live music and special events, including championship or all-star events, or signing of a marquee player. Cross-promotional efforts can also provide additional initiatives in relation to selling the sport object such as hosting a pre- or post-gathering at a local pub or restaurant. This social approach also provides the opportunity for social bonding, where participants can continue to share food, drink and their sport event experiences. In addition, other social marketing strategies including sport festivals and supporting events to provide various entertainment offerings (e.g. bands, gala and auctions) to create an inclusive, celebratory community component for the sport brand. The use of corporate social responsibility initiatives can also be beneficial in enhancing the image of a sport event and attracting consumers because it is a common expectation among consumers.

- Managing the sport experience represents another strategy to create attraction. First, service quality is important and when service delivery performs poorly at a sport event, negative experiences can result, creating negative evaluations. The knowledge, behaviour and attitudes of a sport organizations' employees are important for fostering attraction. The creation and implementation of 5-star service training programmes for volunteers and event day personnel is advisable. Second, the sport experience can also be enhanced through theming that involves the use of symbols, colours and decorations to enhance the sport event experience. The key aspect for creating attraction is to emphasize the role of positive experience from an initial trial behaviour, such as in the phrase 'I went to watch a basketball game and had fun'.

- Sport events can use corporate sponsorship as a vehicle to provide additional benefits to attract sport consumers. It can be used to add value without increasing costs by the sport organization such as via premium give-aways and lotteries. Relevant marketing communications should concentrate on building and reinforcing attractive attributes and benefits that sport consumers associate with a specific sport team or event. These sport marketing activities should provide repetitive advertising and information, encourage familiarity, offer a variety of inducements, create attention-grabbing point-of-purchase (POP) displays and, if possible, be distributed in multiple outlets.

- The emergence of the internet to initiate sport marketing activities has become an effective and efficient means to create attraction. The determination of what information content to provide on a website can be developed from understanding the psychological, personal and environment forces that shape sport consumer decision-making. The internet and social media represent a low-cost marketing mechanism for potential spectators to search for information during the pre-consumption search. However, such marketing activities will need to help sport consumers overcome perceived constraints that may prohibit attending or watching games during busy periods of their lives.

9.5.3 Sport marketing in the attachment stage

Sport marketing activities within the attachment stage should focus on personalization. Personalization basically involves customizing the marketing mix to selected target sport consumer markets to increase personal meaning of the sport product or service. The use of additional social and interpersonal strategies can help the sport consumer feel important and make the sport object more personally relevant. This can be implemented at the stadium operations or through social media platforms. Activities designed to learn sport consumer names, engage with them on a one-on-one basis, acknowledge them through special services, invite them to team and event functions and provide opportunities to communicate with players, owners and coaches are beneficial. For example, this could be done at fitness clubs by offering personalized services such as personal training for members. Social and interpersonal strategies can also be used to foster emotional and symbolic meaning, through forming running, hiking or cycling groups, using blogs and web communities to exchange personal information and experiences.

Customization strategies should also be used to personalize attachment to the sport object. In a sport team context, marketers can determine how consumer needs and benefits can be personalized and work to provide those opportunities. For example, the Australian Football League's Brisbane Lions has a number of membership levels with various attributes and benefits that allow fans to become more involved with the organization. In line with this, flexible ticketing packages and broadcast opportunities can also be offered. However, this customization approach requires detailed attention to a range of elements related to the tangible service aspects of the sport experience, including food choices at the venue, accessibility of parking, cleanliness of the venue, crowd control and safety.

The sport marketer should consider himself/herself as the event host and make the fan or participant feel 'special' and unique. Relevant marketing schemes include incrementally moving the sport consumer toward a better seat location, premium club seating, access to hospitality events, fan appreciation events and preferential parking and restrooms. Other means include a money-back guarantee to reduce the potential risk of purchasing expensive ticket packages or other related merchandise and services during the event.

Furthermore, web-based forums are beneficial for returning or exchanging tickets throughout the sport team's season, receiving information on new logos and mascots and purchasing personalized merchandise. These online communities and forums also allow sport marketers access to data on consumer satisfaction, feedback for personalizing and customizing benefits and services and tracking changes in consumer attitudes. In addition, online forums provide sport consumers with a voice, fostering discussion regarding sport event management practices and enhancing social interaction among members long after the sport event is over.

Sport marketing activities can also utilize corporate sponsors to move interested consumers toward attachment. For example, sport events can use sponsorship as a vehicle to integrate products and services such as cars, banks, mobile phones and restaurants into the personality of the team brand. Such integration can be personalized, allowing sport consumers to use, for example, a sport team credit card, ring-tones on their mobile phone, the homepage for internet access or VIP special events cards at local restaurants. In addition, corporate partnerships can be established to foster more involvement with the team. For example, fantasy sports leagues and competitions can enhance attachment with the sport team.

9.5.4 Sport marketing in the allegiance stage

Allegiance contributes to a sport marketer's ability to charge premium prices for licensed merchandise, tickets and registration, seating and amenities and corporate sponsors. In addition, most sport marketers continually have to face the 'leaky bucket syndrome', which is the loss or churn of existing consumers. It has been recognized that attracting a new customer is six times more expensive than keeping an existing one. Allegiant consumers acting as socializing agents have the ability to combat the leaky bucket syndrome as well as expand the customer base by creating awareness and attraction. Whether generating word-of-mouth or using formal marketing channels, sport marketing activities need to capitalize on the allegiant consumer. For example, an allegiant sport team fan may pass down season tickets to his/her children. Likewise, a golfer may decide to transfer their club membership to a sibling. Season ticket holders and members often have children and relatives who may be the next generation of allegiant consumers.

A key aspect for sport marketers to remember in fostering allegiance is to continue the marketing activities that originally helped move the consumer from the attraction stage to the attachment stage. In other words, maintain the marketing strategies that fostered attachment to the sport object. Sport marketers should focus on why the individual became attached in the first place and revisit the key reasons for why the passion and meaning of the sport object developed in the first place. For example, do not stop servicing the consumer needs. There are many customer loyalty and affinity marketing programmes that can be used to build sport allegiance.

The passion and meaning created in the attachment stage may fluctuate, but commitment within the allegiance stage generally endures. As in any relationship, whether it is between an individual and a sport object, or between two individuals in a relationship, the passion and experience of attachment is likely to fluctuate. Thus, the sport marketer must continually help the allegiant consumer revisit why they are passionate about the sport product or service. For example, attending or participating in a sport event is much like preparing and taking a romantic holiday, to rekindle the passion in a committed relationship. Based on this analogy, a committed recreational runner can renew her passion for running while preparing for a marathon event; a die-hard football fan can renew his passion for a team as it plays in the soccer league championship. The emotional, functional and symbolic meaning is also rekindled while watching or participating in the actual event (e.g. marathon or league final).

In addition, the allegiance stage will often necessitate the use of technology and a comprehensive information system. That is, sport marketing activities within the allegiance stage often require the integration of marketing within the overall sport organization (e.g. finance, operations, human resources). Allegiance strategies must therefore be consistent with the overall mission of the sport organization, as marketing is only one respective department with the business's operations.

9.6 PSYCHOLOGICAL AND BEHAVIOURAL ENGAGEMENT

This chapter has described the PCM framework, which identifies how a sport consumer's psychological connection to a sport object forms and changes. In general, this connection forms in a step-by-step developmental progression along four psychological stages of awareness, attraction, attachment and allegiance. As the connection grows stronger, a sport consumer's behaviour would also be influenced. The PCM can be used to examine both psychological and behavioural outcomes in relation to sport consumerism. As part of this, a linear relationship based on the four PCM stages can be used to understand how attitudes and behaviour should correspond. Here the PCM stages are placed in a linear progression of grey boxes, as shown in Figure 9.6, in relation to a sport object. This linear representation suggests that psychological and behavioural engagement is positively correlated.

Figure 9.6 illustrates how psychological and behavioural outcomes increase as the sport consumer progresses through the stages of the PCM (Funk, Beaton & Pritchard, 2011).

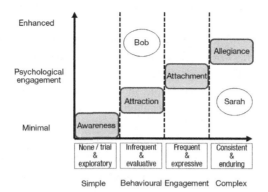

FIGURE 9.6 Correspondence between sport consumer's attitude and behaviour within the PCM

The level of psychological engagement is represented on the vertical axis and ranges from 'minimal' to 'enhanced' – it represents the degree of attitude formation that has occurred. As the sport consumer moves upward through the PCM stages, his/her attitude changes, becoming more highly formed. Behavioural engagement is represented on the horizontal axis and ranges from 'simple' to 'complex', which is further divided into four boxes to represent the type and frequency of consumption activities, progressing from trial and exploratory, to infrequent and evaluative, to frequent and expressive, to consistent and enduring.

9.6.1 Psychological and behavioural engagement – using golf as an example

The example of engagement in recreational golf will help illustrate the sport consumer progression shown in Figure 9.6. Initially, awareness of golf is based more upon preconceptions of the game created from various socializing agents and information sources than actual direct experiences. Minimal attitude formation has occurred at this initial awareness stage, as indicated by the phrase 'I know about golf'. Behavioural engagement occurs through search and trial behaviour, and can range from non-existent to unplanned, and corresponds to limited knowledge and minimal prior experiences with golf. For example, the individual may know about golf as a recreational and professional sport, may have played a bit of golf during a work-related function, or played putt-putt golf, or even watched a golf event on TV.

The attraction stage occurs when an individual evaluates the merits of golf in terms of obtaining benefits and satisfying needs, which introduces an emotional element to the connection. Psychological engagement is enhanced as the previous weak attitude toward golf changes and continues to form and take shape. This creates psychological engagement, such as 'I like golf' or the opposing 'golf is a bit ordinary'. Behavioural engagement ranges from infrequent to what is required to participate and increases through learning and evaluation. This occurs as the consumer begins to participate and watch golf, internalize golf experiences, interpret and assign value and meaning to golf actions, learn golf rules and etiquette and interact with fellow golfers via mutual experiences. For example, the consumer would like to play more golf so they can learn the rules and etiquette, be able to play better and not embarrass herself/himself, enjoy the outdoors, spend time with friends and family and network with work colleagues and potential clients.

The connection to golf in the attachment stage is when it becomes more meaningful. This is where the individual begins to define him or herself in terms of being a golfer, such as 'I am a golfer'. Behavioural engagement increases in complexity as the type of golf behaviours performed and their frequency are linked to functional, emotional and symbolic meaning. Behaviour becomes standard and repetitive, creating opportunities for self-expression that can form the basis of behaviour related to self-developmental tasks and integration within the subculture of golf. Although behaviours may still fluctuate due to traits and values that the consumer already possesses as part of self-concept, behaviours will generally conform to the norms and expectations that exist within the golf community. For example, playing golf once a month, buying golf clubs, wearing golf-related clothing to work and other non-related activities, subscribing to *Golf Digest*, following the PGA and European tour on the internet, watching the British Open, and joining a golf club are all examples of expressive and frequent behaviour.

The final stage of allegiance represents an attitude that is highly formed. This creates the most enhanced level of psychological engagement and the statement 'I live for golf' embodies this level of engagement. Behavioural engagement also increases in complexity as the behavioural actions that occur in attachment continue to increase in terms of breadth, depth and frequency. Behavioural engagement forms the basis of continuance that represents behavioural consistency in terms of complex actions that are enduring and consistent. For example, an allegiant golfer would frequently play golf, consume golf media and purchase a wide range of golf merchandise and most likely play golf over a number of years.

The preceding golf example provides an example of how a consumer's connection with a sport object progressively develops. This progression is depicted as occurring in a linear fashion with corresponding levels of psychological and behavioural engagement. However, it should be noted that human behaviour is often complex and rarely follows such a simplified linear pattern. In addition, some behaviour is more difficult to perform or differs from one individual to the next, such as watching a sport event live versus watching it on TV. Thus, Figure 9.6 includes dotted lines that separate each stage into boundaries, to indicate that psychological and behavioural engagement may not follow such a simplified linear progression.

9.6.2 Psychological and behavioural engagement – using the sport spectator as an example

This next example illustrates a professional sport and will further clarify the impact of psychological and behavioural engagement on the sport consumer. Bob is a die-hard English Football League Manchester United fan, but only attends a few games during the season, mainly on the weekends. In Figure 9.6, this is represented by the oval labelled 'Bob'. Bob's behaviour would place him in the attraction stage, but as a loyal team supporter, he also has a strong psychological connection as found in the allegiance stage.

Bob would therefore be considered a latent loyal consumer – strong psychological connection but weak observed behaviour. The inconsistency observed between psychological engagement and actual game attendance may occur because of various constraints that Bob has or perceives such as family, injury, work, money and lack of friends to attend with.

Bob's example is next compared with Sarah, who goes to every Manchester United match during the season. This is represented by the oval labelled 'Sarah' in Figure 9.6. Sarah's behaviour in terms of attending games would suggest she is in the allegiance stage. However, Sarah admits that she does not really care about Manchester United as a team and only attends and watches matches to spend time with her friends and have a good time. Hence, Sarah's behaviour appears to be enduring and routine, but her psychological connection to the team is similar to that found in the attraction stage. Sarah would be considered a spuriously loyal consumer – weak psychological connection but strong observed behaviour. These two examples highlight the importance of considering multiple spectatorship behaviours in terms of breadth and depth, and not just frequency.

9.6.3 Psychological and behavioural engagement – using sport participation as an example

Within participant sport, one can also observe similar inconsistent patterns between psychological and behavioural engagement. For example, Sarah jogs 5 km – five times a week after work – and would appear to be in the allegiance stage of the PCM in relation to recreational running. However, Sarah finds no joy in 'pounding the pavement' five times a week and only runs this frequently to gain positive exercise-related health benefits. Hence, Sarah is actually in the attraction stage of the PCM as depicted in Figure 9.6. In fact, if Sarah could figure out how to eat more healthily at lunch and dinner, running would be reduced to a few times a week and replaced with a good movie. The inconsistent pattern emerges because Sarah jogs because her doctor insists that cardiovascular exercise is needed to avoid heart issues, which run in her family. As a result, Sarah would be considered spuriously loyal to recreational running.

Bob represents a latent loyal consumer in relation to recreational golf. Bob loves golf, placing him in the allegiance stage of the PCM. He watches golf on TV, reads *Golf Digest* weekly, wears golf polo shirts to work and talks about golf constantly to his friends and workmates. However, Bob has not played golf for six months at his local 18-hole course. He only plays golf every few months in order to network with business partners. From a golf course management perspective, Bob's behavioural pattern in terms of actual rounds played per year would put him in the attraction stage of the PCM; but this would be incorrect. This example illustrates the importance of understanding the type and frequency of behaviour that is relevant to a sport marketer in order to better identify how to promote a sport experience to a customer.

In general, attitudes and behaviours are correlated, as was discussed in Chapter 7 section 7.1. That is, we can generally observe a sport consumer's behaviour and make inferences about what he/she likes and make predictions about future consumption actions (Funk *et al.*, 2011). However, the examples provided above illustrate how an individual's behavioural engagement level sometimes does not match her/his psychological engagement level. Most often, an enhanced psychological engagement does not correspond with greater behavioural complexity, making the engagement relationship appear vertical, as was highlighted by the dotted lines in Figure 9.6. As a result, it is important to identify the breadth and depth of behaviour, as well as those behavioural acts that are more restrictive to perform (e.g. paying 18 holes of golf vs watching golf on TV). In addition, in order to understand an observed behaviour, one must determine the personal meaning placed on that behaviour by the consumer. In other words, behaviour itself is not as important as the personal meaning a sport consumer attaches to the behaviour.

9.7 CHAPTER SUMMARY

This chapter introduced the PCM to help understand how a psychological connection toward a sport or recreational activity develops. The PCM is a stage-based framework and proposes that an individual may progress upward along four hierarchical stages: 1) awareness; 2) attraction; 3) attachment; and 4) allegiance. Each stage represents a stronger attitudinal connection with unique antecedents and outcomes. Awareness occurs from the influence of social learning and socializing agents that introduce the sport team or recreational activity and shape initial attitude formation. The attraction stage indicates that further attitude formation and change has occurred, and creates positive associations and knowledge that opportunities to satisfy needs and benefits can be acquired through behavioural engagement. The attachment stage occurs through internalization, as the connection is based on emotional, functional and symbolic meaning. The final stage of allegiance represents a highly formed attitude that is resistant to change, stable across context and time, influential on the cognitive processing of information and predictive of behaviour.

Potential movement within the stage-based framework is based on how an individual evaluates personal, psychological and environmental inputs. The evaluation process that occurs within each stage is an important mechanism that accounts for observed behaviours among different sport consumers. Relevant marketing strategies at each PCM stage were also discussed to provide ideas to sport marketers to facilitate movement upward with the PCM. Finally, a discussion of how attitudinal and behavioural outcomes may or may not correspond as the individual progresses through the stages has been provided. The next chapter will provide a detailed discussion of each of the four PCM stages.

DISCUSSION QUESTIONS

The discussion questions presented below are designed to help students review what is important in the chapter. You can answer them on your own, but they are also suitable for discussion work in small groups.

1) What are the different antecedents and outcomes for each stage of the PCM?
2) What is the internal mechanism that accounts for movement within the PCM framework and how does it differ between stages?
3) What sport marketing activities could be utilized to help a consumer progress from the awareness stage to the attraction stage?

4) What type of sport marketing strategies could be implemented to help a consumer progress from attraction to attachment stage?
5) Why does psychological and behavioural engagement change as the sport consumer progresses up the PCM?

CLASS ACTIVITY: PCM

Three class activities are designed to use information learned in this chapter to identify and promote a stronger psychological connection to a sport organization. The fourth activity is designed to explore how new technology in the form of a wearable fitness device can influence attitudes and behaviour toward a recreational activity.

a) Identify potential transitional stages within the PCM. These stages could be used to identify individuals ready to transition upward or downward to a new stage.
b) How could marketers persuade a regular professional football fan to become a basketball fan?
c) As head of marketing for a professional football club, you have been asked to develop an affinity marketing programme with the intent of facilitating sport team allegiance. Detail two marketing activities that could be implemented.
d) Apple introduced an Apple Watch Sport line in 2015 with the marketing strategy of promoting health and fitness. Click on this link (http://abcnews.go.com/Technology/inside-apples-top-secret-health-fitness-lab-apple/story?id=29765653), which takes you to a short video on the research that was used to develop the watch. Discuss how an Apple Watch Sport could influence individuals at different stages of the PCM framework.

REFERENCES

Beaton, A., Funk, D.C. & Alexandris, A. (2009). Operationalizing a theory of participation in physically active leisure. *Journal of Leisure Research, 41*, 177–203.

Funk, D.C. (2008). *Consumer Behaviour for Sport & Events: Marketing Action.* Jordon Hill, Oxford Elsevier: UK.

Funk, D.C., Beaton, A.A. & Pritchard, M. (2011). The stage-based development of physically active leisure: A recreational golf context. *Journal of Leisure Research, 43*, 268–269.

Funk, D.C., Filo, K., Beaton, A. & Pritchard, M. (2009). Measuring motives for sport event attendance: Bridging the academic-practitioner divide. *Sport Marketing Quarterly, 18*, 126–138.

Funk, D.C. & James, J. (2001). The psychological continuum model: A conceptual framework for understanding an individual's psychological connection to sport. *Sport Management Review, 2*, 119–150.

Funk, D.C. & James, J., (2006). Consumer loyalty: The meaning of attachment in the development of sport team allegiance. *Journal of Sport Management, 20*, 189–217.

Gladden, J.M. & Funk, D.C. (2002). Developing an understanding of brand associations in team sport: Empirical evidence from consumers of professional sport. *Journal of Sport Management, 16*(1), 54–81.

James, J.D. (2001). The role of cognitive development and socialization in the initial development of team loyalty. *Leisure Sciences, 23*, 233–262.

CHAPTER 10

Stages of the Psychological Continuum Model

This chapter's objectives are to:

- introduce each stage of the Psychological Continuum Model (PCM)
- identify key external forces that operate within each stage
- identify key internal forces that operate within each stage
- identify stage-based outcomes within each stage.

10.0 INTRODUCTION

Chapter 9 introduced the Psychological Continuum Model (PCM), which describes how a consumer's connection to a sport may progress through four stages of awareness, attraction, attachment and allegiance (Funk & James, 2001; 2006). This framework is useful in understanding how the sport experience creates psychological responses in the form of attitude formation and change that occur before, during and after the use or anticipated use of a sport product or service. In addition, the framework integrates the sport consumer decision-making sequence previously discussed in Chapter 1 section 1.3. This chapter provides a detailed discussion of each stage of the PCM, with key inputs and outcomes that influence and define the stage-based progression. The following story has been used to introduce each stage, followed by a discussion of the relevant inputs and outcomes.

10.1 AWARENESS STAGE

Awareness marks the initial introduction of an individual to a sport object, which can occur at different life stages. As the below example of Mike illustrates, his initial introduction to the Offenbach Kickers (the Kickers) occurred from attending a football match with his relative Helco while visiting Germany. The PCM proposes that the awareness stage represents the initial point at which an individual forms a psychological connection with a sport object. This connection relates to an acknowledgement that a sport team or event exist; a general level of understanding.

In August, Mike travelled to Darmstadt, Germany from his home in Toronto, Canada to celebrate the 95th birthday of his partner's grandfather. During his visit, Mike's cousin Helko invited him to attend a football match on a Saturday. The match was held in Sparda Bank Hessen Stadium outside of Darmstadt, which is where the Offenbach Kickers (the Kickers) play in the Bundesliga. Mike has watched many FIFA World Cup matches on TV, but had no prior knowledge of the Bundesliga, the Kickers, nor had ever attended a football match. While travelling to the match, Mike asked Helko many questions about the Kickers, the Bundesliga and football in general. Upon entering the stadium, Mike along with other spectators received an official Kickers flag provided by the team's telecommunications sponsor. Helko also purchased a match day program for Mike and translated the information. During the match, Mike watched and learned how and when to participate in the rituals at the match, and was amazed at the exciting atmosphere created by 20,000 plus fans. Mike also enjoyed cheering the Kickers on to a 3-2 win in the 87th minute.

10.1.1 Awareness stage external forces

External forces at the awareness stage are primarily environmental. Sport consumers will form impressions and opinions from information provided by a variety of external sources (Eitzen & Sage, 2003). These sources are often referred to as 'socializing agents' and represent persons, institutions and organizations that communicate norms, attitudes and behaviour through social learning (James, 2001).

10.1.2 Social learning in awareness stage

Socializing agents such as parents, peers and mass media represent environmental forces that interact with an individual to convey and exchange information, social mores and values. Social learning influences the development of preferences for sport and recreation products and services from early childhood through to maturity (Funk & James, 2001). Awareness of sport objects can stem from observational learning, modelling behaviour, reinforcement of appropriate behaviour in a given situation and social interaction. In the case of Mike, his attendance at the Kickers game fits within the awareness stage and social learning. Mike knows about European football as a recreational and competitive professional sport, but has never played, rarely watches the sport on TV and only occasionally reads a story about it in the newspaper. However, he is now specifically aware of a Bundesliga football team in Germany, and the type of experience that results from attending a live football match. In this example, Helko is considered a key socializing agent.

The impact of some socializing agents is likely to lessen as an individual matures and transitions through different life stages, while other socializing agents will probably continue to influence and shape the awareness of various sport and recreation objects. The sport consumer's socio-cultural environment creates many socializing agents as in Chapter 4, described in sections 4.1 to 4.4. The following subsections provide a brief discussion of key agents.

Family and friends

Family is an influential socializing agent, with family members often developing similar preferences for sport leagues, teams and recreational activities. For example, if one family member plays golf, children or siblings will often adopt that activity. Parents are particularly strong socializing agents in the early years. If a parent is a fan of football or a team such as Manchester United, many family members will also support that team. However, as the child matures, peers also become key socializing agents, often based on the pressure to conform to the social group. For example, a teenage girl who plays basketball is likely to have a group of friends who play and watch the same sport.

Physical environment

The geographic environment has an important role to play in sport awareness. Geographic considerations often determine the type of sport activities that are most popular in a country (Funk, 2008). For example, an individual who grew up in Austria is more likely to ski, while an Australian is more likely to surf. Environmental considerations such as pollution, overpopulation, urban sprawl and drought also have important implications for accessibility to sport activities. For example, recreational running in large populated cities such as Mexico City or Athens is often marred by heavy traffic and a lack of open green spaces.

Mass media

Mass media can shape awareness by influencing the way individuals think and feel about their social, political and economic environments (Emmers-Sommer & Allen, 1999). For example, media coverage of a sport event often influences the level of awareness by controlling what individuals know about a sport event in the absence of actual observation or first-hand experience. TV, newspapers and the internet represent key mass media sources for sport consumers, which can influence awareness directly or indirectly via word-of-mouth or other socializing agents (e.g. friends, family and work colleagues). In particular, mass media becomes increasingly important in shaping the attitudes and behaviour of sport consumers as they mature (Pritchard & Funk, 2006).

Sport subculture

A sport subculture is a subgroup of society that self-selects based on shared beliefs, rituals and commitment to a particular sport or recreational activity. Schools and universities often have sport clubs that influence the introduction of sport through curriculum and programmes. Awareness of a sport activity occurs as information about a specific sport subculture is learned from reference groups (Donnelly & Young, 1988). Reference groups play a key role in such awareness, as the individual has less information and direct experience with the sport object. Initial awareness forms from positive or negative preconceptions and misconceptions about the subculture.

The PCM proposes that external forces are important for establishing a sport consumer's initial connection to a sport object in the awareness stage. These external forces include socializing agents, socio-cultural influences and the built environment and provide the sport consumer with information related to a sport experience. See Chapter 9, Figure 9.1. A sport consumer also possesses unique characteristics that may influence the evaluation of information from external forces. For example, the ability to evaluate new information is based upon knowledge and prior experience; however, an individual must also be internally motivated to evaluate the information. A number of personal and psychological forces influence this evaluation.

10.1.3 Awareness stage internal forces

Internal forces represent person-specific, intrinsic characteristics such as gender, body image, life stage, ethnicity, culture, personality and prior experiences. For example, physical characteristics can influence sport consumption decisions based on body type. That is, an individual weighing 100 kg and standing 80 cm may find team and contact sports more enjoyable than running and biking, which are more suited to a lighter frame. In addition, an individual's life stage in terms of being young, middle-aged, elderly, single, married or with or without children may determine potential sport opportunities. An individual may also find sports that are embedded in their ethnic and cultural fabric more enjoyable, such as basketball among African-American males in the United States. As another example, a British immigrant in Japan is more likely to follow a sport that resonates with their nationality such as cricket rather than sumo wrestling.

An individual's personality can also influence the evaluation of sport and recreation opportunities. As discussed in Chapter 8, personality traits can explain why a person prefers football, cricket, tennis, skydiving, bushwalking, skiing or yoga. It has been recognized that consumers often purchase products that most closely match their own personality. In most cases, personalities usually emerge in the early stages of an individual's development and often coincide with the awareness stage. In the sport context, prior experience and exposure to a sport product or service is important for awareness and can create positive or negative experiences in the initial stages of awareness.

Intrinsic forces also represent beliefs and feelings regarding the benefits of a particular sport product or service, which can be hedonic or utilitarian. Hedonic benefits are experiential in nature, involving emotional responses that are subjective and create a desire to satisfy internal needs or receive intangible benefits through acquisition. These benefits represent intrinsic motivation described in the Self-determination Theory in Chapter 5 section 5.4 and include sport motives described in Chapter 5 section 5.8. Utilitarian benefits represent the functional tangible attributes of a product or service that an individual desires, and can be a function of price, product features and accessibility. Utilitarian benefits represent extrinsic motivation described in Chapter 5 section 5.4 on the Self-determination Theory.

Self-concept is also an important psychological force. Self-concept is the interaction of how we view ourselves (own view), how we think others view us (perceived self), how we would like to be viewed by others (desired or ideal self) and how we interact with references groups and how we think this group views us (public self). The different perspectives on self-concept can influence how information is evaluated in relation to a sport experience.

10.1.4 Awareness stage outcomes

Awareness describes how external and internal forces influence outcomes such as knowledge and initial attitude formation toward a sport object. An illustration of the awareness stage outcomes was presented in Figure 9.1 in Chapter 9. The awareness stage as an output indicates how an individual has formed an initial psychological connection with a sport object. For example, you may know a great deal about a sport team and have attended or watched a number of games on TV, but still not have favourable feelings toward the team. In the context of Mike, he can now state: 'I know about the Offenbach Kickers'. Mike's awareness reflects a connection based upon the knowledge and realization that the team exists.

Awareness outcomes generally reflect a psychological connection with a sport object that lacks an emotional component. The level of awareness can range from simply acknowledging that a sport object exist, to understanding basic rules and etiquette of a specific sport, to distinguishing between different leagues, events and athletes, to being able to associate the sport object with specific geographic locations and corporate sponsors. For Mike, he may now be aware of the Kickers, but emotionally he is neutral or does not necessarily like the team over other sport objects. Yet the positive experience of attending the sport event may have a subsequent influence on Mike's future sport entertainment decisions.

10.2 ATTRACTION STAGE

The attraction stage indicates when an individual's psychological connection with a sport object has progressed from the awareness stage. Introducing another analogy in relation to Julie the sport consumer, a passage from the Beach Boys' song *Catch a Wave* illustrates how Julie became attracted to surfing (see below). Julie recently moved to San Diego, California from Austin, Texas, and works in public relations for the San Diego Padres of MLB. Julie has been aware of surfing for as long as she can remember, sourced from movies, songs, magazines and advertising. Now that she lives in San Diego where the surfing culture is strong, she is keen to give it a go. A work colleague invites her to catch a wave one Saturday morning and she agrees. Julie stops by the local surf shop to buy some baggies before she goes surfing. After more than a few attempts, Julie is able to stand up and rides her first wave. After one particularly long ride, she begins to understand what it feels like to be 'sittin' on top of the world'.

Catch a wave and you're sittin on top of the world!

"Don't be afraid to try the greatest sport around
Everybody tries it once
Those who don't just have to put it down
You paddle out turn around and raise
And baby that's all there is to the coastline craze
You gotta catch a wave and you're sittin' on top of the world"

Julie decides surfing is something she might like to do more often and enrols in four Saturday morning lessons at the local surf club. During her third Saturday morning session, she gets a friend to video her surfing and posts it on a video-sharing website for her friends back in Texas. After her final morning lesson, Julie decides to buy a used long-board and a rash shirt. A few months later, a friend she met in class invites Julie to stick around after surfing and play beach volleyball. At first she declines, but then decides to participate because she has always wanted to play beach volleyball. The next Saturday she plays volleyball after surfing. The next Saturday, only three months after catching her first wave, Julie decides to skip surfing at 6:00am and sleep in so she can meet her new friends at midday to play beach volleyball.

The emergence of Julie's temporary surfing activity illustrates the attraction stage within the PCM. The attraction stage represents an increased psychological connection with a sport object from the awareness stage, and results from the evaluation of internal and external forces. The outcome of this interaction creates interest and liking for a sport object because it provides opportunities to satisfy needs and receive benefits.

10.2.1 Attraction stage forces

Attraction forces represent newly established awareness outcomes related to the sport object as well as external and internal forces previously discussed in the awareness stage. The awareness stage is when acknowledgement that a sport object exists first occurs. Building upon this knowledge acquisition, increasing levels of awareness allow an individual to compare and contrast different sport activities, engage in search and trial behaviour and make the conscious decision that one activity provides outcomes that are more desirable (Funk, 2008). In the context of Julie the surfer, prior to moving to San Diego, she was aware of surfing but did not consider it a favourite sport activity. However, within a month, the introduction of external forces combined with internal forces helped shape her attitude and behaviour toward surfing.

The PCM proposes that external forces that create awareness stage outcomes remain influential in the other three stages; but this influence diminishes. The awareness stage connection represents the low end of the vertical continuum and as a sport consumer moves upward to higher stages, personal and psychological forces begin to have more influence on sport consumer decision-making. That is, as the sport consumer moves upward through the stages of attraction, attachment and allegiance, the relative influence of external forces weakens.

The attraction stage forces stem from characteristics of the individual and the sport consumption environment to create a person x situation interaction (Funk & James, 2004). At the attraction stage, sport and recreational experiences are considered subjective in nature and based on interactions between individuals and physical environments encountered during consumption. This interaction creates a sport experience, which involves a person's physical and psychological responses such as attitudes, beliefs, emotions and perceptions that occur before, during and after use or anticipated use.

To leverage this consumer attraction stage, many sport organizations attempt to design an experiential journal for consumers, to optimize the interaction between the individual and the contextual environment. That is, each interaction represents a touch-point where an individual encounters information or external stimuli managed by the sport

TABLE 10.1 Internal and external forces of the sport experience

An individual evaluates whether a sport experience provides opportunity to satisfy needs and receive benefits based on environmental and internal forces

Internal forces	External forces	
• **Psychological**	Parking	Management practices
socialization,	Food service	Special events
performance,	Venue cleanliness	Promotions
entertainment,	Quality of sport	Price discounts
esteem, diversion,	facilities/services	Nostalgia/tradition
self-efficacy,	Crowding effect	Marquee athletes
perceived constraints	Crowd control	Community pride
• **Demographic**	Technology access	Customer service
gender, age,	Destination attributes	Wholesome environment
ethnicity/culture,	Merchandise design	Sport knowledge
direct experience,	Charity/cause	Entertainment value
knowledge, learning	Athlete role model	Geographic proximity
skills and ability,	Price	Event/team success
physical	Heritage & culture	Media
characteristics,	Safety & security	Type of sport
lifecycle,	Style of play	Mobile devices
personality	Subculture	Mobile apps

organization (e.g. advertising, promotions, website, parking, venue atmosphere, concessions, bathrooms, email, social media and mobile devices). External forces are more tangible and include aspects of the sport experience design created by the person x context interaction via marketing activities and service delivery.

As a result, there are a wide variety of potential interactions with the sport organization that serve as antecedents in the attraction stage (Funk, 2008). Table 10.1 below provides a list of internal and external forces derived from sport-related research that can shape consumer attitudes toward sport experiences in the attraction stage.

The internal forces listed in Table 10.1 include psychological and person-specific inputs that influence the sport consumer decision-making sequence. Psychological forces are intangible and include hedonic needs and motives, self-efficacy and perceived constraints. As a hedonic service, sport and recreation can stimulate sensory arousal and pleasure (Holbrook & Hirschman, 1982). For example, playing golf versus basketball is different; watching a football match live versus watching it at a pub is different. Different activities can arouse different senses and produce different experiences. As an example, the SPEED motives discussed in Chapter 5 section 5.8 are listed as key psychological forces. Self-efficacy, which is a similar construct to the perceived behavioural control (PBC) variable, as discussed in the Theory of Planned Behaviour in Chapter 7, refers to an individual's belief in his/her ability to perform a required behaviour as part of the sport consumption activity. Based on this theory, as one feels more confident in executing various behaviours, positive feelings are generated. Perceived constraints are the perception of constraints and obstacles that an individual attempts to overcome, which were previously discussed in Chapter 6 sections 6.5 and 6.6. Person-specific forces are based on dispositional characteristics, as previously discussed above in relation to the awareness stage.

The complexity of sport consumer behaviour often makes it difficult to develop an exhaustive list of internal and external forces. The various internal and external forces that influence attraction are numerous. In addition to those listed in Table 10.1, there are many other forces specific to a sport or recreation experiences that should be considered. For example, technology can also shape sport awareness through innovation of equipment and services, and the movement toward online experiences and mobile devices.

10.2.2 Attraction stage outcomes

The attraction stage outcome represents a psychological connection with a sport object based on various beliefs, feelings and direct experiences. This sport connection helps individuals evaluate whether they like or dislike a sport or recreational activity, with three possible outcomes. First, actual performance matches expectations, leading to a neutral feeling. Second, if performance exceeds expectations, positive disconfirmation of expectations occurs and leads to satisfaction. Third, when performance is below expectations, negative disconfirmation of expectations occurs and leads to dissatisfaction. When the evaluation produces positive effect and the sport consumer volitionally selects a sport experience, the attraction stage has been reached. This evaluation process will be discussed in further detail in Chapter 13.

Using the analogy of Julie the surfer, her initial attitude toward surfing was weak, but over a three-month period her attitude continued to take shape as she devoted more psychological and behavioural effort to surfing. This formation occurred via learning and evaluation after she began participating in surfing, including internalizing various surfing experiences, learning surfing etiquette, interpreting and assigning value and meaning to her surfing behaviours, constructing value judgements regarding situations and people related to surfing, and interacting with fellow surfers via a mutual experience.

Attraction stage outcomes indicate the development of positive beliefs and feelings associated with the sport object. The association network formerly illustrated in Figure 9.3 in Chapter 9 provides a number of associations linked to a sport team. In addition, as discussed in Chapter 3 section 3.3.4, sport team associations represent thoughts, images and ideas that come to mind, which can be evaluated by the sport consumer as positive or negative. Attraction outcomes signify when a sport consumer begins to attach positive feelings toward various sport team associations, and begins to develop a preference for a specific recreational activity. For example, an individual may attend a football game because they believe the experience provides opportunities for socialization, which is a highly desirable outcome. Another individual may enter a 10 km running event because they believe it provides opportunities for personal accomplishment, which is highly desirable.

However, if the sport experience evaluation is negative or conflicting positive and negative associations occur, the connection may not continue to develop and remain unstable. A key characteristic of the attraction stage is that psychological connection with the sport object is still forming and preferences are not yet enduring. That is, the attraction outcomes are relatively unstable. A decision not to participate indicates a negative evaluation of the potential outcomes or the presence of constraints. For example, in Julie's situation, she decided to stop surfing and begin playing beach volleyball. This suggests attraction still represents a relative low-level psychological connection with a sport object. That is, positive associations with a sport object are present, but the association network is still forming and not complex (e.g. the 'spider web' is a work in progress). The type of unstable connection found within the attraction stage can often lead to behavioural discontinuation, as the greatest number of dropouts from a sport activity occurs within the first three months of initial participation (Guillot *et al.*, 2004). This timeframe corresponds with Julie's transition from surfing to beach volleyball – her connection with surfing was not able to withstand attractive alternatives.

10.3 ATTACHMENT STAGE

The next story below illustrates Alex's attachment to the Australian Football League's Brisbane Lions. Alex has moved beyond merely liking the team in the attraction stage, and the question is how Alex developed such a personal connection toward this sport team. That is, how did Alex transform from 'I like the Lions' to 'I am a Lion'? Alex is in the attachment stage of the PCM and places greater meaning on the Lions. For Alex, the Lions have become integrated into his self-concept.

The Brisbane Lions are important to Alex. Alex likes to watch football and after moving from Sydney to Brisbane, began following the Lions in the Australian Football League. Alex's initial attraction came from the club's success of three premiership wins. Over the past few years, Alex's friends and co-workers have noticed a change in his behaviour. Alex watches nearly every Lions game on TV, often becoming quite emotional during the game. Alex became a Cat club member to get access to tickets, visits the club's website and online chat forum for news, wears Lions merchandise to work on casual Friday and is rarely seen at the pub, supermarket or a barbeque without some sort of Lions gear. In addition, during every season, Alex contemplates getting a team tattoo. Alex feels that being a Lions fan is about supporting the team regardless of success. The club runs the Read to Succeed after-school clinic on Wednesdays, and during the off-season offers a monthly clinic to teach football skills and get teenagers more physically active. Alex enrolled in the Lions' Skills for Life seminar in conjunction with the local university.

10.3.1 Attachment stage forces

Attachment stage inputs involve attraction stage outcomes, self-concept and personal meaning and personal importance. In the context of Alex, this can be readily observed when he chooses to enter social and work situations that promote the benefits of expressing a desired self-concept related to being observed as a supporter of the Brisbane Lions. His psychological connection with the Lions is more meaningful because of an internal alignment between the team and Alex. The PCM proposes that as a sport consumer internalizes a sport object, the object becomes part of a larger, more complex network of associations that contribute to an individual's self-concept. Self-concept can include personal and group identities that are volitionally adopted and help define a sport consumer (Heere & James, 2007). Based on this, a sport consumer can choose to enter situations that promote the expression of a desired self-concept, which will satisfy how they view themselves, how they think others view them, how they would like to be viewed and how important reference groups view them. For Alex, the Lions still provide the opportunity to satisfy needs and receive benefits, but the team is now considered more personally relevant and important.

Personal relevance and importance refer to a sport consumer's level of attitudinal involvement with a sport object or experience. In general, consumers can have attitudes toward numerous products, services, people and issues, but some attitudes are considered to be more personally relevant than others because they have significant consequences for the consumer. For Alex, the team is personally relevant based on multiple interactions and experiences, and he will spend time and effort seeking out and evaluating further information about the Lions, as well as engaging in various behaviours such as attending games, using social media and wearing team clothing. Importance represents the consumer's perception of the psychological significance and value he/she attaches to a sport team (Funk & Pastore, 2000). As the perceived value derived from the team becomes more important, the attitude becomes more salient and accessible. Attitudes can fluctuate within a given situation, but personal relevance and importance serve to strengthen attitude formation.

Attachment builds upon the attraction stage by creating a stronger connection. Within the attraction stage, external and internal forces influence an individual to begin liking a sport object and engaging in sport consumption activities. Within the attachment stage, internal forces, especially psychological, begin to play a more influential role. As discussed in Chapter 9 and illustrated in Figure 9.4, the attachment stage introduces more passion and emotion, which creates stability and meaning to the connection through a collective strengthening of internal associations linked to a sport object.

10.3.2 Attachment stage outcomes

Attachment outcomes represent the emotional, functional and symbolic meaning a sport consumer places on a sport object (Funk & James, 2006). The story of Alex illustrates how functional meaning relates to the amount of relevant knowledge and direct experience that accompanies an individual's attitude toward a sport team. That is, a sport consumer can evaluate, interpret and assign value and meaning to behaviours related to the sport team. For example, Alex can now construct value judgements regarding how he should behave among other team supporters at games. Emotional meaning represents the type of affective reaction or potency of feeling that an individual has toward a particular sport object. For Alex, going to Brisbane Lions games allows him to experience passion and joy, as well as frustration and pain. Symbolic meaning represents how team-related behaviour conveys information about the sport consumer. For Alex, he no longer merely prefers the Lions team; by making it a part of himself, the team has become an extension of himself.

With the purchase or use of any sport product or service, there is an element of risk. As a result, most sport consumers at the attachment stage place a level of trust in the organization to adequately deliver the product or service to satisfy their needs and acquire benefits. Such trust can develop through a number of different factors including satisfaction. Satisfaction stems from the actual performance of the sport product or service in terms of matching or exceeding prior expectations. The notion of trust suggests that an individual who has confidence in the organization that delivers the sport product or service is more likely to invest emotional, functional and symbolic meaning in that sport object (Filo, Funk & O'Brien, 2010). For sport activities such as jogging or bicycling, trust can develop within the sport consumer through the experience of participating and satisfying the expected benefits. For example, 'I know that if I go running, I will feel good'.

10.4 ALLEGIANCE STAGE

The narrative below illustrates Kevin's allegiance to a sport event, the Lance Armstrong Foundation (LAF) LIVESTRONG Challenge. The LIVESTRONG challenge is a cycling and running event held every October in Austin, Texas. The personal meaning of this sport event for Kevin reveals a psychological connection that is durable and impacts behaviour. For Kevin, the LIVESTRONG still has emotional, functional and symbolic meaning found in the attachment stage. However, somehow the event's meaning has strengthened internally and become centrally embedded in his daily life. Allegiance represents the strongest connection within the PCM framework.

> It's something that's a big part of my life. A major event for me, my family, and the community. You look toward the calendar, like when you were in college and you had your 21st birthday, you had a date; like when you moved out of the dorms; and when finals started. Now it's when the LIVESTRONG Challenge is. Yes, I live for this event. It's on my calendar every year along with Thanksgiving, Christmas, and my son's birthday. I know what I'm doing the first weekend of October every year. Period! End of story!! And I know what I need to do to get there the other 11 months out of the year.
> (Kevin, LIVESTRONG Challenge, 3rd year participant)

Kevin's position within the PCM framework suggests external and internal forces have influenced his upward movement to the allegiance stage. The PCM defines allegiance as loyalty or devotion to a certain sport. Allegiance is commonly known as loyalty, which includes the core elements of commitment and continuance (Funk, Haugtvedt & Howard, 2000). Allegiance stage outcomes differ from attachment stage outcomes in terms of the extent to which the internal collective meaning contributes to a stable psychological connection with a sport object and consistent behaviour. As Kevin's story illustrates, the meaning of the sport event is woven into the everyday fabric of his life.

10.4.1 Allegiance stage forces

Allegiance stage forces represent prior attachment outcomes as well as personal values and identification. In general, personal values are concepts and beliefs related to desirable end states or behaviours regardless of specific situations (Schwartz & Bilsky, 1987). That is, the sport consumer will evaluate whether a sport or recreational activity is congruent with these personal values. In sport, personal values include self-respect, security, warm relationships with others, sense of accomplishment, self-fulfilment, sense of belonging, being well-respected and experiencing fun and enjoyment in life (Kahle, Duncan, Dalakas & Aiken, 2001). For Kevin, the LIVESTRONG sport event provides a chance to enjoy the fun and excitement of a sport event in a safe environment. While at the event or in other social contexts related to the event, Kevin feels part of a group that shares a common purpose to support the event, and Kevin gains a sense of achievement and self-respect. Supporting the event also allows him to foster meaningful relationships with friends and family.

In regard to the LAF event, three personal values were recognized: 1) camaraderie; 2) cause; and 3) competency (Filo, Funk & O'Brien, 2009). Camaraderie represents the solidarity and friendship developed by participants. Sport events provide a strong social component, which facilitates social interaction, allowing individuals to express a connection with others and integrate the self with others. Competency represents the physical challenge a sport event provides, along with the excitement and enjoyment of participating. It reflects the individual's belief in what they can achieve by challenging themselves physically, and provides a way to differentiate themselves from others via the training and successful completion of the event. Cause represents the inspiration and instrumental goal of participation, including raising awareness and supporting the cause. It portrays a self-definitional aspect, where participants use sport as a means to express themselves and support a cause in which they believe.

Adopting a sport identity is an important component in developing allegiance to a sport team (Funk & James, 2004). The connection and shared experiences a sport consumer feels with other spectators and fans of a sport team are often referred to as 'team identification' (Lock, Funk, Doyle & McDonald 2014). Sport research indicates that highly identified consumers are more emotionally involved with the team and more likely to attend and watch games compared with less identified consumers. In the example of attending a sport event, a consumer who attends the event does so to watch the game, but also to show support for a team. Sport consumers can use the sport event as a means to associate themselves with other spectators and fans, and categorize themselves within a distinct group. A sport consumer can express an identity with any number of sport objects including a team, a star player, an influential head coach, a recreational activity, an event or a sport league (Robinson & Trail, 2005). Scholars have used the term identification as a means to describe a meaningful relationship between a sport consumer and a sport team. This section will therefore focus on the concept of identification in a sport team context and how it shapes attitudes and behaviour. Chapter 12 then provides a more detailed discussion in relation to sport team identification.

10.4.2 Allegiance stage outcomes

Allegiance is the loyalty and devotion a sport consumer expresses toward a sport or recreational activity. Allegiance represents the strongest psychological connection and creates the most enhanced level of attitudinal engagement and complex behavioural engagement (Funk, Beaton & Pritchard, 2011) as previously shown in Figure 9.6 in

TABLE 10.2 Allegiance stage outcomes
Durability: persistence
Activation frequency and duration of the psychological connection
Cognitive activity that occurs daily, weekly, monthly, yearly, lifetime
Cognitive activity increases in a specific situation in response to information being encountered
Durability: resistance
Stability in the complexity of the psychological connection
Commitment – resist changing affiliation when confronted with personal, psychological and environmental inputs
Speed of retrieval from memory, personal relevance and importance to self
Impact: cognitive processing
Cognitive mechanism activated by the psychological connection
Creates information processing bias to ignore or suppress conflicting information by recalling fewer facts, refuting messages by generating counter arguments and favourable thoughts
Increases mental elaboration to evaluate and re-evaluate information to restore internal consistency and reduce tension if information conflicts with current beliefs and feelings
Impact: behaviour
Behavioural intent and actual behaviour activated by the psychological connection
Biased, behavioural response, expressed over time
Behavioural complexity in terms of breadth, depth and frequency

Chapter 9. That is, allegiance stabilizes the emotional, functional and symbolic meaning of the sport object. This perspective suggests that allegiance is the continuation of the attitude formation process that created the meaningful connection within the attachment stage. This connection is characterized by allegiance strength outcomes as further discussed in the following subsections (and shown in Table 10.2).

Durability

Durability of the connection consists of two key aspects: persistence and resistance. Persistence represents the degree to which a sport consumer's connection toward a sport object remains unchanged over a period of time. For example, a loyal sport fan will constantly think about his/her team all year round. In the context of Kevin, he has marked the calendar and continually thinks about the LIVESTRONG challenge and what it takes to get there. Resistance reflects the degree of commitment toward the sport event, which often results from increased knowledge, certainty in one's own opinion and consistency between feelings and beliefs. Resistance can also reduce discrepancy between one's initial belief about the sport event and conflicting information related to evaluating whether or not to participate in the sport event.

Impact

Impact is related to cognitive processing and behaviour intent. A strong connection can bias how the sport consumer evaluates new information regarding that object. For example, committed fans of a professional team will recall more facts in news editorials about the team than non-fans (Funk & Pritchard, 2006). The psychological connection in allegiance will correspond to behavioural intentions. Behavioural intent consists of a sport consumer's readiness to participate in a specific activity, and increases the likelihood of engaging in various types of behaviour (e.g. attend, read, watch, listen, purchase) related to the sport object. For example, an avid golfer is more likely to purchase merchandise, spend on golf products, actively participate and spend longer amounts of time playing golf. Over time, these types of golf behaviours will become more enduring and routine.

10.5 CHAPTER SUMMARY

The PCM framework provides a stage-based perspective on how an individual's psychological connection initially forms and changes over time. The awareness stage represents the point at which an individual becomes aware that a sport or recreational activity exists, and has a general level of knowledge. The attraction stage is reached when positive effect occurs, and is triggered when the individual realizes that hedonic and dispositional needs can be fulfilled through some form of consumption behaviour. The attachment stage represents the formation of a meaningful psychological connection generated when the sport or recreational activity becomes internalized into the individual's self-concept. The final stage of allegiance represents the strongest psychological connection on the vertical continuum, and is reached when the connection toward the team becomes durable and impactful, leading to commitment, loyalty and devotion.

10.6 DISCUSSION QUESTIONS

The discussion questions presented below are designed to help students review what is important in the chapter. You can answer them on your own, but they are also suitable for discussion work in small groups.

1) What are the key socializing agents that would influence an adolescent to play a sport?
2) What are the key environmental forces that attract individuals to attend a live sporting event or participate in a recreational activity?
3) The act of free will or volition represents an important psychological characteristic to distinguish which two stages of the PCM?
4) Identify and describe each of the three dimensions of meaning placed on a sport object within attachment, and provide a sport-based example of each?
5) What is the main difference between the attachment and allegiance stages?

10.7 CLASS ACTIVITY: STAGES OF THE PCM

The class activities are designed to use information learned in this chapter to describe how and why a sport consumer progresses through stages of the PCM and investigate how sport marketers could potentially influence this progression at a live sporting event.

a) Thilo is a die-hard Bayern Munich football supporter, and has been a member of the club since 1996. He frequently wears team apparel, follows the team online and on TV and his friends and co-workers are well-aware of his strong support of the team. Based upon the PCM, describe how Thilo became such a passionate Bayern Munich supporter by tracing his progression through the four stages and the types of behaviour that may have occurred within each stage.

b) The sport experience represents the interaction between the sport consumer, the sport context and the delivery of the product or service. Within professional sport, there are many ways sport managers can design and deliver the spectator experience to create positive interactions and foster a stronger connection. Table 10.3 lists various touchpoints that a spectator would experience when attending a live sporting event. Compare and contrast the relevance of each touchpoint across each stage of the PCM.

TABLE 10.3 Sport spectator touchpoints and PCM stages

Touchpoints	PCM stages			
	Awareness	Attraction	Attachment	Allegiance
Pace of game				
Duration				
Intermission				
Concessions				
Pre-game activities				
Post-game activities				
Noise level				
Mobile devices				
Time of game				
Venue				
Star player				
Team website				
Opposing team				

REFERENCES

Donnelly, P. & Young, K. (1988). The construction and confirmation of identity in sport subcultures. *Sociology of Sport Journal, 5,* 223–240.

Eitzen, D.S. & Sage, G.H. (2003). *Sociology of North American Sport* 7th Ed. New York, NY: McGraw-Hill.

Emmers-Sommer, T.M. & Allen, M. (1999). Surveying the effect of media effects: A meta-analytic summary of the media effects research in human communication research. *Human Communication Research, 4,* 478–497.

Filo, K., Funk, D.C. & O'Brien, D. (2009). The meaning behind attachment: Exploring camaraderie, cause, and competency at a charity sport event. *Journal of Sport Management, 23,* 361–387.

Filo, K., Funk, D.C. & O'Brien, D. (2010). The antecedents and outcomes of attachment and sponsor image within charity sport events. *Journal of Sport Management, 24,* 623–648.

Funk, D.C. (2008). *Consumer Behaviour for Sport & Events: Marketing Action.* Elsevier: Jordon Hill, Oxford UK.

Funk, D.C., Beaton, A.A. & Pritchard, M. (2011). The stage-based development of physically active leisure: A recreational golf context. *Journal of Leisure Research, 43,* 268–269.

Funk, D.C., Haugtvedt, C.P. & Howard, D.R. (2000). Contemporary attitude theory in sport: Theoretical considerations and implications. *Sport Management Review, 3,* 125–144.

Funk, D.C. & James, J.D. (2001). The psychological continuum model: A conceptual framework for understanding an individual's psychological connection to sport. *Sport Management Review, 2,* 119–150.

Funk, D.C. & James, J.D. (2004). The Fan Attitude Network (FAN) Model: Propositions for exploring identity and attitude formation among sport consumers. *Sport Management Review, 7,* 1–26.

Funk, D.C. & James, J.D. (2006). Consumer loyalty: The meaning of attachment in the development of sport team allegiance. *Journal of Sport Management, 20,* 189–217.

Funk, D.C. & Pastore, D.L. (2000). Equating attitudes to allegiance: The usefulness of selected attitudinal information in segmenting loyalty to professional sports teams. *Sport Marketing Quarterly, 9,* 175–184.

Funk, D.C. & Pritchard, M. (2006). Responses to publicity in sports: commitment's moderation of message effects. *Journal of Business Research, 59,* 613–621.

Guillot, J., Kilpatrick, M., Hebert, E. & Hollander, D. (2004). Applying the transtheoretical model to exercise adherence in clinical settings. *American Journal of Health Studies, 19,* 1–10.

Heere, B. & James, J. (2007). Sport teams and their communities: Examining the influence of external group identities on team identity. *Journal of Sport Management, 21,* 319–337.

Holbrook, M.B. & Hirschman, E.C. (1982). The experiential aspects of consumption: Consumer fantasies, feelings, and fun. *Journal of Consumer Research, 9,* 132–141.

James, J.D. (2001). The role of cognitive development and socialization in the initial development of team loyalty, *Leisure Sciences, 23,* 233–262.

Kahle, L., Duncan, M., Dalakas, V. & Aiken, D. (2001). The social values of fans for men's versus women's university basketball. *Sport Marketing Quarterly, 10*(2), 156–162.

Lock, D., Funk, D.C., Doyle, J. & McDonald, H. (2014). Examining the longitudinal structure, stability and dimensional interrelationships of team identification. *Journal of Sport Management, 28,* 119–135.

Pritchard, M. & Funk, D.C. (2006). Dual routes to consumption: Examining the symbiotic and substitutionary nature of sport attendance and media use. *Journal of Sport Management, 20*(3), 299–321.

Robinson, M.J. & Trail, G.J. (2005). Relationships among spectator, gender, motives, points of attachment, and sport preference, *Journal of Sport Management, 19,* 58–80.

Schwartz, S.H. & Bilsky, W. (1987). Toward a universal psychological structure of human values. *Journal of Personality and Social Psychology, 53*(3), 550–562.

CHAPTER 11

Sport involvement

This chapter's objectives are to:

- introduce sport involvement
- understand the origin of sport involvement
- discuss the types and nature of sport involvement
- describe how sport involvement is measured
- operationalize sport involvement in sport marketing research.

11.0 INTRODUCTION

Involvement is a term often used to describe an individual's level of interest in sport and recreation activities. For example, an individual who plays golf twice a week would be considered a highly involved golfer; whereas someone who plays once every six months would not be considered as highly involved. In addition, a fan of Bayern Munich football club who attends every home match, watches away games on TV and wears merchandise of the club would be considered highly involved. As a result, involvement provides a useful means for measuring attitudes and behaviours of sport consumers toward a sport or recreation activity, and can help make predictions about future behaviour. This chapter will therefore discuss the concept of involvement and its application to sport consumer behaviour.

Sport involvement represents an attitudinal concept. However, it generally has different qualities and meaning than sport consumer attitudes discussed in Chapter 7. Within the decision-making sequence introduced in Chapter 1 section 1.3, sport involvement is considered an attitudinal outcome of internal processing. As an attitudinal outcome, it reflects the degree of personal relevance a sport object has for a sport consumer and can range across a continuum from low involvement to high involvement. Such involvement can relate to the strength of personal relevance as well as the degree to which sport consumers devote themselves to a recreational hobby (Beaton, Funk, Ridinger & Jordan, 2011). For example, the individual who spends considerable time, effort and money playing golf each week would have developed a high level of sport involvement toward recreational golf. Sport involvement can progressively develop based upon positive and pleasurable sport experiences (Funk, 2008).

Sport involvement is also linked to consumer motivation as discussed in Chapter 5, which can help sport marketers to design sport products and services to enhance the experience. For example, the purchase, use or anticipated use of a sport product or service is very important to a highly involved sport consumer. This sport experience will have a high degree of personal relevance and he/she will likely devote more cognitive effort in processing external information and evaluating the sport experience. In contrast, a less involved consumer will consider the sport experience as having little relevance and will probably devote less effort in processing information about the sport product or service. Sport involvement has two characteristics. First, it is an attitudinal outcome in the sport decision-making sequence that reflects the level or degree of attitude formation. Second, it operates as a psychological factor in the internal processing phase of decision making by influencing the amount of cognitive effort directed at evaluating external inputs related to a sport experience.

11.1 THE ORIGIN OF SPORT INVOLVEMENT

The concept of involvement was introduced by social psychologists interested in studying how individuals evaluate information and make decisions (Sherif & Cantril, 1947). Subsequent work in the area of consumer behaviour has predominately utilized Rothschild's (1984) definition of involvement as a psychological state of motivation, arousal or interest with regards to a product, activity or object. The concept represents a useful means in numerous service contexts to understand how personally relevant a product, brand or organization is to a consumer. It has also been linked to customer satisfaction and purchase behaviours.

From a sport experience perspective, psychological involvement communicates how motivated an individual is to attend a basketball game, for example, how interested someone is in playing tennis or how aroused a person becomes watching a sport event. This perspective allows sport involvement to be measured as a psychological construct, to understand it as an attitudinal outcome, as well as how it shapes a sport consumer's internal state when making decisions related to attending sporting events or purchasing team merchandise. As a result, sport involvement is useful to measure preferences, commitment, and loyalty to a particular sport team, league or recreational activity (Kunkel, Funk & Hill, 2013).

The use of involvement to study sport and recreational activities became attractive in the 1990s due to its ability to examine motivation and predict intentions and behaviour (Havitz & Dimanche, 1990; 1999). Academic researchers focused on understanding the antecedents and behavioural consequences of sport involvement. The reason for this focus was that leisure is considered free discretionary time that can be enjoyed via many activities and situations; and an experience that can be engaged in at various levels and by a wide variety of individuals from diverse backgrounds and cultures. Among practitioners, the ability to understand what features of the leisure experience influence behaviour was commonly used to design sport product and services, and how to communicate this information effectively to sport consumers. For example, sport marketers are interested in knowing how to gain consumers' attention to communicate relevant information about attractive attributes and benefits of attending sport events or joining a fitness club. In addition, knowing which sport consumer is more likely to purchase team merchandise, watch games on TV and use the internet and social media to follow the sport team is important for sport consumer segmentation strategies.

11.2 THE CHARACTERISTICS OF SPORT INVOLVEMENT

Determining how involved a sport consumer is with a sport product or service appears relatively straightforward. One can simply observe and record how much time, effort and money a sport consumer spends on a specific sport experience. However, the characteristics of sport involvement are more complex due to the interaction that occurs between the sport consumer and the sport context (Beaton, Funk, Ridinger & Jordan, 2011). As a result, academic studies commonly use two types of sport involvement to examine sport consumers: 1) situational involvement (SI); and 2) enduring involvement (EI) (Funk, Ridinger & Moorman, 2004). The key difference between EI and SI is based on the strength or degree of attitude formation that has occurred and how it operates in the sport consumer decision-making process. This difference is highlighted by the psychological and physical responses that result from the sport experience. SI represents a condition, instance or circumstance, which stimulates a consumer to engage in a specific sport behaviour (Filo, Funk & O'Brien, 2009). The nature of SI is temporary and dependent upon the context in which the sport experience takes place. In contrast, EI is stable across both time and situations. As a result, EI has been shown to be a good predictor of behaviour in a variety of sport experiences (Doyle, Kunkel & Funk, 2013; Havitz, Kaczynski & Mannell, 2013; Havitz & Mannell, 2005; Kunkel et al., 2013).

As further explanation, the following scenario provides an example of the key differences between EI and SI. A member of Arsenal Football Club in the English Premier League would be considered as having a high level of EI with the club; irrespective of how many games he/she attended. In contrast, a resident of Holloway in London who knows about Arsenal but has never attended a match would have a low level of EI. If both individuals decided to attend a match next Saturday, they would both experience an increase in SI that would then recede after the match. However, the EI levels for both would not change. As such, SI reflects temporary feelings of heightened involvement that accompany a particular situation, while EI represents a stable attitudinal state.

Consider a second example of EI and SI related to CrossFit; a competitive sport fitness workout, (www.youtube.com/watch?v=eBvy_A2jTmk).

Assume there are two sport consumers, Sarah and Veronica, who like to exercise and stay in shape and are members of the same fitness facility. In this example, Sarah and Veronica have equally high levels of EI in relation to exercising; but their SI is different. Sarah prefers to engage in strength training and fitness at a local sport facility with a friend, and does not want to sign up for a strengthening and conditioning training programme at a local CrossFit facility despite its popularity. In contrast, Veronica who works out at the same sport facility prefers to hire a trainer to improve her strength and conditioning, and decides to sign up for a CrossFit programme at the CrossFit facility. In this example, Sarah and Veronica both consider the dynamics of their current sport facility experience and compare this to the potential CrossFit experience. Based upon SI, two different decisions are made. The opposing SI is based on the physical environment and peer influence at the facility, but is also influenced by individual personality traits, such as level of anxiety, sense of self-esteem and power of concentration. This example highlights why individuals may have equal levels of EI toward fitness, but differ in their desire to seek out SI behaviour.

The differences between EI and SI highlight the value of examining the sport experience from the perspective of the three sport design factors previously introduced in Chapter 1 section 1.1: 1) sport consumer; 2) sport context; and 3) sport management system. From a sport consumer behaviour perspective, EI relates solely to the sport consumer. The level of enduring sport consumer involvement is generally fixed regardless of the sport contexts or the quality of service provided by the sport organization. For example, a loyal fan of Arsenal FC is unlikely to change his/her level of support for the club across various situations such as attending games, watching games on TV, using the internet to follow team news and talking with mates about the club. In contrast, situational sport involvement is more complex due to the three sport experience design factors interacting to generate the physical and psychological responses that occur.

For consumers with low or moderate levels of EI, improving the pleasure provided in the interactions between them and the delivery of the sport experience can increase the level of EI. Positive sport experiences have the ability to incrementally influence EI levels over time; whereas negative experiences could erode EI. As a result, sport managers focus on SI in order to help build a sport consumer's EI.

11.3 MEASURING ENDURING SPORT INVOLVEMENT

Enduring sport involvement has generally been conceptualized and measured in two different ways depending upon the needs of the research. The first approach is to examine enduring sport involvement as a unidimensional measurement construct. The second approach is to examine sport involvement as a multidimensional construct with various attribute measurements, often called 'facets'. Both approaches conceptualize sport involvement as an attitudinal construct; however, the second approach deconstructs sport involvement into multiple facets to create unique sport consumer profiles. Further discussion of each approach is provided in the next section.

11.3.1 Unidimensional approach

The unidimensional approach treats sport involvement as 'an unobservable attitudinal variable that reflects the strength or extent of the cognitive linkage between the self and stimuli or social and environmental situation that mediates an individual's behaviour' (Rothschild, 1984, p. 216). Researchers use survey questions completed by sport consumers to measure sport involvement. A widely used survey is the Personal Involvement Inventory (PII) introduced by Zaichkowsky (1985). Since the PII was introduced, subsequent research has utilized shorter versions of the PII to assess an individual's level of enduring sport involvement. For example, Funk and Bruun (2007) examined why sport consumers registered for and travelled internationally to an Australian marathon event, utilizing five survey questions to measure participants' prior involvement in recreational running.

Table 11.1 presents an example of a condensed version of the PII that has been used in sport research in relation to running (Beaton *et al.*, 2011; Funk & Bruun, 2007). The five

TABLE 11.1 Enduring running involvement		
Personal judgement as to how an individual perceives a sport activity	Survey questions measured using 7-point semantic differential scales	Running is . . .
		Mundane__:__:__:__:__:__:__Fascinating
		Valuable__:__:__:__:__:__:__Worthless
		Not needed__:__:__:__:__:__:__Needed
		Involving__:__:__:__:__:__:__Not involving
		Important__:__:__:__:__:__:__Not important

semantic differential scales are used to calculate a summated score to represent an individual's level of enduring running involvement. This measurement approach is simple and efficient in assessing a consumer's level of sport involvement. As such, the PII is beneficial when researchers want to examine the relationship between sport involvement and potential causes and consequences. In addition, this approach reduces the number of questions required when a survey is administered to sport consumers.

11.3.2 Multidimensional approach

The multidimensional perspective of sport involvement is more complex than the unidimensional approach. However, this complexity often gives researchers the ability to understand different patterns of involvement among sport consumers through the measurement of facets. The facets allow for the creation of consumer profiles. Within the general study of consumer behaviour, Laurent and Kapferer (1985) proposed a multidimensional Consumer Involvement Profile (CIP) with a scale that included five facets of involvement: 1) perceived importance of the product (importance); 2) perceived importance of negative consequences/risks associated with purchase of the product (risk importance); 3) perceived probability of making a poor purchase decision (risk probability); 4) congruence between the perceived identity of the object and the individual's own identity (sign); and 5) hedonic value or pleasure provided by the product (pleasure). Each facet can be measured by using a survey given to consumers.

Sport scholars have since used the multidimensional approach to measure enduring sport involvement. Numerous facets have been used, with three main facets particularly beneficial: 1) pleasure; 2) sign; and 3) centrality. Specifically, pleasure is similar to attraction and refers to the hedonic value or enjoyment derived from involvement with a sport activity or object. Centrality encompasses interaction with friends and family, and the central role a sport activity or an object plays in an individual's life. Sign represents self-expression and the unspoken statement or self-representation/impression that sport consumers wish to convey to others.

Theoretically, enduring sport involvement is present when sport consumers' evaluate their sport experience as a central component of their life, and can provide them with both hedonic and symbolic values (Beaton *et al.*, 2011). Table 11.2 provides items used to

TABLE 11.2 Multidimensional measure of sport involvement

Measure specification	Facet	Example of items
Sport involvement (Beaton et al., 2011)	Pleasure	I really enjoy participating in sport.
		Participating in sport is fun.
		Participating in sport is one of the most satisfying things that I do.
	Sign	Participating in sport says a lot about who I am.
		Participating in sport tells something about me.
		Participating in sport is what defines me.
	Centrality	I find a lot of my time is organized around participating in sport.
		Participating in sport has a central role in my life.
		I find a lot of my life is organized around participating in sport.

measure each facet of sport involvement as a psychological construct. The survey includes multiple questions measured with 7-point Likert scales ranging from 1= strongly disagree to 7= strongly agree.

The unidimensional approach to measure enduring sport involvement is a preferred option for field-based research due to its simplicity and requiring less time for sport consumer to complete. The multidimensional approach is longer but provides more valuable and in-depth information that would be otherwise lost if treated as unidimensional.

11.4 THE USE OF SPORT INVOLVEMENT IN SPORT MARKETING RESEARCH

The majority of sport involvement research has been directed at characterizing sport consumers based on the composition of various involvement facets to create unique consumer profiles. The multidimensional approach can be used to segment sport consumers based on a profile of involvement facets rather than a using single overall involvement score (Beaton, Funk & Alexandris, 2009). A mean score could be calculated for each of the three sport involvement facets and used to create a profile. For example, the sport involvement profile for sport consumer 'A' could be high on pleasure, low on centrality and medium on sign. For sport consumer 'B', the sport involvement profile could be low on pleasure, high on centrality and low on sign.

The PCM proposes that in general, sport involvement profiles are likely to vary across the four stages of the PCM. That is, the awareness profile is likely to have low scores across all facets; the attraction profile will probably have high scores on the pleasure facet but low scores on the sign and centrality facets; the attachment profile will likely have higher scores for sign and centrality, and have the most diverse involvement profiles; the allegiance profile will probably have high values across all facets of involvement. As a result, each stage of the PCM has a unique set of profiles based on the level and combination of the three involvement facets. The appendix located at the conclusion of these chapters list the various facet profile for each stage of the PCM. The following section provides further discussion of how to utilize information contained in an enduring sport involvement profile.

11.5 SEGMENTATION USING ENDURING SPORT INVOLVEMENT PROFILES

Sport involvement profiles can be used within the Psychological Continuum Model (PCM) previously discussed in Chapters 9 and 10. The PCM provides a segmentation method to allocate sport consumers into one of the four stages to help examine different needs and benefits deemed useful in developing marketing strategies and customizing promotion activities. This method enables a quick and simple procedure for segmenting sport consumers into one of the four PCM stages: 1) awareness; 2) attraction; 3) attachment; and 4) allegiance. It has been well used across a number of sport contexts including recreational activities and spectator sport. Consider the Australia Sports Commission's (2013) visual explanation of the benefits of market segmentation for sport participation (www.youtube.com/watch?v=V0v92-JfpW8). The video articulates the benefits of segmenting people into homogeneous groups to understand different motivations, attitudes, needs and constraints that influence their decisions and participation in club-based sport in Australia.

The PCM staging protocol utilizes a three-step technique as shown in Table 11.3. The first step is to measure three facets of sport involvement: pleasure, centrality and sign using survey questions and then calculate mean scores for each facet ranging from 1 to 7. The second step utilizes the mean score for each facet to develop profiles of high, medium and low for each sport involvement facet. The third and final step employs an algorithm based on a configuration of 27 unique sport involvement profiles to allocate a sport consumer into a PCM stage. There are three sport involvement facets (i.e. pleasure, sign and centrality) that could be classified at three different levels (i.e. high, medium or low). The following subsections provide examples of this PCM staging procedure in specific sporting contexts.

TABLE 11.3 PCM staging protocol	
Step 1:	Measure three sport involvement facets of pleasure, centrality and sign; then calculate mean scores for each facet.
Step 2:	Create facet profiles of high, medium and low levels on each sport involvement facet.
Step 3:	Use staging algorithm to allocate PCM stage membership.

TABLE 11.4 Three facets of sport involvement

Pleasure	Hedonic value – the enjoyment derived from the experience or activity.
Centrality	Importance – how central the activity is to the individual's lifestyle.
Sign	Symbolic value – the self-expression value or level of symbolism that an activity has for an individual.

11.5.1 PCM stage protocol example 1: running involvement

Recreational running represents a sport activity, which requires moderately intense physical exertion, and is often chosen on a volitional basis (Beaton & Funk, 2008). The National Runner Survey conducted by Running USA (2013) provides insights into the demographics, lifestyle, habits and product preferences of the running population in the USA. As running becomes an increasingly popular activity within a country like the USA, it has the capacity to attract a broad range of participants (Du, Jordan & Funk, 2015). As a result, information beyond traditional segmentation strategies is beneficial in that it includes more advanced psychographic methods.

A sport consumer's level of involvement in running can be determined by measuring each of the three sport involvement facets described in Table 11.4 to create a specific sport consumer involvement profile. For example, data can be collected from a running event held using an online questionnaire after the event. Participants can be asked to rate their agreement with a series of sport involvement statements on a 7-point Likert scale, where 1 = strongly disagree and 7 = strongly agree. The sport involvement statements can be used to measure the three facets of pleasure, centrality and sign. The PCM staging protocol can then be used to place each sport consumer into one of the PCM stages related to attraction, attachment or allegiance. Next, the entire sample of running participants could be segmented into three different groups in order to make comparisons using other information collected from the survey.

The three sport involvement facets are also beneficial because unique information about the sport consumer can be obtained. Such differences are shown in Table 11.5, where even though participants A and B have identical overall sport involvement scores of 15, the individual scores across the three facets vary. Using an aggregated score approach, two participants would appear similar at 15, but it would be a mistake to assume both participants A and B have similar levels of running involvement. As a result, different facet profiles could produce different behavioural and psychological outcomes and the creation of segments should always be the goal.

TABLE 11.5 Running involvement facet scores

	Pleasure facet	Centrality facet	Sign facet	Total score
Participant A	6	3	6	15
Participant B	7	4	4	15

As shown in Table 11.5, participant B recorded values of 7 for the pleasure facet, and 4 on each of the centrality and sign facets. Participant B could therefore be described as someone who participates for the inherent pleasure of running, but does not consider running as a central part of his or her life, or as a tool for expressing their identity to others. As participant B mostly runs for fun, he/she is susceptible to changing preference to other recreational activities.

Participant A recorded values of 6 for pleasure, 3 for centrality and 6 for sign. These results indicate that participant A derives pleasure from running, and utilizes this activity to express an identity to other runners. Participant A does not consider running a central part of their lifestyle. Participant A may have initially started running for the enjoyment of the activity, but it has now taken on more personal meaning in terms of self-expression to others. Participant A is unlikely to change their preference from running to another recreational activity.

11.5.2 PCM stage protocol example 2: spectator involvement

The second example is taken from research conducted on the Australian Football League (AFL) (Doyle *et al.*, 2013). Information was collected using an online survey from 1,384 spectators who attended at least one match during a season. The survey contained questions related to league involvement using the three involvement facets as well as other demographic and behavioural questions. Each involvement facet was measured using three statements to ensure reliability. See Table 11.A.1 in the chapter Appendix for example statements of each sport involvement facet.

The PCM staging protocol briefly described and presented in Table 11.3 is now employed to place spectators into one of the PCM stages. The first step was to use information collected from the survey in order to assess the three facets of sport involvement: pleasure, centrality and sign and then calculate mean scores for each facet. Table 11.6 presents an example of one AFL spectator response for each of nine involvement statements used. There were three statements for each sport involvement facet and are labelled P for pleasure, C for centrality and S for sign. Looking at the pleasure facet,

TABLE 11.6 Step 1: Sport involvement item responses and mean facet scores

Calculating involvement facets

	Pleasure	Centrality	Sign
Item 1	P1 = 5	C1 = 4	S1 = 7
Item 2	P2 = 6	C2 = 3	S2 = 6
Item 3	P3 = 5	C3 = 4	S3 = 6
Total score	16	11	19
Average	Mean = 5.33	Mean = 3.67	Mean = 6.33

TABLE 11.7 Step 2: Creation of sport involvement facet profile

Classification of involvement facets

Low (L)	Medium (M)	High (H)
Mean score ≤ 4.49	Mean score 4.50 – 5.74	Mean score ≥ 5.75

there are two scores for P1 and P3 with a score of 5, and one score of 6 for P2, resulting in a mean pleasure score of 5.33 (16 ÷ 3 = 5.33). The individual item scores and mean scores for centrality (3.67) and sign (6.33) are also presented.

Once a mean score for each sport involvement facet were calculated, Step 2 of the PCM staging protocol was employed. Step 2 created a high, medium or low classification from the mean score for each sport involvement facet. The high, medium or low classification utilized intervals based on the work of Beaton *et al.* (2009) and Doyle *et al.* (2013). A low classification is when the facet's mean score ranges between 1.00 and 4.49; a medium classification when it ranges between 4.5 and 5.74; and a high classification is when it is 5.75. See Table 11.7 for classification ranges.

Based upon the information collected and presented in Table 11.6, the classification intervals listed in Table 11.7 were used to create the spectator's AFL involvement profile. The unique spectator profile created is presented in Table 11.8: pleasure at 5.33 is considered medium (M); centrality at 3.67 is considered low (L); sign at 6.33 is considered high (H).

TABLE 11.8 Step 2 continued: AFL involvement profile

Centrality	Pleasure	Sign
3.67 = Low (L)	5.33 = Medium (M)	6.33 = High (H)

Once the spectator profile was created, Step 3 of the PCM staging protocol was next employed. Step 3 utilized an algorithm developed for the PCM. The staging algorithm is presented in Table 11.9.

The spectator profile created in Step 2 and presented in Table 11.8 was used to place the spectator in the attachment stage of the PCM. The profile of centrality = L, pleasure = M and sign = H was applied to staging algorithm in Table 11.9. Based upon following the action sequence from 1 to 4, the attachment stage was determined. This means the spectator would be considered attached to the AFL.

The PCM staging protocol used in the above AFL example can at first seem complex, but it is relatively simple once it has been completed a few times. The following two additional examples using AFL spectators will help clarify the application of the PCM staging protocol. The first relates to Pat and is represented in Table 11.10. The second is for Cary as shown in Table 11.11.

TABLE 11.9 Step 3: Determine stage using PCM algorithm

Using the involvement profile in Step 2, complete the following six actions below IN ORDER until stage is determined.

Action 1: if **all** three facets rated low (L), stage = awareness

If condition not satisfied then next action;

Action 2: if **pleasure** facet is rated low (L), stage = attachment

If condition not satisfied then next action;

Action 3: if **both** centrality and sign facets are rated low (L), stage = attraction

If condition not satisfied then next action;

Action 4: if **either** centrality or sign facet is rated low (L), stage = attachment;

If condition not satisfied then next action;

Action 5: if **any two** facets are rated as high (H), stage = allegiance;

If condition not satisfied then next action;

Action 6: all **remaining**, stage = attachment.

TABLE 11.10 Pat's involvement in the AFL

Pat's involvement mean scores

Facets	Pleasure	Centrality	Sign
Scores	6.25	5.25	4.25
Classification	H	M	L

Consider action 1: Pat's involvement scores are not all low (L). As a result, this condition is not satisfied, so proceed to next action;

Consider action 2: Pat's pleasure facet is not low (L), so second action is not satisfied, so proceed to next action;

Consider action 3: both of Pat's centrality and sign facets are not low (L), so third action is not satisfied, so proceed to next action;

Consider action 4: Pat has a sign facet rated as low (L) – hence, fourth action is affirmative and classification is attachment stage.

The preceding examples in relation to the AFL illustrate how the sport involvement facets can be used within the PCM to place spectators into one of the four stages. They have shown that the process of creating a unique profile using the staging protocol for one spectator can be extended to generate unique involvement profiles for the entire sample of spectators. In the current example, this PCM staging protocol can be used to place all 1,384 spectators that completed the online survey into one of the four PCM segments of awareness, attraction, attachment and allegiance.

Table 11.12 displays AFL spectator profiles segments based upon stage of the PCM. The PCM staging protocol was used for all spectators in the data sample to place a consumer into one of four stages. Additional information was also collected on the survey

TABLE 11.11 Cary's involvement in the AFL

Cary's involvement mean scores

Facets	Pleasure	Centrality	Sign
Scores	6.5	6.5	6.5
Classification	H	H	H

Action 1: Cary's involvement scores are not all low (L), first action is negative, so consider next action;

Action 2: pleasure facet is not low (L), second action is negative, so consider next action;

Action 3: both centrality and sign facets are not low (L), third action is negative, so consider next action;

Action 4: neither centrality or sign facets are rated as low (L), fourth action is negative, so consider next action;

Action 5: two facets are rated as high (H) – hence, fifth action is affirmative and Cary's classification is allegiance stage.

TABLE 11.12 PCM stages and AFL spectator segments

Awareness stage:	Casual spectator
	Motivation: AFL
	Attends: 0–15% of team games
	Size of members: under 1%
	League I s. . .: 'not a large part of who I am, but it has a role as an outlet for socialization, expression, and fun'
Attraction stage:	AFL supporter
	Motivation: AFL then team
	Attends: 16–39% of team games
	Size of members: under 10%
	League is . . .: 'an interest that I enjoy – it provides entertainment and relaxation'
Attachment stage:	Dedicated team patron
	Motivation: team then AFL
	Attends: 41–74% of team games
	Size of members: under 30%
	League is . . .: 'one of life's great passions – a big part of my life'
Allegiance stage:	Avid team fan
	Motivation: team
	Attends: 75% of team games
	Size of members: Over 60%
	League is . . .: 'integral, I can't imagine life without AFL, it's part of the joy of life'

about the AFL and teams that play in the league. This information was used to help describe each segment as shown in the right-hand column. Each segment was also given a label in order to help communicate the characteristics of the segment. For example, an AFL Supporter is a consumer who is motivated to attend games primarily because of his/her interest in the league, but also because he/she has a secondary interest in a particular team. This consumer attends 16 to 39 % of a team's games. However, the size of the AFL Supporter segment is relatively small consisting of 138 spectators (10 % of the 1,384). The use of additional demographic and psychographic information beyond the sport involvement facets is recommended when conducting research to help describe differences and similarities between segments.

The AFL example illustrates how a consumer's involvement with a sport league can be determined and subsequently used within a theoretical framework to allocate individuals into different segments. The additional use of sport involvement facets and the PCM staging protocol can be applied in various sport contexts including teams, recreational activities, tourist destinations and consumer brands. This approach is beneficial to study existing consumers, and provides the ability to examine key target markets by exploring how personal, psychological and environmental factors influence identified segments. The final section of this chapter provides a more complex example that utilizes sport involvement facets and the PCM staging protocol.

11.5.3 PCM stage procedure example 3: team and league involvement

This professional sport example will help clarify the application of the PCM staging protocol using sport involvement facets. The example also explores the concept of sport brand architecture. Sport brand architecture describes the brand relationship between a professional sport league and a team that competes in that league. The league is considered the master brand, while the team is considered the sub-brand (Kunkel, Funk & Hill, 2013). For example, the US National Football League (NFL) and the Philadelphia Eagles are two distinct brands that are connected. Similarly, Manchester City FC is a unique team brand connected to the English Premier League brand. From a branding perspective, the league and team each utilize specific marketing activities to attract new consumers, maintain support among existing consumers and sale merchandize. In addition, due to their brand relationship, league and team marketing activities can also provide mutual benefits. For example, the league benefits from the teams' branding efforts and the team benefits from the league's branding activities. An important question for sport marketers to consider and answer is how these marketing activities influence sport consumer behaviour toward the league and team.

In particular, comparing the level of team involvement with the level of league involvement allows sport marketers to identify the degree to which each brand influences behaviour such as attending games, using social media and purchasing merchandize. This information is useful to determine which brand – the team or league – is driving behaviour, or whether both are equally contributing to certain behaviours. Sport consumer involvement can be used to determine the relative contribution of each sport brand on sport consumer behaviour.

The data for this example comes from a study of Australian professional sport leagues conducted by Kunkel *et al.* (2013). The investigators recruited 752 sport consumers to complete a survey who supported a sport team playing in one of the following four football leagues within Australia. The leagues were the National Rugby League (NRL); AFL; Super 15 Rugby Union; and Hyundai A-League (soccer). The survey measured the three facets of sport involvement (e.g. pleasure, centrality and sign) for both the sport league and the sport team. This required collecting responses from sport consumers using nine items for team and nine items for league.

Using the PCM staging protocol, all 752 consumers were placed into one of the four PCM stages based on: 1) sport team involvement profile and 2) sport league involvement profile. A detailed breakdown of the distribution resulting from the PCM staging protocol has been depicted in the sport brand involvement matrix in Figure 11.1. The team stage placements and league stage placements were then compared in a matrix format, as shown in Figure 11.1. The grid matrix was developed by matching the league stage on the X axis, with the team stage on the Y axis for each sport consumer.

Placement within a PCM stage for both the team and league was used to create three different groups: 1) team dominant; 2) league dominant; and 3) co-dominant. Team dominant describes placement in a team stage that is higher than a league stage (e.g. team = attachment vs. league = attraction); league dominant describes placement in a league stage, which is higher than a team stage (e.g., league = attachment vs. team = attraction); co-dominant is placement in equal stages (e.g. team = attraction vs. league = attraction).

This matrix indicated that sport consumers are mainly co-driven by both team and league brands; that is, most sport consumers were classified in identical stages and

	Allegiance	0	6	35	65
	Attachment	18	58	110	22
Team	Attraction	50	189	50	4
	Awareness	65	66	14	0
		Awareness	Attraction	Attachment	Allegiance

League

☐ Team dominant   ■ League dominant   ☐ Co-dominant

FIGURE 11.1 Sport brand involvement matrix

represented a co-dominant group. For example, 429 sport consumers were placed in the same stage for both team and league as depicted by the dark grey boxes. The remaining sport consumers were placed in either team dominant (167) or league dominant (156). The team dominant group contains sport consumers who were classified into one or more higher stages on team involvement than on league involvement, and is represented by the light grey boxes. In contrast, sport consumers in the league dominant group were classified into one or more higher stages on league involvement than team involvement, and are depicted with white boxes.

The sport brand involvement matrix offers a beneficial method to exam the relationship that exists between sport teams and their professional league as perceived by sport consumers. The matrix illustrates the mutual brand benefits that team and leagues can receive from each other's marketing activities. The co-dependent brand perspective suggests that professional sport teams and leagues should focus on cooperative strategies in addition to activities specific to their respective brand.

The use of sport involvement information in conjunction with the PCM staging protocol to create a brand matrix can help compare and examine different sport consumer segments. Additional demographic, psychographic and behavioural data could be collected from sport consumers to examine the differences and similarities such as attendance frequency, TV viewership, membership type, ticket price sensitivity and social media usage among team dominant, league dominant or co-dominant segments. A brand matrix could also be created using player/athlete involvement stage and team involvement stage (i.e. player X team matrix) or a corporate sponsor involvement stage and team involvement stage (i.e. sponsor X team matrix) to develop promotions and assess return on investment for each of the three segments. Finally, a matrix for a running event could be developed by comparing running involvement stage versus sport event involvement stage (i.e. running X sport event matrix) to investigate different sport consumer segments.

11.6 CHAPTER SUMMARY

Sport involvement represents an attitudinal construct that describes a sport consumers' level of interest, desire and motivation to engage in a sport and related consumption activities. The sport involvement construct has received considerable attention among researchers for its usefulness in studying consumer behaviour in various sport and recreation organizations. A beneficial approach to study the construct is by using the three facets of pleasure, centrality and sign to determine the degree to which individuals evaluate their connection with a sport based on the extent to which the sport provides hedonic and symbolic value, and is central to their lives. Sport involvement can also be used to develop profiles of sport consumers to examine behaviour toward sport products and services and collect information about evaluation of sport experiences. In addition, sport involvement information can be used to segment sport consumers into stages of the PCM. Industry professionals can utilize analytical techniques to personalize an effective mixture of marketing strategies for specific consumer segments to meet sport consumers' increasing demand for quality experiences.

11.7 DISCUSSION QUESTIONS

The discussion questions presented below are designed to help students review what is important in the chapter. You can answer them on your own, but they are also suitable for discussion work in small groups.

1) Why is it important to understand sport involvement?
2) What are the two different approaches to measure sport involvement?
3) What are the key antecedents and consequences of sport involvement?
4) How can sport involvement be used to create different profiles of sport consumers?
5) How can sport involvement information be used as a segmentation technique within the PCM?

11.8 CLASS ACTIVITY: SPORT INVOLVEMENT

Two class activities are designed to use information learned in this chapter to examine sport consumer involvement in relation to a sport team and a recreational sport.

a) Sport team activity

- Step 1:

    i. Complete the survey in Table 11.13. Think of a sport team as you respond to each statement.
    ii. Place your response to each statement in Table 11.13.1.
    iii. Calculate the mean scores on each sport involvement facet.
    iv. Divide each column total score by three to obtain an average score for each sport team involvement facet

- Step 2:

    i. Use Table 11.13.2 to create sport team involvement profile. Record the appropriate high, medium or low rating for each sport team involvement facet

- Step 3:

    i. Use Table 11.9 to determine your PCM stage

b) Recreational sport activity

- Download an SPSS dataset collected from runners who participated in a marathon or half marathon event in the USA. The dataset can be found on the companion website. SPSS syntax is also provided to accomplish the staging procedure for the entire sample, and can be found on the companion website.
- Use the PCM staging protocol to place all runners into the four stages of the PCM.
- Compare and contrast different stages using demographic, psychographic and behavioural information found in the dataset.

TABLE 11.13 Sport team involvement survey example

Rank your level of agreement with the following statements using the guide below:

	1	2	3	4	5	6	7
	Strongly disagree	Disagree	Slightly disagree	Neither agree nor disagree	Slightly agree	Agree	Strongly agree
Watching the [TEAM] is one of the most satisfying things I do.	1	2	3	4	5	6	7
Watching the [TEAM] says a lot about who I am.	1	2	3	4	5	6	7
I find a lot of my life is organized around following the [TEAM].	1	2	3	4	5	6	7
I really enjoy watching [TEAM] matches.	1	2	3	4	5	6	7
You can tell a lot about a person by the [TEAM] he/she follows.	1	2	3	4	5	6	7
A lot of my time is organized around following the [TEAM].	1	2	3	4	5	6	7
Compared to other activities, watching the [TEAM] is very interesting.	1	2	3	4	5	6	7
When I watch the [TEAM], I can really be myself.	1	2	3	4	5	6	7
Following the [TEAM] has a central role in my life.	1	2	3	4	5	6	7

Notes: Pleasure facet = Questions: 1, 4 & 7, Sign facet = Questions: 2, 5 & 8, Centrality facet = Questions: 3, 6 & 9.

TABLE 11.13.1 Mean scores on sport team involvement facets

Pleasure facet	Centrality facet	Sign facet
Q1 =	Q3 =	Q2 =
Q4 =	Q6 =	Q5 =
Q7 =	Q9 =	Q8 =
Total score =	Total score =	Total score =
Mean =	Mean =	Mean =

TABLE 11.13.2 Profile classifications on sport team involvement facets

Low (L)	Medium (M)	High (H)
Mean score ≤ 4.49	Mean score 4.50–5.74	Mean score ≥ 5.75
	Pleasure facet =	
	Sign facet =	
	Centrality facet =	

- Discuss potential reasons for the differentiation among the four stages.
- Create a persona for an average consumer within each PCM stage.
- Identify potential marketing strategies for the various PCM stages.

REFERENCES

Australian Sports Commission. (2013). Market Segmentation for Sport Participation [Video File]. Retrieved from www.youtube.com/watch?v=V0v92-JfpW8

Beaton, A.A. & Funk, D.C. (2008). An evaluation of theoretical frameworks for studying physically active leisure. *Leisure Sciences, 30*(1), 53–70.

Beaton, A.A., Funk, D.C. & Alexandris, K. (2009). Operationalizing a theory of participation in physically active leisure. *Journal of Leisure Research, 41*(2), 177.

Beaton, A.A., Funk, D.C., Ridinger, L. & Jordan, J. (2011). Sport involvement: A conceptual and empirical analysis. *Sport Management Review, 14*(2), 126–140.

CrossFit. (2012). Crossfit 101 – The basics [Video File]. Retrieved from www.youtube.com/watch?v=eBvy_A2jTmk

Doyle, J.P., Kunkel, T. & Funk, D.C. (2013). Sport spectator segmentation: Examining the differing psychological connections amongst spectators of leagues and teams. *International Journal of Sports Marketing and Sponsorship, 14*(2), 95–111.

Du, J., Funk, D.C. & Jordan, J. (2015). Managing mass sport participation: Adding a personal performance perspective to remodel antecedents and consequences of participant sport event satisfaction. *Journal of Sport Management, 29*(6), 688–704.

Filo, K., Funk, D.C. & O'Brien, D. (2009). The meaning behind attachment: Exploring camaraderie, cause, and competency at a charity sport event. *Journal of Sport Management, 23*(3), 361–387.

Funk, D.C. (2008). *Consumer Behaviour for Sport & Events: Marketing Action.* Jordon Hill, Oxford Elsevier: UK.

Funk, D.C. & Bruun, T. J. (2007). The role of socio-psychological and culture-education motives in marketing international sport tourism: A cross-cultural perspective. *Tourism Management, 28*(3), 806–819.

Funk, D.C. & James, J. (2001). The psychological continuum model: A conceptual framework for understanding an individual's psychological connection to sport. *Sport Management Review, 4*(2), 119–150.

Funk, D.C., Ridinger, L.L. & Moorman, A.M. (2004). Exploring origins of involvement: Understanding the relationship between consumer motives and involvement with professional sport teams. *Leisure Sciences, 26*(1), 35–61.

Havitz, M.E. & Dimache, F. (1990). Proposition for testing the involvement construct in leisure and recreation contexts. *Leisure Sciences,* 12, 179–195.

Havitz, M.E. & Dimache, F. (1999). Leisure involvement revisited: Drive properties and paradoxes. *Journal of Leisure Research, 31*(2), 122–149.

Havitz, M.E., Kaczynski, A.T. & Mannell, R.C. (2013). Exploring relationships between physical activity, leisure involvement, self-efficacy, and motivation via participant segmentation. *Leisure Sciences, 35*(1), 45–62.

Havitz, M.E. & Mannell, R.C. (2005). Enduring involvement, situational involvement, and flow in leisure and non-leisure activities. *Journal of Leisure Research, 37*(2), 152.

Kunkel, T., Funk, D. & Hill, B. (2013). Brand architecture, drivers of consumer involvement, and brand loyalty with professional sport leagues and teams. *Journal of Sport Management, 27*(3), 177–192.

Laurent, G. & Kapferer, J.N. (1985). Measuring consumer involvement profiles. *Journal of Marketing Research, 22*(1), 41–53.

Rothschild, M.L. (1984). Perspectives on involvement: Current problems and future directions. *Advances in Consumer Research, 11*(1), 216–217.

Running USA. (2013). *The 2013 National Runner Survey.* Retrieved from www.runningusa.org/2013-national-runner-survey

Sherif, M. & Cantril, H. (1947). *The Psychology of Ego Involvement: Social Attitudes and Identifications.* New York: John Wiley.

Zaichkowsky, J.L. (1985). Measuring the involvement construct. *Journal of Consumer Research, 12*(3), 341–352.

APPENDIX 11.A

Theoretical distribution of involvement profiles across PCM stages

Awareness			Attraction			Attachment			Allegiance		
P	C	S	P	C	S	P	C	S	P	C	S
L	L	L	M	L	L	L	L	M	M	H	H
			H	L	L	L	L	H	H	H	M
						L	M	L	H	M	H
						L	M	M	H	H	H
						L	M	H			
						L	H	L			
						L	H	M			
						L	H	H			
						M	L	M			
						M	L	H			
						M	M	L			
						M	H	L			
						M	M	M			
						M	M	H			
						M	H	M			
						H	L	M			
						H	M	L			
						H	M	M			
						H	L	H			
						H	H	L			

Note: P = Pleasure facet; C = Centrality facet; S = Sign facet

CHAPTER 12

Sport team identification

This chapter's objectives are to:

- introduce and provide an overview of team identification
- discuss the origin of team identification and social identity theory
- describe within-group differences and similarities
- discuss the presence of multiple in-groups that exist
- present measurement approaches to examine team identification
- discuss the consequences of team identification.

12.0 INTRODUCTION

Sport team fandom is a widespread phenomenon. Few consumer experiences cultivate greater interest and passion than watching sport teams compete. The interactions that occur at live sporting events between the sport consumer, the sport context and the sport management system generate a number of physical and psychological responses. Attending a match at a sport venue is similar to the excitement of attending a political rally or a religious event. The atmosphere found in stadiums across the globe is mostly created by the spectators who attend the match to support a team.

Thus sport teams often have a competitive advantage when playing at home due to the overwhelming support of hometown spectators. Leveraging this hometown advantage, the home crowd is often considered the 12th team member for a US NFL team. In general, sport team spectators and fans express their support for a team by wearing apparel with a team logo, cheering and engaging in match day rituals, purchasing club memberships, watching a game in a pub or attending a watch party and using social media to receive and share information about the team. When the sport consumer displays such observable behaviour in relation to a specific team, this represents an expression of sport team identification.

This chapter focuses on the concept of sport team identification and how it shapes the sport experience. Sport team identification represents an attitudinal concept, however it has differing qualities and meaning than the general attitudes discussed in Chapter 7, and sport involvement as discussed in Chapter 11. Within the sport consumer decision-making sequence introduced in Chapter 1 section 1.3, team identification represents an attitudinal outcome of internal processing phase. As an attitudinal outcome, it reflects the degree to which a consumer feels a sense of belonging and connection with other spectators and fans of the sport team and can range on a continuum from low to high.

The psychological responses and shared experiences a sport consumer feels with other spectators and fans of a sport team are often referred to as 'team identification'. This chapter focuses on sport team identification and the concept of identification can be used in a number of sport and recreation contexts. For example, a sport consumer can identify with numerous recreational activities such as running, golfing and surfing as well as numerous organized sport events.

12.1 TEAM IDENTIFICATION

Team identification is a key concept for understanding consumer group behaviours in sport settings and therefore is an important topic in sport marketing research (Theodorakis, Wann & Weaver, 2012). Relevant research has indicated that highly identified sport consumers are more emotionally involved with the team and more likely to attend and watch games compared with less identified sport consumers (Sutton, McDonald, Milne & Cimperman, 1997; Underwood, Bond & Baer, 2001). In the US at the University of Wisconsin's home football games, the playing of the song *Jump Around* is a good example of both physical and positive psychological responses that can occur within the live sport experience. This game-day tradition occurs between the third and fourth quarters of each Wisconsin Badgers home game – the stadium shakes and 80,000 fans follow the theme song's instructions – and has become a media sensation in the US (GameDayESPN, 2011).

A live sport event creates numerous opportunities for the consumer to engage in the sport experience. The sport consumer attending a sport event usually does so to watch the game as well as to show united support for a team. In addition, sport consumers can use the sport event as a means to associate themselves with other spectators and fans, and categorize themselves within a group, which is distinct from others, such as opposing fans. The sport consumer can also express their identity via any number of sport objects at a live sport event, including the team, a star player, an influential head coach or the sport league. Sport marketing research often uses team identification to gauge the sport consumer relationships with various sport products and services.

Within general society, most individuals express an identity by publicly associating themselves with smaller social groups within a society. There are numerous social groups to which they may belong, with the sport team a highly relevant context for the individual to identify with a group of like-minded individuals. Identification with a sport team often creates a sense of belonging. For example, imagine the sense of belonging felt when wearing a team jersey at the stadium while watching your favourite NFL team play a home game. Combined with thousands of other fans wearing the same team apparel and cheering for the same team, this experience is likely to make the individual feel like the 12th member of the team.

12.2 ORIGINS OF TEAM IDENTIFICATION

The concept of team identification evolved from social identity. Social identity is the subjective perception of the self, and how this perception is communicated and perceived by others in various social contexts. In the most basic sense, identification involves an individual stereotyping himself/herself as a member of a group based on shared characteristics. Thus, sport team identification needs two or more sport consumers to exist. Branscombe and Wann (1992) defined team identification as the 'extent to which individuals perceive themselves as fans of the team, are involved in the team, are concerned with the team's performance, and view their team as a representative of themselves' (p. 3). Sport consumers who adopt a sport team identity can differentiate themselves from other spectators attending or watching a game.

Various scholars have made distinctions between spectators and fans. It has often been concluded that most spectators will watch a sport match on Sunday and then forget about it by Monday; while fans will generally demonstrate more intensity and devote more effort to following the team during the other six days of the week. Spinrad (1981) suggested that a sport fan is 'the person who thinks, talks about and is oriented towards sports even when [the fan] is not actually observing, or reading, or listening to an account of a specific sports event' (p. 354). The key difference is that fans demonstrate more passion and engagement than spectators, which reflects an identity in the individual's self-concept. From this perspective, identification with a sport team represents the development of a psychological connection based on a sense of belonging to a larger social structure created by the sport team context (Wann & Branscombe, 1991).

However, contributions to this psychological connection can be more complicated to determine. According to social psychologists, individuals in relation to social situations categorize themselves based on perceived membership in social groups (Tajfel & Turner, 1985). That is, each individual classifies themselves as a member of a social group, and this membership distinguishes 'in-group' members from 'out-group' members. Team identification often reflects a sport consumer's self-concept based on knowledge of in-group membership and its perceived value and emotional significance (Tajfel, 1978). As a result, team identification represents a specific form of social identity that a group of individuals develop and maintain in relation to a sport team. The next section discusses the relationship between team identification and social identity further.

12.3 TEAM IDENTIFICATION AND SOCIAL IDENTITY

Social identity theory often emphasizes the role of self-concept. Self-concept is derived from a combination of unique personal attributes and the repertoire of group memberships that define an individual. That is, social identity is an individual's sense of who they are, based on a constellation of social groups to which they belong. Membership in a group often gives the individual a sense of belonging to a social 'world'. Based on social group memberships, individuals can divide their world into 'us' and 'them'.

The social identity perspective is often observed when pronouns like 'we' and 'us' are used to describe an individual's connection to a group (Hogg, 2006). This social identity also allows in-group members to distinguish themselves from out-group members (Tajfel & Turner, 1979). A key point for understanding team identification is the difference between in-group versus out-group membership status.

12.3.1 In-group versus out-group membership

Think of your favourite sport team. If you categorize yourself as a fan of that team, you immediately form a set of perceptions that favour other supporters of the team in comparison with those who do not support the team. This comparison process is referred to as 'self-categorization', and creates in-group versus out-group membership status. The psychological processes that underpin the evaluation of in-group versus out-group membership depend on social contexts, and determine when and how social structures impact on group and individual behaviour. Sport represents a strong example of in-group versus out-group comparisons, where the out-group normally changes from week to week. That is, even though each sport team will have traditional rivals in its league, matches against all teams can create a social context for intergroup evaluation.

In general, social identity theory proposes that members of the in-group make attitudinal and behavioural comparisons with members of out-groups (Turner, Hogg, Oakes & Wetherell, 1987). A key aspect of social identity theory is that most in-group members will seek to differentiate themselves from out-group members via self-perceived positive characteristics, and will correspondingly highlight the perceived negative characteristics of out-group members. This way, in-group members can enhance their own self-concept, which creates between-group differences as well as within-group similarities (Tajfel & Turner, 1979). Most individuals join social groups that reflect positively on their self-concept because of a perceived congruence between the values of an individual and values of the group. The self-categorization process therefore explains why prejudicial attitudes occur between in-groups and out-groups.

Tajfel and Turner (1979) identified the following three stages as part of evaluating the self in relation to social groups: 1) social categorization; 2) social identification; and 3) social comparison. The first stage of social categorization describes the process through which individuals categorize groups and objects to understand and identify themselves within their social environment. As there are numerous social groups and objects encountered in everyday life, this categorization enables more simplistic decision making and allows individuals to make quicker judgements and immediately engage in appropriate behaviour. Social categorization can help define the individual's place within society and can involve age, gender, race and membership of a team, religion, club or corporation (Bhattacharya, Rao & Glynn, 1995).

In the second stage of social identification, this is where the individual classifies him or herself as belonging to a specific group. At this point, self-esteem is attached to group membership, as the in-group status conveys characteristics that are attractive and positive to others.

The last stage in relation to social comparison occurs when the individual compares in-group versus out-group membership. For example, Manchester City football fans can differentiate themselves from Manchester United fans by wearing the sky blue and white strip, and singing *Blue Moon*. Similarly, Manchester United fans can differentiate themselves from their across-town rivals, particularly when Manchester City ends the season higher on the English Premier League ladder, by focusing on the historical success of their team, the home ground Old Trafford and the Red Devils logo. Such social comparison allows in-group members to achieve a sense of positive psychological distinctiveness in relation to out-group members (McNamara, 1997). Sport fans can use various social comparison strategies. For example, if their team loses a match, fans may still claim a distinctive group identity based on fair play in the absence of team success. This comparison includes highlighting differences with out-group members, as well as positively confirming similarities with in-group members (Brewer & Campbell, 1976). An individual can also distinguish himself/herself from other members within the same in-group to achieve benefits, as discussed further below in relation to optimizing in-group membership.

12.3.2 Optimizing in-group membership

The traditional definition of social identity is that individuals distinguish in-group members from out-group members by emphasizing intergroup differences. However, this approach fails to explain intragroup differences that can occur within the same in-group. Brewer's (1991) work on optimal distinctiveness surmised that individuals often struggle to balance two conflicting motives within an in-group: a desire for similarity versus a desire for distinctiveness. Figure 12.1 illustrates the combination of opposite needs for assimilation versus differentiation.

The diagonal lines in Figure 12.1 labelled 'assimilation' and 'differentiation' represent two conflicting forces, which determine how much an individual desires to either be just like everyone else in the in-group or stay unique within the in-group. The slope of each line increases from low to high, representing how strongly the individual perceives being similar or different from other members of the in-group. For example, an individual that is high on differentiation may perceive himself/herself as too different from the in-group and could experience a negative feeling of isolation. In contrast, an individual who is high on assimilation may feel he/she is too similar to other in-group members, and could

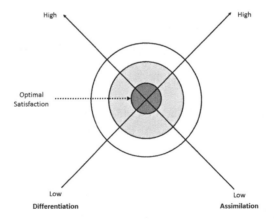

FIGURE 12.1 In-group membership satisfaction

experience a negative feeling of low self-esteem. These two opposing forces of being 'too unique' or 'not unique enough' can create feelings of dissatisfaction with in-group membership.

As shown in Figure 12.1, the optimal level of in-group membership is achieved when the degree of assimilation and differentiation are perceived as similar – represented in the diagram as an intersection point of the two lines. For example, an association with an in-group that is too inclusive could motivate an individual to behave somewhat differently from other in-group members to return to the optimal point of satisfaction. In contrast, if the individual feels too different from other in-group members, he/she may strive for more similarity to return to this optimal point of satisfaction.

The three circles in Figure 12.1 surrounding the intersection point represent three different levels of satisfaction, resulting from the benefits derived from in-group membership. The centre ring or 'bullseye' is the optimal level of satisfaction with in-group membership and represents the ideal position to maximize benefits of similarity and distinctiveness as well as self-esteem. The middle ring indicates moderate satisfaction with membership and occurs when the level of assimilation and differentiation begins to diverge; thus providing some additional benefits. The outer ring indicates the lowest level of satisfaction with membership, caused by increasing differences between assimilation and differentiation levels, which only provide marginal benefits. The following sport example will help illustrate how optimal distinctiveness works within in-group memberships.

This example uses a hypothetical case of a Bayern Munich football team fan named Thilo. Thilo identifies himself as a Bayern Munich fan and will meet his need for assimilation by wearing the team's jersey and attending home matches at Allianz Arena along with 60,000 other team supporters. At the stadium, Thilo will chant, cheer and sing the team's song *Stern des Südens*, and feel a high level of inclusion with other fans (see www.youtube.com/watch?v=Vo7Vuu9gJlI). However, if Thilo achieves too much inclusion within this in-group, a competing need for differentiation may be activated to return to optimal distinctiveness. In such a scenario, Thilo may reframe his membership within the group by taking on a special cheerleading role at the stadium or becoming a member of a smaller fan club related to the team. He may even become one of the 'hardcore' fans who can often be seen in sport stadiums, demonstrating what others perceive as fanatical behaviour.

The above discussion of social identity theory provides the basis for understanding sport consumer perceptions of groups and behaviours among in-group members for a team. Previous sport researchers have primarily focused on the emotional relationship of a sport consumer with a particular group such as a sport team or organization. From this perspective, team identification more accurately reflects a consumer's identification with the group of athletes who compete for a sport organization. This highlights a fundamental difference between social identity and team identity. This is because the concept of team identification in sport research does not generally conceptualize the presence of multiple in-group identities (i.e. social identification). The next section therefore provides a discussion of the implications of considering multiple in-group identities in the sport team identification context.

12.4 MULTIPLE IN-GROUP IDENTITIES

The focus on one type of in-group can overlook the interrelationships that often exist between multiple in-group identities. As a result of being overlooked, multiple group identities should be considered within a larger social context (Heere & James, 2007). In the sport context, if a sport team serves as a distinct source of social identity, this identity could also be influenced by relationships between the individual and larger social networks surrounding the team. The individual can generally identify with numerous groups – one group identity does not exist in isolation (Foreman & Whetten, 2002). For example, university students who have developed a team identity with their collegiate football team will also possess an identity as students of the university. Likewise, a fan of the Dallas Cowboys in the NFL may also have an identity with the city of Dallas and the state of Texas. Each of these multiple identities contributes to the individual's self-concept. Thus, a single group identity will fail to adequately define an individual's multiple social identities.

The concept of social identity is no doubt complicated. In everyday life, most people simultaneously encounter members of numerous social groups. From this perspective, social identity also represents the degree of overlap between various groups in which an individual is simultaneously a group member (Roccas & Brewer, 2002). Based on the notion that multiple group identities exist in addition to team identity, these other group identities will likely affect team identification (Heere, James, Yoshida & Scremin, 2011). A key point to remember here is that an individual's identity does not exist in isolation within one group, and that multiple social identities can be activated in different contexts as well as within a specific context. Recent research in sport management has provided a theoretical framework to examine how multiple in-groups form and operate in a sport team setting, as discussed below.

12.4.1 Multiple in-group identity framework

Lock and Funk (in press) first proposed the Multiple In-group Identity Framework (MIIF) to help understand the vast array of in-groups that can exist for one sport organization (see Figure 12.2). The MIIF consists of three identity levels: 1) superordinate team group identity; 2) subgroup identity; and 3) relational group identity. Each level represents an in-group with different degrees of inclusiveness and opportunities for interpersonal relationships between members.

As illustrated in Figure 12.2, the superordinate team identity level is represented by the largest circle and relates to the traditional notion of team identity. Each triangle represents sport consumers who belong to this superordinate team identity group. The superordinate group is the most inclusive and includes all consumers of a sport team. For example, the entire number of spectators that attend a football match and support a specific team. However, due to its larger size, it often provides fewer opportunities for interpersonal relationships.

The black dotted circles in Figure 12.2 represent the subgroup identity level, which includes in-groups with a smaller number of consumers than the superordinate level. These groups are less inclusive than the superordinate level, but provide more opportunities

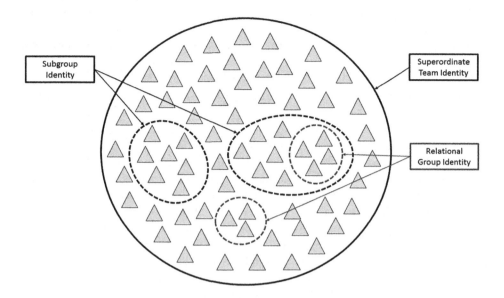

FIGURE 12.2 Multiple in-group identities

for interpersonal interaction. An example of this would be an in-group of spectators that sit in a specific section of a stadium.

The smaller black dotted circles in Figure 12.2 represent the relational group identity level, which relates to the smallest amount of consumers. Relational in-groups are the least inclusive but provide the most opportunities for interpersonal relationships. An example of this would be an in-group of spectators that attend a game who are friends, family, work colleagues or belong to other social groups that exist outside of the sport team context. The dotted circles for both the subgroup and relational group identities indicate that the boundaries of each in-group are not permanent – a consumer may transition between in-groups and levels.

Based on Figure 12.2, the following example further illustrates the MIIF. In the context of sport consumers attending a Philadelphia Eagles game in the NFL, there can be various degrees of superordinate team identification. For instance, these consumers may have shared knowledge about Eagles' players, the home ground of Lincoln Financial Field, club traditions and its history as a franchise. They may also know that the team's traditional rival, the Dallas Cowboys, has beaten the Eagles in the last four contests and plays in the best stadium in the NFL. As a result, they share one in-group superordinate identity as fans of the Philadelphia Eagles. However, within the superordinate team identity, a smaller subgroup of consumers called the 'Green Machine' exists. The Green Machine members sit in the north-end zone of the stadium and engage in in-group rituals and expressive behaviour during the game. For example, they wear Eagles clothing from head to toe, cheer the loudest, arrive early and stay late, abuse opposing players and fans, and generally attract the attention of other spectators during the game. Hence, this smaller in-group is less inclusive but has more opportunities for interpersonal interaction than the superordinate identity.

These Philadelphia Eagle consumers can share two identities: a fan of the Philadelphia Eagles and a member of the Green Machine. However, to add another layer of in-group team identification to the mix, within the Green Machine section of the stadium, some members attend with family and relatives. This relational group is the smallest and least inclusive, but emphasizes interpersonal relationships more than the superordinate and subgroup. This group has three in-group identities: 1) a fan of the Eagles; 2) a member of the Green Machine; and 3) a member of a family. At various times during the game, each of these three identities can be activated.

It should be noted here that the above MIIF illustration and the corresponding Eagles fans example do not necessarily capture the potential amount of multiple in-groups that could exist. Although not illustrated in Figure 12.2, the MIIF proposes that a large number of distinct subgroups can exist within the superordinate identity, which can be spatially based in terms of location in the stadium, or attitudinally based in terms of attitudes, interests and opinions of members. They can also be socially based in terms of group ticket sales to organizations at sporting events. In addition, a vast number of small relational groups can exist within the superordinate and subgroup levels. Thus, returning to Figure 12.2, one could add in further subgroup and relational circles among the triangles. As an example, if a stadium holds 50,000 spectators, the vast number of subgroup and relational groups that could form during a contest should be considered.

Overall, the MIIF highlights how various self-concept benefits can be obtained from team membership of multiple in-groups. The superordinate team identity can provide members with a broader sense of community and allows for intragroup distinctiveness in relation to opposing teams' spectators and fans. The subgroup identity allows consumers to gain further distinctiveness and sense of belonging by self-classifying into a smaller group that shares unique values and symbols in relation to the sport team. The relational group identity allows consumers to maintain existing relationships outside of the sport setting, and experience new ones within the larger superordinate team identity. Due to the clear complexity of considering the multitude of in-groups, sport scholars have largely focused on measuring the superordinate team identity, as discussed below.

12.5 MEASURING TEAM IDENTIFICATION

The evaluation of in-group membership is fundamental to understanding team identification in sport management. Sport scholars have therefore utilized a number of approaches to measure team identification, ranging from a unidimensional to a multidimensional construct. The unidimensional approach was introduced by Wann and Branscombe (1991, 1993) via the development of their Sport Spectator Identification Scale (SSIS). A subsequent Team Identification Index (TII) measure was introduced by Trail and James (2001). Both the SSIS and TII measure a sense of belonging to a sport team based on the degree of the sport consumer's psychological connection, which equates team identification to an attitudinal evaluation of in-group membership. Subsequent scholars have developed other measures for team identification citing the complexity of understanding how a sport consumer evaluates a sense of belonging to a sport team.

Most sport scholars agree that team identification has cognitive, affective and evaluative dimensions (Lock, Taylor, Funk & Darcy, 2012), which can be measured. However, some

TABLE 12.1 Example of team identification measurement scales

Scale	Dimension	Measurement items
Sport Spectator Identification Scale (SSIS) (Wann & Branscombe, 1991, 1993)	1	Individual's perceptions of being a fan of the particular team The importance of winning The degree to which they see themselves as a fan of that team The extent to which their friends view them as a fan How closely the individual follows the progress of the team How often the fan displays or wears team memorabilia or team apparel The degree to which they dislike their team's principal rivals
Team Identity Index (TII) (Trail & James, 2001)	1	I consider myself to be a real fan of the team I would experience a loss if I had to stop being a fan of the team Being a fan of the team is very important to me
Team*ID Scale (Heere & James, 2007)	6	*Private evaluation* Feel good about being a fan Glad to be a fan Proud to think of myself as a fan *Public evaluation* Overall, the team is viewed positively by others In general, others respect the team Overall, people hold a favourable opinion of the team *Sense of interdependence from the group* What happens to the team will influence what happens in my life Changes that impact the team will have an impact on my life What happens to the team will have an impact on my life *Interconnection with the group* When someone criticizes the team, it feels like a personal insult Being associated with the team is an important part of my self-image When someone compliments the team, it feels like a personal compliment *Behavioural involvement* I participate in activities supporting the team I am actively involved in activities that relate to the team I participate in activities with other fans of the team *Cognitive awareness* I am aware of the tradition and history of the team I know the ins and outs of the team I have knowledge of the successes and failures of the team

have created additional dimensions for measuring team identification. For instance, Heere and James (2007) proposed the Team*ID Scale with the following six dimensions: 1) public evaluation; 2) private evaluation; 3) interconnection of self with group; 4) sense of interdependence; 5) behavioural involvement; and 6) cognitive awareness.

Table 12.1 presents each of the scales referred to above, with sample items that can be used to measure team identification. While many other approaches exist for measuring team identification, the three scales listed in Table 12.1 provide an exemplar of the most common in the context of sport research. In general, such scales are important for measuring the level or degree of team identification, which helps to understand why some consumers form a connection with sport organizations while others do not. In addition, researchers can use these to evaluate how team identification operates and leads to subsequent psychological and physical consequences that are part of the overall sport experience, as discussed below.

12.6 CONSEQUENCES OF TEAM IDENTIFICATION

Sport researchers have directed considerable attention to examining the consequences of team identification. The bulk of this research has observed and reported on various behaviours that are triggered among in-group members based on the outcome of team performances. For example, most in-group members will rejoice in victory and demonstrate their passion and affiliation with a sport team by wearing team clothing, placing bumper stickers on their cars and posting pictures on their Facebook pages.

Sport scholars have suggested that sport consumers can fulfil inner-achievement needs by watching, following and supporting sport teams. From this perspective, a sport consumer can create a positive self-image via their strategic association with successful sport teams. As the association becomes stronger, a sport consumer is more likely to engage in various forms of consumption that require time, money and effort to follow the team. For example, highly identified fans will likely seek out more opportunities to attend games by purchasing memberships, multi-game ticket packages and team-licensed merchandise which will help them express their team support. In addition, a highly identified fan will frequently visit a team's website, watch games on TV or pay for a subscription channel, read news articles and communicate with others about team news. In the highly competitive spectator sport industry, most sport marketers will strive to develop effective strategies to motivate these consumer behaviours.

12.6.1 Team performance-based behaviours

The fundamental assumption is that team performance will create different psychological and physical responses within the sport consumer, depending on the level of team identification. That is, how sport consumers respond to a team's win or loss is determined by the in-group membership status. For example, to express identification with a sport team, the sport consumer might purchase and wear a team's sweatshirt. Then when the team wins on a Saturday, wearing the sweatshirt to class on Monday reflects the team's success, but more importantly allows the sport consumer to express self-success to others by basking in the glory of victory, which has been referred to as 'basking in reflected glory' (BIRGing) (Cialdini *et al.*, 1976). In this scenario, the self-esteem derived from the success of the sport team turns into vicarious achievement for the consumer who has publicly associated himself/herself with the team. The BIRGing phenomenon helps explain why licensed merchandise sales increase for teams that win championships across numerous leagues. Most sport consumers like to associate themselves with winners, expressing a form of in-group status to receive self-esteem benefits. However, what happens when the team loses?

On the flipside of winning, sport consumers that dissociate themselves from a losing sport team often do so to protect their self-esteem. The team identification behaviour termed as 'cutting off reflected failure' (CORFing) occurs when individuals want to distance themselves from team failure, especially from in-groups that are perceived as negative because of the team's failure (Hirt, Zillmann, Erickson & Kennedy, 1992). For example, if the team loses on Saturday, the individual is unlikely to wear the team sweatshirt on Monday, to avoid being associated with the losing team. CORFing refers to an impression management technique that allows an individual to avoid a negative evaluation by others and a potential loss to self-esteem. As such, CORFing is individual-centric behaviour, where the in-group status is not activated publicly.

The individual's use of pronouns after a team's performance often articulates the differences in CORFing versus BIRGing behaviour. For example, someone who uses the phrase 'we won' or 'we played well on Saturday' is BIRGing. In contrast, someone who uses the phrase 'they lost' or 'they played poorly on Saturday' is CORFing.

The impression management techniques of BIRGing and CORFing have been well documented. While anyone can BIRG, many loyal fans will not CORF. That is, a highly identified sport fan is not likely to turn their back on their favourite sport team just because of a loss. The highly identified sport fan will probably maintain the connection regardless of wins or losses. This indicates that even though a team's on-field performance does matter, behaviour must be consistent with expectations of this in-group membership status. In this scenario, highly identified sport fans can utilize other techniques that do not require them to dissociate from the in-group of team supporters. For example, 'blasting' occurs when the individual justifies a loss by blaming others such as referees, opposing players, the poor performance of the coach, individual players or even opposing fans and players (Kozub, 2011; Trail & James, 2011). The key is to blame some external force for the negative outcome.

Highly identified fans can also use optimistic predictions of future performance to protect their self-esteem and maintain the in-group status, including 'basking in reflected failure' (BIRFing) and 'cutting off reflected success' (CORSing) (Campbell, Aiken & Kent, 2004). BIRFing occurs when sport consumers that identify with a team that fails to win on a consistent basis maintain their in-group membership status through continuing their association with the team and attending games. In this context, the losing aspect can actually become a badge of honour and provide unique characteristics for this in-group. CORSing occurs when an individual withdraws their support following repeated success of a team, to differentiate themselves from the new group of fans that now support the team due to its popularity.

12.6.2 Team loyalty

One of the main consequences of team identification is loyalty. In general, loyalty refers to a high degree of commitment to re-buy or re-patronize a preferred product or service (Oliver, 1999). A loyal consumer is one who consistently purchases goods and services of a specific brand, and spreads information about that brand via word-of-mouth. Such loyalty is often developed over time through relationship building that makes it difficult for consumers to change preferences to other brands or services (Jones, Mothersbaugh & Beatty, 2000; Liu, Guo & Lee, 2011). Based on this perspective, team loyalty is regarded as a positive outcome or consequence of team identification. That is, the more an individual identifies with a team, the more likely it is that they will become allegiant (McDonald, 2010).

As an example of sport team loyalty, imagine yourself watching a live football match against a rival team that has gone into penalty kicks to decide the outcome. For the entire match, you have demonstrated BIRGing behaviour by wearing team apparel, waving the team flag, singing the team's song, using the pronoun 'we' and 'us' in conversations with other spectators and participating in rituals and chants. You now place your hands together and pray for a goal before the next penalty kick attempt. Unfortunately, the shot is missed and your team loses the game. You become upset or angry. You want to CORF, but you have been a fan of this team for 10 years. You may instead blast, but this only helps a bit. As you commute home, you feel depressed and this mood stays with you for two days. Such emotions and behaviours are unlikely to happen unless you feel a strong sense of belonging to the team and other fans and spectators that are part of the in-group. The notion that team identification leads to team loyalty therefore makes it an important asset for sport marketers. Increasing the number of highly identified fans is critical for sport team organizations, as this in-group is more likely to engage in actual consumption that generates revenue.

12.7 CHAPTER SUMMARY

Team identification is a highly influential concept in sport consumer behaviour. For example, sport consumers can publicly express a social identity to others by associating themselves with a group of like-minded individuals who support a sport team. Team identification provides an in-group membership status for a sport consumer, and establishes a sense of belonging and connection with other spectators and fans of the team. This self-categorization can promote a positive self-image based on the strategic association with sport teams, especially when successful. Team identification can also provide a basis for differentiating from others who are not members of the in-group. The reasons sport consumers join team supporter groups often relate to a desire for inclusion and differentiation.

However, it has also been emphasized in this chapter that team identity does not generally exist in isolation, with most sport consumers possessing multiple group identities due to the various social and organizational groups to which one can belong. Sport marketers also need to take into account that not all in-group members behave and think the same, as there is an optimal level of sameness and uniqueness that exists for each consumer that accounts for their behaviour. This is particularly important in the context of sport organizations, for developing strategic partnerships with corporate partners who promote the activation of different in-group identities. Sport marketers can also measure team identification to help understand why some individuals spend more time, money and effort following a team than others. Such knowledge will enable marketers to develop revenue streams such as from membership and ticket packages, sponsorships and online content, as well as creating team-related merchandise that helps consumers express their team connection.

12.8 DISCUSSION QUESTIONS

The discussion questions presented below are designed to help students review what is important in the chapter. You can answer them on your own, but they are also suitable for discussion work in small groups.

1) Think of an example of sport team fandom based on your own experience. How do you experience 'the sense of belongingness with a sport team' differently than others?
2) What prejudicial attitudes and different behaviours have you observed among in-group fans versus out-group spectators when attending a game?
3) What is the key difference between sport team identification and social identity?
4) Imagine yourself as a member of a sport in-group. What is the optimal level of distinctiveness that you desire?
5) Imagine yourself participating in a 10 km road race. What are the number of multiple in-groups that could exist?
6) What are the various strategies that a sport organization can use to increase the level of team identification?

12.9 CLASS ACTIVITY: TEAM IDENTIFICATION

Three class activities are designed to use information learned in this chapter to examine sport consumer team identification.

1) Pick a sport team with which you are familiar and use one of the team identification measurement scales presented in Table 12.1 to determine your level of sport team identification.
2) When a sport team wins or loses, the outcome creates a range of psychological and behavioural consequences, depending upon the level of team identification. Drawing on information learned in this chapter related to team performance-based behaviours, think of a positive and negative result and explain what types of behaviour would be expected. What influences this behaviour? How could a sport organization manage these behaviours to optimize the sport experience?
3) Team loyalty is an important consequence of team identification. Using online and secondary sources, find the following information: 1) attendance figures of teams in a professional sport league for a given year; 2) sales of licensed merchandise of teams in the league; 3) success of each team in the league in terms of wins or losses. Compare and discuss the results found in 1, 2 and 3.

REFERENCES

Bhattacharya, C.B., Rao, H. & Glynn, M.A. (1995). Understanding the bond of identification: An investigation of its correlates among art museum members. *The Journal of Marketing, 4*, 46–57.

Branscombe, N.R. & Wann, D.L. (1992). Role of identification with a group, arousal, categorization processes, and self-esteem in sports spectator aggression. *Human Relations, 45*(10), 1013–1033.

Brewer, M.B. (1991). The social self: On being the same and different at the same time. *Personality and Social Psychology Bulletin, 17*, 475–482.

Brewer, M.B. & Campbell, D.T. (1976). *Ethnocentrism and Intergroup Attitudes: East African Evidence.* New York: Sage.

Campbell Jr, R.M., Aiken, D. & Kent, A. (2004). Beyond BIRGing and CORFing: Continuing the exploration of fan behavior. *Sport Marketing Quarterly, 13*(3), 151–157.

Cialdini, R.B., Borden, R.J., Thorne, A., Walker, M.R., Freeman, S. & Sloan, L.R. (1976). Basking in reflected glory: Three (football) field studies. *Journal of Personality and Social Psychology, 34*, 366–375.

Foreman, P. & Whetten, D.A. (2002). Members' identification with multiple-identity organizations. *Organization Science, 13*, 618–635.

GameDayESPN. (2011, October 11). *Game Day Tradition – Wisconsin's Jump Around* [Video file]. Retrieved from www.youtube.com/watch?v=WHYgwC4fyhM

Heere, B. & James, J.D. (2007). Stepping outside the lines: Developing a multi-dimensional team identity scale based on social identity theory. *Sport Management Review, 10*, 65–91.

Heere, B., James, J., Yoshida, M. & Scremin, G. (2011). The effect of associated group identities on team identity. *Journal of Sport Management, 25*, 606–621.

Hirt, E.R., Zillmann, D., Erickson, G.A. & Kennedy, C. (1992). Costs and benefits of allegiance: Changes in fan's self-ascribed competencies after team victory versus defeat. *Journal of Personality and Social Psychology, 63*, 724–738.

Hogg, M.A. (2006). Social identity theory. In P.J. Burke (ed.), *Contemporary Social Psychological Theories*. Stanford, CA: Stanford University Press.

Jones, M.A., Mothersbaugh, D.L. & Beatty, S.E. (2000). Switching barriers and repurchase intentions in services. *Journal of Retailing, 76*(2), 259–274.

Kozub, J. (2011). *Ottawa Senators v Winnipeg Jets* [Online image]. Retrieved from www.gettyimages. com/detail/news-photo/referee-chris-lee-maintains-his-composure-despite-the-news-photo/134649837

Liu, C., Guo, Y.M. & Lee, C. (2011). The effects of relationship quality and switching barriers on customer loyalty. *International Journal of Information Management, 31*(1), 71–79.

Lock, D. & Funk, D.C. (in press). The multiple in-group identity framework. *Sport Management Review.*

Lock, D., Taylor, T., Funk, D. & Darcy, S. (2012). Exploring the development of team identification. *Journal of Sport Management, 26*(4), 283–294.

McDonald, H. (2010). The factors influencing churn rates among season ticket holders: An empirical analysis. *Journal of Sport Management, 24*(6), 676–701.

McNamara, T. (1997). Theorizing social identity: What do we mean by social identity? Competing frameworks, competing discourses. *TESOL Quarterly, 31*(3), 561–567.

Metz, T. (2013, May 25). *Stern Des Südens Allianz Arena 25.05.2013 Champions League Finale BVB Dortmund FC Bayern München* [Video file]. Retrieved from www.youtube.com/watch?v=Vo7Vuu9gJll

Oliver, R.L. (1999). Whence consumer loyalty? *Journal of Marketing, 63*, 33–44.

Roccas, S. & Brewer, M.B. (2002). Social identity complexity. *Personality and Social Psychology Review, 6*(2), 88–106.

Spinrad, W. (1981). The function of spectator sports. In G.R.F. Lüschen & G.H. Sage (eds), *Handbook of Social Science of Sport: With an international classified bibliography* (354–365). Champaign, IL: Stipes Publishing Company.

Sutton, W.A., McDonald, M.A., Milne, G.R. & Cimperman, J. (1997). Creating and fostering fan identification in professional sports. *Sports Marketing Quarterly, 6*(1), 15–22.

Tajfel, H. (1978). *Differentiation between social groups: Studies in the social psychology of intergroup relations* (27–60). London: Academic Press.

Tajfel, H. & Turner, J.C. (1979). An integrative theory of intergroup conflict. In W.G. Austin & W. Worchel (eds), *The Psychology of Intergroup Relations* (33–47). Monterey, CA: Brooks/Cole.

Tajfel, H. & Turner, J.C. (1985). The social identity theory of intergroup behavior. In S. Worchel & W.G. Austin (eds), *Psychology of Intergroup Relations* (2nd ed., 7–24). Chicago, IL: Nelson-Hall.

Theodorakis, N.D., Wann, D.L. & Weaver, S. (2012). Identification. *Sport Marketing Quarterly, 21,* 80–90.

Trail, G. & James, J. (2001). An analysis of the sport fan motivation scale. *Journal of Sport Behavior, 24,* 108–127.

Trail, G.T. & James, J.D. (2011). *Sport Consumer Behavior.* Seattle, WA: Sport Consumer Research Consultants LLC.

Turner, J.C., Hogg, M.A., Oakes, P.J. & Wetherell, M.S. (1987). *Rediscovering the Social Group: A self-categorization theory.* New York: Basil Blackwell.

Wann, D.L. & Branscombe, N.R. (1991). The positive social and self-concept consequences of sports team identification. *Journal of Sport and Social Issues, 15*(2), 115–127.

Wann, D.L. & Branscombe, N.R. (1993). Sports fans: Measuring degree of identification with the team. *International Journal of Sport Psychology, 24,* 1–17.

Underwood, R., Bond, E. & Baer, R. (2001). Building service brands via social identity: Lessons from the marketplace. *Journal of Marketing Theory and Practice, 9*(1), 1–13.

CHAPTER 13

Service quality and customer satisfaction

This chapter's objectives are to:

- introduce and provide an overview of service quality and customer satisfaction
- detail how customer perceptions of quality are formed and how they can be managed
- describe the determinants of customer satisfaction
- discuss the relationship between perceived quality and satisfaction
- describe how customer satisfaction impacts on other business outcomes such as customer loyalty and word-of-mouth.

13.0 INTRODUCTION: QUALITY AND SATISFACTION IN SPORT

Customer management is a complex blend of understanding what a customer requires and delivering it profitably, in the right way at the right time. So how can organizations gauge how well they are meeting customer needs? This is a difficult question, which has yielded a number of different approaches. The most common approach is to focus on managing the quality of both services and goods, based on an understanding of the relationship between quality and customer satisfaction.

Satisfaction is an attitude (see Chapter 7), and is perhaps one of the most important in determining how customers behave in the future. This future behaviour not only includes their own actions (i.e. whether they use product again), but also how consumers impact on other consumers (e.g. whether they spread positive word-of-mouth). Accordingly, this chapter focuses on the management of quality in sports settings, and understanding how such quality impacts on customer satisfaction, advocacy, repurchase and retention.

Traditional Customer Relationship Management theory (CRM) suggests that careful management and monitoring of customer expectations, followed by the provision of service quality at a standard that consistently meet those needs, are key to long-term success (Grönroos, 1990). However, alternative views suggest that attitudes more often form after (and in line with) behaviour, such that people feel positively about brands they choose, provided they meet their needs (Sharp, 2010). Yet regardless of whether attitudes form before or after behaviour, it is clear that positive attitudes correlate with repurchase; thus, managing customer attitudes is important. This chapter therefore discusses how sport managers can control the perceived quality of their products to drive higher customer satisfaction and, in turn, how to take full advantage of that satisfaction.

13.1 QUALITY: GOODS VERSUS SERVICES

Quality could be broadly defined as fitness for purpose. It is a significant forerunner to concepts such as value (e.g. Did I receive adequate benefit for the costs involved?) and satisfaction (e.g. Were my needs met?). Quality is often viewed only from an organizational perspective, measured in terms of technical aspects of the product. For example, the quality of carpet might be described in terms of the materials it is made from (e.g. nylon, wool), the density of the fibres or its overall durability (i.e. how well it wears over time). However, such technical measures may mean very little to the consumer. Thus, taking into account consumer perceptions has been an important recent development in product quality management.

Based on this shift in focus to include customers' perceptions, quality is now more commonly defined as the degree to which a product satisfies customers' needs, and in particular the degree to which it meets their expectations. The concept of 'expectations' is a particularly important one in regard to the management of satisfaction, as further discussed later in this chapter (section 13.4).

Quality is most easily interpreted in the context of physical goods where, like the carpet example, there are objective technical measures of how well an individual product meets quality standards. All products include a service component, but those with the greatest emphasis on service rather than physical good, such as sport and leisure, are the most difficult to manage.

Such difficulties in managing service quality often stem from the unique characteristics of services. Foremost among these is the inherent *intangibility* of services. That is, many services aspects cannot be held, smelt, tasted or seen; thus, assessing their quality is often challenging. In the sport context, consider your local health club or gymnasium. Membership there generally includes a range of tangible components such as the equipment, the size of the building and the facilities in the change rooms (e.g. lockers and showers). Equally important are the intangible aspects of the gym membership, such as the friendliness and knowledge of staff, how crowded the venue feels and how well the venue is managed.

Another likely complication is the *variability* in service provision, which can also make quality control difficult. Variability stems from the fact that most services rely on human service providers and each service provider is going to be different. Quality therefore fluctuates. For example, on your first visit to a doctor's surgery, hairdressing salon or boot camp fitness session, the first service provider you encounter will set the quality standard you expect on the next visit. Yet if you experience a different doctor, hairdresser or trainer on subsequent visits, your experience is unlikely to be the same due to differences in the way people approach the same job. This is why we usually seek out the same people to provide our personal services, even though they may work in an organization that has several doing the same role.

No discussion of service quality is complete without some reference to *co-creation*. Co-creation is the recognition that customers add value to the consumption experience via the way they select, consume and dispose of products. Co-creation has been highlighted as part of the broader shift in marketing theory toward acknowledging that every product has a service component, and this service component is often the key to value creation. This shift in thinking has been termed 'Service-Dominant Logic' (or SD Logic) by Lusch and Vargo (2006); and complex theory has subsequently developed around how organizations can embrace SD Logic.

SD Logic encourages marketers to consider that the perceived value of the product will depend on the extent to which consumers have been encouraged, and allowed, to add to the experience. For example, in the context of live sport spectatorship, the 'producer' – the professional sport organization – fields a team, which is trained and prepared, secures a venue and organizes pre- and post-match entertainment. The opposition contributes to make a contest and build rivalries. The fans, however (who are 'consumers' in this example), add almost as much value to the event as the teams. For instance, crowd rituals such as tailgating, chanting and making banners all enhance the experience; the crowd also creates atmosphere via its size and their social interactions. In addition, fans who engage in such rituals have been found to be more satisfied with their experience and more likely to engage in other positive behaviours like merchandise purchasing and repeat attendance (McDonald & Karg, 2014). If you doubt this, consider what it would be like to be the only person in the stadium watching a sporting match.

13.2 MEASURING QUALITY

Quality, as a subjective evaluation made by customers post-consumption, can be difficult to measure in a way that is helpful to managers seeking to improve their service. Customers usually have perceptions about both the overall quality of the core service (e.g. the athletic competition in spectator sports) and the functional quality of how that core service is delivered (e.g. the stadium, food and beverages and parking) (Kelley & Turley, 2001). As a result, most attempts to measure quality are multidimensional, in that they cover a range of attitudes a consumer might have toward what they have consumed.

A good starting point is to collect feedback from the customer on their quality perceptions whenever possible. This can be as simple as organizing staff to directly ask customers how their experience was, soliciting feedback via casual interactions wherever possible. Other methods include via observation, such as monitoring whether customers can easily find what they want in a retail setting, or assessing if they actually use the facilities and services provided. Unsolicited comments, where customers provide feedback without being prompted, such as social media commentary, is also highly valuable information. Yet while these methods can all yield beneficial customer feedback, such informal approaches of assessing quality also have weaknesses. For example, customers might feel uncomfortable reporting negative experiences directly to staff. In addition, ensuring the feedback obtained from such informal interactions is logged, considered and acted upon can also be difficult and open to interpretation. Therefore, while these more informal methods can be useful for keeping up-to-date with customers' perceptions, they are not as revealing as formal, systematic data collection on quality and satisfaction.

TABLE 13.1 SERVQUAL dimensions and applications to sport

Service quality dimension (SERVQUAL) (Parasuraman, Ziethaml & Berry, 1988)	Examples from sport spectating (Theodorakis, Alexandris, Tsigilis & Karvounis, 2013)
Tangibles (physical facilities, equipment, appearance of staff)	The stadium is visually appealing The stadium provides comfortable seats
Reliability (dependable and accurate performance)	Delivers services as promised Services are provided right the first time
Responsiveness (promptness and helpfulness)	Provides prompt service Gives individual attention
Assurance (credibility, security, competence)	Car parking availability Feel safe in the stadium
Empathy (easy access, good communications and understanding)	Studies did not support this dimension in sport spectating

Formal measurement of service quality has been subject to a large amount of research, with two main approaches subsequently developed. The first is by Parasuraman, Ziethaml, and Berry (1988), who conceptualized service quality as having five key dimensions, which were developed in the widely used SERVQUAL instrument. Table 13.1 shows these dimensions with specific examples of where past researchers have adapted SERVQUAL to sport spectator context. The full SERVQUAL questionnaire has 22 questions relating to these five dimensions, for which both expectations and performance perceptions data must be collected. This requires two separate data collections, usually before and after the service encounter.

The SERVQUAL approach is widely employed in many industries and is still regarded as the most complete approach to the measurement and management of service quality. However, it is not without its critics and rivals – the main criticisms are as follows:

a) The one instrument has been designed to cover a wide range of service settings, which causes it to be inflexible – that is, the same questions are used for every service setting. Therefore, many researchers find that to make SERVQUAL relevant to respondents, they must adapt the questions to different contexts. As evident from the sport context shown in Table 13.1, many of the items are easily adapted. However, in earlier research, some of those who tried to adapt the 'empathy' dimension to sport spectatorship (Theodorakis & Alexandris 2008) and outdoor recreation services (Crompton, MacKay & Fesenmaier, 1991) could not do so meaningfully. Yoshida and James (2011) argued that sport events need to include 'aesthetic quality', to capture some of the unique aspects of the sport experience including game atmosphere and the crowd experience.

b) Some believe that the reliance on expectations as a theoretical basis (see section 13.4) makes SERVQUAL a more difficult instrument to administer and interpret than it needs to be. SERVQUAL examines the difference between expectations and performance, and this approach has been criticized by those who favour simply collecting perceived performance. Collecting expectations data as well as performance evaluations requires either two separate data collections before and after the service (preferable), or one large survey instrument that collects both at the same time. In particular, this may not be possible at sporting events such as live games or participatory distance runs. Another issue with this expectations-based approach is whether customers are actually able to accurately recall their expectations after the service. Attitudes are often fluid, and most consumers seek consistency between their attitudes and experiences. Therefore, having just experienced a service, it is possible they might shift their expectations to align with that experience. This means that collecting both performance and expectations data together may equate to minimal variation between the two measures, as most respondents seek this consistency.

c) The number of dimensions found in some contexts can vary markedly from the original SERVQUAL five. For example, in some specific sport settings, such as outdoor recreation (Kouthouris & Alexandris, 2005) and indoor sports centres (Ko & Pastore, 2005), this approach has been found to be a poor fit. In sport participation and recreational facilities contexts, SERVQUAL has provided a basis for measurement, but has often had to be heavily adapted to produce a viable measurement tool. For example, in assessing sports centres in Korea, Kim and Kim (1995) identified 12 distinct dimensions of quality, seven of which reflected aspects of SERVQUAL and five that were unique to this context (e.g. exclusivity, stimulation, social opportunity).

d) SERVQUAL focuses more on the quality of service delivery (functional quality) rather than the outcome of the service experience (outcome quality). Accordingly, many researchers have designed and included outcome quality measures in their studies to supplement SERVQUAL.

Such criticism suggests that SERVQUAL cannot simply be used without some consideration of context and relevant adaptation. Therefore, numerous researchers have adapted it, while others have even sought to replace it. The SERVPERF of Cronin and Taylor (1992) is perhaps the best-known alternative, which focused on measuring performance only, using 22 questions. In later work, Brady and Cronin (2001) recognized a hierarchy among service quality evaluations and proposed that measures be taken of the following three quality dimensions:

- physical environment (e.g. stadium seating, cleanliness)
- interactions (e.g. staff friendliness, expertise)
- outcomes (e.g. waiting times, contest result).

Yet despite such research issues and subsequent amendments to SERVQUAL, it would appear that choosing to use this approach or an alternative like SERVPERF is largely irrelevant. A meta-analysis comparing the different approaches concluded that, for the most part, both approaches are valid and effective (Carrillat, Jaramillo & Mulki, 2007); although SERVPERF required less adaptation to context. The common approach taken in more recent service quality studies is to use the SERVPERF approach of only collecting performance data (not expectations for each measure) but use the measures of quality developed for the five SERVQUAL dimensions, adapt those measures to the specific service context, and include the outcome quality measures from Brady and Cronin

(2001). The main necessity is to have a systematic approach to assessing service quality and customer perceptions of it. Actions need to be taken to improve areas that fall short of customer requirements, and process improvements recorded and tested for effectiveness in improving customer perceptions over time.

13.3 IMPROVING QUALITY

When academics and practitioners tried to manage the quality of service-heavy products in a similar way to more tangible goods, they were often unsuccessful. The nature of service-heavy products creates unique problems. Standardizing services, for example, is often difficult because of the personal dimensions involved. That is, every service staff member looks, speaks and behaves differently, so variances can even occur in heavily regimented and scripted services (e.g. telephone call centres). But do we really want to standardize services? The personalized components of service delivery often attract customers, with service provider relationships often formed over long time periods (e.g. hairdressers, doctors, personal trainers). A careful balance often therefore needs to be struck between allowing staff individuality and implementing standardized services for all staff members.

Parasuraman, Ziethaml and Berry (1985) advanced the 'gap theory' of service quality improvement and design as one way of helping managers to identify ways to determine what actions they should take to increase quality perceptions among customers (see Table 13.2). Based on this theory, by understanding gaps in service quality, managers are able to alter relevant practices to improve in this area (see De Knop, Van Hoecke and De Bosscher 2004 for a detailed example of the application of service quality gap management to sporting clubs and federations in Belgium).

13.4 CUSTOMER SATISFACTION

What leads the consumer to be satisfied with a consumption experience? The bulk of research on this topic is based on the concept that most consumers already have preconceived ideas of what they are likely to experience. With products consumers have used before, they have a very clear idea of what to expect. Even with a product not previously experienced, though, some idea of what the experience will be like usually exists. This usually is formed through past experiences of a similar type, the recommendations of others or from marketing communications consumers have seen.

When consuming repeat products, there is no doubt a clear idea of what to expect; yet even with new products, there is generally some perception of the forthcoming consumption experience – which could be based on former experiences with a similar product, recommendations of others or via marketing communications.

Using sport as an example, even though the consumer may not have participated in a fun run before, they are still likely to have some idea of how it will be organized and what the race experience will be like. These preconceived ideas are termed 'expectations'; while attitudes about what is actually experienced, post-consumption, are often referred to as 'perceived performance' or 'perceived quality'.

TABLE 13.2 The five key service gaps

Gaps in service	Sport examples
Gap 1: customer gap – difference between expected and perceived service	At a live sport match, the customer is expecting to have a quick bathroom break during an interval in the game, but finds bathrooms are limited and queues are long
Gap 2: listening gap – difference between what a customer expects and what an organization thinks customers expect	Having played professional sport, the CEO of a professional team knows fans react well to on-field success; they therefore focus organizational resources on winning games rather than on servicing fans and season ticket holders
Gap 3: design and standards gap – difference between how services are designed and what the customer needs	Golf club members are often heard to say they want a 'challenging' course, so the golf club undertakes a redesign of the course to bring it to professional standards; however, member numbers drop off after the redesign, because the course is now 'too hard' for casual players
Gap 4: performance gap – difference between organizational standards promised and what is actually delivered	A charity fun run prides itself on ensuring every runner who completes the course is acknowledged with a medal and follow-up letter; however, due to production problems in China and a last minute growth in registrations, on the day of the race there are not enough medals for each participant, and late finishers are not acknowledged
Gap 5: communication gap – difference between service delivery and external communications about the service	A fitness centre promises new members that they will feel like 'part of the family' and commits to keeping in touch with all members; however, three months in, most new members have not received any communications from the centre's management or had any of the staff introduce themselves

Early theories on satisfaction focused on meeting customer expectations and were commonly known as confirmation of expectations models (Oliver, 2014). The principal idea behind these theories was that if an organization provided customers with what they expected, they would likely be satisfied and return. In such a scenario, small deviations from what was expected, even negative ones, could be tolerated by customers. The confirmation model essentially suggests that consumption is followed by feelings of familiarity (either positive or negative), and that having this familiar feeling confirmed by the consumption experience leads to contentment or discontentment. A decision on whether to repurchase logically follows from that contentment/discontentment.

It may sound strange that consumers would tolerate small negative deviations in service standards from what they expect. In all of our lives, however, small annoyances or inconveniences are often overlooked, and even persistent problems can become part of what is expected by customers. Based on the gym example, while most aspects of the consumption experience may be positive, the customer may be somewhat put off by how crowded the gym is at peak times. Yet even though this is somewhat frustrating, the customer will probably grow to expect to be waiting longer for equipment and to have to tolerate more patrons if attending at peak times. Over time, the customer's behaviour will either change their behaviour to avoid crowding or or simply accept that the gym is busy at this time and go anyway.

Such acceptance of minor consumption inconveniences is usually based on the belief that things will not be better from switching to another product. That is, the customer could change gyms, but would probably question whether all other gyms are also going to be busy at peak times. They may also debate whether changing gyms to fix this insignificant problem is worth sacrificing the aspects they enjoy about their current gym. Such questioning of whether switching is worth it is common among consumers, explaining a range of behaviours including why they choose to continue to use a product that although not perfect, is good enough.

The confirmation of expectations model can be used to understand customer satisfaction and consumption behaviour in situations of low involvement or where consumer choice is obvious or easy. In some situations, for example if the product consumption experience vastly differs from what was expected, we may find that consumers respond more actively. Thus, new models of customer satisfaction, commonly known as disconfirmation models, have been developed to explain what happens in situations where there are large deviations between expectations and performance.

Disconfirmation models also have customer expectations as the foundation, and assess the differences between what was expected and what was received (performance). Based on this theory, where expectations are met by performance (i.e. expectations are confirmed), consumers are satisfied. In contrast, where consumer expectations are not met, there are two situations where expectations are disconfirmed: performance is either below expectations (negative disconfirmation), or above expectations (positive disconfirmation). The outcome of negative disconfirmation is dissatisfaction; the outcome of positive disconfirmation is excess satisfaction, often referred to as 'delight'.

When disconfirmation models became widely used, a large amount of both academic and practitioner attention was paid to delighting customers, and many managers believed this should be the goal of an organization. Customer delight, though a popular catchphrase in the late 1990s and early 2000s, has now been faded in prominence. Consistently satisfying customers by meeting their expectations has been proven to be as effective in encouraging repeat purchase as delighting them. That is, there is little real benefit to the organization in exceeding customer expectations. The other issue with the customer delight goal is that it is difficult to continually achieve this. True delight requires customers to be continually surprised, which can be a daunting task for any organization. Consider that if something special is done once for customers, they may expect this to continue to occur, and could adjust their evaluation of the organization's performance if it does not maintain this additional service. In addition, delighting customers often requires additional resources, which can be expensive and unprofitable for the organization. Therefore, understanding customer expectations of quality and consistently meeting them is a more effective, all-round organizational strategy.

13.5 MEASURING SATISFACTION

Compared with quality, measuring satisfaction is relatively straightforward. There are three common approaches for measuring satisfaction, and the first is to simply ask customers directly to assess their own satisfaction. A typical question might be:

Considering your experience at today's event, would you say you are:

> Very satisfied (7)
> Quite satisfied (6)
> Slightly satisfied (5)
> Neither satisfied or dissatisfied (4)
> Slightly dissatisfied (3)
> Quite dissatisfied (2)
> Very dissatisfied (1).

The second method is to include measures of both satisfaction and expectations. In this scenario, in addition to the satisfaction question shown above, the customer could be asked:

Thinking about your experience in relation to what you expected before you came today, would you say that it was:

> Well above my expectations (7)
> Above my expectations (6)
> Slightly above my expectations (5)
> As I expected (4)
> Slightly below my expectations (3)
> Below my expectations (2)
> Well below my expectations (1).

Finally, it may be useful to include a comparison of customer satisfaction with an 'ideal', which would be particularly beneficial for new organizations entering the market. An example of an ideal question is:

Imagine what an ideal event of this type would look like to you. How well do you think today's event compares with your ideal event?

> Almost exactly my ideal (7)
> Very close to my ideal (6)
> Close to my ideal (5)
> About halfway to my ideal (4)
> Far from my ideal (3)
> Very far from my ideal (2)
> Almost the opposite of my ideal (1).

In addition to the above, some general notes on designing satisfaction questions are worth keeping in mind. These include always using odd numbered scales so there is a mid-point, such as 'As I expected'. In addition, longer response scales have been shown to be better than shorter scales, as they help tease out distinctions between consumer experiences. For example, on a 5-point response scale, respondents only have two positive (4,5) and two negative response (1,2) options. Most will not have experienced very bad or very good service, which means most respondents will give the same response. Longer scales (7- or even 11-point) allow more variability in responses and can help detect important, but subtle differences in customers. There are often large differences, for example, in the future behaviour of respondents who rate a service at 6 on a 0–10 scale, compared with those who rate it at 7. Lastly, labelling each response point, and ensuring the scales are balanced in terms of positive and negative options, will improve the quality of the data received and increase the analysis options.

13.6 MEASURING AND USING CUSTOMER SATISFACTION DATA: AN EXAMPLE OF SEASON TICKET HOLDERS

Previous research into sport season ticket holders illustrates how the concepts of service quality, satisfaction and retention management can be used to improve the product offering and the customer experience. This is one of the few sport-related contexts where the relationship between quality, satisfaction and positive business outcomes has been extensively researched. Over the last 15 years, the authors of the book you are reading have worked with professional sport teams looking to increase their season ticket base and deepen their relationship with season ticket holders. A detailed overview of this work is provided in the following sections, as an illustration of how to develop instruments for measuring sport quality and satisfaction, and then managing these key areas to improve customer outcomes.

13.6.1 What matters to season ticket holders?

When thinking about sports season ticket holders, some obvious questions come to mind. Which components of the season ticket package or experience are most important in determining the overall level of satisfaction? What impact does this have on strategy and how do teams perform overall? We start this review by answering those questions.

A recent study reports on work undertaken with nearly 8,000 season ticket holders (STH) across different sports, where seven core drivers of STH satisfaction with professional sport teams were identified (McDonald, Karg & Vocino, 2013). Each of those drivers was defined by a series of specific management or team actions. Those specific management actions were identified via a series of focus groups with season ticket holders of different sport teams, interviews with managers and observation of industry practices by the researchers. Table 13.3 details the key drivers of satisfaction identified in this context, with each of the five SERVQUAL dimensions represented, along with some additional areas unique to this context.

TABLE 13.3 Satisfaction drivers for season ticket holders

Driver	Individual actions
	Convenience of entering the ground
	Member access to finals tickets
Membership arrangements	Savings on game entry fees
	Quality of the season reserved seats
	Speed in which membership packages were sent
Personal involvement	Opportunities to mix with players
	Efforts to make members feel part of the team
	Opportunity for members to mix with other members
	Team values the importance of its membership base
	Members' contributions are recognized
Home ground	As a place to watch football
	Feeling of a 'home' ground
	Standard of facilities at the ground
	Ease of getting to the ground
	'Family-friendly' ground
Service to members	Helpfulness of team staff
	Number and range of functions
	Quality of the events or functions
	Value of functions
	Staff enquiry handling
Marketing & communications	Clarity of the membership brochure
	Content of the official team website
	Content of the electronic newsletter, email and SMS updates
	Efforts to keep members informed about admin decisions
	Information provided on membership issues
	Social media and networking
On-field performance	Number of games won
	Position on the ladder
	Effort put in by players
	Standard of the play
Team administration	Administration of the team
	Functioning of the team board
	Financial position of the team
	Promotion of the team in general

13.6.2 Relative importance of each satisfaction driver

The satisfaction of season ticket holders has been measured, using a survey tool based on the drivers shown in Table 13.3, across a wide range of sport contexts over the past decade. These sports include rugby union, rugby league, cricket, Australian football (AFL), netball and soccer. The subsequent results have been remarkably consistent in that the seven drivers always account for around 70–80% of season ticket holder satisfaction. The other 20–30% of satisfaction can be attributed to random or unique events, too difficult to capture across a wide range of customers.

The relative importance of each of these drivers (i.e. the contribution of each driver to overall satisfaction) varies between teams and sports based on factors related to the composition of the season ticket holder base and the team's circumstances (e.g. win/loss record). In particular, the importance of each driver may vary based on the number of years someone has been a season ticket holder and the number of games they have attended in a season. For example, depending on how many games they attend, newer season ticket holders may focus on tangible aspects like Membership Arrangements or Service to Members; while more established members are more likely to focus on Personal Involvement and Team Administration. In addition, teams with longer losing streaks may find that On-field Performance is an increasingly important driver, and those who share a home ground with other sporting teams, or have an aging stadium, may also find that Home Ground is highly relevant.

Summarizing over 150 of these studies on various sport teams and sporting codes, the typical contributions of each driver to the overall satisfaction score is shown in Figure 13.1. As an example of what's shown in the diagram below, if a respondent rates their overall satisfaction as a 7/10, 30% of that score has been derived from their attitudes toward the Membership Arrangements components, and 10% from their attitudes toward Home Ground.

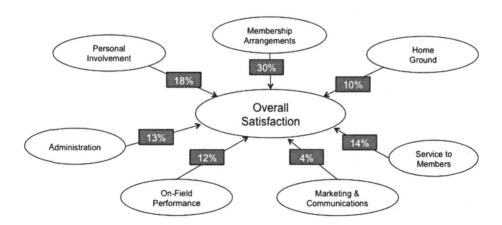

FIGURE 13.1 Typical contribution of the drivers of sport season ticket holder satisfaction

13.6.3 Influencing and benchmarking sport season ticket holder satisfaction

A common question asked by managers is what is a good score on satisfaction ratings? However, the eternal problem with customer satisfaction measurement is that, over time, customers quickly become used to innovations (e.g. digital communications) and their expectations of the service provider increase. This is why benchmarking is also often required to adequately assess customer satisfaction. Table 13.4 is an example of benchmarking, capturing the historical minimum, maximum and average scores against each of the seven satisfaction drivers as measured in one professional league's season ticket holder annual surveys from 2004 to 2014.

13.6.4 Increasing performance on individual drivers

From a management perspective, it is encouraging and empowering to note that out of the seven key drivers of sport season ticket holder satisfaction, all but one (On-field Performance) are directly under the control of the team's commercial managers. Managing these drivers is therefore both desirable and possible. Each of the key drivers is now discussed in more depth, with examples of activities that have influenced season ticket holders' attitudes toward each component.

Membership Arrangements

The umbrella term 'Membership Arrangements' captures the core tangible product offering of the team to its season ticket holders. It is therefore not surprising that it is often the most important driver in terms of overall season ticket holder satisfaction.

TABLE 13.4 Satisfaction scores from one professional sport league: 2004–14 (n=122 surveys)

	MIN.	AVE.	MAX.
Membership arrangements	6.72	7.66	8.73
Service to members	6.33	7.73	8.90
Marketing & communications	6.53	7.82	9.11
On-field performance	0.90	6.07	9.92
Personal involvement	2.59	6.72	9.43
Team administration	2.60	7.08	9.21
Home ground	5.06	7.67	9.62
SATISFACTION	5.44	7.38	9.20
EXPECTATIONS (met or exceeded)	3.97	6.33	8.40
RENEWAL PROBABILITY	6.38	8.93	9.76

Note: All scores are on a 0–10 scale, where 0 = highly dissatisfied and 10 = highly satisfied; except 'expectations' where 0 = well below, 5 = as expected, and 10 = well above.

The importance placed on this, the most tangible aspect of team membership, is relatively high for all season ticket holders, but often declines based on the length of membership and the number of games attended. This decline is a result of season ticket holders' personal links with the team developing and deepening, making them less likely to evaluate their membership experience predominantly via a cost-benefit value analysis. This has significant implications for encouraging season ticket holder retention and managing churn, which will be discussed further (see section 13.7).

Speed of membership ticket delivery is consistently the most important individual satisfaction element, yet what is called 'fulfilment' is often still poorly executed by teams. Fulfilment is action of delivering the tangible components of the season ticket product (e.g. ticket books, merchandise, welcome packs) to the season ticket holder. Improving this activity should be relatively easy to execute from an internal process perspective, which is highly likely to have a notable impact on the overall satisfaction rating. The growing trend toward outsourcing the fulfilment component of season tickets to specialized mailing houses must be balanced with the potential risks of not having control over the delivery. The key to successful fulfilment is not so much the actual time between taking the order and its fulfilment, but the way in which customer expectations are set and met. For example, if orders taken by a certain date are promised to be fulfilled prior to Christmas, meeting that deadline is likely to satisfy the customer, regardless of the interval. In contrast, failure to meet the deadline is likely to cause significant issues for the customer (e.g. uncertainty about whether the order has been lost, or inability to provide promised Christmas gifts), and will likely result in significant dissatisfaction.

Personal Involvement

In stark contrast with the highly tangible Membership Arrangements, Personal Involvement is probably the most intangible of the seven key satisfaction drivers. Yet even though it is a 'feeling' more than a tangible benefit, and therefore hard to judge, season ticket holders typically consider personal involvement to be critical to their overall satisfaction.

Each of the individual dimensions that feed into Personal Involvement are under the direct control of a team but due to their intangible nature, it is often difficult to get the exact mix right. A process of trial and error is therefore often inevitable. In addition, the contribution that Personal Importance makes to overall satisfaction can be expected to increase based on the length of membership. That is, as season ticket holders become more familiar with the team, their loyalty and personal connection is likely to grow, and they are more likely to shift from focusing on the tangible aspect of the membership product, and more toward how well they are made to feel a part of the team.

Establishing, maintaining and developing the feelings of personal connection and involvement is also important in managing season ticket holder churn and renewal, particularly among new members who are often most at risk. The particular dimensions (see Table 13.3) of Personal Involvement can be leveraged to create additional membership products designed for those unable to attend many games – that is, membership options that offer a highly involved and satisfying experience irrespective of on-field performance and the ability to get to games.

Yet despite its notable importance, the overall performance rating (see Table 13.4) for Personal Involvement is relatively low, with only On-field Performance scoring lower for most teams. To improve this performance rating, teams are encouraged to make strategic efforts to increase attachment and activate greater personal involvement, effectively driving fans to higher stages of the PCM. Examples include loyalty schemes that reward season ticket holders based on length of membership, recognition of fans at games (especially having players thank fans) and personalized communications. Although perhaps the most effective way to build personal involvement is to ensure the organization is genuinely season-ticket-holder-centric – that is, considers season ticket holders in all decisions and ensures they are well-informed and acknowledged.

Home Ground

The Home Ground driver captures both tangible and intangible dimensions of a season ticket holder's experience with their home stadium. The measures (Table 13.3) used here are a simplified version of what Wakefield, Blodgett and Sloan (1996) termed the 'Sportscape'. However, for teams experiencing issues such as low crowd attendance and poor satisfaction with the stadium experience, it may be useful to return to the deeper Sportscape measures to gain a fuller assessment of the fan experience at games. However, it is important to note that not all aspects of the home ground are within the control of the team. In particular, where venues or stadiums are shared, there may be limitations on the degree to which an individual team is able to customize the facilities to suit their season ticket holders.

The sport spectator experience is increasingly influenced by technology, with many sport teams seeking to combat the convenience and enhanced viewing experience available at home via digital broadcast. In addition, given the difficulties often faced in getting to a stadium (e.g. traffic, queues) and the impact of uncontrollable factors such as the weather, watching sporting events at home has become increasingly attractive due to improvements in both broadcast technologies (e.g. high definition, better camera angles and detailed player information) and the quality of in-home equipment (e.g. large screen television, surround sound).

Sport teams must therefore continue to improve the home ground experience if they are to effectively compete with broadcasting. Although there are already some aspects of the in-stadium experience that are difficult to replicate elsewhere, such as the feeling of being part of a broader community and having a direct influence over the outcome via fan behaviour (e.g. cheering, intimidating opposition players). Such factors need to be enhanced and further complemented by a team's efforts to reduce barriers to attendance; particularly feelings of safety (e.g. a family-friendly environment) and ease of entry/exit.

A sensory approach can be taken to managing the stadium experience; whereby all five senses are evoked to provide a feeling of 'home' in the stadium (see Lee, Lee, Seo & Green, 2012). Critical among the senses is physical touch – the stadium must be both comfortable and comforting to make fans feel safe and welcome. With stadium redevelopments regularly exceeding USD$1 billion, there has been much attention placed on the functional aspects of the stadium environment – seating, entry points, catering and technology. Yet the other senses all play a role in building a feeling of a home ground.

As an example of a professional sport team that has successfully leveraged the home ground feeling are the Seattle Sounders in the US Major League Soccer (MLS), which has successfully encouraged attendance and a feeling of a true home ground in a shared stadium. Some of the team's main initiatives have included a fan 'march to the match', organized chants and 'fight songs', a marching band, special entrances for season ticket holders, entertainment around the ground and an honour board for season ticket holders' photos.

Service to Members

Service to Members broadly refers to the level of customer focus displayed by a sport team and its staff, and the opportunities given to season ticket holders to interact with each other and the team. Harking back to the SERVQUAL work of Parasuraman, Berry, and Zeithaml (1991), the key aspects of customer service are reliability, responsiveness, building trust and displaying empathy. As discussed, season ticket holders are character- ized by a high degree of involvement with the team, and are therefore more likely to be demanding of team service staff.

One issue notable in many sport organizations is the high use of volunteer labour, and the prevalence of employees who are passionate fans of the organization. Many people dream of working for their favourite sport team, which has its benefits; but this can also be counterproductive in a service role. Highly passionate staff may lack empathy for those fans not as engaged; they may also be critical of those who require high service levels, such as expecting 'real fans' not to complain about the team. Training staff to be responsive and empathetic is therefore highly important in this context.

Another difficult aspect to manage is the interactions between season ticket holders, and between season ticket holders and the sport team. For example, simple benefits like allowing season ticket holders to attend functions and hear from players and coaches can become difficult as season ticket holder numbers increase. Some team functions such as family days can be run in a manner that makes them scalable to large crowds, but others need to be limited for them to be effective. This provides an opportunity to restrict these benefits to high-tier membership products or to reward season ticket holder loyalty. Managing interactions between fans must also be done sensitively. While it is necessary to build a sense of community between fans, it is again worth noting that 'hardcore' fans are often disparaging toward new and less engaged fans. For example, online chat rooms can be intimidating for newer 'non-experts', with abuse commonly hurled at these 'newbies'. Multiple communications might therefore need to be established to cater for the range of season ticket holder experiences being sought.

Marketing & Communications

The Marketing & Communications driver broadly refers to the key communication channels and touchpoints that a sport team has established with its season ticket holder base. As such, it includes traditional forms of communication such as mail-outs and magazines, and also emerging forms such as social media and web content. Regardless of the execution, the purpose is to keep season ticket holders informed and connected to the team.

Communication is a key tool for establishing and maintaining a sense of personal involvement among members, and as such it is somewhat surprising that it does not rate higher in terms of its overall contribution to the satisfaction score (Table 13.4). In terms of opportunities for improvement, qualitative discussions with season ticket holders highlighted the following:

- These members are critical of communications that are overly corporate and contain information that is otherwise available to the general public, or at times even out-of-date.
- They seek a behind-the-scenes perspective into team life and events, or a more passionate 'one-eyed' voice from the team.
- The responsibility for effective and targeted communications lies beyond that of just the marketing department. Senior management and the board also have a role to play.
- Teams should take into consideration the different needs and drivers of cohorts with the season ticket holder base (e.g. foundation members, recent joiners), and customize their communications where practical.

Across the team satisfaction studies conducted, it is noteworthy that Marketing & Communications is often the least important satisfaction driver (contributing only 4% in the aggregate model – see Figure 13.1). Based on discussions with season ticket holders, the overriding reason seems to be that they are mostly satisfied with the marketing communications they receive (i.e. expectations are consistently met, lowering the driver's importance); although it was also commonly noted that the communications they receive from the team are 'bland' or 'generic', such that they are not distinguishable from media reports or other sources of information. Most teams are conservative in their marketing communications, commonly restrained by sport league rules and codes of conduct; yet most fans still expect the team to reflect their passion. For example, if the refereeing was poor, fans would like the team to speak about it in the same passionate and biased tones as they do.

On-field Performance

On-field Performance is unique in that it is the only key satisfaction driver that is mostly outside the short-term control of team management. In a sporting context, the on-field success of a team is perceived as central to the fan experience; thus, it may be surprising to know that winning or losing does not have a strong direct influence on the overall satisfaction score. It is generally possible to provide a satisfying sport membership experience even when the on-field results are poor, such as by ensuring other aspects of the experience are done well, which provides a buffer between any on-field fluctuations.

On-field performance tends to aid season ticket holder acquisition, but does not impact greatly on season ticket holder retention. This is because most long-term season ticket holders accept that on-field results are part of the theatre of sport; the team is so important to their identity that even repeated failure on field does not damage their desire to stay connected to the team.

Yet even though the direct effect of On-field Performance on overall satisfaction is weak, there is evidence of a 'halo effect' around winning and losing. That is, the indirect impact of On-field Performance is usually stronger on satisfaction drivers such as Personal Involvement or Team Administration, and to a lesser extent on the likes of Home Ground and Membership Arrangements. This means that the team's administration is often held responsible for poor performance, and that many people feel less involved and connected to losing teams. Even though this halo effect is not large, teams need to carefully manage season ticket holder expectations in relation to On-field Performance to avoid it becoming an issue.

Team Administration

Team Administration might seem like a strange inclusion for a scale purporting to measure the sport season ticket holder experience. However, season ticket holders can, and frequently do, judge the management and administrators of their team, which notably impacts on their overall satisfaction with the season ticket holder product. Many season ticket products include the ability to vote for board members in general elections – an initiative that often makes season ticket holders feel part of the organization, even if they seldom exercise this right.

Relevant academic research (McDonald & Sherry, 2010) and experience working with sport teams has indicated the following:

- Most season ticket holders have a strong opinion about the performance of the team's board, even if they are uncertain about its exact role and responsibilities (e.g. versus that of team management). In fact, there have been examples of dissatisfied sport team members acting to have team boards overturned.
- Boards have been shown to have a strong impact on promoting a feeling of personal inclusion, and therefore have a direct impact on the Personal Involvement element of season ticket holder satisfaction.
- Boards need to be mindful of governing in an inclusive manner, and taking the time and effort to explain decisions, making them accountable and open to scrutiny.

It is worth bearing in mind that season ticket holder views of Team Administration performance are often based on limited information, usually gleaned from annual reports or media reports. Sport teams can therefore be proactive in managing perceptions of the team administration in their communication efforts, ensuring that positive news about the administration is widely communicated.

13.7 CUSTOMER SATISFACTION AND OUTCOMES

Given all the attention now placed on quality management and customer satisfaction, it is important to assess whether improving in these areas positively impacts on future customer behaviour such as repeat purchase and word-of-mouth. There are generally costs involved in improving quality and satisfaction, and so the question often arises as to whether this investment is profitable for organizations.

The already widespread adoption of quality and satisfaction management means that a large amount of research studies examining their impact have already been conducted. Two large ongoing research projects – the American Customer Satisfaction Index and the Swedish Customer Satisfaction Barometer – have shown that increases in satisfaction can be linked to customer retention, shareholder value and small increments in returns on investment. For example, in commercial organizations, increased customer satisfaction produces a more stable customer base, which in turn allows them to form stronger relationships with suppliers and reduce price elasticity. Satisfied customers also improve acquisition efforts by spreading positive word-of-mouth, particularly in the age of social media.

In sport markets, there is a growing body of data that supports the relationship between quality, satisfaction and customer outcomes. For example, McDonald, Karg and Leckie (2014) revealed that satisfaction is a contributor to whether season ticket holders choose to purchase in future years; although not a strong one. In addition, McDonald and Stavros (2007) found a positive relationship between season ticket holder satisfaction and lapsed intention to rejoin. A subsequent 2010 study of over 4,500 season ticket holders (McDonald, 2010) confirmed that while some non-renewers choose not to repurchase while still satisfied overall, the average satisfaction ratings for renewing season ticket holders is higher.

Other relevant research in a broader industry context has revealed that the highest proportion of churn occurs among the most recently acquired customers. In the sport scenario, converting fans to season ticket holders is a major achievement; however, it is often only part of the story, with an excess of 33% of first-year season ticket holders then leaving at the end of their first year (see Figure 13.2). First-year season ticket holders cannot be considered to be fully engrained in the life of a team – they are new to the season ticket experience and are yet to develop links of mutual trust and commitment. McDonald's 2010 study noted above found that most new season ticket holders remain 'at risk' until year four, upon which time churn likelihood stabilizes. It is therefore worth considering what stage of the PCM customers are at when assessing the relationship between quality, satisfaction and what they will do next.

In other contexts, similar relationships can be seen. Sport participants have been consistently shown to not only have a strong relationship between event quality and repeat participation, but also benefit from a relationship between participation satisfaction and

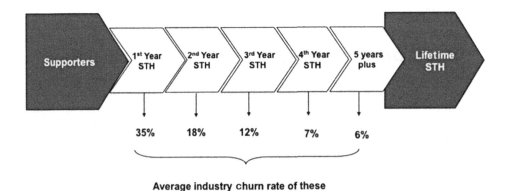

FIGURE 13.2 Churn rate by number of years as a season ticket holder (STH)

life satisfaction (Funk, Jordan, Ridinger & Kaplanidou, 2011). The quality of fitness centres and gymnasiums has been extensively studied in many countries, and the data clearly indicates that improved quality of both staff and facilities increases customer retention (e.g. Smith, Duncan & Howat, 2014; Yo & Pastore, 2004). Similarly, in ski resorts (Alexandris, Kouthouris & Meligdis 2006) and golf clubs (Lee, Kim, Ko & Sagas, 2011), the relationships hold.

Sport spectators across a range of sports have been shown to notice improvements to the quality of their expereince, which has impacted on their satisfaction and likelihood of repeat attendance (Kelley & Turley 2001; Theodorakis *et al.*, 2013). However, managing satisfaction levels takes on a unique twist in a sport spectating context, where even unhappy customers are unlikely to switch their support to another team. To demonstrate their lack of satisfaction, sport team customers are more likely to decrease their level of consumption and revert to being casual supporters. Another unique aspect of sport is that at its heart there is a contest. Where many services can be difficult to assess, sport performance is often clearly signalled via the scoreboard.

Despite such differences between the various sport contexts, it would appear that sport participants and spectators both derive their satisfaction from service quality, favourably responding to higher quality services that leverage positive outcomes for the sport organization.

13.8 CHAPTER SUMMARY

The experience of customers is complex and multidimensional, but their satisfaction (or lack of it) can be expressed as the difference between their expectations prior to consumption and their perceptions of the actual experience.

While acquisition is a critical part of customer management, marketing activities must be designed to balance acquisition with the retention of existing customers. While there has been much debate about where organizations should focus the bulk of their marketing efforts, the simple facts are that acquisition is necessary for growth and replacement of unavoidable churn, and that retention is often easier to manage and less costly to the organization. Customer retention relies on satisfying customers and maintaining high brand awareness. Satisfied customers also spread positive word-of-mouth, which can be useful to the acquisition of new customers. Customer satisfaction is therefore critical to the success of any business, particularly subscription-based organizations that rely on maintaining enduring and interactive relationships with their customers.

This chapter's discussion of service quality, satisfaction and service recovery has been based around one key assumption – that efforts to retain customers are worthwhile. However, to balance this discussion, it is important to note that sometimes the customer is NOT always right. In fact, there are times when a customer should be allowed to leave the relationship with the organization, with minimal effort used to retain them. The main relevant scenario is when the customer is toxic to the organization, such as football hooligans. In all other cases, improving service quality will improve satisfaction and allow organizations to be more successful via stronger customer retention and recommendations, and lower acquisition costs.

13.9 DISCUSSION QUESTIONS

1) What are the relationships between service quality, expectations and satisfaction?
2) What are service quality gaps? Name three that can arise, giving an example of each.
3) If an organization does not want to undertake formal research, what are some of the data sources on customer perceptions of service quality they could access?
4) What are the key differences between SERVQUAL and SERVPERF?
5) Explain the disconfirmation of the customer expectations model.

13.10 CLASS ACTIVITY: SERVICE QUALITY AND CUSTOMER SATISFACTION

Think about the last experience you had as a sport consumer. This could either be as a participant (e.g. playing a round of golf, running a marathon) or as a spectator. Identify the key components of the product you consumed. Develop a questionnaire for measuring the perceived quality of each component and the overall satisfaction with the product. Based on your experience, identify three ways the organization could improve the customer experience, and discuss how that might impact on your future consumption behaviour.

REFERENCES

Alexandris, K., Kouthouris, C. & Meligdis, A. (2006). Increasing customers' loyalty in a skiing resort: The contribution of place attachment and service quality. *International Journal of Contemporary Hospitality Management, 18*(5), 414–425.

Brady, M.K. & Cronin Jr, J.J. (2001). Some new thoughts on conceptualizing perceived service quality: A hierarchical approach. *Journal of Marketing, 65*(3), 34–49.

Carrillat, F.A., Jaramillo, F. & Mulki, J.P. (2007). The validity of the SERVQUAL and SERVPERF scales: A meta-analytic view of 17 years of research across five continents. *International Journal of Service Industry Management, 18*(5), 472–490.

Crompton, J.L., MacKay, K.J. & Fesenmaier, D.R. (1991). Identifying dimensions of service quality in public recreation. *Journal of Park and Recreation Administration, 9*(3), 15–27.

Cronin Jr, J.J. & Taylor, S.A. (1992). Measuring service quality: A re-examination and extension. *Journal of Marketing, 56*(3), 55–68.

De Knop, P., Van Hoecke, J. & De Bosscher, V. (2004). Quality management in sports clubs. *Sport Management Review, 7*(1), 57–77.

Fisher, R. & Wakefield, K. (1998). Factors leading to group identification: A field study of winners and losers. *Psychology & Marketing, 15*(1), 23–40.

Funk, D., Jordan, J., Ridinger, L. & Kaplanidou, K. (2011). Capacity of mass participant sport events for the development of activity commitment and future exercise intention. *Leisure Sciences, 33*(3), 250–268.

Grönroos, C. (1990). *Service Management and Marketing: Managing the moments of truth in service competition.* Lexington, MA: Lexington Books.

Kelley, S.W. & Turley, L.W. (2001). Consumer perceptions of service quality attributes at sporting events. *Journal of Business Research, 54*(2), 161–166.

Kim, D. & Kim, S.Y. (1995). QUESC: An instrument for assessing the service quality of sport centers in Korea. *Journal of Sport Management, 9*(2), 208–220.

Ko, Y.J. & Pastore, D.L. (2005). A hierarchical model of service quality for the recreational sport industry. *Sport Marketing Quarterly, 14*(2), 84–97.

Ko, Y.J. & Pastore, D.L. (2004). Current issues and conceptualizations of service quality in the recreation sport industry. *Sport Marketing Quarterly, 13*(3), 159–166.

Kouthouris, C. & Alexandris, K. (2005). Can service quality predict customer satisfaction and behavioral intentions in the sport tourism industry? An application of the SERVQUAL model in an outdoors setting. *Journal of Sport & Tourism, 10*(2), 101–111.

Lee, J.H., Kim, H.D., Ko, Y.J. & Sagas, M. (2011). The influence of service quality on satisfaction and intention: A gender segmentation strategy. *Sport Management Review, 14*(1), 54–63.

Lee, S., Lee, H.J., Seo, W.J. & Green, C. (2012). A new approach to stadium experience: The dynamics of the sensoryscape, social interaction, and sense of home. *Journal of Sport Management, 26*(6), 490–505.

Lusch, R.F. & Vargo, S.L. (2006). The service-dominant logic of marketing: Dialog. *Debate, and Directions, ME Sharpe, Armonk, NY, 10.*

McDonald, H. (2010). The factors influencing churn rates among season ticket holders: An empirical analysis. *Journal of Sport Management, 24,* 676–701.

McDonald, H. & Karg, A.J. (2014). Managing co-creation in professional sports: The antecedents and consequences of ritualized spectator behavior. *Sport Management Review, 17*(3), 292–309.

McDonald, H., Karg, A.J. & Leckie, C. (2014). Predicting which season ticket holders will renew and which will not. *European Sport Management Quarterly, 14*(5), 503–520.

McDonald, H., Karg, A. & Vocino, A. (2013). Measuring season ticket holder satisfaction: rational, scale development and longitudinal validation. *Sport Management Review, 16*(1), 41–53.

McDonald, H. & Sherry, E. (2010). Evaluating sport club board performance: A customer perspective. *Journal of Sport Management, 24*(5), 524–543.

McDonald, H. & Stavros, C. (2007). A defection analysis of lapsed season ticket holders: A consumer and organizational study. *Sport Marketing Quarterly, 16,* 218–229.

Oliver, R.L. (2014). Satisfaction: A behavioral perspective on the consumer. Armonk, NY: M.E. Sharpe.

Parasuraman, A., Berry, L.L. & Zeithaml, V.A. (1991). Refinement and reassessment of the SERVQUAL Scale. *Journal of Retailing, 67*(4), 420–450.

Parasuraman, A., Zeithaml, V.A. & Berry, L.L. (1985). A conceptual model of service quality and its implications for future research. *The Journal of Marketing, 49*(4), 41–50.

Parasuraman, A., Zeithaml, V.A. & Berry, L.L. (1988). Servqual. *Journal of Retailing, 64*(1), 12–40.

Sharp, B. (2010). *How Brands Grow: What Marketers Don't Know.* South Melbourne: Oxford University Press.

Smith, J., Murray, D. & Howat, G. (2014). How perceptions of physique can influence customer satisfaction in health and fitness centres. *Managing Leisure, 19*(6), 442–460.

Theodorakis, N.D. & Alexandris, K. (2008). Can service quality predict spectators' behavioral intentions in professional soccer? *Managing Leisure, 13*(3–4), 162–178.

Theodorakis, N.D., Alexandris, K., Tsigilis, N. & Karvounis, S. (2013). Predicting spectators' behavioural intentions in professional football: The role of satisfaction and service quality. *Sport Management Review, 16*(1), 85–96.

Wakefield, K.L., Blodgett, J.G. & Sloan, H.J. (1996). Measurement and management of the Sportscape. *Journal of Sport Management, 10*(1), 15–31.

Yoshida, M. & James, J.D. (2011). Service quality at sporting events: Is aesthetic quality a missing dimension? *Sport Management Review, 14*(1), 13–24.

PART 5

An alternative perspective on sport consumer behaviour

CHAPTER 14

Sport consumption and marketing empirical generalizations

This chapter's objectives are to:

- define an empirical generalization
- introduce and provide an overview of the key marketing empirical generalizations
- detail how sport consumption follows those marketing empirical generalizations
- explain how sport managers should adapt their practices to include knowledge of empirical generalizations.

14.0 INTRODUCTION

When we think about the sport fan or participant, the image that comes to mind is often of someone who is highly passionate and committed. It's the extreme fan with painted face, lots of team merchandise and dedication to seeing every game. Or, it's the amateur athlete who trains hard, spends money on the best equipment and commits hours to improving their personal best performances, all as a 'hobby'. The sports consumer is often portrayed as being different from other consumers – more passionate, more commitment and more loyal – especially compared to consumers of typical fast-moving consumer goods (FMCG). Indeed, there are numerous books written about sports consumers, with titles like 'The Elusive Fan' (Rein, Kotler & Shields 2006) or 'The Secret Lives of Sports Fans' (Simons, 2013), which give the impression of a very unusual and distinct group of consumers. This raises the questions – are sports consumers really different from consumers in other product markets and if so, should we adopt different marketing practices?

One way to examine these questions is to understand what is 'normal' consumer behaviour in most markets, and then look at the extent to which sport fans conform or not to that norm. Our understanding of the norms of consumer behaviour have advanced greatly in the last 20 years, and we are now in a position to describe 'laws' of marketing. Most of these laws stem from observing patterns in consumer behaviour.

Although they are not well known, and many believe consumer behaviour to be impossible to predict, there are a number of empirical generalizations that have been identified in the marketing field. For example, a substantial amount of panel data, analysed longitudinally and across multiple product categories, has shown that consumers are rarely 100% loyal to one brand. Instead, they purchase across repertoires of similar brands to satisfy their category requirements (Ehrenberg, Uncles & Goodhardt, 2004). Just as sport consumers represent many diverse types, from casual viewers to die-hard fans (see discussion of the PCM in Chapters 9 and 10), non-sport consumers range from light to heavy buyers (Uncles, Ehrenberg & Hammond, 1995). While it is generally assumed that sport has a higher proportion of consumer fanatics than other products, many products have devotees (e.g. Starbucks, Hello Kitty, Harry Potter, Apple computers). The combined effects of purchases made by consumers along the full spectrum from one-time buyers through to brand devotees create recognizable and predictable patterns – patterns we call 'empirical generalizations'.

14.1 WHAT ARE 'EMPIRICAL GENERALIZATIONS'?

Empirical generalizations are patterns regularly seen in data across multiple fields. Frank Bass, one of the pioneering researchers examining these generalizations in consumer data, defined them as 'a pattern or regularity that repeats over different circumstances and that can be described simply by mathematical, graphic, or symbolic methods' (Bass, 1995 p. 6). They allow us to understand what is 'normal' in most markets by providing benchmarks we can measure. Empirical generalizations flow from having large amounts of data and repeated studies. Often patterns are recognized in data before there is a theoretical explanation for them, so the finding of an empirical generalization sometimes leads us to rethink our theories on how the world operates.

This has been the case in marketing, where the influx of new data has allowed researchers to understand consumer behaviour better, and identify important patterns. This new data has come from many sources – supermarket scanner data, loyalty programmes that link customer demographics to purchase and behaviour, social media data like tweets and Facebook likes and improved data on media consumption (e.g. television ratings). What marketers are seeing in this data is changing marketing theory – and beginning to have a profound impact on marketing practice.

The development of these marketing empirical generalizations ('laws', hereafter for simplicity) began much earlier. Andrew Ehrenberg, a leading researcher and pioneer of the search for laws in marketing, was actively looking for patterns in consumer data back in the mid-1950s. The Bass diffusion model – an accurate method of predicting the manner in which innovations diffuse throughout society – was developed in the late 1960s (Bass, 1969). Given how long many of these patterns have been known, it is surprising to see how slow many marketers have been to adopt this knowledge and its implications. The increased volume of data has shown us that these patterns are indeed law-like and have widespread applicability. The recent adoption of new marketing practices based on these marketing laws by global market leaders like Mars and Coca-Cola has meant that, almost 60 years after they were first discovered, there is now a burgeoning interest in applying marketing laws. In sport marketing practice and research, however, recognition and use of these generalizations is almost unheard of, and few sports organizations could be said to have embraced this new approach.

The marketing laws discovered so far suggest that some practices traditionally encouraged in marketing such as segmentation, target marketing, differentiating your product and developing niche brands are flawed and require a rethink. It is therefore critically important that modern marketing managers are aware of these laws and can assess the implications of those laws for the industry they work in. We begin our look at marketing empirical generalizations, and their relevance to sports, by looking at the characteristics of two key types of markets – repertoire and subscription markets.

14.2 REPERTOIRE VERSUS SUBSCRIPTION MARKETS

The first step in understanding marketing laws is to know your market and its characteristics. Consumer behaviour norms differ in different types of markets. Markets, based on consumer behaviour, can be divided into two categories.

The first type of market is called a 'repertoire' market. A repertoire is a range or full inventory of your possible options. We say that singers have a 'repertoire of songs', meaning the range of songs they know and can perform. In repertoire markets, customers have a repertoire of brands they use to fulfill their needs in each category. In most markets, consumers purchase regularly and do so from a 'repertoire' of competing brands to fulfill their category requirements. Fast moving consumer goods (FMCGs) are typical of repertoire market products. Consider your local supermarket. Almost all of the products stocked there are repertoire market products. That is, for each product category (e.g. canned soup, shampoo, breakfast cereal) consumers will have a repertoire of brands they purchase from over the course of year.

If you are a breakfast cereal eater, you most likely have a favourite product in this category. Let's say that your favourite is Cheerios, given it is still the highest selling cereal in the USA (http://wpo.st/lVN41). Even though Cheerios is your preferred brand and, if asked, you might describe yourself as loyal Cheerios consumer, chances are that over the course of a year you purchased or consumed other brands of cereal as well as Cheerios. You consume brands other than your favourite for a number of reasons. For example, sometimes your favourite brand will be unavailable (e.g. sold out at the store or not available in a hotel you're staying at) or sometimes you simply want to try something different. The brands you consume over the year are your repertoire for that category.

What is typically found in repertoire markets is that consumers are 'loyal' to a few brands. This phenomenon has been called 'polygamous' loyalty (Sharp, 2013, p. 43). We are loyal to a small number of brands in each product category. We know those brands work well for us, and we switch between them based on mood and circumstance. Most people have a strong tendency to be loyal to brands because they are seeking to simplify decisions. Consider your own behaviour. If you are bored one afternoon, the difficult decision is how you will entertain yourself given so many options – go for a run, watch a movie, go out for a meal, etc.? Once it is decided on which category of entertainment you will consume, the specific choice of running location, cinema or restaurant is relatively simple because you have favourites. These favourites are simply a way to reduce the stress of decision making, given how busy people are and the relatively large number of unimportant decisions we make each day. Loyalty to products, as a result, is best viewed as a convenient option for consumers, not as an expression of any deep love or strong emotional attachment.

The other category of market is called a 'subscription' market. Subscription markets require consumers to commit to purchasing the product for a fixed period of time. Such products include phone services, insurance, banking and utilities (see Sharp, Wright & Goodhardt, 2002, for a full discussion). The key differences between subscription markets and the more commonly seen repertoire markets are that: (a) subscription products are bought infrequently, often annually; (b) consumers have much smaller repertoires in subscription markets and are often solely loyal to one provider; and (c) they often involve being formally contracted to one specific provider for the period of purchase, for example, annual cell phone contracts.

As a consequence of the characteristics of subscription markets, subscription market behaviour differs from repertoire market behaviour on two key metrics. First, preferred brands in subscription markets tend to satisfy a much higher percentage of consumers' category needs. For example, if you have a membership to a fitness/health club, it is likely that the vast majority of your exercise is done there. You may occasionally use a hotel or a workplace gym, but as much as 90% of your training could be expected to occur at your primary fitness club (your 'preferred brand' in this case).

The second metric that will differ in subscription markets is that there will be a higher number of solely loyal customers for each brand evident. Solely loyal buyers are present in repertoire markets, but usually they are very light buyers. That is, people who only buy the category once a year, are always solely loyal because they only bought one brand. Sharp (2013) reports an average sole loyalty rate of 11% across three different categories of repertoire products. In subscription markets we see a much higher number of solely loyal buyers, upwards of 70% (Sharp & Wright, 1999). This is a direct consequence of the nature of subscription products. Most people, for example, have only one cell phone contract at any one time, so they will be solely loyal to your contracted provider. There will be some exceptions – people with work and personal phone contracts for example – but across the cell phone customer base, you will see more solely loyal customers than in repertoire markets.

The key differences between repertoire and subscription markets are summarized in Table 14.1.

TABLE 14.1 Differences between repertoire and subscription markets

Characteristic	Repertoire market (e.g. FMCG)	Subscription market (e.g. Fitness Club)
Frequency of purchase	Purchased often	Purchased infrequently (annually or seasonally)
Number of brands bought	Consumers buy many brands over time (large repertoire)	Few brands bought (small repertoire)
Nature of relationship	Informal relationships	Often formal contracts
Degree of involvement	Low consumer involvement	Often high involvement

14.3 SPORTS MARKETS

Both types of market are common in sports industries. Repertoire markets in sports would include sports apparel, free-to-air broadcast sport and casual ticket buying for sport events. Subscription markets in sport include the offering of a team season ticket package or a membership, fitness club membership and paid broadcast subscriptions (e.g. the 'NBA League Pass').

It is worth giving some attention to the relationship between repertoire and subscription markets in sport, because the relationship between them is different in sport than from most markets. If we think about the typical subscription market, the product cannot be readily sampled prior to committing to the subscription. Insurance is a good example of a typical subscription product. In order to insure your house or car, you must take out a 12-month subscription. To switch between brands, you normally need to wait until your subscription is expired. This is true of phone companies, electricity providers and credit cards.

It is common practice for sport teams worldwide, as well as various other arts and leisure organizations (e.g. theatre companies, art galleries, gyms), to offer subscription products to fans. Variations abound, and it is no longer the case that a 'season ticket' constitutes a pass for multiple game entry. Many organizations have moved from using the term season ticket to other expressions such as 'member' or 'patron' to reflect the changing nature of the product. For sport market leaders with capacity attendance, non-ticketed memberships are now the norm and often the major product sold. In all cases, it is likely that the fan considering buying a season ticket (the subscription product) has previously consumed a casual game entry (repertoire product).

In addition, the sport product is inherently unpredictable because its outcome relies on competitive sporting endeavour. On the other hand, the unpredictable nature of sporting contests has been shown to be an important motivator of consumption (Kerstetter & Kovich, 1997). Such unpredictability, however, makes it very difficult to provide accurate or concrete information about the content or quality of sport services in advance, which increases the level of uncertainty for consumers. Participating in a marathon or watching a football match cannot be guaranteed to satisfy or meet expectations, making them high in what Zeithaml (1981) called 'experience qualities'.

For these reasons, sport consumers can be expected to evaluate these products differently from most other consumer products, meaning that simple adaptation of marketing laws may not be appropriate here. Despite (or perhaps because of) these complexities, consumers often become most heavily involved with these products. Fisher and Wakefield's (1998) examination of sport fans typifies the somewhat paradoxical behaviours that can occur in relation to these products. They found evidence of poorly performing teams experiencing increased support and loyalty among their fans. This phenomenon may be explained by the notion that many of these products are hedonic (pleasurable) in nature, and the enjoyment comes in many ways rather than just simple consumption of a single preferred brand.

Accepting that sport markets often comprised both repertoire and subscription product categories, we now discuss two specific marketing laws and their applicability to sport.

14.4 THE DOUBLE JEOPARDY LAW

The double jeopardy law is now perhaps the best known of the market empirical generalizations. Double jeopardy describes the relationship between a brands market share and the loyalty of its customers. Specifically, McPhee's (1963) double jeopardy pattern suggests that smaller market-share brands receive not only fewer customers, but also slightly lower levels of loyalty from their customers than larger brands (Ehrenberg, Goodhardt & Barwise, 1990). Thus, small market-share brands suffer in two ways: (1) fewer customers and (2) lower loyalty among those customers they have.

Researchers have identified double jeopardy patterns in a wide range of products, including packaged goods (Wilbur & Farris, 2014), durable goods (Colombo & Morrison, 1989), B2B (Uncles & Ehrenberg, 1990), store patronage (Uncles & Kwok, 2009), arts and culture (Hand, 2011) and television viewership (Sharp, Beal & Collins, 2009). Fast-moving consumer goods (e.g. instant coffee, toothpaste, laundry detergent) remain the most-studied context. The empirical patterns in purchase data consistently exhibit a number of characteristics related to market share, purchase frequency, loyalty measures and brand switching.

Specifically, as market penetration decreases between brands, so does purchase frequency and 100% loyalty rates (Ehrenberg et al., 2004). Smaller brands having both fewer customers and customers who buy the brand less frequently is the source of the name 'double jeopardy' – the brands lose in two ways. This stream of research has identified a statistical model, the Dirichlet, as a useful tool for predicting these regular patterns based on parameters capturing the market penetration and purchase frequency for the product category and at least one brand (Ehrenberg et al., 2004). Kearns (2004) produced an Excel-based tool for quickly calculating these statistics and it is still widely available on the internet (see Table 14.2 for an example of Dirichlet outputs).

Double jeopardy may sound banal to you – you may think that it is obvious that large brands have more customers, and their customers being 'slightly' more loyal isn't that impressive. But prior to this finding (and even today in some organizations), it was believed that brands might only have a small number of buyers but those buyers could be very loyal, heavy users giving the brand a large market share. This was the idea of 'niche' marketing – finding a specific (and small) group of customers you could satisfy better than anyone else and as a result, gaining all of their purchasing. The double jeopardy law shows us that this scenario does not happen in practice. You cannot have a small number of customers who you 'own' – who are entirely loyal to you – and have a large market share. The implications of this are discussed in section 14.7.

14.5 THE DUPLICATION OF PURCHASE LAW

The duplication of purchase law flows from double jeopardy, but this empirical generalization focuses on how brands share customers with other brands. It states that this sharing is in line with each brand's market share or penetration (Ehrenberg et al., 2004). All brands, within a category, share their customer base with other brands in line with the size of those other brands. Large brands may have more customers who buy other brands, but small brands will have a greater percentage of their customers buying brands – and its usually the bigger brands they buy when they do.

Some variations have been found to this law, with what has been called 'partitioning' existing in some markets (Romaniuk & Dawes, 2005). Partitioning occurs when major functional differences or similarities between brands exist, which has the effect of creating sub-repertoires of brands within a larger market. For example, a customer preferring free trade products may select more heavily among free trade brands than the duplication of purchase law (based solely on market share) would suggest (Winchester, Nencyz-Thiel, Arding & Less, 2011).Partitioning is uncommon, and when it does occur, the impact of it is predictable using the Duplication of Purchase Law.

The duplication of purchase law challenges traditional thinking about who brand buyers are. In particular, it calls into account how deeply connected consumers are with the products they buy. If consumers aren't 100% loyal to brands, and they have a number of brands that suit their needs, then are they really going through the process of finding a brand that expresses their personality or who they are? Are people who support the Green Bay Packers different from people who support the New York Giants? Are soccer fans different from NHL fans? Are marathon runners different from cyclists?

These questions mirror the classic marketing debates – are Coke drinkers different from Pepsi drinkers, Harley Davidson buyers from Kawasaki buyers, Apple users different from PC (as the 66 adverts famously attest: www.youtube.com/watch?v=0eEG5LVXdKo)? These debates have been comprehensively settled with data showing not only that the demographic and attitudinal profiles of buyers of these brands are comparable, but that they are often the same people! That is, Coke buyers drink Pepsi, Harley owners ride other bikes and Apple buyers buy PCs on about one-third of future purchase occasions (see Sharp, 2010 for full data sets and discussion).

14.6 APPLYING THESE LAWS TO SPORT CONSUMPTION

This book has discussed in depth the unique aspects of sport consumption, and the variety of sport consumers that exist. The PCM has, at its heart, the acknowledgement that there is a variety of sport fans and participants at different degrees of involvement and commitment to sport. One point must be made very clear here, and that is that the PCM does not map out a method for marketers to grow their brands by converting all their consumers from Aware to Allegiant. To do so is almost impossible without losing market share – the laws of marketing tell us so. While we can use the insights from the PCM to increase the involvement levels of sport fans or participants and improve retention, in order to grow our sport brand, new customers must be found. These new customers will typically (but not always) come in at the Awareness level. They will consume infrequently or once in their initial stages of involvement, and may stay in the lower stages of the PCM forever. This should not be viewed as a failing, but rather the natural state of growing brands.

Looking specifically at how marketing generalizations might apply to sport, there are some differences that could be expected to impact how well the laws fit. McDonald (2010) noted the low level of customer switching between competing brands (teams), and how consumers tend to lower their engagement rather than change allegiance to a team. Considering the context of professional team sport in particular, there are two further factors that could represent additional distinguishing features. These are the simultaneous consumption of two teams when attending or viewing team sport events and the geographic divisions of teams in most national leagues. Geographic divisions build team identity through connection with locations and communities important to the fan (Heere & James, 2007). What is unclear is how multiple teams from the same region, especially those that compete against each other, might impact on fan behaviour like viewing and attendance. While unusual in sport, this situation is common in other industries, with one example being beer markets where many local beers compete (e.g. Milwaukee). The simultaneous consumption of sport teams or players is something quite unique to sport. Although recognized as a key feature, the impact of consuming two brands at once (one favoured, one possibly disliked strongly) on consumer behaviour has not been examined in detail. Related studies, such as that of Bee and Madrigal (2012), have found that less engaged fans prefer closer contests between opponents.

Previous researchers have speculated these empirical generalizations may not hold in the case of professional team sport brands because of these differences (Gladden & Funk, 2001). At the same time, other researchers have suggested sport team supporters exhibit behavioural and attitudinal loyalty patterns similar to those observed in non-sport contexts, such as supermarket goods (e.g. Tapp, 2004).

Given the applicability of these laws to a wide range of industries, however, questioning whether they apply to team sport brands may seem redundant. In a study of television viewing habits in the United States, Barwise and Ehrenberg (1988) found notable deviations from predicted patterns for Spanish-language and religious-themed programming. Despite relatively low viewership numbers, these two types of programming still generate relatively heavy consumption. As such, while rare, variation from the double jeopardy and duplication of purchase laws is known. Sport brands arguably may experience heavy partitioning due to traditional rivalries, geographic separation or underdog preferences.

So is this the case? Analysis of sports specific data is extremely rare, and only a handful of academic studies have been published on the topic of how well these marketing empirical generalizations apply to sport. Sport is a difficult product category in which to undertake typical brand-level consumption analysis. Complexity is inherent in sport, with team-based sports requiring two brands to be consumed simultaneously as they compete. Loyalty in a sport context is also hard to define in behavioural terms, because fans often watch teams they dislike compete (i.e. consume disliked brands) since the outcomes of those contests impact on their favoured team. Consumption of a competing brand (team) would not always be considered disloyal behaviour in sport contexts, the way it might in FMCG markets.

In order to examine whether sport fan consumption conforms or deviates from established patterns of behaviour in other markets, the context must be carefully selected. Two key studies by Doyle, Filo, McDonald & Funk (2013) and Baker, McDonald & Funk (2016) examine how well the marketing laws fitted data from professional sports leagues in Australia.

Doyle, Filo, McDonald & Funk (2013) examined the extent to which the brand perceptions of fans of teams in professional rugby (NRL) and Australian Football (AFL) leagues followed double jeopardy patterns. They found that on 9 of 13 brand associations, teams with higher market share (number of fans in this case) had higher brand associations. They also found that attitudinal loyalty was stronger among fans of more popular teams than less popular teams.

Baker, McDonald & Funk (2016) examined some unusual data from the Australian Football League, with clear results. The data collected focused on actual live game attendance. They examined a large group of 'members' of the Australian Football League. These members have purchased a season ticket allowing them to attend any of up to 40 football games played live in the state of Victoria during the season. Data was obtained directly from the governing body of the AFL, and provided by the manager of AFL memberships from their consumer database. Two hundred members who nominated each of the 16 teams active in the league prior to 2011 were chosen at random.

The regular AFL season involves 18 teams each playing 11 home and 11 away games each season. Two new teams were introduced into the AFL in Gold Coast (2011) and Western Sydney (2012). The AFL was formed essentially through the incorporation of teams from each of Australia's six states into one existing state-based league operating in Victoria. As a consequence, 10 of the 18 teams in this league are based in the state of Victoria. Fans can purchase tickets on a game by game basis, buy season tickets to their favoured club or buy an AFL membership to access games played by a range of teams.

AFL membership can be thought of as being similar to a stadium membership (e.g. MCC membership at Lords), but it is spread across two stadiums and primarily features only AFL content. All AFL members nominate a team of support as part of their joining process, but it is the wide access to games played by other teams that makes them uniquely suited to this examination.

Baker *et al.* acknowledge this context is atypical, but it is not uncommon. In the EPL, six teams from one city (London) will compete and in the Australian NRL, eight of 16 teams are based in Greater Sydney. Game attendance data was tracked through bar code scanning at stadium. AFL memberships are non-transferable, meaning they cannot be given to others to use. The data from AFL members allows examination of 'double jeopardy' effects – whether high market share brands (teams) have consumers who are slightly more loyal (that is, consume a higher percentage of their team in total games attended) than lower share teams. For each team it is possible to determine how frequently their customers are shared with each other team. The duplication of purchase law dictates that a brand's customer base is expected to overlap with the customer base of each competing brand in line with the relative market share of the brands. Together, this allows a detailed examination of the degree to which observed 'laws' of consumer marketing hold in the sporting context.

Baker *et al.* used the data received from the AFL to run Direchlet modelling, allowing them to see how closely sport consumer behaviour matched the standard patterns. As can be seen in Table 14.2, where Observed (O, actual behaviour data) is compared to Theoretical (T, model derived predictions), a strong double jeopardy pattern was observed in the data.

If this is your first time seeing a table of this type, it is worth spending some time interpreting it. The first column shows the penetration of each team, that is, the number of consumers in the market who consumed that team at least once during the season. Collingwood and Carlton were the two largest teams with 59% observed (actual) penetration. The model predicted that Collingwood would have a larger penetration (66%),

TABLE 14.2 Observed (O) and theoretically predicted (T) brand statistics for AFL attendance

TEAM	Penetration* (%)		Brand purchases*		Category purchases		Share of category requirements (%)	
	O	T	O	T	O	T	O	T
Collingwood	59	66	3.2	2.9	12.4	11.5	26	25
Carlton	59	59	2.6	2.6	12.0	11.8	21	22
Essendon	55	56	2.5	2.5	12.3	11.9	21	21
Richmond	52	49	2.2	2.3	12.4	12.1	17	19
Geelong	50	49	2.3	2.3	12.6	12.1	18	19
Hawthorn	49	49	2.3	2.3	12.8	12.1	18	19
St Kilda	47	48	2.3	2.3	12.7	12.1	18	19
Melbourne	46	42	1.9	1.9	12.6	12.3	15	17
Western Bulldogs	45	43	2.1	2.1	12.8	12.3	16	18
North Melbourne	40	41	2.2	2.2	12.9	12.3	17	17

Note: * Used in fitting the Dirichlet model.
Source: Baker, McDonald & Funk, 2016.

but predicted Carlton's penetration exactly. All other clubs were very closely predicted, so we would say the data closely followed the predicted pattern.

In the second column, we see the average brand purchases (games attended) of each team by consumers. Here, Collingwood was expected to have an average game attendance of 2.9 games a season by consumers, but was observed to have slightly more (3.2). All other teams were closely predicted. As expected under the double jeopardy law, rate of purchase of a brand decreased with lower brand penetration, while rate of purchase of the category increased (column three). Observed share of category requirements for all 10 teams (column four) reflected a nearly-perfect match with the theoretically predicted results.

Examination of duplication of purchase rates allows identification of any partitions in consumption patterns. The traditional duplication of purchase law states that each brand's customer base overlaps with the customer bases of other brands in proportion to its market share. Brands with high market share should overlap with a large portion of the customer base of each competing brand, while those with low market share should capture a relatively smaller portion of the base of each other brand. If Brand A overlaps with 60% of Brand B's customers, Brand A should also overlap with approximately 60% of Brand C's customers and Brand D's customers. As can be seen in Table 3, the duplication of purchase law holds in the case of the observed data. There are no partitions evident between teams in the study, although Hawthorn shares a higher-than-expected share of consumers with most of the other teams. Hawthorn's popularity among fans of other teams may be explained by either their overall success during this period or the presence of exciting individual players (e.g. Lance Franklin, Cyril Rioli). Overall, however, the results indicate that consumers of a team consume other teams in line with the second team's market share. A consequence of this observation is that rivalries do not drive consumption behaviour in the AFL. Consumption of both rival and non-rival teams is in line with the market share of the alternate team and not influenced by the effects of the rivalry.

Baker *et al.* (2106) concluded that high market share teams have consumers who are slightly more loyal than do low market share teams. Customers of the high share teams attend games involving the team more often than do customers of low share teams. Analysis of the duplication of purchase observations indicates that AFL game attendance shows no signs of partitioning. While the AFL offers traditional rivalries, as is common in sport, actual consumption behaviour indicated no such division. Choice of which games to attend and which teams to consume was in line with overall market penetration of each team. As with most other consumer goods, all teams shared their customers and larger teams captured a larger share of the customers of each other team.

As further evidence of the applicability of marketing's laws to sport, consider Table 14.4. This data, produced by the Neilson Scarborough Sport Group, is often used as an example of the differences between sport fans of different leagues. The NBA has more African-American fans than any other leagues. NASCAR has the least female fans. But are these differences meaningful? When you compare each league to the average shown in

TABLE 14.3 Duplication of purchase rates for AFL teams

TEAM	COLL	CARL	ESSE	RICH	GEEL	HAWT	ST K	MELB	WEST	NORTH
COLL	–	77	75	68	68	68	63	61	60	56
CARL	77	–	75	69	66	68	63	59	60	55
ESSE	81	81	–	73	70	73	68	64	64	58
RICH	77	78	77	–	68	70	66	65	65	59
GEEL	81	79	77	71	–	73	69	63	65	58
HAWT	81	81	81	74	73	–	69	66	67	60
ST K	78	79	78	73	72	71	–	63	68	61
MELB	77	75	76	73	68	70	64	–	63	60
WEST	79	79	79	76	72	73	72	65	–	64
NORTH	81	81	79	76	71	74	72	69	71	–
Average	79	79	77	72	70	71	67	64	65	59
Expected	83	83	77	73	70	69	66	64	63	56

Note: Numbers in each cell represent the proportion of people who attended games with team X (row) who also attended games with team Y (column). Coll = Collingwood, Carl = Carlton, Esse = Essendon, Rich = Richmond, Geel = Geelong, Hawt = Hawthorn, St K = St Kilda, Melb = Melbourne, West = Western Bulldogs, North = North Melbourne.

Source: Baker, McDonald & Funk, 2016.

TABLE 14.4 Fan demographics across the five major American sport leagues

DEMOGRAPHIC	MLB (%)	MLS (%)	NASCAR (%)	NBA (%)	NFL (%)	NHL (%)	AVERAGE (%)
GENDER							
Men	59	61	63	60	59	64	61
Women	41	40	37	40	41	36	39
AGE							
Age 18–34	28	38	29	32	30	33	32
Age 35–49	29	32	30	29	29	32	30
Age 50+	43	30	41	39	41	34	38
RACE/ETHNICITY							
White	85	82	86	78	83	86	83
Black/African-American	10	11	10	16	12	9	11
Other	5	7	5	6	5	6	6
Spanish/Hispanic origin	12	23	9	14	11	9	13
HOUSEHOLD INCOME							
<$25K	11	11	13	12	11	9	11
$25–35K	11	11	12	11	11	9	11
$35–50K	18	17	20	18	18	17	18
$50–75K	18	17	19	18	18	19	18

Source: sport business daily http://sportsbusinessdaily.com/Daily/Issues/2010/06/Issue-185/The-Back-Of-The-Book/Fan-Demographics-Among-Major-North-American-Sports-Leagues.aspx.

Table 14.4, the differences are not large. In fact, it could easily be argued that all of these leagues have very similar fans, most likely because they are the same people switching from one sport to another in line with marketing's laws.

14.7 IMPLICATIONS FOR SPORTS MARKETERS

There are many important implications of this work for sports marketers, but some specific issues are:

- Being a small share brand is not good. Defining the size of your brand, however, is not clear-cut in sports, the way it is in FMCG categories, where sales are a clear indicator. In sports, we might look at the number of fans in the league, television ratings, ticket sales, number of participants, Facebook followers or a range of other measures to define size versus your competitors. This is easy to examine at a league level, but harder within a league to evaluate team market share. However defined, if you are small share, your sports brand will suffer from the double jeopardy effect. Growing market share is the only option to improve.

- Growth in market share comes from two sources – improving physical availability (ease of purchase or consumption) and mental availability (ease of recall at the right time). Improve your physical availability by increasing the number of events or games played, the channels through which it can be consumed (e.g. wider broadcast deals) and stadium/event capacity. Improvements to mental availability come through better sponsorship arrangements, wider media coverage, simple and repeated messaging and brand consistency (don't change cities, logos, colours, uniforms unless you have to). See Sharp (2010) for a detailed discussion about building what he calls 'market-based assets'.

- Your fans/participants will be consuming similar products to yours. It should be acknowledged that they consume your competitors and leverage where possible. This might involve teaming up with similar events in different regions to form a 'tour' or linking with other teams in your region to build local allegiances.

- Mass marketing is more effective than a targeted approach, given that if you want a large brand, you'll need to attract a diverse range of buyers. This will include infrequent buyers and less involved consumers. Keep messages simple and communications' reach broad, to have the best chance of them recalling your brand.

- Be kind to 'light buyers'. Resist the temptation to dismiss them as 'not true fans' or 'once a year athletes'. Light buyers are critical to brand growth, and you can use tools such as the PCM to develop greater involvement over time. Acquisition is important though, and light buyers will be most of what you acquire.

- Collect important metrics like:

  - Market penetration (how many customers bought the brand over a time period)
  - Market share (sales of brand/sales of product category)
  - Share of category requirements (proportion of consumers' category purchases that went to a particular brand)
  - Purchase frequency (how often a consumer buys a brand)
  - Brand awareness (how many customers know the brand)
  - Overall customer satisfaction
  - Availability metrics (number of distribution points/ease of purchase) (Sharp, 2013).

14.8 CHAPTER SUMMARY

Two key law-like patterns – the *double jeopardy* and *duplication of purchase* laws – have consistently been found to explain and predict consumer behaviour across a wide range of industries. There has been speculation that these empirical generalizations may not hold in the case of professional team sport brands. The reasons given include the passionate loyalty of sport fans, the fact that two sport teams must be consumed at once in any contest, and the strong geographic dominance of sport brands. Although limited in number, the studies undertaken to date that examine the applicability of these two law-like generalizations to professional team sport show that these concerns are unfounded. With a few caveats, these law-like patterns hold, suggesting that sport team brands operate in line with what is known about other consumer markets. The results suggest the unique aspects of the sport market do not meaningfully impact consumer behaviour and therefore sport brands should be managed in fundamentally the same way as most consumer markets.

14.9 DISCUSSION QUESTIONS

1) What are the two key metrics a marketing manager needs to know in order to assess the performance of their brand?
2) What is 'partitioning'? Can you think of some circumstances where a professional sport team might experience some partitioning with other brands?
3) A manager of a professional sport team notices that as the number of season ticket holders has grown, the average games attended per ticket holder has dropped. Should the manager be concerned? Explain why or why not.
4) Explain the duplication of purchase law, and how it might explain the behaviour of sports fans watching teams they don't support play.

14.10 CLASS ACTIVITY

Imagine you are the manager of a fun run being organized in a mid-size city. Early registrations were strong, particularly among people who have run in the race in previous years. You know, however, that if you are to grow the number of participants from previous years, you must appeal to more 'light buyers'. What are light buyers in this context and how would you build the important market-based assets (distribution and awareness) needed to attract them?

REFERENCES

Apple. (2012). Complete 66 Mac vs PC ads + Mac & PC WWDC Intro + Siri Intro [Video File]. Retrieved from www.youtube.com/watch?v=0eEG5LVXdKo

Baker, B., McDonald, H. & Funk, D. (2016, forthcoming). The uniqueness of sport: testing against marketing's empirical laws. *Sport Management Review.*

Barwise, P. & Ehrenberg, A. (1988). *Television and its audience* (Volume 3). London: Sage.

Bass, F. (1969). A new product growth for model consumer durables. *Management Science, 15*(5), 215–227.

Bass, F. (1995). Empirical generalizations and marketing science: A personal view. *Marketing Science, 14*(3 supplement), G6-G19.

Bee, C. & Madrigal, R. (2012). Outcomes are in the eye of the beholder, *Journal of Media Psychology, 24*(4), 143–153.

Colombo, R.A. & Morrison, D.G. (1989). A brand switching model with implications for marketing strategies. *Marketing Science, 8*(1), 89–99.

Doyle, J.P., Filo, K., McDonald, H. & Funk, D.C. (2013). Exploring sport brand double jeopardy: The link between team market share and attitudinal loyalty. *Sport Management Review, 16*(3), 286–297.

Ehrenberg, A.S., Goodhardt, G.J. & Barwise, T.P. (1990). Double jeopardy revisited. *The Journal of Marketing, 54*(3), 82–91.

Ehrenberg, A.S., Uncles, M.D. & Goodhardt, G.J. (2004). Understanding brand performance measures: using Dirichlet benchmarks. *Journal of Business Research, 57*(12), 1307–1325.

Fisher, R. & Wakefield, K. (1998). Factors leading to group identification: A field study of winners and losers. *Psychology & Marketing, 15*(1), 23–40.

Gladden, J.M. & Funk, D.C. (2001). Understanding brand loyalty in professional sport: Examining the link between brand association and brand loyalty. *International Journal of Sports Marketing and Sponsorship, 3*(1), 67–94.

Hand, C. (2011). Do arts audiences act like consumers? *Managing Leisure, 16*(2), 88–97.

Heere, B. & James, J.D. (2007). Sports teams and their communities: Examining the influence of external group identities on team identity. *Journal of Sport Management, 21*(3), 319.

Kearns, Z. (2004). Dirichlet VB [Computer Software].

Kerstetter, D.L. & Kovich, G.M. (1997). An involvement profile of division 1 women's basketball spectators. *Journal of Sport Management, 11*(3), 234–249.

McDonald, H. (2010). The factors influencing churn rates among season ticket holders: An empirical analysis. *Journal of Sport Management, 24*(6), 676–701.

McDonald, H. & Stavros, C. (2007). A defection analysis of lapsed season ticket holders: a consumer and organizational study. *Sport Marketing Quarterly, 16*, 218–229.

McPhee, W.N. (1963). *Formal Theories of Mass Behavior*. New York: The Free Press.

Rein, I., Kotler, P. & Shields, B.R. (2006). *The Elusive Fan: Reinventing sports in a crowded marketplace*. New York: McGraw-Hill Professional.

Romaniuk, J. & Dawes, J. (2005). Loyalty to price tiers in purchases of bottled wine. *Journal of Product & Brand Management, 14*(1), 57–64.

Sharp, B. (2010). *How Brands Grow: What marketers don't know*. South Melbourne: Oxford University Press.

Sharp, B. (2013). *Marketing: Theory, evidence, practice. 1st pub.* South Melbourne: Oxford University Press.

Sharp, B., Beal, V. & Collins, M. (2009). Television: Back to the future. *Journal of Advertising Research, 49*(2), 211–219.

Sharp, B., Wright, M. & Goodhardt, G. (2002). Purchase loyalty is polarised into either repertoire or subscription patterns. *Australasian Marketing Journal (AMJ), 10*(3), 7–20.

Sharp, B. & Wright, M. (1999). There are two types of repeat purchase markets. In *28th European Marketing Academy Conference* (Vol. 400). Berlin: Humboldt-University.

Simons, E. (2013). *The Secret Lives of Sports Fans*. New York: Penguin.

Sport Business Daily. (2010). Fan Demographics among Major North American Sports Leagues. Retrieved from http://www.sportsbusinessdaily.com/Daily/Issues/2010/06/Issue-185/The-Back-Of-The-Book/Fan-Demographics-Among-Major-North-American-Sports-Leagues.aspx

Tapp, A. (2004). The loyalty of football fans—We'll support you evermore? *The Journal of Database Marketing & Customer Strategy Management, 11*(3), 203–215.

Uncles, M., Ehrenberg, A.S. & Hammond, K. (1995). Patterns of buyer behavior: Regularities, models, and extensions. *Marketing Science, 14*(3), G71–G78.

Uncles, M.D. & Kwok, S. (2009). Patterns of store patronage in urban China. *Journal of Business Research, 62*(1), 68–81.

Uncles, M.D. & Ehrenberg, A.S. (1990). Industrial buying behavior: Aviation fuel contracts. *International Journal of Research in Marketing, 7*(1), 57–68.

Wilbur, K.C. & Farris, P.W. (2014). Distribution and market share. *Journal of Retailing, 90*(2), 154–167.

Winchester, M., Nencyz Thiel, M., Arding, R. & Lees, G. (2011). The importance of prior knowledge in understanding consumer purchases of fair trade brands. In Martin MacCarthy (ed.), *Australia New Zealand Marketing Academy Conference 2011*: Proceedings. Perth: School of Marketing, Edith Cowan University.

Zeithaml, V.A. (1981). How consumer evaluation processes differ between goods and services. *Marketing of Services, 9*(1), 25–32.

PART 6

Case studies

US college sports: insights into the dynamic commercial environment of intercollegiate athletics in the United States

(http://issuu.com/repucom.net/docs/repucom-us-college-sports-report-pr/8?e=11968292/12209085)

by REPUCOM (http://repucom.net/)

While intercollegiate athletic competition exists around the world, nowhere does it have the level of participation and popularity than in the United States. Each year, more than 460,000 men and women complete in 23 different sports at nearly 1,100 colleges and universities in the US, according to the NCAA.

COLLEGE SPORTS POPULARITY BY US REGION

The southern US has the biggest college sports fan base. College sports are especially popular in states such as Alabama, Arkansas, Kentucky, Mississippi, Nebraska, North Dakota, South Carolina and South Dakota where NFL and NBA franchises don't exist. Overall, college sports are more accessible to fans than professional sports, with competition taking place in every state in multiple regions (Table 1).

Table 1: Popularity of college sport fans by region

1.	40% South
2.	22% Midwest
3.	22% West
4.	16% Northeast

TOP FIVE LARGEST US SPORT FAN BASES

The popularity of NCAA college football and men's basketball is on a par with professional sports in the United States. College sports occupy two of the top five largest fan bases, with college football drawing more fans than the National Basketball Association (Table 2).

Table 2: Top five largest US sport fan bases

1.	NFL Professional Football	169.3 M
2.	MLB Professional Baseball	147.6 M
3.	NCAA College Football	143.6 M
4.	NBA Professional Basketball	129.3 M
5.	NCAA Men's College Basketball	126.0 M

Based on Repucom's monthly sports tracker SponsorLink, which surveys 1,000 nationally representative 18+ adults in the US each month, the following numbers can be extrapolated. Each respondent is asked to rate his or her fan avidity toward a variety of sports and leagues on a 0–10 scale, with 10 being a die-hard fan and 0 not a fan at all. Anyone scoring 2–10 on that scale is considered a fan.

Top 10 'Can't miss' sporting events

Interest in the marquee college football and basketball events is strong, with three earning top 10 'can't miss' sporting event designations. More than half of the US adults surveyed in Sponsor Link named the College Football Sponsorship game, the College Football Sponsorship playoff and the NCAA Men's Basketball March Madness as 'can't miss' sporting events in 2015 (Table 3).

Table 3: Top 10 can't miss sporting events

1.	73.9%	NFL Super Bowl
2.	62.5%	Olympic Games (Summer)
3.	62.1%	Olympic Games (Winter)
4.	57.8%	MLB World Series
5.	54.7%	College Football Championships
6.	53.9%	College Football Playoffs
7.	53.5%	Daytona 500
8.	53.2%	NBA Finals
9.	52.2%	NCAA March Madness
10.	52.2%	Kentucky Derby

COLLEGE BASKETBALL

According to the NCAA, total Division I game attendance for men's basketball was just over 25 million in 2014. Syracuse had the largest overall season attendance with average individual game attendance of more than 26,000 people. Two schools have owned the title of 'attendance champions' for a season since 1977 – Syracuse and Kentucky.

MARCH MADNESS CONSUMER BEHAVIOUR

NCAA March Madness, which is composed of conference tournaments and culminates with the NCAA Championship, draws the attention of everyone ranging from game experts to armchair fans to individuals who don't follow college basketball at all but want to partake in an office or family bracket competition.

The power of March Madness to bring together a myriad of individuals is what produces immense on-screen exposure value for brands associated with tournament games (Table 4). In the case of sponsor Buffalo Wild Wings, this power has even led to an augmentation of stock performance. Shares of the Minneapolis-based chain restaurant, which has strong advertising and activation presence during the tournament, have outperformed the S&P 500 Index by an average of 5.8 percentage points each March in the past 10 years.

Table 4: March Madness

76M Adults Follow March Madness
50M On Laptop/Desktop
31M On Smartphone
19M On Tablet

MEDIA VALUE FOR NCAA MEN'S BASKETBALL FINAL FOUR

The NCAA men's College Basketball Tournament appears on CBS, TBS, TNT, truTV and ESPN International. Having every game aired on national television has heightened viewership of the tournament. Just a few years ago, there was only one game being televised at a time, with a regional game of choice being shown. Nielsen reported that 21.2 million people watched the 2014 NCAA Men's Basketball Championship game, 18% higher than game five of the NBA Finals when the San Antonio Spurs defeated the Miami Heat to win their fifth NBA Championship. The Final Four broadcasts earned more than $15.6n million of in-game media value for sponsors in 2014.

The fans

College sports fans are a desirable audience for many reasons. The combination of buying power and sponsor loyalty is attractive for corporate sponsors. College sports fans are more likely to have earned a bachelor's or graduate degree and have a 9% higher average income than the general public.

Repucom found the overlap between college sports fan and professional golf fans to be as high as 90%, signifying the affluence of the college sports fan base compared to the general population and to NFL and NBA fans.

College basketball and football fans have a unique ethnicity breakout versus other sports in that they over-index in being African-American and Asian or Pacific Islander versus the general population and professional sports fans.

College sport fans are

More Ethnically Diverse

61% males
39% females
9% average high income
34% more likely to be college graduates than the general population and overall sport
fans

More Likely to Own a Business than the General Population

More Likely to Create and Respond to Content on Social Media

Fan avidity

Nearly half of all college football fans consider themselves avid, while roughly 4 out of 10 college basketball fans are avid. The levels of fan avidity for college basketball fans are nearly identical to those of the NBA. However, there is a significant difference between the levels of college football fans and NFL fans. While 48% of college football fans are avid, 70% of NFL fans identify themselves as avid (Table 5).

Table 5: Fan avidity

College football fans	
1.	Low: 20%
2.	Moderate: 32%
3.	Avid: 48%
College basketball fans	
1.	Low: 23%
2.	Moderate: 34%
3.	Avid: 43%

Characteristics of college sports as described by fans

The attributes that fans most associate with college sports are very similar to their professional counterparts; however, 'youthful', 'inspirational' and 'community-minded' are more likely to be associated with college sports versus the pros.

Loyalty and passion

College sports fan loyalty is something that comes through in traditions of various campuses. On the Duke University campus in Durham, North California, students set up Krzyzewskiville, named in honour of the head basketball coach. They camp out for hours, even the night before games featuring arch rival University of North Carolina. Wake Forest University students 'roll the quad' to celebrate big wins, tossing streams of toilet paper into the trees. Texas A&M has even trademarked its '12th Man' tradition. The entire student body stands throughout football games to show their 'readiness, desire and enthusiasm' to join the 11 players on the field if needed.

Social and digital media

College sports fans are heavy users of social media and more likely to visit YouTube and Twitter than the general adult public. Facebook is the most popular social media channel among college sports fans with 74% usage.

The value of digital and social exposure through college sports is just beginning to be realized. Looking at one post from Match 8 that contained an athlete image with the Nike 'swoosh' front and centre, it would generate approximately $6,250 in Media Value per day, or $2,275 million per year, if posted daily on Ohio State Athletics' Facebook and Twitter accounts and on OhioStateBuckeyes.com.

Social media ranking

Ohio State University won the NCAA Football Championship in 2015 and also wins the social media popularity contest. Ohio State has more combined Facebook and Twitter followers than any other college athletics department, with more than two million Facebook fans alone (Table 6).

Table 6: Social media ranking

1. Ohio State University
2. University of Florida
3. University of Texas
4. University of North Carolina
5. University of Alabama
6. University of Oregon
7. University of Wisconsin
8. University of Nebraska
9. University of Kentucky
10. Michigan State University

QUESTIONS

1) Profile the US college sport fans by using demographic and psychographic variables.
2) Compare college vs. professional sport fans, in terms of their socio-demographic and psychographic profiles. Point out the main differences and their common characteristics.
3) In which of the age generations do college fans belong? Discuss aspects that describe the characteristics and behaviour of their age generation, and in relation to the development of marketing strategies for targeting them.

4) Discuss the main positive and negative characteristics of the college sport fans for sponsorship investment. Use segmentation and attitude theory to support your answer.

5) Using motivation theory, explain the popularity of March Madness.

6) Do you see any differences between college and professional sport fans in terms of their motives to become fans and attend games? If yes, discuss possible reasons for these differences.

7 a) Compare college and professional sport fans in terms of their sport involvement and identity levels; b) What are the factors that influence the development of involvement and identity among college and professional sport fans? c) Do you see any differences? Use the Psychological Continuum Model to answer the questions.

8) College football and basketball fans have more diverse cultural and ethnicity backgrounds, in comparison to the general population and the professional sport fans: Is this a positive or a negative sign for marketing and sponsorship? Justify your answer.

9) Considering the profiles of college and professional sport fans, discuss indicative differences in the marketing approaches between college and professional associations and bodies.

Report spotlights female NFL fans

David Broughton and Staff Writer (2014). Sports Business, www.sportsbusinessdaily.com/Journal/Issues/2013/10/ 14/Leagues-and-Governing-Bodies/NFL-women.aspx

Female fans of the NFL feel like they are valued by the league, but believe there are a number of ways to make the game-day experience better for them, according to an NFL-commissioned study completed this month by the University of Central Florida.

SportsBusiness Journal obtained a copy of the internal study, titled 'I'm Part of the Shield, Too: Examining the NFL Game Day Experiences of Female Spectators and Their Influential Patterns', the second research effort to come out of the league's 'Diversity and Inclusion With Good Business' campaign.

The report, overseen by C. Keith Harrison, Associate Professor at the University of Central Florida, is based on data collected by Harrison and his staff during four NFL games last season, two each at Sun Life Stadium in Miami and O.co Coliseum in Oakland. Approximately 1,600 female spectators were asked a series of questions about their NFL game-day experience. Participation was voluntary, and no incentives were provided. Each woman wrote her individual responses directly on the survey.

'The core objective was to learn more about the female decision-making process and overall experiences at NFL games', Harrison said. 'This will most certainly help the NFL, individual NFL teams, sponsors and the league's other stakeholders to make more informed strategic business decisions.'

In the report, 72% of the women felt that they are a 'valued participant' of the NFL or a specific team, while 20% did not feel valued with respect to their game-day experiences.

More than half (51%) of the participants indicated that they were attending the game with family, and 22% said that they were attending the game with their husband. Eight per cent said they were there 'just with girlfriends'.

Women represent approximately 45% of the NFL fan base, according to Scarborough Research, and approximately 33% of the NFL viewing audience based on Nielsen data.

One area where women felt somewhat left out was in the league's tailgating culture. In the survey, 28% felt that tailgating is exclusively male focused. One of the top suggestions from respondents on how to improve that part of the game-day experience was that teams have women-only port-a-potties.

Robert Gulliver, chief human resources officer at the NFL, said the decision to field the study, and others like it being conducted by UCF for the league, shows how the league recognizes the diversity of its fan base.

Faithful fans, frequent buyers

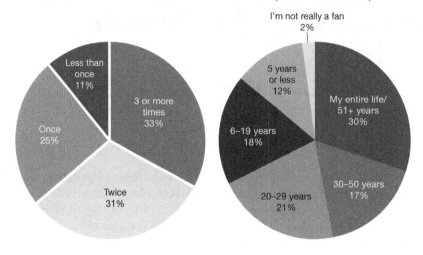

How often each year do you purchase NFL products/merchandise/apparel?

How long have you been a fan of the NFL (and/or relative team)?

- ■ **Total number of women who purchased merchandise at the team's stores: 151**
- ■ **Total number of items purchased: 264**
- ■ **Percentage of all items purchased that were characterized as "women's merchandise": 63%**
- ■ **Percentage of women who purchased multiple items: 53%**

MOST FREQUENT ITEMS PURCHASED:

Women's T-shirt	18%
Women's hat/visor	12%
Women's accessories	12%
Men's T-shirt	10%
Women's jersey	6%

Methodology: A total of 1,600 female spectators were surveyed at four NFL games in 2012, two games each at Sun Life Stadium in Miami and at O.co Coliseum in Oakland

'When you look across our operation, you see success stories as a result of integrating diversity into our business', he said. 'The marketing department has ads that celebrate our female fans. Our consumer products department has had a lot of success with the launch of our women's apparel line. And on the game-day front, our security department continues to make sure our game-day experience is family friendly, which obviously resonates with women.'

Gulliver does not expect any leaguewide game-day mandates to come out of this specific study, but said it will be shared with teams and the information could lead to a better game-day experience.

The women's study is being replicated at select NFL stadiums, and coincides with the league's fifth annual Breast Cancer Awareness Month activation. Additionally, this summer the league launched the Women's Resource Initiative, an outreach effort aimed at engaging players' mothers, wives and girlfriends in areas of career, health and safety, wellness and lifestyle.

Female NFL fans want to see more variety when it comes to the licensed merchandise and apparel, according to the results of a recent study that examined the NFL game-day experiences of female spectators.

Approximately 38% of female spectators who participated in the study indicated that there was not sufficient variety of apparel at the sporting event.

QUESTIONS

1) Define the term 'game experience', using the three levels of the sport service product (core, tangible and augmented). Discuss differences between male and female fans in terms of the 'game experience' expectations.
2) Based on demographic trends, socio-cultural factors and consumer trends, justify the importance of females as a target group for NFL.
3) Using motivation theory, explain females' decision-making process for becoming NFL fans.
4) Using constraint theory, discuss the main factors that might limit females attending NFL games.
5) Propose marketing strategies for the development of involvement among female fans, using the PCM model. Should these strategies be different for females and males? If yes, discuss the main differences.
6) Is it possible for female fans to develop the same levels of team identification as male fans? Justify your answer, by using the theory on team identification.
7) Robert Guilliver, the Chief Human Resources Officer at the NFL said that: 'When you look across our operation, you see success stories as a result of integrating diversity into our business.' Review recent NFL marketing and communication strategy, and present more examples which show how NFL recognizes the diversity of its fans.

Rising participation, significant economic impact and community engagement: major marathons and their contribution to host cities

Colin Stewart and Guntur Dwiarmein
Sportcal – Sports Market Intelligence
(http://www.sportcal.com/Home/Default.aspx)

There are more than 80 international marathons taking place between now and the New Year, with thousands scheduled throughout 2015. Sportcal looks at the continuing popularity of major international marathons and how they have affected host cities in various nations. The World Marathon Majors (WMM) Series, created in January 2006, originally consisted of the world's five leading races: Berlin, Boston, Chicago, London and New York. Tokyo came on board in 2013. The demand for a starting position in each marathon is always high, with all six marathons reaching capacity in 2014. Out of the approximate 400,000 applicants of all races combined, 185,000 are accepted as participants. According to the series organizers, the six majors attract 300 million television viewers and more than five million on-course spectators.

This year's New York Marathon will take place on 2 November. It will be the 44th edition of the race, since the first New York City Marathon took place in 1970. With more than 60,000 registrants every year, this year's race is expected to reach 55,000 participants, the marathon's official capacity.

ENTRANT NUMBERS INCREASING YEAR-ON-YEAR

New York has the highest capacity of all the majors and has cemented its place as a firm favourite with international and domestic participants. In 2013, it surpassed the 50,000 mark with 50,740 runners starting the race. The race was cancelled in 2012 due to the after-effects of Hurricane Sandy, having previously hosted 45,350 and 47,763 participants in 2010 and 2011, respectively.

The Boston Marathon has always been the least well attended of the WMM series despite entrance numbers increasing by 50% to 35,755 in 2014. This is the first time the Boston Marathon has reached over 35,000 entries and there are plans to grow the marathon further. In September, Tom Grilk, Boston Athletic Association executive director, said: 'As we look forward to 2015, our goal is to accommodate as many participants as possible in the Boston Marathon, while maintaining the exceptional race experience and unique characteristics that make this event special.' In 2012, the number of starters in the Boston Marathon significantly decreased from 26,907 in 2011 to 21,616. This was due to a heat wave that resulted in organizers offering participants the option to defer entry to 2013 as a result of the weather. The significant increase in numbers between 2013 and 2014 was a response to the terrorist bombings that occurred at the end of the 2013 marathon. Applications to participate reached a record high with participants wishing to run the race to show their support.

The third of the US-based majors, the Chicago Marathon, took place earlier this month and also reached record numbers in participation. The 2014 edition represented Chicago's highest ever turnout with 40,802 runners starting the race, up from 38,883 in 2013, and 60% greater than 2007. This makes Chicago the fastest-growing marathon in the WMM series and marked the first time a marathon other than New York had hosted more than 40,000 participants.

This year, the Berlin, London and Tokyo marathons all hosted over 36,000 participants. The 2014 series is the first in which all six races have reached this total in the same year. Despite the high turnouts, when we compare 2007 with 2014, the Berlin, London and Tokyo marathons have not produced the same level of participation growth as their US counterparts. There has been a 13% overall growth in participation at the Berlin Marathon, although numbers have fluctuated over the eight-year period. The London Marathon has the lowest participation increase with less than a 1% difference from 2007, reaching its official capacity every year. The largest rise in participation of the non-US majors is at the Tokyo Marathon. A 17% increase since 2007 makes it the fifth largest marathon in 2014 of the WMM series, placing it narrowly ahead of Boston (Table 1).

Table 1: World Marathon Majors participants, 2007–2014

	Starters 2007	Starters 2014	Increase
Berlin	32.497	36.755	13%
Boston	23.869	35.755	50%
Chicago	25.522	40.802	60%
London	36.396	36.621	<1%
New York	39.265	55.000*	40%
Tokyo	30.870	36.030	17%

*Entrance cap

Source: Various.

SIGNIFICANT CONTRIBUTION TO THE ECONOMY

Each marathon of the WMM series contributes significantly to their respective economies. Every year, the thousands of entrants, guests and spectators provide a welcome economic boost to the host city, particularly impacting the hospitality industry. The WMM series estimates that two million spectators gather along the course of the New York Marathon each year, the largest spectator following of the six races. Tokyo has the second largest spectator following, with 1.72 million spectators estimated to line the course each year, closely followed by Chicago with 1.7 million. Berlin attracts one million and London, 750,000 spectators each year. Boston has the smallest following with half a million spectators lining the course (Table 2).

Table 2: Estimated spectators at World Marathon Majors (in millions)

New York	2.0
Tokyo	1.72
Chicago	1.70
Berlin	1.0
London	0.75
Boston	0.50
Total:	7.67 million on-course spectators

According to research undertaken by the UK's Sheffield Hallam University, the 2010 London Marathon contributed £110.1 million ($175.3 million) of economic activity in the UK. Of this figure, £31.7 million was attributed to spending by participants, spectators, organizers and visitors. The Berlin Marathon is the largest event organized by SCC Events, a leading Germany-based event organizer. A report by the University of Hamburg in 2003 estimated that the series of races organized by SCC contribute a combined ⇔35 million ($44.3 million) in economic impact. This consists of a ⇔23 million direct impact to Berlin, created by the spending of out-of-town participants and visitors. New York, Chicago and Boston report the highest economic impact figures out of the marathons of the WMM series. In 2010, the New York Marathon generated a record $340 million, nearly double the figure of London's marathon in the same year.

The Chicago Marathon estimated that the 2013 race generated a $253.5 million economic impact. Race director, Carey Pinkowski, said he hopes the recent sponsorship deal with healthcare giant Abbott will help boost this 'already huge economic influx'. The Boston Marathon generates the least economic impact out of the major marathons held in USA, although this year's marathon did generate a record $175.8 million economic impact, beating the previous high of $172 million set in 1996 (Figure 1).

US ENTRY FEES ON THE RISE

Each marathon requires specific levels of policing, traffic management and volunteer support, provided by local government and the community, which is paid for by the organizers. As organizers increase the entrance capacity of each marathon, local governments increase their fees to provide additional personnel to support staging the race. The appetite to meet the demand for places remains higher in the USA, resulting in higher organizational costs and therefore entrance fees. Between 2008 and 2014, the cost of entering the Boston Marathon increased by almost 60%. The Chicago Marathon has

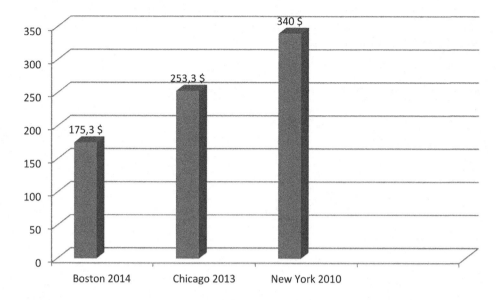

FIGURE 1 Economic impact of recent American major marathons ($ in millions)

increased the most, from $110 in 2008 to $185 in 2014, a 68% hike. The New York Marathon is the most expensive to enter at $255.

Participants have often voiced their concern at the ever-increasing costs, especially at a time when lucrative television and sponsorship deals are being struck with organizers. The series recently announced its first ever title sponsor, Abbott, a global healthcare company based in Illinois, USA. However, there are signs that the increase in fees may be slowing; the organizers of the Boston Marathon announced that the 2015 entry fee will remain the same as 2014, at $175 for US citizens (Table 3).

Table 3: World Marathon Majors entrance fees

2014	Entrance Fees	Increase since 2008
Boston	$175	59%
Chicago	$185	68%
New York	$255	65%

VOLUNTEERS AND RESOURCES

This year, Boston had to turn away nearly 5,000 volunteer applications, despite increasing volunteer capacity to 10,000, up from the 8,500 in 2013. Chicago has in excess of 12,000 volunteers on hand and New York estimates that around 8,000 to 12,000 volunteers are present each year. Volunteer applications are extremely popular. 'I always felt we would have more support than we could handle,' said Elisabeth Worthing, volunteer programme manager for the Boston Athletic Association. 'We have such a dedicated group that comes back year after year.' The organizers of the Tokyo marathon employ some 10,000 volunteers each year. These volunteers form 'TEAM SMILE', and help to ensure that the event runs smoothly (Table 4).

Table 4: Estimated number of volunteers at WMM series

Marathon	Estimated volunteers
Berlin	5,900
Boston	10,000
Chicago	12,000+
London	6,000
New York	8,000–12,000
Tokyo	10,000

Source: Various.

The 2010 report by Sheffield Hallam University estimates that 6,000 volunteers were mobilized for the London Marathon in that year. Some 68% of these volunteers were from local London boroughs. These 6,000 volunteers provide an average of 6.5 hours of work, which resulted in a combined total of 39,000 man hours provided on the marathon day. This represents close to £500,000 in 'free' labour, using the 2010 average wage of £12.50, according to the authors of the report. In addition to the 5,900 volunteers required to run the Berlin Marathon, an estimated 7,369 members of the police force are on hand. Organizers provide participants with 240,000 litres of water, 145,000 bananas, 80,000 biscuits and 45,000 apples. Organizers of the London Marathon provide around 750,000 bottles of water, 200,000 isotonic energy drinks and 50,000 carbohydrate energy gels. Tokyo estimates that 850,000 drinks and 100,000 bananas are distributed throughout the day of its race.

COMMUNITIES BENEFIT AS WELL AS CHARITIES

The marathons of the WMM series are well known to raise substantial amounts of charitable contributions. In America, Boston raised a record $38.4 million in 2014, nearly doubling its previous record of $20 million raised in 2013. New York raised $34 million in 2011, and despite the 2012 event being cancelled, it still raised $31 million. It is estimated that the Chicago Marathon has raised $115 million since 2002.

In 2014, the London Marathon raised a record £53.2 million, beating its previous record of £53 million achieved in 2013. This is the highest amount of any single race among the majors. London has raised in excess of £716 million in charitable donations since 1981. The Greater London Authority highlighted other benefits such as community involvement and participation in sport. Organizers of the New York Marathon cite community action as a benefit, with educational programmes reaching over 200,000 children.

RANKING THE MARATHONS AGAINST INDICATORS

When comparing the marathon majors, we find that the three US marathons are the most expensive races to enter. London is the cheapest of the six majors to enter, with ballot entries costing as little as £35. Despite Boston's low rankings for number of participants and estimated spectators, it boasts the largest pool of prize money available. The USA leads the way, topping every category with New York ranking highest for three of the four indicators considered. Only Tokyo breaks into the top three in terms of spectators while Berlin ranks third for number of participants, which consolidates the US-based marathons' commanding position among the majors (Table 5).

The demand exists for organizers to raise the capacity in all the major marathons; however, organizers must take into account road capacity, and whether they are prepared to change the format of their event to meet the demand.

Table 5: World Marathon Majors rankings

Position	Entrance fee	Participants	Prize money	Spectators
1.	New York	New York	Boston	New York
2.	Chicago	Chicago	New York =	Tokyo
3.	Boston	Berlin	= Chicago	Chicago
4.	Berlin	London	Tokyo	Berlin
5.	Tokyo	Tokyo	Berlin	London
6.	London	Boston	London	Boston

QUESTIONS

1) Discuss the main environmental and individual/psychological factors that have influenced the growth of city marathons over the last ten years.
2) Define the term 'race experience', by using the analysis of the three levels of sport product (core, tangible and augmented).
3) Go to the websites of the six biggest marathons (as presented in Table 1) and discuss the main marketing and communication strategies for each of them. Considering that they take place in different continents (North America, Europe and Asia), do you see any differences in the marketing and communication strategies, in relation to the profile of their runners?
4) Define city marathon runners by using segmentation variables (socio-demographic, psychographic, geographical etc). Do you see any differences among the six major city marathons in terms of the profile of the runners?
5) Using motivation theory, discuss the main motives for marathon runners and spectators. Based on your analysis, propose marketing strategies for marathon organizers.
6) Based on branding theory, and considering that city marathons take place in cities that are strong tourism destinations, discuss the main factors that influence the development of a strong marathon brand.

7) Using leisure constraint theory and taking one of the major marathons as an example, discuss possible constraints that might influence an individual's decision to participate in an international marathon.

8) Using the Psychological Continuum Model, discuss the development of runners' loyalty with a city marathon. Propose marketing and communication strategies to increase runners' loyalty with a city marathon.

Coke gets 'Zero' recognition in college sports

David Broughton, Staff Writer (2015)

Sports Business, www.sportsbusinessdaily.com/Journal/ Issues/2015/04/27/Research-and-Ratings/NCAA-Sponsor- Loyalty.aspx

Coca-Cola's college sports-themed tagline this spring was 'You Don't Know Zero 'Til You've Tried It', but fans certainly know who is the NCAA's official soft drink.

More than 37% of fans polled in a Sponsor Loyalty survey conducted for *SportsBusiness Journal/Daily* by Turnkey Sports & Entertainment correctly identified Coca-Cola as the NCAA's official soft drink, making it the most recognized NCAA sponsor in the polling. It's the first time that Capital One, another NCAA sponsor, did not score highest in the survey's three-year history.

Coke Zero was featured in at least two dozen ads during this year's Final Four coverage on TBS and CBS. Its most unique activation, however, may have been its 'drinkable billboard'. The 26 by 36-foot structure, concocted by Coke's new advertising agency, Ogilvy & Mather, featured a giant straw that shot the soda into drinking fountains for fan sampling at the Final Four experiential site near Lucas Oil Stadium, host of the tournament's last three games.

A mobile extension of the campaign involving music app Shazam allowed fans to pour a virtual Coke Zero into a glass on their smartphones.

Those efforts followed Coke Zero being promoted in several spots during the college football season under the 'Zero means it's gameday' campaign.

Coca-Cola fared especially well in the survey's polling among avid fans: 45% of that group of respondents recognized the company's NCAA relationship, the highest such rate ever registered by a brand in the three years of the NCAA study. In fact, only Coke's relationship with NASCAR, which has averaged a 56% recognition rate among avid fans over the eight years of the Sponsor Loyalty study for NASCAR, has ranked higher when considering all league-soda relationships tracked in the survey's history.

The Sponsor Loyalty series, which debuted in 2007, also includes annual studies of MLB, NBA, NFL, NHL, MLS and PGA Tour fans.

Coca-Cola in 2013 renewed its NCAA sponsorship, which began in 2002, with an 11-year deal.

IMPACT ON SAMPLING AND SUPPORT

■ Are you more or less likely to *consider trying* a product/service if that product/service is an official NCAA sponsor?

	AVID			CASUAL		
	2015	2014	2013	2015	2014	2013
More likely	46.0%	48.0%	43.5%	29.2%	38.5%	25.5%
Unaffected or less likely	54.0%	52.0%	56.5%	70.8%	61.5%	74.5%

■ Are you more or less likely to *consciously support* a company by purchasing its products/service if the company is an official NCAA sponsor?

	AVID			CASUAL		
	2015	2014	2013	2015	2014	2013
More likely	48.5%	49.0%	46.0%	29.2%	37.5%	31.5%
Unaffected or less likely	51.5%	51.0%	54.0%	70.3%	62.5%	68.5%

■ Are you more or less likely to *recommend* a product/service to a friend or family member if that product/service is an official sponsor of the NCAA?

	AVID			CASUAL		
	2015	2014	2013	2015	2014	2013
More likely	40.0%	45.5%	44.0%	25.7%	32.0%	28.0%
Unaffected or less likely	60.0%	54.5%	56.0%	74.3%	68.0%	72.0%

FIGURE 1

Among the 11 categories tracked in the study, Coca-Cola, Enterprise, Buick, Allstate and Reese's, each enjoyed a second straight year of improved awareness levels among avid fans. Buick has seen a seven percentage point improvement among avid fans since the inaugural 2013 survey, the largest increase of the more than 70 brands tracked each year.

Other notable findings (see Figure 2):

- Capital One ranks with Coca-Cola and AT&T in the NCAA's corporate champions tier, the organization's highest level of sponsor involvement. Capital One's affiliation with college sports began in 2001, and it was the most recognized brand in the study among casual fans surveyed for a third consecutive year.
- AT&T, whose Dallas-based global headquarters is not far from AT&T Stadium, site of this year's CFP National Championship game, was recognized correctly as an NCAA sponsor by 28% of all 400 fans surveyed, down four percentage points from last year
- Buffalo Wild Wings has shown the most stability in score among sponsors over the survey's three-year history. Its overall awareness level among fans has ranged between 30% and 32% across the three years.

SPONSORSHIP SIGNIFICANCE AND ASSESSMENT

■ **Subject:** How much more likely are fans to consider purchasing/using an NCAA sponsor's product/service if they are aware of the relationship?
■ **To read:** 32 percent of NCAA basketball fans said they would be more likely to consider purchasing consumer electronics from a company that is the NCAA's official sponsor in that category if they knew which company had that designation. That response rate increased to 48 percent when considering only those fans who correctly knew that LG is the NCAA's official consumer electronics sponsor.

CATEGORY (NCAA SPONSOR)	AMONG ALL NCAA FANS	AMONG NCAA FANS WHO CORRECTLY IDENTIFIED THE SPONSOR	DIFFERENCE
Shipping services (UPS)	30%	48%	+18 pct. points
Consumer electronics (LG)	32%	48%	+16 pct. points
Rental car (Enterprise)	36%	50%	+14 pct. points
Soft drink (Coca-Cola)	37%	48%	+11 pct. points
Life insurance/financial advisory services (Northwestern Mutual)	26%	36%	+10 pct. points
Wireless service (AT&T)	31%	40%	+9 pct. points
Casual dining (Buffalo Wild Wings)	33%	41%	+8 pct. points
Insurance (Allstate)	28%	36%	+8 pct. points
Automobile (Buick*)	27%	33%	+6 pct. points
Candy (Reese's)	35%	39%	+4 pct. points
Credit card (Capital One)	31%	32%	+1 pct. points

* Both Buick and Infiniti are NCAA sponsors in the automobile category, but only Buick was featured in this element of the survey.

FIGURE 2

- Each of the NCAA sponsors tracked saw its awareness score among casual fans decline compared to last year's survey results.

Methodology

For this project, Turnkey Sports & Entertainment, through its Turnkey Intelligence operation, conducted national consumer research surveys among a sample of more than 400 members of the Toluna online panel who were at least 18 years old.

This year's data was collected between 30 March and 8 April, a period leading up to and continuing through the men's and women's Final Fours. In 2014 and 2013, the data was collected ahead of the Final Four weekend of each of those years.

Respondents were screened and analysed based on their general avidity levels. Fans

■ **Subject:** What brands do fans think should be NCAA sponsors?
■ **To read:** 67 percent of NCAA basketball fans said they think Coca-Cola should be an NCAA sponsor compared to 39 percent who think Pepsi should have such a partnership. Those numbers became 81 percent and 39 percent, respectively, when considering only those NCAA basketball fans who correctly knew that Coca-Cola is the NCAA's official soft drink

NCAA SPONSOR/ COMPETITOR	AMONG ALL NCAA FANS		AMONG NCAA FANS WHO CORRECTLY IDENTIFIED THE SPONSOR	
	RESPONSE RATES	DIFFERENCE	RESPONSE RATES	DIFFERENCE
Buffalo Wild Wings/ Fox & Hound	29%/3%	+25 pct. points	51%/3%	+48 pct. points
Coca-Cola/Pepsi	67%/39%	+28 pct. points	81%/39%	+42 pct. points
Allstate/Nationwide	39%/23%	+16 pct. points	62%/24%	+38 pct. points
AT&T/Verizon	51%/44%	+7 pct. points	68%/35%	+33 pct. points
UPS/FedEx	47%/46%	+1 pct. points	63%/32%	+31 pct. points
Reese's/Snickers	31%/33%	−2 pct. points	60%/29%	+31 pct. points
Northwestern Mutual/ New York Life	10%/13%	−3 pct. points	28%/4%	+24 pct. points
Capital One/Case	39%/33%	+6 pct. points	55%/32%	+23 pct. points
Enterprise/Hertz	31%/24%	+7 pct. points	46%/24%	+22 pct. points
LG/Samsung	26%/45%	−19 pct. points	57%/38%	+19 pct. points
Buick*/Chrysler	18%/13%	+5 pct. points	36%/21%	+15 pct. points

* Both Buick and Infiniti are NCAA sponsors in the automobile category, but only Buick was featured in this element of the survey. Notes: Fans could select both the official sponsor and the competitor if they chose to do so. The listed companies were selected by Turnkey for consideration in the survey file.

FIGURE 3

categorized as 'avid' were those who responded '4' or '5' to the questions 'How big a fan are you of NCAA basketball?' and 'How big a fan are you of NCAA football?', then claimed to 'Look up NCAA basketball news, scores and standings several times a week or more often', 'Watch/listen/attend at least 20 NCAA basketball games per season' and 'Have a favorite NCAA basketball team'. Fans categorized as 'casual' responded '3' to the same initial questions, then claimed to 'Look up NCAA basketball news, scores and standings several times a month or more often', 'Watch/listen/attend at least five NCAA basketball games per season' and 'Have a favorite NCAA basketball team'.

When asked to identify official sponsors, respondents selected from a field of companies and brands that was provided to them for each business sector. Only the top-scoring companies and brands are listed in the results published here. The percentage responses listed have been rounded. The margin of error for each survey is +/− 4.9 percentage points.

Turnkey Intelligence performs research work for more than 30 conferences and schools as well as for numerous sponsors that are involved in college sports.

QUESTIONS

1) You were assigned to develop a report in order to evaluate how attractive is NCAA for sponsorship investment. Present the main arguments by emphasizing on the profile (e.g. socio-cultural, psychographic) of the college sport fans.
2) Critically discuss the methodology of categorizing fans as 'avid' and 'causal'. Using attitude theory (e.g. team identity, consumer involvement etc) and the PCM model, provide alternative and more detailed categorization of fans. Do you think that such an approach would benefit sponsorship research?
3) Propose alternative fan segmentation variables that could be used in the survey in order to examine sponsorship recognition in more depth.
4) Discuss the main strategies developed by Coke Zero in order to promote their sponsorship and achieve high sponsorship awareness among NCAA fans. How would you explain Coke's Zero high rate of sponsorship recognition?
5) In the survey discussed in the Case Study, sponsorship recognition and fans' behavioural intentions (try a sponsor's product/service, support a sponsor, recommend a sponsor's product/service) were measured as sponsorship outcomes. Propose alternative sponsorship outcomes that could be measured in the survey.
6) Using the constructs of 'team identification' and 'team involvement', compare NCAA and NBA fans. Which of the two would you consider as the most identified and involved? Justify your answer.
7) Check the official sponsors of NCAA, NBA, NFL, MLS, MHL and UEFA Champions League. Do you see any differences in the profile of the fans of each league? If yes, can you present some arguments that justify the sponsors' decisions to invest on these leagues? On doing the analyses, consider the fit between the sponsors' marketing strategy and fan base of each of the leagues.

Running, the people's sport

Juli Anne Patty (2014, June)

Sports Destination Management www.sportsdestinations. com/sports/running-events/running-people%E2%80% 99s-sport-7856

In 2010, running's second boom was in full swing, brought about largely by a surge in the popularity of the half marathon. That surge inspired a new research report from Running USA, the industry's research, marketing and communications hub.

Since 2003, says the report, the half marathon has been the fastest-growing standard distance in the US with a 24% record rise in both 2009 and 2010 (1).

While the half marathon is still holding its own, particularly among women runners, the running world now has its eyes on a new sort of prize.

'The half marathon is still at record levels, the fastest-growing traditional distance in this country', says Ryan Lamppa, media director, Running USA. 'But non-traditional races have just exploded in the past few years, going from low six figure finishers in 2009 to over four million in 2013. There's no doubt we're still in the second running boom, and what we may be looking at, thanks to the non-traditional mud, obstacle, and theme runs, is the start of a third running boom.'

THE NEW RACE

'Non-traditional' is a broad term for the new class of running events that have emerged in the last few years. They range from obstacle races and mud runs to theme races of all kinds. Though these types of races are varied and unique, they have one thing in common, says Lamppa: they appeal to participants who have a strong interest in fun, social physical activities, but who are less interested in competition. Many of these races aren't timed, and that's part of their appeal.

The Color Run is a prime example of the non-traditional running boom. In just its first two years, The Color Run registered more than a million people to dash through the event's signature 5 kilometres of coloured powder.

'The Color Run has had more first time 5 km runners than any other event in history', says Travis Snyder, founder and executive director. 'For most of these runners it will lead to more participation in fun runs and competitive events.'

Obstacle and mud runs are another vein of the exploding non-traditional race. These races are enjoying such popularity that two obstacle racers teamed up in early 2014 to establish a governing body for the sport, United States Obstacle Course Racing (USOCR). Following the death of a Tough Mudder participant in 2013 (and a subsequent wrongful death lawsuit filed by the participant's mother in 2014), obstacle course and mud runs face growing scrutiny about their safety regulations and preparation. The USOCR will address 'safety protocols and procedures, quality control, and rules and regulation for competition'.

Regardless of issues, the alternative race market continues to make record sales. According to Running USA's 2014 *State of the Sport: Non-Traditional Running Events* report, 'With a business strategy driven by a large social media footprint, start-up companies such as Tough Mudder and The Color Run have attracted hundreds of millions of revenue dollars in just a few years of operation.'

But has the high demand created an over-saturated market? Recently, countless theme and obstacle races have emerged, which could be a cause for concern regarding the future of these events, particularly ones that depend on large numbers of participants travelling to races.

'I think that the market is becoming so saturated with similar races that people always have one if not multiple ones nearby. They don't necessarily have to travel, unless it's for a prestigious race like The Color Run, which definitely brings people to Grand Rapids', says Katy Tigchelaar, events manager, West Michigan Sports Commission. 'Add to that the fact that a lot of the trendy races are so expensive, people might start to do fewer runs overall.'

THE TRAVELLING RUNNER

With a potentially oversaturated running events market, participants certainly have lots of options, many of them right outside their front doors. So what characteristics make some running events' travel-worthy appeal?

In some cases, says Lamppa, the choice to travel for races is tied to the type of runner as much as the type of race:

> Per our 2013 National Runner Survey, more than 60% of runners do overnight travel to an event, usually traditional runners who want to do different races per a certain checklist that they've created for their running career, a marathon per state for example. The typical non-traditional runner is much more passive. They're doing events with their friends locally.

The Color Run, for one, is disproving this idea.

'We do have repeat runners, especially for our big events such as Los Angeles and Chicago. We do have some other runners that are much more dedicated and have been to The Color Run events all around the US and World', says Lisa Nunes, marketing special projects lead, The Color Run. 'We have a couple ladies we call "The Legends" that have been to 13 events to date. They even have The Color Run tattoos. We love them!'

But what about the rest of the races, both traditional and convention breaking? As it turns out, a survey of successful races across the US reveals a number of strategies that help these events draw visitors and tourism dollars, even when there's no mud, fire or glow paint involved.

Make a weekend of it

Races that benefit a non-profit or cause are common enough, but when they offer runners a chance for a weekend of homecoming excitement that also benefits a community they care about, the registrations start rolling in.

'Our main event, which draws the most out of state runners and even some internationally, is the Five Points of Life Marathon and Half Marathon', says Joleen Cacciatore, executive director, Gainesville Sports Commission (Florida). 'It started in 2006, beginning as just a half and full marathon. We grew the marathon, added a 5 km, a marathon relay and a kids' marathon, and it's the Five Points of Life race weekend. We get runners from all parts of the country, especially people who want to come back to Gainesville, who went to school here. The nostalgia factor helps.'

The Livermore Half Marathon (California) takes advantage of a weekend of existing activities, giving not just runners but whole families a reason to make the trip to Livermore. 'We're fortunate to have five distinct towns and cities that can offer appealing events and activities so that there's something for everyone', says Geoffrey Sarabia-Mason, vice president of sales, Visit Tri-Valley. 'Also, at Visit Tri-Valley, we act as the conduit for all the cities, and our calendar holds everyone's events. We look for peaks and valleys and help event directors choose strategic dates that will help their events be successful.'

Go to extremes

As the push-your-limits mud obstacle race genre suggests, there's a huge market of participants who will jump at the opportunity to test their mettle. But you don't necessarily need barbed wire or climbing walls. Just ask organizers of the Point Bock Run in Stevens Point, Wisconsin.

'The Point Bock Run is one of the most popular local races, but it also brings in a lot of people from out of town', says Melissa Sabel, director of marketing, Stevens Point Area Convention and Visitors Bureau. 'The race is capped at 2,000, and usually it sells out in 24 hours. This year, it shocked everyone when it sold out in just three hours.'

The five-mile traditional out-and-back road race begins and ends at its sponsor's doorstep – the Stevens Point Brewery. But what really gives this race its magnetic draw is its timing, taking place each year on the first Saturday in March. In Wisconsin, that means cold and snow. In 2014, the three-hour sellout race, runners faced 5-degree temperatures, and only 300 of the sellout 2,000 decided not to run. Busloads of out-of-town runners still showed up despite the record low race temperatures, and the party continued.

Races that take advantage of unique local venues or courses also tend to draw more travellers, such as a number of races near Rapid City.

'Trail running has had a really big spike in numbers of late. People like to run in the elements, and here, in the Black Hills, we have a lot of beautiful places to do that', says Domico Rodriguez, director of sports and events, Rapid City Convention and Visitors Bureau. 'The Crazy Horse Marathon is an event that winds around the base of the Crazy Horse monument, and the Deadwood Mickelson Trail Marathon is another popular iconic course.'

Keep it local

Even for the large, multi-city events like The Color Run, a localized approach is critical.

'Every market is pretty different. With new race directors, if they're in a market they know well, they're going to be a step ahead of someone coming into a new market', says Jim Estes, director of events, USA Track & Field (USATF), the American national governing body for running events. 'If you're looking to start a new race in a market that's not your home, getting in touch with the local running community is very important. Even for the big races you see duplicating themselves throughout the country, they rely on some level of local knowledge.'

Become a brand. XTERRA is an off-road triathlon and trail run series. By branding a race under the XTERRA banner, race directors not only get the support and marketing reach of the organization, but also association with the XTERRA brand promise.

'Except for our championships, we work with local race directors who have established their own races. There are no dictated distances or guidelines. Just run a solid event that satisfies runners', says Emily McIlvaine, trail running series manager, XTERRA. 'Tim Schroer, for example, runs Dirty Spokes in Georgia. He knows his runners better than I would ever know them. We rely on the directors' expertise. They know the market, and that's why the program works so well.'

A successful race doesn't necessarily mean a big race, however. XTERRA's trail running series includes races of all sizes.

'We have races that are 50 people, 100 people, and some that are 2,500 people', says McIlvaine. 'I don't always think that the size of a race is the evidence of how good a race is.'

In the case of trail running, small races are often dictated by the trail itself. Certain trails require that numbers be capped. That works in favour of these races, in some cases, as well, creating a high demand. Many trail races sell out in a matter of hours, some signing up long rosters of hopeful participants (a helpful marketing tool) for race entrance lotteries.

GIVE RACERS A REASON

Part of the reason that XTERRA has been successful is its points system. Each trail run offers three to seven races that runners can compete in to accumulate points towards their series championship totals. Top age group points winners receive free entry into the XTERRA Trail Run National Championship, an off-road half marathon, which will be hosted this year in Snowbasin, Ogden, Utah.

Kalamazoo, Michigan, already has a passionate running community, which is why its Borgess Run for the Health of It, which includes a marathon, half marathon, 10 km, 5 km run, 5 km walk, kids' fun run and motivational mile, has grown to more than 8,000 participants in its 35 years.

'One of the things we've been doing is the 50 State Challenge', says Greg Ayers, president and CEO, Discover Kalamazoo. 'The goal of this promotion is to secure one marathon registrant from all 50 states. We're lucky because Kalamazoo is very strong in the running world, and we have some well-connected, great advocates.'

THE FINISH LINE

Of all the event strategies, though, there's one that will ensure a successful, growing event above all else, says Lamppa: Keep your customer satisfied. If you have happy racers, they will tell people. If you make your runners happy, more will come.

[1] 'Running USA Annual Half-Marathon Report'. 6 April 2014. Running USA State of the Sport Reports.

QUESTIONS

1) Based on environmental (e.g. socio-cultural, demographic and lifestyle trends) and individual/psychological factors, explain the rapid growth of running, as a worldwide recreation activity today.
2) Discuss the main differences in motivation among participants in traditional vs. non-traditional running races. Can you find other segmentation variables that might differentiate runners in the two forms of races?
3) Using social identity theory, explain the development of running identification.
4) Discuss the main running segments, which are presented in the case study. Further profile these segments by using demographic and psychographic variables.
5) Using the PCM model, discuss how loyalty can be developed in running races. Use the Color Run event as an example to justify your answer.
6) What are the main personality traits that can be used to explain runners' decision making to participate in the different types of running races (e.g. traditional, non-traditional, trail, mountain etc.).
7) It is reported in the Case Study that the running race market (especially the alternative) has started to become over-saturated. As a result only prestigious races will probably survive. Using branding theory: a) define what it means for a running race to have a strong brand; b) apply the construct of brand personality in the case of a running race (traditional and non-traditional), by defining each one of Aakers' five personality facets; c) propose strategies for the development of branding in the running races; d) make a list of five non-traditional running events with a strong brand. Based on what criteria did you select them?
8) Using branding theory, discuss why and how races under the brand of 'XTERRA' are getting marketing and communication benefits.
9) Discuss the main factors that influence the development of runners' satisfaction, after participating in a running event.

Women and sport: insights into the growing rise and importance of female fans and female athletes

(http://repucom.net/wp-content/uploads/2014/09/Women-and-Sport-Repucom.pdf)

by REPUCOM (http://repucom.net/)

WOMEN FANS

From music to museums, theatre to travel, we are all fans of something. Being a sports fan might have been more associated with men in the past, but women are increasingly consuming sports both in terms of attending sporting events and watching sports on TV and other media. The number of women participating in sport is also on the up. Understanding which sports women watch and how is paramount to sponsors, brands, broadcasters as well as national and international sports bodies in order to further increase attendance figures and participation levels around the world.

WOMEN'S AND MEN'S INTERESTS

Music, movies and travel generally top the ranking of interests for both men and women around the world. Differences in interest between men and women usually emerge lower down the list with women tending to prefer arts, culture and social interests while men focus more on technology and sport. But the gap between men's and women's interest in sport has narrowed hugely in the last 50 years. On average across 24 major countries representing the Americas, Europe and Asia, nearly half of all women now declare themselves either interested or very interested in sport compared to 69% of men. And some of the dynamic markets of Asia – UAE, India and Indonesia – lead the field with more than half of all women switched on to sport, particularly sport on TV. Across the rest of the world, Brazil, Russia, Italy, Japan and Turkey all show above average interest in sport among women as well. UAE, Brazil, India and Russia are the countries with the smallest gender gaps between male and female interest in sport.

WOMEN'S AND MEN'S INTEREST IN WATCHING SPORT ON TV

While tennis and basketball frequently come out as the sports women are most interested in across eight key markets, women report football as the sport they are most likely to watch sometimes or regularly during their respective seasons – and this is increasingly true with younger women across the world.

The female audience for tennis and Olympic sports such as athletics and figure skating is often actually larger than their male audience. Of the mainstream 'global' sports considered here, motorsport is the sport with the biggest gender gap with a female audience less than 70% of the size of the male one on average across these countries.

WOMEN'S SPORTS MEDIA CONSUMPTION

In addition to the diversity of different sports women are interested in across the world, we can see some important changes happening between younger and older women. The most significant of these changes is the rise of the percentage of women who watch football. It is noticeable that women aged 30 to 49 have the highest percentage of interest in sport. And two-thirds of them are at least a little interested in any sport. Subsequently, this age group will often be encouraging their children to participate in sport. In general, women keep track of their sporting interests in much the same way as men with the internet and free-to-air TV being the most important media on a weekly basis. Across eight key markets women are more likely to be incorporating radio vs mobile and free-to-air rather than Pay TV – and younger women are more focused on internet and mobile apps. When we compare media habits in the under-30 age group, however, we can see that internet and mobile behaviour is converging with fewer differences between men and women than older generations. The gap is not narrowing in Pay TV and thus reflects differences in the types of sports men and women are interested in and the way they can be accessed in different countries.

THE INFLUENCE OF SPORTS AT SCHOOL

So what is driving these changes in the number of female fans and the type of sports they are interested in? Academic research over the last 50 years shows that the biggest influences on developing sports fans are parents, friends, schools and communities. But, it is the dramatic change in the level of participation of girls in sports at school from the 1970s onwards which has made this aspect the most important driver of change for women. The daughters of that generation of girls at school in the 1970s and 1980s are the new generation of female athletes and fans today. In the under-30 group of women across the diverse markets studied here, we see more than 50% participated in sports at school. There are some marked differences between markets though – with fewer than 15% of young women in China who did not participate to over 84% still not playing sports in Japan. So there is plenty of opportunity left to broaden women's participation further. The link between taking part in sport at school for women and their subsequent level of interest as an adult is very clear. Across these diverse markets, a high level of sports participation at school translates to a 76% chance of an enduring interest in sport compared to a less than a 50% chance for those that did not play sports at school.

TRIGGERS AND BARRIERS FOR PARTICIPATION IN SPORTS AMONG MEN AND WOMEN

What about actual participation in sports for adult women? Running and cycling top the league of sports women enjoy most around the world and the explosion of organized mass participation events for running in particular is self-evident. But what triggers women's participation in sport and what holds it back? Repucom qualitative research shows some similarities between men and women such as the desire for health and stress relief. Men tend to focus more on achievement listing, competing and winning as key drivers, while women are more likely to focus on connection and emotional benefits.

Thinking about barriers to participation, men talk about tangible obstacles such as fitness level, age, location – and while women list these too, they are also more likely to cite emotional barriers such as fear of failure and embarrassment.

WOMEN, SPORT AND SPONSORSHIP

Brands have focused on sponsorship opportunities with mens' individual and team sports for many years. But over the last decade we have seen sponsors and broadcasters engaging more with female athletes at both grassroots and elite levels, reflecting a broader realization of the value of female role models and women's purchasing power around the world.

TURNING OF THE TIDE?

When assessing finances in sport as a whole, women are far from achieving equality in terms of endorsements and sponsorship with their male counterparts. For instance, in UK advertising campaigns that followed on from the London 2012 Olympic Games, the only two British female athletes who featured prominently were athletics star Jessica Ennis-Hill (Santander and PruHealth) and up-and-coming tennis player Heather Watson (BT Sport). So why do brands continue to underleverage female athletes and teams when they certainly match their male counterparts in terms of success on-field and on-court? One obvious explanation is the media coverage. Sarah Juggins of the UK Sports Journalist Association asserts: 'In the past two to three years, there has been a bit of a shift in perceptions about women's sports. The 2012 Olympics did a great job in putting sports-women on the front and back pages, and in some cases they have remained there. However, the back pages are still mainly football and racing.' But, it is important to note that there is an increasing awareness of women's tennis, women's rugby and particularly women's football in the media, especially as the FIFA Women's World Cup is taking place this summer. Juggins adds: 'There is a growing sense of responsibility along the media to give a form of parity to women's sport.' Outside the media, public policy and sports industry forums are concentrating more and more on the women and sport opportunity, and 2015 has seen the launch of Female Sports Group. The agency, an extensive user of Repucom data, is the first sports consultancy in the UK to focus exclusively on mixed gender and female sports.

As we have already seen, football and tennis are incredibly important sports for female fans, so we have looked at the share of the TV audience of two major global events for these sports in 2014 – the FIFA World Cup in Brazil and the Wimbledon Championships. Perhaps unsurprising that these events were particularly popular among women in the event's home markets, but more significant is that the female share of audience for the World Cup is now above 25% in markets like the US and Australia where football is not one of the largest national sports. And for Wimbledon, we see women actually have a larger share of audience than men in Australia and the UK with other major markets not far behind. Consequently, the huge audience events such as Wimbledon attract no doubt had an impact on the large monetary value of the groundbreaking WTA deal with PERFORM, which was announced at the end of last year.

WOMEN'S ATTITUDE AND BEHAVIOUR IN RELATION TO SPONSORSHIP

During 2014 Repucom conducted foundational research relating to women's attitudes and behaviour in response to sponsorship and saw some common themes emerge around the world in both similarities and differences to the attitudes and behaviour of men. Beyond these general statements, there are a number of important variations in women's attitudes to sponsorship in different countries. For example, in the UK, Mexico and Australia, women more than men look to sponsors to contribute expertise as well as money and appreciate when sponsors focus on local small teams and community programmes. In the US, Germany and China, women are more likely to focus only on the biggest events when thinking about sponsorship. Examples of statements in Germany and China show that women are more likely to be sceptical about sponsorship as 'a necessary evil' (China) and 'ruining the purity of sport' (Germany). Finally, in Japan women are more likely than men to see sport sponsors as 'credible' especially when their products 'fit' the sport being sponsored. And they are more likely to enjoy prize draws offered by sponsors as well. Earlier in the report we discussed how important the participation of women in sport at school has been in changing their level of interest as sports fans and the chances of them taking part in sport in their adult life. Our foundational research in 2014 shows that this change in participation levels has had a profound impact on how sponsorship changes women's behaviour – with women who fully participated in sport at school three to six times more likely to have subsequently shown 'fan behaviour' relating to the brands involved in sport sponsorship.

We also asked both men and women to estimate their annual spend in different aspects of being a sports spectator (buying tickets and merchandise) and a sports participant (clothing and equipment). While men still outspend women in general, it is noticeable that the gap is narrowest with women aged 30 to 49, who actually exceed mens' average spend level on clothing for sport across these countries. Money spent by them on the rest of their family's sporting activities will be an important factor here.

WOMEN TOMORROW

Repucom has a vast mountain of data tracking shifts in women's attitudes and behaviour in relation to sport over the last decade. The selection of insights in this report shows that these recent changes are the latest development in even bigger differences in our society stretching back to the 1970s and before, which the media revolution in this last decade has accelerated and amplified. In our mobile and digital world, both men and women can access a much broader range of interests, including sport – and the gap between how men and women partake in sport and which sports they are interested in is shrinking. A major driver of this change is women's participation in sport both as children and adults. Taking part in sport drives life-long interest, but it also drives engagement with the brands associated with sport and the level of behaviour change sponsors can expect to inspire in women. Understanding the triggers and barriers to participation, and how these differ for men and women, is therefore one of the future keys to success in the sports marketing industry. The year 2015 is the next chapter in the history of women and sport. The FIFA Women's World Cup in Canada this year will be an important marker, but the combination of public policy focus in this area and the underlying need for brands and sports to connect with women in a relevant and authentic way has created unstoppable momentum. The second generation of women in sport has arrived.

QUESTIONS

1) Considering the socio-demographic and consumer trends, justify the importance of the female sport market.
2) How can you interpret the differences in the popularity of sports among men and women in various countries, as reported in the case study?
3) Can you interpret the increasing popularity of football among females? What is the key female age group for marketing football, according to the case?
4) Are there any differences in the type of media that should be used, when targeting males and females?
5) Justify the role of parents on developing sport fans.
6) What are the most important barriers for womens' participation in sports, according to the case study? Use the hierarchical model of leisure constraints to better explain and group these barriers.
7) Using motivation theory, explain differences between males' and females' sport participation.
8) Why do brands underleverage female athletes and teams with respect to sport sponsorship?
9) Using attitudinal variables, discuss the attractiveness of female fans as a promising market for sponsors.
10) What are the main differences between men and women, in terms of their behaviour and attitudes towards sponsorship? Justify your answer.
11) How do you see the future of the female sport market? Justify your answer.

PART 7

Topics of interest for sport marketing

Topics of interest for sport marketers

There are a number of topics with respect to sport marketing that can be examined.

The following information provides a list of various topics:

- selection of applicable and combined segmentation criteria
- use of secondary data (e.g. demographics) for segmentation analysis
- application of psychographic and behavioural segmentation
- collection of primary data related to psychographic and behavioural patterns
- link between segmentation analysis, marketing and communication strategy
- use of social media (e.g. Facebook) as a tool to segment sport consumers
- studying changing demographics (e.g. aging of the population) to develop sport and recreation services appropriate for baby boomers
- studying the changing structure of the modern family in relation to sport consumer behaviour
- leveraging the increasing consumer power of the female market
- understanding the characteristics of the different age cohorts and developing appropriate sport services for each of them
- developing marketing and communication strategies targeted to generations X, Y and Z
- considering the growing populations within race and ethnicity groups, and studying their different cultures
- developing marketing and communication strategies targeted at ethnic and race groups (e.g. Hispanics)
- identification of sport consumer motives based on primary data collection (market research) and the development of appropriate marketing strategies
- selection of a reliable and valid sport consumer motivation scale, adjusted to the context of each study
- use of sport motivation data as the basis for psychographic segmentation (e.g. cluster analysis)
- satisfaction of sport consumer needs and expectations via appropriate provision of sport products and services
- satisfaction of sport consumer needs and expectations, as a prerequisite for developing consumer loyalty

- diversity of sport consumer motives, such as those based on demographics and different sport services and contexts
- understanding of how the different types/dimensions of motivation influence consumer loyalty and commitment
- development of strategies to strengthen sport consumer intrinsic motivation – those associated with the most positive behavioural outcomes
- creation of a sport/recreation environment that fosters opportunities for task-oriented goals/incentives (e.g. fun, enjoyment)
- creation of a sport/recreation environment that promotes opportunities for social interaction
- provision of sport services that emphasize personal experiences and make sport participants/consumers feel competent
- use of marketing campaigns on social media (e.g. blogs, Facebook, Twitter) to motivate prospective sport consumers
- incorporation of leisure constraint theory within other social/psychological and marketing models that aim to explain sport/consumer behaviour, such as the Psychological Continuum Model and the Transtheoretical Model of Behaviour Change
- use of leisure constraint theory to understand sport behaviour of specific socio-demographic groups of the population, such as elderly, disabled and individuals with chronic diseases
- use of leisure constraint data in psychographic research, with the aim of improving sport marketers' knowledge of sport consumer segmentation
- refocus of constraint research on specific sport activities, sport events (local and international) and sport leagues, with the aim of capturing contextual aspects and making the data useful for sport marketing applications
- expansion of cross-cultural research in relation to sport consumer behaviour with the use of standardized measurement tools
- measurement of leisure constraints by using valid and reliable scales
- collection of primary data and the incorporation of constraint research within marketing research projects
- recognition of the diversity of constraints among individuals within different socio-demographic groups
- use of constraints data for segmenting sport consumers (creation of clusters)
- development of appropriate marketing and communication strategies to alleviate the impact of constraints
- recognition of the important role of intrapersonal constraints on individuals' decision making for sport engagement, especially in relation to active sport participation
- use of social media (blogs, Facebook, Twitter and other online social networks) as a means to educate and motivate prospective sport consumers and overcome perception of constraints they face
- measurement of the cognitive and affective component of attitudes, with reference to sport commercials and new sport products/services
- collection of primary attitude research data to minimize the risk of failure in the process of new product developments

- development of specific marketing and communication strategies to target the cognitive or affective components of consumer attitudes, depending on the product positioning strategy
- understanding of the role that the social environment plays on the development of sport consumer attitudes
- use of social and digital media in influencing the development of sport consumer attitudes
- development of marketing and communication strategies, aiming to change consumer attitudes, if required
- collection of primary attitude research data to measure the antecedents and outcomes of sport sponsorship success
- selection of the human personality traits, which can be associated with the choice of sport services and products
- measurement of sport product and service brand personality profiles
- development of appropriate marketing and communication strategies to build the personality of a sport product and service
- influence of traditional, social and digital media on the development of sport brand personality
- how alternative communication strategies, such as sport sponsorship and corporate social responsibility actions, can influence the development of sport brand personality
- role of consumers' socio-cultural backgrounds on the development of brand personality perceptions
- examination of the fit between the personality of the destination (the place where an event takes place) and the sport event
- use of brand personality research for guiding marketing and communication strategy.

Index

Taylor & Francis eBooks

Helping you to choose the right eBooks for your Library

Add Routledge titles to your library's digital collection today. Taylor and Francis ebooks contains over 50,000 titles in the Humanities, Social Sciences, Behavioural Sciences, Built Environment and Law.

Choose from a range of subject packages or create your own!

Benefits for you

» Free MARC records
» COUNTER-compliant usage statistics
» Flexible purchase and pricing options
» All titles DRM-free.

Benefits for your user

» Off-site, anytime access via Athens or referring URL
» Print or copy pages or chapters
» Full content search
» Bookmark, highlight and annotate text
» Access to thousands of pages of quality research at the click of a button.

REQUEST YOUR **FREE** INSTITUTIONAL TRIAL TODAY	**Free Trials Available** We offer free trials to qualifying academic, corporate and government customers.

eCollections – Choose from over 30 subject eCollections, including:

Archaeology	Language Learning
Architecture	Law
Asian Studies	Literature
Business & Management	Media & Communication
Classical Studies	Middle East Studies
Construction	Music
Creative & Media Arts	Philosophy
Criminology & Criminal Justice	Planning
Economics	Politics
Education	Psychology & Mental Health
Energy	Religion
Engineering	Security
English Language & Linguistics	Social Work
Environment & Sustainability	Sociology
Geography	Sport
Health Studies	Theatre & Performance
History	Tourism, Hospitality & Events

For more information, pricing enquiries or to order a free trial, please contact your local sales team:
www.tandfebooks.com/page/sales

 Routledge Taylor & Francis Group | The home of Routledge books | www.tandfebooks.com

Made in the USA
Middletown, DE
12 September 2019